# Equality in Asia-Pacific: Reality or a Contradiction in Terms?

In 1948, the United Nations General Assembly proclaimed the Universal Declaration of Human Rights, stating every human being's right of equality in dignity and right. However, notwithstanding recognition by the international community of its importance and codification in numerous national and sub-national constitutions and legislation, reinforced by various multilateral and regional human rights treaties, the right of equality continues to be unable to take complete firm hold in all regions and countries.

Evidence, as presented in this book dedicated to exploring the place of equality in Asia-Pacific societies, suggests that although progress is being made the right of equality has not yet fully materialised, both in law and in reality, in the world's most populous region. Many factors, particularly entrenched cultural heritage and practices, the lingering effects of colonialism and newly found independence, and, above all, pervasive ignorance and prejudices, continue to impede the recognition, development and protection of equality in this region. Of course, equality, a normative right and entitlement by virtue of our humanity, has neither been fully achieved in societies outside the region. Such neo-colonial thinking in fact perpetuates and assists in the subjugation of the right of equality in the Asia-Pacific Region as a matter of relevance and concern only to Western countries. This collection sheds light on realities outside as interlinked with our aim.

This book was previously published as a special double issue of *The International Journal of Human Rights*.

**Phil C. W. Chan** is currently Visiting Scholar/Visiting Professor at the Faculty of Law, Common Law Section, University of Ottawa, and Visiting Scholar at the Asian Institute, Munk Centre for International Studies, University of Toronto.

# Equality in Asia-Pacific

Reality or a Contradiction in Terms?

Edited by
Phil C. W. Chan

With Foreword by
Archbishop Desmond Tutu

LONDON AND NEW YORK

First published 2008 by Routledge

2 Park Square, Milton Park, Abingdon, Oxon OX14 4RN
711 Third Avenue, New York, NY 10017, USA

*Routledge is an imprint of the Taylor & Francis Group, an informa business*

First issued in paperback 2016

Copyright © 2007 edited by Phil C. W. Chan

Typeset in Times Roman by Techset Composition, Salisbury, UK

All rights reserved. No part of this book may be reprinted or reproduced or utilised in any form or by any electronic, mechanical, or other means, now known or hereafter invented, including photocopying and recording, or in any information storage or retrieval system, without permission in writing from the publishers.

Notice:
Product or corporate names may be trademarks or registered trademarks, and are used only for identification and explanation without intent to infringe.

*British Library Cataloguing in Publication Data*
A catalogue record for this book is available from the British Library

*Library of Congress Cataloging in Publication Data*
A catalog record for this book has been requested

ISBN 13: 978-0-415-37329-6 (hbk)
ISBN 13: 978-1-138-99350-1 (pbk)

# Contents

Foreword
*Archbishop Desmond Tutu*     vii

Preface
*Frank Barnaby*     ix

1. Equality in Asia-Pacific: Reality or a Contradiction in Terms? – An Introduction
   *Phil C. W. Chan*     1

2. What's in a Name? Bisexuality, Transnational Sexuality Studies and Western Colonial Legacies
   *Clare Hemmings*     9

3. Same-Sex Marriage/Constitutionalism and their Centrality to Equality Rights in Hong Kong: A Comparative–Socio-Legal Appraisal
   *Phil C. W. Chan*     29

4. Changing Times, Changing Minds, Changing Law – Sexual Orientation and New Zealand Law, 1960 to 2005
   *Paul Rishworth*     81

5. The Same-Sex Marriage Debate in Australia
   *Kristen Walker*     104

6. Non-Governmental Organising for Gender Equality in China – Joining a Global Emancipatory Epistemic Community
   *Cecilia Milwertz and Wei Bu*     126

7. On China's Slow Boat to Women's Rights: Revisions to the Women's Protection Law, 2005
   *Michael Palmer*     145

8. Inequality of Educational Opportunity in Korea by Gender, Socio-Economic Background, and Family Structure
   *Hyunjoon Park*     172

9. Official Languages and Bilingualism in the Courtroom: Hong Kong, Canada, the Republic of Ireland, and International Law
   *Phil C. W. Chan*   191

10. Constitutionalising Affirmative Action in the Fiji Islands
    *Jill Cottrell and Yash Ghai*   218

Notes on Contributors   249

*Index*   253

# Foreword

Human nature entails fear of differences, and it is only natural that the majority of us will seek to maintain the status quo such that our perceived superiority (whatever it be) over others who are, or are perceived to be, different from us may continue to subsist. Nonetheless, it is precisely these differences that make up humanity, and it is affirmation and respect for these differences that make it so truly wonderful to be humans. The Holocaust and South Africa's decades-long sufferings from apartheid, to name but two, vividly illuminated the dangers and perils into which prejudices and stereotypes are capable of degenerating. Equality is thus not an abstract notion: to be treated equally on the basis of one's merits alone is integral to the human experience and the integrity of each and every human society. This is not to say that life is or must be fair; human experience perforce dictates otherwise. It is, however, incumbent upon all of us to make life fairer.

Whilst equality is now a principle legally celebrated in all international human rights treaties and most national and sub-national constitutions, the full and complete implementation of these equality guarantees continues to be impeded if not entirely disregarded in and by many countries. I therefore commend and congratulate *The International Journal of Human Rights*' dedication and Phil C. W. Chan's editorship of a Special Double Issue that examines the status of achievement of equality in Asia-Pacific, the most populous region of the world. The range of coverage in this interdisciplinary Special Double Issue is impressive. These contributions, by leading scholars in their fields, assist us in our global understanding and appreciation of equality in law, in practice and, most importantly, in its being normative. Readers within and without the Asia-Pacific Region therefore have much to gain from the insights this Special Double Issue contains, for equality, upon which all human rights are premised, can all but be taken away with alacrity by those in a position of domination who will seek to maintain and exploit the status quo for their selfish concerns, and must be strengthened, by all of us, at all costs.

Archbishop Desmond Tutu<br>
Truth and Reconciliation Commission<br>
Cape Town, South Africa

# Preface

This Special Double Issue of *The International Journal of Human Rights* contains a selection of nine papers dealing with various aspects of achievement or otherwise of full and complete equality in the Asia-Pacific Region. The topic is of core importance to all scholars, policy-makers, human rights practitioners and activists, and students who are concerned about human rights in the world's most populous region. Moreover, it is obviously the case that achievement of full and complete equality is an essential, and basic, requirement for the improvement of all human rights.

Phil C. W. Chan, as Guest Editor, has superbly assembled a group of first-rate scholars to be authors of the papers in this Special Double Issue and prepared the Special Double Issue for publication. He is to be much congratulated and I am grateful to him.

I am confident that this Special Double Issue of the *Journal* will be regarded as a standard text by and essential reading for all who are concerned about the status and place of equality in Asia-Pacific.

Frank Barnaby
Editor
*The International Journal of Human Rights*

# Equality in Asia-Pacific: Reality or a Contradiction in Terms? – An Introduction

PHIL C. W. CHAN

The Holocaust brought to the fore consequences of oppressing individuals and groups by virtue of their respective particular personal characteristics, and of ignoring such oppression. Thus, in 1948, as the United Nations General Assembly proclaimed the Universal Declaration of Human Rights, since taken as largely reflecting norms of customary international law binding on all States, it was agreed by consensus in its first provision that '[a]ll human beings are born free and equal in dignity and rights. They are endowed with reason and conscience and should act towards one another in a spirit of brotherhood'.

However, notwithstanding such recognition by the international community of the importance of the right of equality in dignity and rights and its codification in numerous national and sub-national constitutions and legislation, reinforced by various multilateral and regional human rights treaties, the right of equality continues to be unable to take complete firm hold in all regions and countries. Evidence, as presented by the nine insightful papers in this Special Double Issue dedicated to exploring the place of equality in Asia-Pacific societies, suggests that although progress is being made, the right of equality has not yet fully materialised, in law or in reality, in the world's most populous region. Many factors, particularly entrenched cultural heritage and practices, the lingering effects of colonialism and newly found independence, and, above all, pervasive ignorance and prejudices, continue to impede the recognition, development and protection of equality in this region. Of course, as we begin to introduce our discussions, we by no means imply that equality, a normative right and entitlement by virtue of our humanity, has been fully achieved in societies outside the region, as it has not. Such neo-colonial thinking, as our discussions will point out, in fact perpetuates and assists in the subjugation of the right of equality in the Asia-Pacific Region. Accordingly, we hope that our discussions will also be able to shed light and generate reflections on realities outside the region as interlinked with our aim.

This Special Double Issue will begin with Clare Hemmings' 'What's in a Name? Bisexuality, Transnational Sexuality Studies and Western Colonial Legacies'. In her thought-provoking study exploring the role of bisexuality in transnational sexuality studies, Hemmings argues that bisexuality is either absent or inscribed as potential or behaviour, which by definition is alterable and fluctuating, rather than as a stable inborn identity, so much so that lesbians and gay men are considered the only proper subjects of sexuality studies and of sexuality discrimination and prejudices. 'The conceptualisation of bisexuality as potential', the author argues, 'refers not only to the development of individuals, but also to the relations between societies within colonialism'. Its absence or subordinated role in Western queer discourse on account of its behavioural primitivity thus reflects an equivalent and continuing Western conceptualisation of societies that have previously suffered colonisation. Such conceptualisations, as the author elaborates, perpetuate the lingering effects of colonialism in the newly independent Asia-Pacific (and African) countries and assist the notion that homosexuality is a Western/imported identity *and* behaviour and HIV/AIDS a Western/imported disease, hindering sexuality equality protection as well as sexual health measures. In the process, both heterosexual men and heterosexual women are also endangered, with the enforced masculinity – which subjects heterosexual men to constant and pervasive guards and attacks of their heterosexual identity and heterosexual women to domestic violence, as Phil C. W. Chan and Cecilia Milwertz and Wei Bu will discuss in their respective papers to follow – that ensues.

Phil C. W. Chan, then, in his comprehensive 'Same-Sex Marriage/Constitutionalism and their Centrality to Equality Rights in Hong Kong: A Comparative–Socio-Legal Appraisal', refutes the notion that homosexuality and protection of sexual minorities, including recognition of the right of a person to marry another person of the same sex, are Western concepts inapplicable in Hong Kong, a conservative Confucian society. Rather, Chan argues that it was the classification of homosexuality as criminal and the higher age of consent for anal intercourse and sexual intimacy between men, since ruled by Hong Kong courts as constituting discrimination on grounds of sexual orientation and thus unconstitutional, that were Western imports through Great Britain's colonisation of Hong Kong. Adopting a comparative and socio-legal approach, the author discusses the evolution of homosexuality in law from a sin to a capital crime and finally to a personal characteristic entitled to and warranting equal protection, in jurisdictions including the United Kingdom, the United States, Canada, South Africa, and Ireland as well as under various multilateral and regional human rights agreements such as the International Covenant on Civil and Political Rights and the European Convention on Human Rights. The author elucidates the unique circumstances, including two scandals and ultimately a tragedy in far-flung Beijing, that changed the status of homosexuality from being a crime punishable by life imprisonment in all circumstances, to one permissible if engaged in by two parties both aged 21 or above and invisible to others, to a personal characteristic on par with heterosexuality and constitutionally protected against discrimination. The author proceeds to explain that recognition in Hong Kong of a right to same-sex marriage is not constrained by a Chinese/Confucian culture; same-sex marriage, and not just same-sex civil partnership, is in fact essential both for its own sake and for the protection of *everyone*, and that cultural relativist arguments against full and complete sexual orientation equality are misguided and fall prey to the conceptualisations which Clare Hemmings has dissected. In doing so, Chan also questions the place of Christianity and the Bible in Hong Kong society and dissects those verses in the Bible on which opponents of homosexuality and sexual minority rights rely. Then, referring to debates on the issue and on judicial activism in academia and in legislatures and the courtrooms in various jurisdictions, Chan maintains that recognition of the right of a person to marry another person of the same sex constitutes a constitutional and democratic requirement which an impartial and responsible judiciary must uphold. Finally, the author concludes with an analysis of Hong Kong's international treaty obligations in relation to same-sex marriage and to active protection of the right of equality of all persons, irrespective of their sexual orientations, within its jurisdiction.

Oppression of homosexuality and sexual minorities, as it originated from Henry VIII's Buggery Act 1533, is, expectedly, present also in countries settled primarily by those sailing from Great Britain, with New Zealand and Australia being two examples. In his 'Changing Times, Changing Minds, Changing Laws – Sexual Orientation and New Zealand Law, 1960 to 2005', Paul Rishworth lucidly traces the legal developments on homosexuality and sexual orientation equality in New Zealand. His paper illustrates both that homosexuality and sexual minorities had until the mid-1980s been treated, both in law and in reality, as an aberration, and that it was thanks to generation of knowledge that in New Zealand, as in Hong Kong and other former colonies, lesbians and gay men have now finally freed themselves from legal discrimination. Reasoning that 'a human rights *culture* is the best protection of rights from infringement', the author elucidates recent developments in New Zealand recognising same-sex (and different-sex) relationships as civil unions, with similar rights and obligations as are owed through marriage, and banning hate speech attributable to sexual orientation as well as other personal characteristics, and discusses the impact of sexual orientation equality and non-discrimination rights on religious institutions in New Zealand.

Same-sex marriage, of course, may not be the desired outcome for every lesbian or gay man. In her interesting 'The Same-Sex Marriage Debate in Australia', Kristen Walker argues that the institution of marriage is an inherently heterosexist and heterosexualising mechanism by which, if available to same-sex couples, members of sexual minorities will be judged and into which their freedom to engage in relations as lesbians and gay men will be subjugated. Walker's position is thus a good contrast and comparison with Phil C. W. Chan's, which, whilst silent on the issue of whether same-sex marriage is self-defeating for giving in to hetero-normative pressures, emphasises that it is equal *access* to the civil institution of marriage that is essential to the full and complete realisation of sexual orientation equality in law and in society. Before she begins her discussion on the normative implications of same-sex marriage, Walker analyses the recent amendment by the federal Parliament in Australia to federal marriage law in response to constitutional litigation which sought that same-sex marriages validly entered into in foreign jurisdictions be recognised and given effect as similarly valid in Australia, as different-sex marriages are. The author proceeds to discuss the debate against Australian constitutional jurisprudence as to the mode of interpretation – whether the intentions of the framers of the Australian Constitution or contemporary developments in law and society should control the issue of same-sex marriage – and as to whether the federal and state legislatures may enact or amend laws in order to provide for same-sex marriage. Then, Walker points out the current political climate surrounding same-sex marriage and concludes that instead of fighting for same-sex marriage, one should insist that the linkage between marriage and the state be removed and that 'a more tailored system of recognition, with a combination of presumptive recognition and a registration system for various purposes and allowing for the recognition of a more diverse range of relationship forms', such as that available in New Zealand, would be more appropriate.

The linkage between marriage and the state, in fact, raises another significant concern, that is, domestic violence within marriage and family and the role of the state in perpetuating or preventing and punishing domestic violence, particularly in a country where a man is culturally entrenched as superior to, if not owning, his wife (and children). In their insightful 'Non-Governmental Organising for Gender Equality in China – Joining a Global Emancipatory Epistemic Community', Cecilia Milwertz and Wei Bu allude to the anti-domestic violence activism in China in the 1990s and early 2000s as a quintessential case study in examining the benefits and process which non-governmental women's rights organisations in China may gain – and have gained – through engagement with similar organisations in other countries and through a greater familiarity with global human rights norms. The authors demonstrate that instead of imposing their own beliefs and non-beliefs in relation to human rights and cultural practices which they may believe to reflect universal norms which developing and other countries may reject as neo-colonialist, developed countries stand capable of communicating global human rights norms for the recipients' own reflections and generation of knowledge. Milwertz and Bu's paper shows that in merely a decade domestic violence has been transformed from a non-issue in China to establishing women's rights as a human rights and anti-domestic violence as a health issue, in the light of prevailing global human rights norms. Such generation of knowledge, insight and perspectives on domestic violence amongst anti-domestic violence activists in China is particularly encouraging as 'the construction of new knowledge has not been imposed from without as a top-down education process but has instead been shaped by the activists themselves in the context of international interactions. They have engaged in what Jean Lave and Etienne Wenger generally regard as a situated learning process within a global community of practice, and by engaging in such processes the activists have joined a global emancipatory epistemic community'.

The development on protection of women against domestic violence, of course, must be supported and reinforced by the legal system in order to be truly and fully effective. In his comprehensive 'On China's Slow Boat to Women's Rights: Revisions to the Women's Protection Law, 2005', Michael Palmer examines the nature and significance of the recent amendment to China's Women's Protection Law to discern whether women's rights in China have been advanced or in fact continue to be stalled. In doing so, the author scrutinises the recent amendment against its predecessor as well as related Laws of the 'socialist-market' country. The author concludes that whilst the amendment suggests a growing concern on the part of the state with the protection of equality between men and women and of women's rights and interests *in se*, its tendency 'to mandate people on what not to do, rather than to lay the foundations for positive conduct and thinking by, for example, providing detailed actionable provisions, ensuring women a much greater role in public life, and promoting enthusiastically the rights of women to educational benefits'. Thus, protection of women in China continues to suffer cultural and state resistance and the progress as manifested in the amendments reveals that full and complete realisation of women's rights and interests, including their right of equality, *in se* in China remains a long and intricate struggle.

As abuse and disadvantages travel across generations, it is essential that we remedy and prevent inequalities as soon as, if not before, they are revealed. In his empirical 'Inequality of Educational Opportunity in Korea by Gender, Socio-Economic Background, and Family Structure', Hyunjoon Park, using comparative statistics and data, discusses the degree of and trend in inequality of educational opportunity in South Korea caused by South Korean children's personal and ascribed characteristics including their respective genders, socio-economic backgrounds, and the structures of their families – specifically as to whether they reside in a nuclear family or in a single-parent family and if so whether the single parenthood was caused by parental divorce or death. In addition, the author argues that recent demographic changes in South Korea brought about by a rising prevalence of marriages between Koreans and foreigners in South Korea, a country that regards itself as ethnically and culturally homogenous, will constitute a significant variable in children's educational achievement and attainment unless perceptions of ethnic and cultural homogeneity are altered.

Then, returning to Hong Kong, our attention shifts to the courtroom and the legal process itself. Whilst Hong Kong is now part of China, enjoying a high degree of autonomy, English continues to be the *lingua franca* of education, commence, and the legal process, with the common law legal system constitutionally preserved. In the process, however, the Chinese language (Cantonese) continues to be subjugated in Hong Kong's judicial and legal practice, even though since 1 July 1997 it is constitutionally and by legislation recognised as an official language in the former British colony. In *Re Cheng Kai Nam Gary*, the defendant, facing trial which might, and ultimately did, lead to his imprisonment, sought that the judge presiding over his trial be able to directly understand Chinese, with which he self-identified most intimately. His application for leave to apply for judicial review was, nonetheless, rejected. Adopting a comparative approach by reference to and scrutinising Canadian, Irish, and international jurisprudence, Phil C. W. Chan, in his 'Official Languages and Bilingualism in the Courtroom: Hong Kong, Canada, the Republic of Ireland, and International Law', argues that an individual is entitled to choose to use an official language with which he or she self-identifies most intimately in judicial services or proceedings affecting his or her rights and interests. Such entitlement, the author maintains, stems from an individual's language use rights and right to a fair trial. Furthermore, the author insists, one's fluency in the dominant official language and availability of interpretation during the relevant proceedings are immaterial and do not affect the individual's aforementioned rights. The author concludes that the unfortunate outcome and reasoning in *Re Cheng Kai Nam Gary* illuminated that the adverse effects of colonialism, which has long been recognised as causing and perpetuating inequalities, continue, in colonialism's altered neo-colonial ego, to be pervasive in postcolonial Hong Kong.

Finally, we conclude our Special Double Issue on equality in Asia-Pacific with Jill Cottrell and Yash Ghai's 'Constitutionalising Affirmative Action in the Fiji Islands' to reflect on whether affirmative action, whereby historically disadvantaged groups are given discriminatorily positive rights, benefits or advantages in order to redress their past disadvantages and assist them in advancing economically, socially and politically, is suitable, appropriate and effective in achieving full and complete realisation of the right of equality or merely causes and perpetuates existing inequalities only that the identities of the victims are reversed. In their reflective paper, Cottrell and Ghai, with their hands-on experience in the constitution-making process in Fiji, argue that Fiji's constitutional provision for affirmative action programmes in fact merely strengthen the existing dominant position of ethnic Fijians which the Fijian government claims to have been disadvantaged by ethnic Indo-Fijians who descend from those emigrating from India – then also under British control – to Fiji during Great Britain's colonisation, at the expense of

Indo-Fijians. In the meantime, groups historically disadvantaged in Fiji other than for reason of ethnicity receive little or, in the case of sexual minorities, no attention from the Fijian government under the constitutional provision. In addition, the criteria for eligibility for and the standards of affirmative action programmes in Fiji have largely been indeterminate or contradictory – or in fact unconstitutional – and the implementation of these programmes faulty or ineffective, and the end result has so far been that resentment, and not equity, has grown within all sectors of Fijian Islands society. Such resentment culminated in four military coups in Fiji, with the latest one in December 2006. The core of the problem, the authors discern, lies at the heart of Fijian Islands society: 'can Fijian values, society and tradition (or perhaps a parody of tradition) be preserved, and how far are they compatible with market economy, globalisation and individualism?' The dilemma, it ought to be noted, inheres in all societies, in and beyond the Fiji Islands and the Asia-Pacific Region.

These nine critical analyses on issues of equality and inequalities in the Asia-Pacific Region, on subject matters that have not been adequately addressed either in other forums or at all, should therefore be able to provide important insight into the process of development of a person's right of equality as guaranteed in Article 1 of the Universal Declaration of Human Rights in this most populous and yet ethnically and culturally diverse region of the world, and into whether or not it has materialised and how it has been implemented or violated. However, we are conscious that our undertaking may be critiqued, in at least three respects. We are, first and foremost, conscious that this forum has not the benefit of analyses on the religious inequalities and conflicts in Thailand between the majority Buddhist population and minority Muslims and in the Philippines between majority Roman Catholics and minority Muslims, matters of great consequence not only to the guarantee of equality to take firm hold in Asia-Pacific but also to peace and stability in the respective countries and the region. We have also been unable to have the ethnic and religious minorities in China addressed in our forum. Japan's wealth, also, cannot disguise and certainly does not excuse its continuing discriminatory treatment of foreigners and Korean-Japanese persons. In addition, during our preparations we have been alerted to the religious genocide in Bhutan, a Buddhist country that prides itself on its 'Gross National Happiness', and the resulting plight of Hindu refugees in neighbouring Nepal; however, on account of time constraints we were unable to include an expert discussion on the subject. Accordingly, we urge that experts in these fields continue their essential research and cordially encourage these experts to consider submitting their important works to our *Journal*.

Also, we are conscious that by devoting substantial attention to issues relating to sexuality and gender equality, this forum may be perceived as having a sexuality/ gender agenda and our focus as not being evenly balanced. However, whilst such an agenda was not initially in mind, we can only be delighted with the resulting dialogues on sexuality and gender equality issues as they pertain to the Asia-Pacific Region, particularly as they are reinforced by discussions on the implications of post- and neo-colonialism, manifestations of continuing grave inequalities, that inhere in the region. Furthermore, given the continuing dearth of discussions on sexuality and gender equality issues, often perceived to be of concern only to Western countries, in and by the Asia-Pacific Region, we are proud in serving as host to six scholarly discussions on what sexualities actually are, the roles of sexualities in Asia-Pacific societies and of Western and former colonial countries in their being oppressed and empowered in the Asia-Pacific

Region, and their correlation with and contribution to a person's right of equality and the development and well-being of society.

The third critique that we may envisage may, perhaps, go directly to the title of the Special Double Issue itself, that equality and Asia-Pacific cannot be a contradiction in terms. We certainly hope that they cannot, and there is only one way to find out – through informed and constructive dialogues had in, and hopefully opened up by, this forum amongst others, and through the necessary legal reform and generation and dissemination of knowledge and insight to which we hope to serve an authoritative contribution.

**Acknowledgements**

Its planning, preparation and production spanning more than two years, this Special Double Issue would not have materialised but for the insightful contributions by the leading scholars in the fields, and I am honoured to be responsible for their general well-being. I am grateful to Frank Barnaby, Editor of the *Journal*, for engaging me in such an invaluable undertaking and to Taylor & Francis, in particular Caroline Broughton, Amber Bulkley, Sarah Elvins, and especially Josephine Oakley, for their enthusiastic support of the project. I thank consultancy firm Yenji Limited for its generous financial assistance to my ongoing research and editorial work. I also thank the British Institute of International and Comparative Law, the Gender, Sexuality and Law Research Group at Keele University School of Law, the Lauterpacht Research Centre for International Law at the University of Cambridge, and the Asia-Pacific College of Diplomacy at the Australian National University for welcoming me, respectively, as Visiting Fellow during which this Special Double Issue was substantially prepared. Special thanks also extend to the ANU College of Law and the Centre for International and Public Law at the Australian National University for welcoming me as their unofficial visitor during the final stage of preparation, from which it benefited greatly. Last but not least, I thank all the anonymous reviewers who so kindly volunteered their valuable time to enable this Special Double Issue to be an authoritative source of analyses on issues of equality and inequalities as they pertain to the Asia-Pacific Region.

In the course of the years, I have had the good fortune to make the acquaintance of many amazing individuals who have helped me one way or the other in my transition through adolescence as a person and as an academic, and I must selfishly take this opportunity to express my gratitude to these individuals without whom I would not have been able to have a life and academic career with its share of joy and despair: Jon Austin, principal of Imperial College Toronto, for completely changing my life as he guided me with indescribable kindness and patience through from a Form 4 secondary school student from Hong Kong with a gloomy academic future to someone offered law school admissions in an amazing five months (under circumstances and with memories I would not wish to relive but which I will forever cherish); Sylvia Acevedo, Professor Andrew Byrnes, Professor Johannes Chan, Robin Corcos, John Harris, and Robert Morgan for their kindness and patience in helping me survive law school and Professor Andrew Byrnes, Jill Cottrell, and Donald Lewis for introducing me to legal research and writing with which I am since ever preoccupied; Dapo Akande for his model of academic qualities and his continuing support to my academic endeavours and Alisoun Roberts for helping me withstand the Durham winter and other matters of concern; and Jon Austin, Anita and Terry in Hamilton,

Sylvia Acevedo, Robin Corcos, Jill Cottrell, Michelle Chong, Sarah Gardiner, Monica Hall, Juyon Kim, Julie Wong, Detlev Pusch, Tamara McKen, Marianne in Berlin, Alisoun Roberts, Linn Edvartsen, Felizmina Lutucuta, Aisling O'Sullivan, Sarah Wennberg, Richard Gardiner, Philip Ridgway, Linda Christie, Annalisa Meloni, Nicky Priaulx, and Mark Nolan for tolerating my many flaws and extending to me their warmest company and friendships and the many wonderful and cherished memories. I wish also to thank the staff and students at St. Stephen's College (Stanley), Hong Kong, for showing me the need and fostering in me the resolve and resiliency to strive to be a kind and truthful person in spite and because of ignorance, prejudice, oppression, and, above all, self-enforced silence, and Au Tak-ming at my primary school (which was not so long ago) for giving me opportunities for responsibility and a sense of purpose. Above all, I am grateful to my mother and my grandmother, who gave me as best they could the opportunities that had been denied them, and Paul Serfaty, with his years of unquestioning confidence, unreasonable dedication, wonderful company, intelligent conversations, and love.

# What's in a Name? Bisexuality, Transnational Sexuality Studies and Western Colonial Legacies

CLARE HEMMINGS

This paper explores the work that bisexuality does within the expanding field of transnational sexuality studies. I want to ask why it is that bisexuality matters in relation to dilemmas within the field, particularly those concerning naming of sexual practices globally. My focus is thus not on what bisexuality is, or which practices, where, might nestle under the term, but on what the absence or presence of bisexuality means for transnational sexuality studies. In this I draw on Eve Kosofsky Sedgwick's 1990s insistence that queer theorists need 'repeatedly to ask how certain categorisations work, what enactments they are performing and what relations they are creating, rather than what they essentially *mean*'.[1]

In Western theorisation of sexual identities, particularly queer theory, bisexuality has faded somewhat from view in the last decade. While bisexual theorists in the early to mid 1990s embraced queer approaches to sexuality, albeit critically,[2] bisexuality's position within the field has not been institutionalised in the same way as transgender studies' has. While theorists seem to know that bisexuality needs to be acknowledged, this tends to take place only in footnote glosses, or tacked-on mentions that have no impact on sexual epistemology or methodology. In part, this must be due to the dual form that queer resistance to bisexuality has taken within queer theory and politics. On one hand, bisexuality has been understood as undermining lesbian or gay claims to legitimacy, bringing opposite-sex relationships very firmly into the frame that only ambivalently seemed able to contain them.[3] On the other hand, it has been understood to reproduce the oppositional identity categories queer theorists wanted to challenge, the 'bi' in bisexuality figuring as the 'tie that binds' sexual poles. As a variety of bisexual theorists noted at the time, bisexuality was simultaneously viewed as a challenge to and reproducer of Western sexual categories.[4] Yet this dual role has also typified a transgendered position within queer studies, and its fate has not been the same, so something else appears to have happened to disqualify bisexuality from a visible role in the field.[5]

It is my contention, and one I have also made elsewhere, that bisexuality continues to be invisible within Western lesbian and gay and queer studies because that invisibility is fundamental to ensuring that lesbians and gay men remain the *de facto* subjects of queer studies.[6] This does not occur through erasure alone, though that is certainly part of the process. It occurs primarily through the harnessing of particular definitions of bisexuality – as pre-oedipal potential or androgyny, rather than sexual identity – to understandings of how a gendered queer subject position is formed.[7] Thus, in her influential article 'Melancholy Gender/Refused Identification', Judith Butler indicates that sexual and gendered identity is formed through object-choice repudiation, such that heterosexuals come to *embody* the gender of lost homosexual object-choice, and homosexuals the gender of lost heterosexual object-choice.[8] This framework foregrounds the importance of cross-gender identification in the formation of gay and lesbian subjectivity, but assumes that object-choice repudiation is always both gendered and exclusive – a sexual subject becomes such through the repudiation of one or other gender of object-choice. Bisexuality is thus not an empirical possibility, but its role as sexual or gendered potential is critical to explaining why people can choose to 'go either way' in the first instance. In effect, then, bisexuality as identity or critical perspective cannot be taken up by queer theory because it is already rendered as that which facilitates sexual subject formation.

That use of bisexuality locks queer theory into a developmental paradigm it might otherwise wish to challenge. The conceptualisation of bisexuality as potential refers not only to the development of individuals, but also to the relations between societies within colonialism. In psychoanalysis and sexology, bisexual potential is what allows gendered and sexual identity to emerge in the *civilised* individual, who leaves bisexuality behind as a kind of innocence. Thus, for Freud, active bisexuality in adulthood is understood as a failure to grow up, less innocence than adolescent strop, a refusal to choose when choice must be made.[9] For Merl Storr, an understanding of bisexuality as raw materials for modern sexual identity development underwrites and is mirrored by the colonial understanding of civilisation developing out of primitivism, with its attendant symbol of the 'noble savage'. In her reading of Wilhelm von Krafft-Ebing, Storr highlights his (and others') conviction that more advanced (white, Western) races are understood as more sexually differentiated, and more primitive races (black, African or Asian) as less so, and thus more likely to display deviance.[10] Bisexuality, as potential or behaviour, thus becomes associated with primitive societies, while homosexual or heterosexual monosexuality becomes a marker of modern civilisation.

In the context of this study, then, I am interested in exploring how transnational sexuality studies' use of bisexual potential for its conception of sexual subjectivity utilises and disavows the colonial, as well as gendered, meanings that underwrite it. In this emergent field, as I shall elaborate in the rest of the paper, bisexuality emerges and disappears in sporadic and contradictory ways. It is by turns completely ignored, brought in as an example of the problems of Western identity, or reframed as a neutral description of 'local' sexual behaviour. I will argue that bisexuality, whether absent or present, is mobilised in this field in order to fix a clear distinction between Western and non-Western sexual meanings, histories and practices. Bisexuality is key here because it can carry or deflect the burden of the colonial histories of modern sexual identity, and, in this respect, its role in transnational sexuality studies mirrors its ambivalent status in more Western-focused queer accounts. The paper as a whole, then, is intended to highlight both the continued importance of theorising bisexuality, and the need for a more nuanced account of the work that it does as a Western sexual identity category when it travels.

In the rest of this paper, I aim both to give the reader a clearer sense of the terrain of transnational sexuality studies within which I am situating my discussion of bisexuality, and to focus on the forms that bisexual meaning takes therein. Part I, Transnational Sexuality Studies, provides an overview of some of the debates within the field and the reasons why theorising sexuality in a global framework matters in the first instance. Here, too, I highlight the key issue of nomenclature for feminist, lesbian, gay and queer theorists. Why does it matter what we call the project of global sexual justice? How have different theorists engaged this question? Part II, Imagining Bisexuality, returns to the question of bisexual presence and absence within these debates, and maps its location in relation to the issue of naming. I ask why and how queer theorists are unwilling to include bisexuality in global accounts, and the conditions under which it surfaces and is erased. I move on to thinking about the more curious emergence of 'bisexuality as behaviour' in some transnational sexuality studies work, particularly sexual health and social movement accounts, discussing the desire for 'bisexual' here to be a neutral term unharnessed from its Western history.

## I. Transnational Sexuality Studies

I understand transnational sexuality studies as an interdisciplinary field engaging both the role sexuality plays in transnational relations and formations in an era of globalisation, and the complex discourses of nation, gender, sexuality and ethnicity that make this intervention so essential. Transnational sexuality studies cuts across sexuality and gender studies, postcolonial theory, queer theory, anthropology, critical race studies, literary studies, development studies, globalisation theory, reproductive health studies, among others, and, in fact, might be said to constitute one way of bringing these disciplinary or interdisciplinary concerns together. Transnational sexuality studies thus offers a useful way of bridging the gap between humanities and social/political science work in feminist studies, and particularly between critical accounts of subjectivity and international feminist politics.[11]

Part of my interest in this field arises from my location as a lecturer at the Gender Institute at the London School of Economics, where within an annual intake of between 65 and 75 graduate students around 40 per cent register for the Masters programme in Gender, Development and Globalisation, which is emblematic of the increasingly international focus of feminist studies in Western contexts. Despite sexuality's central place in feminist studies (nationally or internationally), students on our Master's programmes are often initially resistant to including an analysis of sexuality in their work. And they are not alone – sexuality may be understood variously as a 'Western concern' (particularly when homosexuality is invoked), a distraction from the real task of poverty analysis and prevention, or a prioritisation of private over public concerns. From a critical sexuality perspective, such responses reproduce rather than challenge pervasive transnational sexual discourses, and it is in engaging with, contesting and seeking to transform these discourses that transnational sexuality studies gains its theoretical vibrancy and political *raison d'être*.

Given these perspectives on sexuality as an unworthy topic, one of the first issues that writers in the field have to address is why sexuality is significant globally as both an interpersonal and a structural concern. The dilemma of sexuality's status is phrased nicely, I think, by Amanda Lock Swarr and Richa Nagar, who ask: 'Can we analyze the politics of sexuality and intimacy in [women's] lives without diminishing the centrality of neo-colonial histories and geographies and their everyday struggles over access to material resources?'[12] Transnational sexuality studies work tries to answer in the affirmative by highlighting the importance of legal and social control over sexuality for both modern and postcolonial states,[13] and by emphasising that one problem lies in the definition of sexuality as mere sexual practice rather than as a diffuse set of social, political and interpersonal expectations with particular histories and effects.[14] A rather different answer to the question of how to balance material and sexual rights comes from Susie Jolly, who challenges the implicit assumption in this division that 'while in the North people need sex and love, in the South they just need to eat'.[15] More mainstream political theorists are also developing some understanding of individuals' sexual rights as critical for ensuring people's ability to live meaningful, as well as economically viable, lives, rather than be simply economically viable.[16]

Theorising sexuality transnationally is essential for thinking through the relationship between gender, ethnicity and nationalism in several ways. We are by now familiar with sexuality's role in maintaining gendered racial divisions in slavery, for example, through discourses and practices of lynching, and with the reification of white European male bodies in colonialism as victims rather than perpetrators of sexually transmitted diseases.[17] Importantly, transnational sexuality scholars have also focused on the continued use by nation states of sexuality as signifying religious, cultural and political allegiances.[18] Thus, racially and ethnically appropriate heterosexual family life is reinforced as the bedrock of nation in a range of different postcolonial contexts, and challenges to this are framed as not only personally or socially deviant, but as national betrayals.[19] For national spokesmen for a range of African and Asian nation-states, among others, homosexuality is a framed as a betrayal in two ways: as a failure of appropriate gendered and sexual citizenship, and as a marker of Western influence. By suturing nation to heterosexuality through positing 'gayness ... as a polluting foreign influence', state representatives can deny any history of same-sex practice in the national context at stake, and dismiss global sexual rights movements as straightforwardly imperialistic.[20] The impact of such discourses is devastating for sexual health awareness and provision, and for people whose desires do not fit the expected heterosexual frame. Suturing nationalism to heteronormativity in this way also plays into the Western conviction that developing nations are less advanced, less tolerant and less concerned with individual rights, such that gay and lesbian tolerance can stand as a dubious symbol of Western democratic freedom. In this respect, sexuality's intersection with gender and nation is of critical importance to unpacking contemporary, global political networks of exchange.

*Sexual Translations*

Within this insistence that sexuality is a primary concern for anyone interested in nationalism, state regulation and globalisation, questions remain as to how to understand sexual practice transnationally without replicating the above dynamics. In other words, how might Western sexuality scholars engage with and challenge violence and homophobic constraint transnationally without imposing Western terms and social conditions as universals? Vincanne Adams and Stacy Leigh Pigg helpfully articulate this concern as 'an epistemological question concerning the limits of all projects of representation, especially those pertaining to cross-cultural interpretation or translation'.[21] The problem of nomenclature is a key issue for transnational 'queer' studies, in its emphasis both on the dangers of over-association of sexual rights with Westernisation, as suggested, and the need to develop a transnational sexual rights agenda sensitive to differences of experience and history of 'same-sex' sexual behaviour. It is in the context of transnational 'queer' studies that I take forward this discussion.[22]

The use of time- and place-specific identity categories such as 'gay' and 'lesbian' as universals by Western scholars and activists has been critiqued as inaccurate and ethnocentric.[23] While justification for such universalisation tends to stress the political and ethical importance of identifying 'transcultural features inherent in the experience of same-sex attraction itself',[24] critics point instead to the ways that universalisation often tells us more about the observer than it does the context under scrutiny. Thus, as Carole Vance notes, '[t]he literature routinely regards opposite gender sexual contact as "heterosexuality" and same gender contact as "homosexuality", as if the same phenomena were being observed in all societies in which these acts occurred'.[25] Such presumptions frequently represent the reification of existing categories of analysis and the identity of the researcher in ways that prevent practices being understood in context.[26] As Swarr and Nagar suggest, 'terms like lesbian can be incomplete, inapplicable, or even offensive depending on contexts and histories. But scholarship and organisations often rely on such terms, concepts, and identities – including their Western and imperialist trappings – with little or no interrogation'.[27] This debate is not only restricted to the politics of identity naming, but also to the epistemologies and tropes that attend the privileging of Western sexual identity, such as 'voice, visibility, and coming out' and 'closet', or indeed 'homophobia'.[28]

These discussions are similar to those operating within sexual historiography, where the terms of the debate are focused on whether one can legitimately name sexual practices lesbian, gay, bisexual and so on, if the term was not historically available.[29] This is an important link for transnational 'queer' studies, because it both underlines the dangers of assuming that contemporary Western identity categories are universally applicable, and, importantly, raises questions about the teleological assumptions embedded in understanding same-sex behaviour cross-culturally as being 'really' or eventually becoming 'gay'. The latter assumption takes its strongest form in work on social movements, where it is common to understand emergent gay and lesbian movements in different part of the globe as directly mirroring Western gay and lesbian movements from the 1960s and 1970s on.[30] Denis Altman thus uses his own experience of travelling to insist on the transnational valence of the term 'gay' for people outside the West. 'Last year in Morocco', Altman writes, 'I met several men who identified as gay, and felt they would need to emigrate to escape family pressures.'[31] Altman's rendition of his experience, which he repeats throughout his work, is emblematic of the way lesbian and gay rights come to stand not only for freedom from 'compulsory heterosexuality',[32] but from national constraint. In such narratives, women are frequently stereotyped as bearers of those national strictures (the disappointed mother; the passive asexual wife). As Mark Chiang suggests in his provocative reading of *The Wedding Banquet*, desire for both men and women can thus only be narrated as a failure to become fully gay or lesbian, which is also to say fully transnational.[33] For Altman, in contrast, gay and lesbian subjects are imaginatively freed to participate in a realm of transnational identification beyond time and space, as if there were no national histories to the development of lesbian and gay rights. Indeed, this cosmopolitan identification actively works to obscure the privileges of nation that allow certain people and not others to travel and participate in 'global gay culture'.[34]

Such developmental paradigms do of course have certain positive effects in rights terms. Sexual persecution asylum claims rely on discourses of Western spaces as providing safe havens from homophobic violence, and this allows people to flee contexts in which they are indeed under threat. Yet such claims tend to be successful to the extent that they underscore the idea of 'gay' as fundamental and transnationally applicable, and as the country of origin as backward and needing to be brought up to Western standards. In this respect, the framework of these rights claims is unacceptably – often impossibly – narrow, leaving many people unable to access those rights. As Lionel Cantú Jr, Eithne Luibhéid and Minna Stern point out in the context of Mexico, only certain subjects fit the bill in gendered as well as sexual terms.[35] They argue that in the United States' imagined Latin America it is the effeminate gay man, counterposed to the 'macho' heterosexual penetrator, who is the recognisable subject in rights terms. He can be understood to embody the pernicious effects of Latin America's backward and oppressive sex/gender system in ways that other 'homosexual' subjects cannot, and in ways that naturalise the hierarchical political relationship between the US and Mexico.[36] Similar issues pertain to the question of lesbian rights. As Vivien Ng argues in the context of China, and Mariam Fraser indicates in the context of the UK, the linking of rights to identity assumes not only that identity is available to all subjects equally, but that those able to articulate their sexualities as (Western) identities are the most in need, thus obscuring question of class in particular.[37]

The above critiques of 'gay' travels across time and space do, however, run the risk of assuming a radical *discontinuity* among global formations of same-sex meaning. While the term 'gay' as a same-sex identity marker should not be universally imposed, a number of commentators also point to the dangers of assuming that it is 'inherently Western and alien'.[38] As discussed above, the nationalist insistence on gay and lesbian identities as Western feeds into the denial of the history of same-sex practices in many non-Western contexts. In this respect, as Ng points out, well-meaning anti-imperial gestures can confirm restrictive or coercive contexts that Chinese women currently experience with respect to freedom of sexual expression.[39] And in his analysis of same-sex sex between men in Calcutta, Paul Boyce argues that such a cordoning off of Indian sexual authenticity denies the history of English as an Indian language, and he insists that '"Gay" can be, and is, Indian, even if, or because, it refers to Western ideas, language and influences'.[40] Writers in this vein argue for a more complex global history of modern sexual identities that explores the overlaps between contextual sexual histories and meanings as well as the important differences among them. Histories such as Peter Jackson's of Thailand, where 'the word "gay" was being used as a self-identificatory label by homosexually active men ... some years before the 1969 Stonewall riots in New York City saw the establishment of the modern gay liberation movement', and Martin F. Manalansan's of 'the bakla or the Filipino gay man' who is 'a subject in constant mediation whose modernity is not always dependent on Western mainstream queer culture', offer important challenges to the fantasy of the West as a point of origin for modern 'homosexuality'.[41] This work promises to offer a challenge to simplistic understandings of 'gay and lesbian identity' as either imperialistic or transnationally liberating.

*Queer Interventions*

Queer theory is appealing as a way of making sense of transnational sexual meaning largely because of its focus on challenges to identity categories and heteronormative discourses.[42] In her foundational work, *The Epistemology of the Closet*, Eve Kosofsky Sedgwick stresses the importance of uncoupling sexual behaviour and identity as a way of challenging the dominant discursive opposition of heterosexuality and homosexuality in modern Western culture. For Sedgwick, 'queer' operates both as a verb, *to queer*, and as a descriptive noun for sexual subjects whose practices do not coalesce easily in identity terms, while in *Gender Trouble*, Judith Butler argues against the dominant vision of 'sex' as the ground of 'gender', suggesting instead that heteronormativity naturalises their relationship. For Butler, causing 'gender trouble' thus has the capacity to transform power relations, by exposing the relationships between sex, gender and sexuality as fictional and regulatory.[43] Importantly for transnational sexuality studies, queer theory as it has developed in the United States has also focused on sexual oppositions as raced, gendered and classed, emphasising the formation of modern sexual subjectivity in colonialism and the intersectional nature of sexual experience.[44]

These strands of argument have been taken up in transnational contexts across a range of disciplines. So, for example, within development studies, Susie Jolly uses a Butlerian framework to challenge the dominant 'gender and development' paradigm's affirmation of sex and gender as naturally linked, and Boyce draws on Sedgwick to challenge the over-association between sexual identity and behaviour in HIV/AIDS health measures in India.[45] In a similar vein, Sasho Lambevski uses queer methodology to interrogate the assumption that active/passive sexual practices between men in Macedonia primarily correlate with homosexual or heterosexual identities. For Lambevski, the importance of active/passive sexual positioning is its regulation of hierarchical national and class differences in that sphere, and he argues strongly that a queer approach can help challenge nationalism at the everyday level.[46] Work such as Jyoti Puri's on the relationship between gender, sexuality and religion in New Delhi also extends queer's promise of destabilising modern Western heterosexual/homosexual oppositions to critically examine the mobilisation of homosexuality as Westernisation versus heterosexuality as postcolonial nationalism, and particularly this contest's effects on women and sexual minorities.[47] As one might expect, exponents of transnational 'queer' studies also engage in the question of nomenclature directly. Proponents of its use take up Sedgwick's celebration of queer as both a descriptive noun and active verb, and stress the term's openness as critical to reflexive, attentive transnational work on sexual meaning. Queer is not only understood as distinct from Western sexual categories, but is also credited with highlighting the limits of these, as indicated above. Thus, Eithne Luibhéid suggests that the term 'queer' marks 'the fact that many standard sexuality categories were historically formed through specific epistemologies and social relations that upheld colonialist, xenophobic, racist, and sexist regimes'.[48]

Yet despite being initially enthusiastic about queer's capacity for transnational analysis, lately I have become concerned about its function in Western transnational sexuality studies as a 'way out' of the ongoing dilemmas that characterise the field. The first suspicion I have relates to the way in which queer very often loses its specificity in transnational work and comes to mean whatever the author needs it to in context. Thus, in his work on law, social change and sexuality Arvind Narrain chooses 'queer' over 'lesbian and gay' as a better, less imposing way of describing Indian same-sex sexuality, yet in fact he utilises 'queer' as a universal in much the same way he critiques, noting that in India 'though the word queer is not commonly used, "the realities" of the queer experience ... have traditionally existed and continue to exist in the contemporary context'.[49] Similarly, Alyssa Howe argues for 'a universal queer subject' who is able 'to enact queer politics that engage international discourses of identity and human rights, but [is] not ruled by them', in order to rethink same-sex sexual practice between women in non-identitarian terms.[50] But Howe offers no clear sense of what these politics are, how one might avoid being ruled by such discourses, or, indeed, who this universal queer subject might be. What appears to be happening in such work is an acknowledgement of the problems of sexual translation, but a rather hasty instantiation of 'queer' as the answer to those problems with no concomitant paradigmatic or methodological shift.

In a similar vein, Ian Barnard interrogates queer theory's current pervasiveness in the field by asking suggestively, 'is wanting queer to be everything not just a new kind of Western white male imperialism, another instance of white male desire to be everywhere, talk about everything, be everything'.[51] Both Barnard and Jasbir Puar have, rightly I believe, pointed out that such uses of queer theory are predominantly gestural, and work to avoid delineating queer theory itself as having a history or location that marks it.[52] As I have suggested in this section so far, queer theory does of course have a history and location firmly anchored in the academy and political activism in the United States of the 1990s. I want to suggest, again with Barnard, that part of how queer wish-fulfilment works is that it *performs* separation of queer inquiry from Western lesbian and gay identities, but remains underwritten and motivated by those identities. Barnard thus protests that '[d]espite the denotative potential of "queer" to apply to anything that stays from the norm, its historical legacy and current usage sutures it to lesbian and gay sexualities'.[53]

## II. Imagining Bisexuality

Bisexuality has an ambivalent relationship to this queer history, as suggested in my introduction. In political terms, the use of 'queer' as an umbrella term to include a range of sexually marginal behaviours, so wittily articulated by Sedgwick, offered the hope of bisexual inclusion.[54] As too did the Butlerian challenge to the necessary correlation between sexed body, gender and sexual identity.[55] Bisexual queer theory and politics focused particularly on animating the 'sexual middle ground' between hetero- and homosexuality as part of a broader transgression of Western sexual oppositions seen as limiting or oppressive.[56] That development of bisexuality as a middle ground between oppositions was also the basis for bisexual theorists' claims that bisexuality was for sexual oppositions what 'mixed race' identity was for racial oppositions, and that bisexuals faced a similar oppression to lesbians and gay men of colour within the queer movement.[57] It seems to me now that this insistence on the bisexual middle ground as always subversive, rather than as part of the history of Western sexual categorisation, including colonial racial hierarchisation, weakened bisexual claims to queer political inclusion, however. It may also have facilitated both its decreased visibility within queer theory and its reinscription as either the tie that binds identity, or as unacknowledged pre-oedipal primitive potential (itself a form of racial erasure, as suggested in my introduction). Neither is it common for Western bisexual theorists to take a transnational turn, except through a universal discovery of it everywhere unchanged, in history, culture and representation.[58] To date, no bisexual theory seems to address questions of bisexuality in ways that take the problems of transnational nomenclature as axiomatic.

In this part of the paper, then, I map instead the role bisexual meaning continues to play in transnational sexuality studies, focusing on the critical effects of its presence and absence. To begin with, I discuss the significance of bisexual absence in shaping transnational 'queer' studies as *de facto* authored by lesbian and gay subjects. I follow this with an analysis of the importance of bisexual presence in transnational sexual health, development and anthropological perspectives. In relation to the latter arena in particular, the texts I engage with concern male-to-male sexual meanings. This is not intended to sideline material on same-sex sexual practice among women, but is rather a reflection of the paucity of research on women in these fields. There are several reasons for this: the first is that much of the work in sexual health focuses on men in the context of HIV/AIDS; the second is that, as Ng, Y. Antonia Chao, Ara Wilson and Swarr and Nagar all note, questions of recognition and naming work very differently in relation to women, in part because of their usually more precarious social position.[59] In effect, this is one of the dangers of a mapping of existing critical work in the field; it reproduces the same margins as the original material.

*Bisexual Erasure*

What Barnard, above, calls the 'suturing' of queer to lesbian and gay sexualities is partly effected by bisexual erasure. Although I am not the kind of bisexual theorist that wants to insist on bisexual identity recognition, I have found myself rather relentlessly called upon to notice the absence of bisexual naming in transnational 'queer' studies work. 'Gay' and 'lesbian' might be used interchangeably or negatively contrasted with 'queer', and an occasional 'transgender' might be called upon, but 'bisexual' is consistently neither part of the mix, nor superseded by the transnational powers of 'queer'. So, for example, in Jon Binnie's *The Globalization of Sexuality*, which challenges the limits of a 'gay' agenda for understanding sexual formations transnationally, bisexuality is completely absent. Binnie thus contrasts limited gay and lesbian rights and movements with the mobility and fluidity of queer theory, both in the West and in its analytical capacities 'elsewhere'. In the process of repetition of this distinction, 'gay and lesbian' and 'queer' become a closed circle, a performative iteration of inverse colonial logic.[60] Even in work that is critical of queer's capacity for transnational exploration, such as Puar's on sexual meaning in Trinidad and Jackson's on the complex histories of same-sex sexual meaning in Thailand, the certainty that gay and lesbian, and later queer, are accurate descriptors of what is 'left behind' in temporal or geographical terms, remains uninterrogated.[61]

However damning these writers are of the imperialism of Western naming practices, what counts as Western is flattened by what I would term this 'bisexual disappearing'. It is as if there were no histories of contest over Western sexual meaning, as if lesbian and gay were empirically accurate descriptive categories of Western sexual behaviour and identity.[62] Thus, although Jackson is clear that queer studies' 'emphasis on multiplicity and diversity [hides] ... a tendency to be enchanted by the three letters "gay"', he does little to challenge the field's presumption that those 'three letters' do in fact describe Western sexual identities accurately.[63] Of course, it is not just bisexuality that is absent from such histories, but in restricting Western non-heterosexual *identities* to gay and lesbian, the absence of that other major Western sexual identity, bisexuality, is particularly glaring. In addition, and as I discuss below, this absence provides the broader context within which bisexuality's minor appearances take place.

As suggested above, bisexuality is not marked only by its absence from transnational 'queer' studies, it is also present as identity at certain moments and in specific ways that are worth further investigation. In particular, I have been struck in my reading within this field by bisexuality's 'identity appearance' in work otherwise uninterested in exploring the theoretical value of the term. It emerges as a series of asides that ask whether or not to call certain sexual acts 'bisexual', almost immediately insisting on the limits of this reification of Western identity categories. This move mirrors that effected by more Western-focused queer work, where, as I have discussed, bisexuality is framed as having an almost *unique* capacity for reinforcing dominant sexual discourse.[64] Despite the fact that queer theorists acknowledge the ability to resignify homosexual identities through their resistant community histories and interpersonal practices, bisexuality is rarely accorded the same dignity.[65] What is odd about bisexuality's invocation in the context of transnational 'queer' studies is that it tends to occur in articles that continue to use the terms 'lesbian', 'gay' or 'homosexual' to describe same-sex behaviour transnationally, however problematised those terms otherwise are in the argument of the text. It is as if 'lesbian' and 'gay' can be understood as strategic uses of identity, but 'bisexual' cannot be.

Mark McLelland's article querying Japanese 'gay identity' introduces bisexuality into his discussion in ways typical of the trend I am describing. McLelland is explicit from the outset that uncritical nomenclature '[leaves] out what is difficult to fit into the picture', yet as indicated continues to use the term gay, either with or without scare quotes, throughout his piece.[66] Yet in his dicussion of Barbara Summerhawk's insistence that Japanese 'queer' people need identity labels in order 'to form and benefit from supportive communities' McLelland is summarily dismissive.[67] Introduced by McLelland as 'a bisexual woman herself', he critiques Summerhawk's suggestion that Japanese failure to come to 'bi consciousness' is a temporary problem that will be rectified with appropriate development of sexual communities along Western lines. I would generally agree with McLelland that the presumption 'that there are empirical states which can be labelled "lesbian", "gay", or "bi" 'is problematic for transnational sexuality studies, for reasons discussed throughout this paper.[68] What interests me here, however, is the author's choice of bisexual Summerhawk to make this point effectively, a move which transfers his simmering anxieties about retaining 'gay' that run through the article onto bisexuality.

Shortly after his brief but, it emerges, essential dismissal of bisexuality, McLelland relates that in the course of conducting interviews for his research, he discovered that '[t]he "marriage problem" (*kekkon mondai*) is a very common theme on gay internet chat sites, and many gay magazines contain personal ads from lesbians and some straight women who wish to enter into marriage with gay men'.[69] Since the reader already knows that to call these men 'bisexual' would be an unacceptable Western imposition, McLelland's continued use of 'gay' is refigured as more neutral and, indeed, as an opening out of the category to include relationships with women as cultural location requires it (keeping cultural location radically 'other' to Western categorisation in the process). Women, who McLelland can only imagine to be drawn to these 'gay' men for their less misogynistic femininity in a world hostile to straight women, are unproblematically lesbian, straight or asexual; sites and publications, and the men within them, reiterated as 'gay'; while Summerhawk is castigated once again for her naïve insistence on these men's false consciousness. An enormous amount of energy is expended here on preserving, while seeming to keep open, these men's status as gay. I am not, as I hope is clear, saying that these men are really bisexual – that is not my point here. But I am interested in the mechanisms through which 'gay' is released from the Western identity burden that McLelland wishes it did not carry to become a more accurate description of opposite and same-sex behaviour than 'bisexual', despite the Western context marking both terms. Gillian Dunne performs a similar manoeuvre in her work on 'gay dads' in the United Kingdom. Dunne continues to call her research participants 'gay' despite their own resistance to such a label. She uses her adherence to social constructionism as the basis of her dismissal of bisexuality (which marks a return to identity in familiar ways), but not as a way of interrogating gayness. In strikingly similar ways to McLelland, one result of the refusal to relinquish 'gay', but willingness to banish 'bisexual', is the framing of the women involved in these relationships as straight and seemingly desireless.[70]

My discussion of McLelland and Dunne has not given a very accurate picture of the tone of these bisexual dismissals, a tone I think is rather important. Writers such as McLelland, Dunne and previously Sedgwick, are impatient with the imagined person on the sidelines of their work, insisting they take bisexuality seriously. They are irritated that this fantasy bisexual wants to reintroduce identity at this period of sophistication in transnational sexuality studies. The poor imagined bisexual is assigned the role of central protagonist in the Western past we are busy surpassing, the Western past that transnational 'queer' theory wants to leave behind. Such a figuring of bisexuality frames it as a kind of 'identity remnant', one antithetical, even oppositional, to transnational 'queer' inquiry. Thinking through bisexuality's perverse placement as both routinely absent from a queer teleology and as a uniquely Western-saturated identity, it seems that bisexuality performs considerable work. Yet its paradoxical positioning within queer theory allows it to carry the burden of Western sexual identity failings, while gay and lesbian identities are re-associated with a history of increasing openness and fluidity, culminating in the transnational queer present.

Not all considerations of bisexual naming that reject its accuracy dismiss it in this way. Boyce's work, for example, considers the possibility of applying 'bisexual' to the experiences of the men he interviewed in his ethnography of male-to-male sexuality in Calcutta, but he decides against it, for similar reasons to his rejection of the term 'gay'. He emphasises that bisexuality, like other sexual identities, has a cultural specificity belied by such casual use. Concluding his short discussion of this issue, Boyce insists that the 'label would not only be meaningless to the men described, but would imply a coherent sphere of bisexual experience dissonant from the inherently fragmented and irregular sexual practices indicated'.[71] The difference in such work is that Boyce is clearly not using the limits of bisexual identity naming as a way of presenting queer credentials while retaining a gay reading position.

Deflecting the necessity for *locating* queer inquiry has effects that I think transnational 'queer' studies needs to be concerned about beyond issues of bisexual representation. It provides the researcher with a sure gay and lesbian past and home from which to explore complex otherness elsewhere, whether the researcher accepts or rejects queer as useful in that search. My anxiety is that, whatever the researcher's intention, this exploration mirrors rather than challenges the developmental model of sexual subjectivity and social movements, in which the non-West is more amorphous and harder to pin down than the teleologically over-determined West. It also means that the burden of representation is placed fully 'elsewhere', with the only challenges to Western sexual categorisation coming from non-Western contexts. The unidirectionality of this gaze risks fetishising the local as authentic, and further insulates the researcher from needing to reflect upon their motivations for wanting to find difference or sameness in particular places and times.[72]

*Bisexual Neutrality*

I want to shift now to look at a further instance of bisexual appearance within transnational sexuality studies: bisexuality is most visible as *behaviour* in international policy and development work, particularly that focusing on sexual health and HIV/AIDS, where the concept of 'behavioural bisexuality' has often been used interchangeably with the term MSM (men who have sex with men). Here, as in the queer theory literature, concern is with finding terms and concepts to describe individual and community behaviour in context,[73] rather than imposing Western (or other) identity categories that target subjects who do not recognise themselves in those terms.[74] Bisexuality is thus commonly used as an attempt to describe sexual practices involving both men and women in ways that are neutral rather than value laden, partly to try and circumvent the problems of over-association of homosexual identity with Westernisation discussed earlier.[75] Yet what occurs in this desire for bisexuality to be neutral is that its own specific history as a Western sexual category is frequently obscured.

Peter Aggleton's edited collection *Bisexualities and AIDS* provides ample examples of this use of bisexuality as behaviour, as the multiple 'bisexualities' of the title would indicate.[76] Aggleton begins the collection promisingly with the caveat that use of bisexuality as a behaviour or description needs to be interrogated carefully in relation to the epidemic, and opens up possible bisexual meanings by asking 'to what extent is male "bisexuality" the same all over the world'?[77] His cautious tone is echoed by Shivananda Khan, who stresses the importance of cultural sensitivity in work on AIDS globally, and by Richard Parker who asserts that 'the constitution of one's sexual identity (or identities) must necessarily be negotiated in the flow of social interaction, and interaction, in turn, is necessarily shaped by the specific contexts or situations in which it takes place'.[78] Parker further cautions that without such negotiation HIV/AIDS messages have limited impact, 'precisely because many men who have sex with other men, as well as with women, fail to identify themselves as either *homosexual* or *bisexual*'.[79]

Despite these moments of reflexivity, however, bisexuality remains radically under-theorised by the authors in this collection. Despite his opening question, Aggleton continues to use the term as if it referred to the same practices globally, i.e. simply sex with both men and women.[80] And whatever the salience of his earlier point about identification, Parker also uses the term as a neutral description of behaviour throughout his article.[81] Neither is the universal use of bisexuality restricted to the analysis of contemporary behaviour. Pan and Aggleton correct the Chinese record book by declaring that 'viewed behaviourally, the so-called male homosexuality of Chinese classical literature would seem to have been bisexual', writing against the grain of sexual historiography.[82] To mobilise bisexuality as part of an unbiased 'recording' of sexual behaviour across time and space is to lose sight of the importance of location in ways these authors otherwise emphasise. There is no sense here of the term 'bisexuality' as already representing a particular interpretation of sexual behaviour, as referencing an identity with a specific history, or of the significance of people's *experience* of desire that is sidelined in these empiricist accounts.[83] If bisexuality is not a meaningful concept in a given context, its use as a universal will restrict its value in understanding what these behaviours mean to the people bisexuality is used to describe. What is striking is that these authors are otherwise fully aware that interpretations and the experience of desire have a direct impact on the effectiveness of HIV prevention strategies.

One function of bisexual appearance as behaviour rather than identity is to reserve the category of 'homosexual' for 'the real thing'. So, still in the same Aggleton volume, Ana Luisa Liguori *et al.* use the term 'behavioural bisexuality' to describe men's actions as inserters with men and women in Costa Rica, and 'homosexual' for men whose sexual patterns resemble those associated with Western gay men.[84] And while anthropologist James Green makes what initially appears to be a more open statement in relation to sexual practice in Brazil, suggesting that, '[i]ndeed, one must think of multiple homosexualities or sexualities since a form of bisexuality, the phenomenon of married men who have sex with other men, yet maintain heterosexual relationships, also remains common', it is only the realisation of this 'form of bisexuality' that causes Green to multiply his terms.[85] Homosexuality in the singular remains something that does not include these kinds of practices, as also underlined by his slip into 'sexualities' as an alternative term once 'homosexuality' has been multiplied. Sensitivity to questions of sexual translation is thus reserved for what are perceived as *cultural differences* in sexual practice; what homosexuality is presumed to mean in a Western context is never seriously challenged.

Denis Altman provides a further example of this bisexual/homosexual separation when he speaks approvingly of 'a Moroccan friend who defined himself as homosexual, not bisexual, and thus consciously set himself apart from other presumed bisexual men'.[86] Bisexuality as an identity cannot find any space in Altman's rhetoric, negatively squashed as it is between homosexual (identity) and 'presumed' bisexual (behaviour). The conscious choice to 'set himself apart' marks Altman's friend's decision as a sign of his coming of age in identity terms, as being prepared to take the risk that 'presumed bisexual men' are not. Bisexuality as a form of closeting, or over-emphasis on the sexual rather than community or political aspects of identity, is an ongoing theme in lesbian and gay writing on bisexuality in Western contexts.[87] In Altman's work the common perception of bisexuality as a phase in individual terms is mirrored by his investment in the clear developmental move from 'premodern forms of sexual organization' to modern acknowledgment and visibility of homosexual or gay subjects and communities.[88] For Altman, bisexual behaviour belongs to a premodern era, wherever or whenever that may be.

In developmental models of global sexual movements, the relationship between pre-modern and modern sexual organisation is geographically imagined in ways that invest the past, or pre-modern, spaces with an innocence that needs to be surpassed. Altman's parallel between a move from bisexuality to homosexuality, and from pre-modern to modern subjectivity and community, constitutes a sleight of hand that indicates how very far from neutral using bisexuality to describe behaviour is in a global context. In fact, if leaving bisexuality behind is a precondition for access to sexual modernity, its framing as 'merely behavioural' reinforces rather than challenges power imbalances between Western sexual researchers and the contexts under scrutiny.[89]

## III. Conclusion

My analysis of bisexual appearance and disappearance within transnational 'queer' studies has highlighted two primary issues that I would like to close on. Rather than go back through the various 'findings' of my reading of the field, I want to use these as the springboard for thinking about how the field might strengthen its research while remaining vigilant about the reproduction of power relations between nations and subjects.

Firstly, I have come to the conclusion a number of times in the paper that the appearance or disappearance of bisexuality serves to retain the imagined integrity of the category of 'Western homosexual'. This occurs through its performative articulation as distinct from bisexuality (identity or behaviour) and thus as the *de facto* ground of queerness. In addition, homosexuality maintains its integrity by finding, and seriously considering, difference elsewhere, but not folding that difference into a transnational understanding of homosexuality. The primary 'difference' I am signalling here is of course opposite-sex desire. In this respect, the desire not to be culturally imperialist by imposing homosexuality can easily slip into a mechanism for 'self-preservation' instead. We know from Eve Sedgwick's analysis of the nature of men's heterosexuality that homosociality is essential to its functioning;[90] what queer theory has yet to address is whether the inverse is also true. Is there a heteronormativity within homosexuality that needs to be disavowed by queer theory? And might there be a way of thinking this through transnationally in terms other than the oppositional, psychoanalytically informed ones we have now? One starting point might be to bring transnational feminist and 'queer' studies together in more direct ways to look at how transnational queer subjectivity is often formed through rejection of the family, and therefore nation. As I suggested earlier on, such framing assumes that women are stereotypically passive, feminine and heterosexual (leaving little analytic or representational room for women who do not fit this description), and places a burden of 'homosexual' self-representation on those seeking asylum, where homosexuality is evidenced by absolute distance from heterosexual acts and gendering. Transnational 'queer' studies clearly needs to take this issue seriously if it is not to continue to reproduce anxieties about 'opposite sex difference' in the process of translation of sexual meanings globally. Such an approach would also mean taking seriously the importance of empirical studies on same-sex sexual behaviour among women as part of such an inquiry.

Secondly, it seems to me that the idea of transnational sexual epistemology needs to be more fully explored. I have already suggested that an epistemology that assumes a singular homosexual subject, even with a multiple object, runs the risk of defensive rather than fully speculative 'encounters'. This is also true of work from a bisexual perspective that assumes presence, rather than absence, is necessarily a good thing. A focus on bisexual identity as antidote to the effects of mobilising bisexuality as behaviour, for example, is likely to fail to address both the work that bisexual identity does, and the limits of what comes under that term. A broader project of thinking through what it means to engage in transnational sexuality studies with difference at the heart of that inquiry rather than as peripheral to it seems urgent. In a context of global sexual violence and compromise, as well as pleasures and rights, it can also never be enough simply to conclude that we need to highlight partiality, or focus more fully on critique. We also need to be able make meaningful connections across contexts that are not simply comparative, but provide epistemological approaches that are flexible but allow us to make particular *judgments*.[91]

One certainty for me is that we need to turn our attention to the ways in which we *go about* finding out about sexuality, rather than deciding what our object of inquiry is in advance, or expecting it spontaneously to reveal itself.[92] We can assume certain things about this 'difference project', I think. We can assume it comprises encounters between subjects who mis-recognise and mis-translate one another continually, and that sexual meanings will change as subjects negotiate and experience them in their daily lives. We can assume that these meanings are not only observed but also experienced by the transnational researcher. And we can assume that we need to ask different questions, such as, 'what kinds of complex compromises allow survival in this context?' rather than 'which subjects do what, and what are they called?' A few more questions: What kinds of contradictions (of language, history and so forth) might be operational in this context? What work does identity or its refusal do in particular contexts? Lastly, can we assume that a politics of accountability needs to be at the centre of this project, in the sense of sustained attention to what difference our research makes and for whom? What do my analysis and conclusions enable to happen next?

## Acknowledgements

Thanks to Phil C. W. Chan for his support throughout, and to the Sexualities Reading Group at the Gender Institute, LSE, for helping clarify many of the thoughts in this paper.

## Notes

1. Eve Kosofsky Sedgwick, *The Epistemology of the Closet* (London: Harvester Wheatsheaf 1991), p.27.
2. See, e.g., Bi Academic Intervention (ed.), *The Bisexual Imaginary: Representation, Identity and Desire* (London: Cassell 1997); Sharon Morris and Merl Storr (eds), 'Bisexual Special Issue', *Journal of Gay, Lesbian, and Bisexual Identity*, Vol.2, No.1 (1997); Maria Pramaggiore and Donald Hall (eds), *Representing Bisexualities: Subjects and Cultures of Fluid Desire* (New York: New York University Press 1996).
3. For critiques of this position, see Amber Ault, 'Hegemonic Discourse in an Oppositional Community: Lesbian Feminist Stigmatization of Bisexual Women', in B. Beemyn and M. Eliason (eds), *Queer Studies: A Lesbian, Gay Bisexual, and Transgender Anthology* (New York: New York University Press 1996), pp.204–16; Jo Eadie, 'Activating Bisexuality: Towards a Bi/Sexual Politics', in J. Bristow and A. Wilson (eds), *Activating Theory: Lesbian, Gay, Bisexual Politics* (London: Cassell 1993), pp.139–70; Ann Kaloski, 'Returning to the Lesbian *Bildungsroman*: a Bisexual Reading (of) Nancy Toder's *Choices*', in Bi Academic Intervention (note 2) pp.90–105; Paula Rust, *Bisexuality and the Challenge to Lesbian Politics: Sex, Loyalty and Revolution* (New York: New York University Press 1995).
4. Marjorie Garber, *Bisexuality and the Eroticism of Everyday Life* (London: Penguin 1995); Merl Storr (ed.), *Bisexuality: A Critical Reader* (London: Routledge 1999); Clare Hemmings, *Bisexual Spaces: A Geography of Sexuality and Gender* (New York: Routledge 2002).
5. For transgender studies critiques, see Judith Halberstam, *Female Masculinity* (Durham, NC: Duke University Press 1998); Judith Halberstam, *In a Queer Time and Place: Transgender Bodies, Subcultural Lives* (New York: New York University Press 2005); Jay Prosser, *Second Skins: The Body Narratives of Trannsexuality* (New York: Columbia University Press 1998); and Susan Stryker, 'Transgender Studies: Queer Theory's Evil Twin', *GLQ: Journal of Lesbian and Gay Studies*, Vol.10, No.2 (2004), pp.212–15. There are, of course, a range of possible reasons for the disparity in the take-up of bisexual and transgendered perspectives. The success of Judith Butler's *Gender Trouble*, which favours drag as performative, must be one such factor. In addition, the distinction between *transgender* and *transsexual* has also enabled the former to denote gender ambiguity, and the latter gender identity, in ways that mean 'trans studies' can fore-

ground both performativity and the importance of embodiment in critical ways. In contrast, there is no distinction in terminology between bisexuality as action or identity. Judith Butler, *Gender Trouble: Feminism and the Subversion of Identity* (New York: Routledge 1990).

6. Hemmings, *Bisexual Spaces* (note 4); Clare Hemmings, 'Waiting for No Man: Bisexual Femme Subjectivity and Cultural Repudiation', in Ken Gelder (ed.), *The Subcultures Reader* (New York: Routledge 2005), pp.418–32; and Clare Hemmings, 'Rescuing Lesbian Camp', *Journal of Lesbian Studies*, Vol.11, No.1/2 (2007), pp.175–82.
7. Malcolm Bowie's description of the competing definitions of bisexuality remains useful. Malcolm Bowie, 'Bisexuality', in E. Wright (ed.), *Feminism and Psychoanalysis: A Critical Dictionary* (Oxford: Basil Blackwell 1992), pp.26–31.
8. Judith Butler, 'Melancholy Gender/Refused Identification', in J. Butler, *The Psychic Life of Power: Theories in Subjection* (Stanford, CA: Stanford University Press 1997), pp.132–50.
9. Sigmund Freud (1905), 'Three Essays on the Theory of Sexuality', *Volume 7. On Sexuality: Three Essays on the Theory of Sexuality and Other Works*, in A. Richards (ed.), *The Penguin Freud Library* (London: Penguin 1977), pp.31–169.
10. Merl Storr, 'The Sexual Reproduction of "Race": Bisexuality, History and Racialization', in Bi Academic Intervention (note 2) pp.73–88. For more general accounts of the relationship between homosexuality and colonialism, see Siobhan Somerville, 'Scientific Racism and the Invention of the Homosexual Body', in R. N. Lancaster and M. di Leonardo (eds), *The Gender Sexuality Reader: Culture, History, Political Economy* (New York: Routledge 1997), pp.37–52; and Jennifer Terry, *An American Obsession: Science, Medicine, and Homosexuality in Modern Society* (Chicago: University of Chicago Press 1999).
11. Of course, there are feminist writers within humanities or social/political sciences who achieve this without a particular sexuality focus – Rey Chow and V. Spike Peterson, respectively, come to mind. But transnational sexuality studies' bridging is constitutive of the field rather than exceptional. Rey Chow, *The Age of the World Target: Self-Referentiality in War, Theory, and Comparative Work* (Durham, NC: Duke University Press 2006); V. Spike Peterson, 'How (the Meaning of) Gender Matters in Political Economy', *New Political Economy*, Vol.10, No.4 (2005), pp.499–521.
12. Amanda Lock Swarr and Richa Nagar, 'Dismantling Assumptions: Interrogating "Lesbian" Struggles for Identity and Survival in India and South Africa', *Signs*, Vol.29, No.2 (2003), pp.491–516.
13. Theorists such as Jyoti Puri and Jon Binnie thus adapt Michel Foucault's delineation of the centrality of sexuality to the emergence of the subject of the modern state to postcolonial contexts. More directly, Laura Ann Stoler seeks to critically integrate his interrogation of sexuality with an analysis of colonialism. Jyoti Puri, 'Sex, Sexuality and the Nation State', in *Woman, Body, Desire in Post-colonial India: Narratives of Gender and Sexuality* (New York: Routledge 1999), pp.25–42; Jon Binnie, *The Globalization of Sexuality* (London: Sage 2004); Michel Foucault, *The History of Sexuality, Vol.I: An Introduction* (New York: Vintage Books 1978); Laura Ann Stoler, *Race and the Education of Desire: Foucault's History of Sexuality and the Colonial Order of Things* (Durham, NC: Duke University Press 1995).
14. See Adrienne Rich, 'Compulsory Heterosexuality and Lesbian Existence', in C. Stimpson and E. S. Person (eds), *Women: Sex and Sexuality* (Chicago: University of Chicago Press 1980), pp.62–91; and Carole S. Vance, 'Anthropology Rediscovers Sexuality: a Theoretical Comment', in R. Parker and P. Aggleton (eds), *Culture, Society and Sexuality: A Reader* (London: University College Press 2002), pp.39–54.
15. Susie Jolly, '"Queering" Development: Exploring the Links Between Same Sex Sexualities, Gender, and Development', *Gender and Development*, Vol.8, No.1 (2000), pp.78–88.
16. Thus Nancy Fraser and Martha Nussbaum address the relevance of sexuality for a nuanced politics of global justice. That said, mainstream theorists typically position sexuality as concerned with a politics of 'recognition', which is to say culture or identity, rather than political economy, marking one of the differences between the fields. The debate between Judith Butler and Nancy Fraser in the late 1990s is understood as key to the outlining of both positions in this regard. Nancy Fraser, *Justice Interruptus: Critical Reflections on the 'Postsocialist' Condition* (New York: Routledge 1996); Martha Nussbaum, *Sex and Social Justice* (Oxford: Oxford University Press 2002); Judith Butler, 'Merely Cultural', *Social Text*, Vols.52/53 (1997), pp.265–77; Nancy Fraser, 'Heterosexism, Misrecognition, and Capitalism: a Response to Judith Butler', *Social Text*, Vols.52/53 (1997), pp.279–89.
17. See, e.g., Angela Y. Davis, 'Rape, Racism and the Myth of the Black Racist', in K.-K. Bhavnani (ed.), *Feminism and Race* (Oxford: Oxford University Press 2001), pp.50–64; Philippa Levine, 'Orientalist Sociology and the Creation of Colonial Sexualities', *Feminist Review*, Vol.65 (2000), pp.5–21; Philippa

Levine, *Prostitution, Race and Politics: Policing Venereal Disease in the British Empire* (New York: Routledge 2003); Frank Mort, *Dangerous Sexualities: Medico-Moral Politics in England since 1830* (London and New York: Routledge 2000).
18. Lila Abu-Lughod, 'Movie Stars and Islamic Moralism in Egypt', in R. N. Lancaster and M. di Leonardo (eds), *The Gender Sexuality Reader: Culture, History, Political Economy* (New York: Routledge 1997), p.502; M. Jacqui Alexander, *Pedagogies of Crossing Meditations on Feminism, Sexual Politics, and the Sacred* (Durham, NC: Duke University Press 2005); and Almas Sayeed, 'Making Political Hay of Sex and Slavery: Kansas Conservatism, Feminism and the Global Regulation of Sexual Moralities', *Feminist Review*, Vol.83 (2006), pp.119–31.
19. The rape and torture of women and men as part of strategies of ethnic cleansing in conflict situations has been extensively discussed in public and theoretical arenas. Although the failure to be an appropriate sexual citizen is forced rather than chosen here, national humiliation is both aim and result. See, in particular, Katrina Lee Koo, 'Confronting Disciplinary Blindness: Women, War and Rape in the International Politics of Security', *Australian Journal of Political Science*, Vol.37, No.3 (2002), pp.525–36; Wendy Bracewell, 'Rape in Kosovo: Masculinity and Serbian Nationalism', *Nations and Nationalism*, Vol.6, No.4 (2000), pp.563–90; Kirsten Campbell, 'Legal Memories: Sexual Assault, Memory and International Humanitarian Law', *Signs*, Vol.28, No.1 (2002), pp.149–78.
20. Peter A. Jackson, 'Pre-Gay, Post-Queer: Thai Perspectives on Proliferating Gender/Sex Diversity in Asia', *Journal of Homosexuality*, Vol.40, No.3/4 (2001), pp.1–25. As Phil C. W. Chan notes in relation to Hong Kong in his paper in this Special Double Issue, there is a particular irony in postcolonial nation-states criminalising homosexuality when very often it was colonial administrations that introduced such legal sanctions. In this respect, it would make more sense for postcolonial nations to refer to criminalisation, rather than homosexuality, as Western: Phil C. W. Chan, 'Same-Sex Marriage/Constitutionalism and their Centrality to Equality Rights in Hong Kong: A Comparative–Socio-Legal Appraisal', in this Special Double Issue, pp.33–84.
21. Vincanne Adams and Stacy Leigh Pigg, 'Introduction', in V. Adams and A. L. Pigg (eds), *Sex in Development: Science, Sexuality, and Morality in Global Perspective* (Durham, NC: Duke University Press 2005), p.9.
22. I put 'queer' in inverted commas when part of transnational 'queer' studies to indicate the contested nature of the proper name for this project.
23. Vance (note 14).
24. Mark McLelland, 'Is There a Japanese "Gay Identity"?', *Culture, Health and Sexuality*, Vol.2, No.4 (2000), pp.459–72.
25. Vance (note 14) p.45.
26. See Jackson (note 20); Neville Hoad, 'Arrested Development', *Postcolonial Studies*, Vol.3, No.2 (2000), pp.133–58.
27. Swarr and Nagar (note 12) p.514.
28. Mark Chiang, 'Coming Out into the Global System: Postmodern Patriarchies and Transnational Sexualities in *The Wedding Banquet*', in D. L. Eng and A. Y. Hom (eds), *Q and A: Queer in Asian America* (Philadelphia: Temple University Press 1998), pp.374–96; Martin F. Manalansan IV, 'In the Shadows of Stonewall: Examining Gay Transnational Politics and the Transnational Dilemma', *GLQ: Journal of Lesbian and Gay Studies*, Vol.2 (1995), pp.425–38.
29. See variously Robert A. Padgug, 'Sexual Matters: on Conceptualizing Sexuality in History', *Radical History Review*, Vol.20 (1979), pp.3–23; Jeffrey Weeks, 'Sexuality and the Historian', *Sex, Politics and Society: The Regulation of Sexuality Since 1800* (London: Longman 1989), pp.1–18; Jennifer Terry, 'Theorizing Deviant Historiography', *Differences*, Vol.3, No.2 (1991), pp.53–71; Terry, *An American Obsession* (note 10). In relation to these problems as they attend the historicisation of bisexuality, see Marjorie Garber, *Bisexuality and the Eroticism of Everyday Life* (London: Penguin 1995); and Steven Angelides, *A History of Bisexuality* (Chicago: Chicago University Press 2001).
30. Denis Altman's work on the global nature of gay identity and social movements is characteristic of this trend: Denis Altman, 'On Global Queering', *Australian Humanities Review*, Vol.2, July–August (1996), http://www.lib.latrobe.edu.au/AHR/archive/Issue-July-1996/altman.html; Denis Altman, 'Rupture or Continuity? The Internationalization of Gay Identities', *Social Text*, Vol.48 (1996), pp.77–84; and Altman, *Global Sex* (Chicago: University of Chicago Press 2001). In this context, 'gay' signals both an identity-to-come or in process and a space of sexual freedom associated with Western contexts. As Peter Jackson (note 20) p.19, caustically notes, the presumption is that '"prehistoric" or inchoate sexuality may one day emerge into the light of global discursive history'.

31. Altman, 'On Global Queering' (note 30).
32. Rich (note 14).
33. Chiang (note 28).
34. Ibid. p.386. There is a growing body of literature on lesbian and gay tourism, which covers a range of perspectives from celebratory: e.g. Marie Cieri, 'Between Being and Looking: Queer Tourism Promotion and Lesbian Social Space in Greater Philadelphia', *ACME: International E-Journal for Cultural Geographies*, Vol.2, No.2 (2003), pp.147–66 – to condemnatory: e.g. Jasbir Kuar Puar, 'Circuits of Queer Mobility: Tourism, Travel and Globalization', *GLQ: Journal of Lesbian and Gay Studies*, Vol.8, No.1/2 (2002), pp.107–37. This resonates with writing on sex tourism concerned with sexual practices (between client and provider) as formative of contested sexual subjectivities within globalisation (see three papers on this issue in the recent special issue of *Feminist Review* on 'Sexual Moralities', Vol.83 (2006): Esther Bott, 'Pole Position: How Lapdancing Became Respectable', pp.23–41; Julia O'Connell Davidson, 'Will the Real Sex Slave Please Stand Up?', pp.4–22; Jacqueline Sanchez Taylor, 'Female Sexual Tourism: a Contradiction in Terms?', pp.42–59.
35. Lionel Cantú Jr, Eithne Luibhéid and Minna Stern, 'Well-Founded Fear: Political Asylum and the Boundaries of Sexual Identity in the U.S.–Mexico Borderlands', in E. Luibhéid and L. Cantú Jr (eds), *Queer Migrations: Sexuality, U.S. Citizenship and Border Crossings* (Minneapolis: University of Minnesota Press 2005), pp.64–6.
36. Ibid. p.66. The authors further suggest that the construction of the American legal system as saviour obscures the lack of political, social and cultural rights of gay men in the United States.
37. Vivien W. Ng, 'Looking for Lesbians in Chinese History', in M. Duberman (ed.), *A Queer World: The Center for Lesbian and Gay Studies Reader* (New York: New York University Press 1997), pp.199–204; Mariam Fraser, 'Classing Queer: Politics in Competition', *Theory, Culture and Society*, Vol.16, No.2 (1991), pp.107–31. Lisa Adkins takes up Mariam Fraser's critique of Nancy Fraser's 'politics of recognition' model in this regard, in her analysis of lesbian and gay negotiations of identity within service economies: Lisa Adkins, 'Sexuality and Economy: Historicisation vs Deconstruction', *Australian Feminist Studies*, Vol.17, No.37 (2002), pp.31–41.
38. Paul Boyce, 'Moral Ambivalence and Irregular Practices: Contextualizing Male-to-Male Sexualities in Calcutta/India', *Feminist Review*, Vol.83 (2006), pp.79–98.
39. Ng (note 37).
40. Boyce, 'Moral Ambivalence' (note 38) p.84. James N. Green makes a similar argument in his work on Brazil, where nineteenth century European medico-moral constructions of sexual identity circulated in a context that already had 'same-sex erotic subcultures and identities'. Green and Boyce underscore the ways in which a queer developmental model (with *Western* gay identity as its presumed culmination) necessarily forgets the ways in which colonisation, trade and migration have always had an impact on the sexual construction of a nation. James N. Green, *Beyond Carnival: Male Homosexuality in Twentieth-Century Brazil* (Chicago: University of Chicago Press 1999), p.8.
41. Jackson (note 20) p.3; Martin F. Manalansan IV, 'Migrancy, Modernity, Mobility: Quotidian Struggles and Queer Diasporic Intimacy', in E. Luibhéid and L. Cantú Jr (note 35) pp.146–60.
42. Jennifer Robertson, *Same-Sex Cultures and Sexualities: An Anthropological Reader* (Oxford: Blackwell 2004).
43. Sedgwick (note 1); Butler, *Gender Trouble* (note 5).
44. Gloria Anzaldúa's *Borderlands/La Frontera: The New Mestiza* (San Francisco: Aunt Lute Press 1989), was paradigmatic in this regard. More recent work on queer diasporas in the United States continues this queer focus of thinking race, ethnicity and sexuality together. Indicative work includes: Gayatri Gopinath, 'Funny Boys and Girls: Notes on a Queer South Asian Planet', in R. Leong (ed.), *Asian American Sexualities: Dimensions of the Gay and Lesbian Experience* (London: Routledge 1996), pp.119–27; Gayatri Gopinath, *Impossible Desire: Queer Diasporas and South Asian Public Cultures* (Durham, NC: Duke University Press 2005); David L. Eng, 'Out Here and Over There: Queerness and Diaspora in Asian American Studies', *Social Text*, Vol.15, No.3/4 (1997), pp.31–52; Eng and Hom (note 28); John C. Hawley (ed.), *Postcolonial Queer: Theoretical Intersections* (Albany, NY: State University of New York Press 2001); Cindy Patton and Benigno Sánchez-Eppler (eds), *Queer Diasporas* (Durham, NC: Duke University Press 2000). It should be noted that the majority of this material focuses on Asian or Latin American, rather than African, diasporas within the United States. E. Patrick Johnson's work on 'Quare' studies is one exception, and its critique of 'queer studies' from an African diasporic perspective also suggests why this might be the case: E. Patrick Johnson, '"Quare" Studies, or (Almost) Everything I Know About Queer Studies I Learned from my Grandmother', *Text and Performance Quarterly*, Vol.21, No.1 (2001), pp.1–25.

45. Jolly (note 15); Paul Boyce, 'Men who have Sex with Men in Calcutta: Gender, Discourse and Anthropology' (PhD Dissertation, London School of Economics and Political Science, University of London, 2004).
46. Sasho A. Lambevski, 'Suck My Nation – Masculinity, Ethnicity and the Politics of (Homo)sex', *Sexualities*, Vol.2, No.4 (1999), pp.397–419.
47. Jyoti Puri, 'Stakes and States: Sexual Discourses from New Delhi', *Feminist Review*, Vol.83 (2006), pp.139–48.
48. Eithne Luibhéid, 'Introduction: Queering, Migration and Citizenship', in E. Luibhéid and L. Cantú Jr (note 35) pp.ix–xlvi.
49. Arvind Narrain, *Queer: Despised Sexuality, Law and Social Change* (India: Books for Change Press 2004), p.2.
50. Alyssa Howe, 'Undressing the Universal Queer Subject: Nicaraguan Activism and Transnational Identity', *City and Society*, Vol.XIV, No.2 (2002), pp.237–79.
51. Ian Barnard, 'Queer Race', *Social Semiotics*, Vol.9, No.2 (1999), pp.199–212.
52. Jasbir Kuar Puar, 'Global Circuits: Transnational Sexualities in Trinidad', *Signs*, Vol.26, No.4 (2001), pp.1039–66.
53. Barnard (note 51) p.208.
54. Sedgwick (note 1) pp.25–6.
55. Butler, *Gender Trouble* (note 5).
56. Michael du Plessis, 'Blatantly Bisexual; or, Unthinking Queer Theory', in Hall and Pramaggiore (note 2) pp.19–54; Garber (note 4); Rust (note 3); Rebecca Kaplan, 'Your Fence is Sitting on Me: the Hazards of Binary Thinking', in N. Tucker (ed.), *Bisexual Politics: Theories, Queries, and Visions* (New York: The Haworth Press 1995), pp.267–80.
57. See, e.g., Brenda Marie Blasingame, 'The Roots of Biphobia: Racism and Internalized Heterosexism', in E. R. Weise (ed.), *Closer to Home: Bisexuality and Feminism* (Seattle: Seal Press 1992) pp.47–53; Elias Farajajé-Jones, 'Fluid Desire: Race, HIV/AIDS, and Bisexual Politics', in Tucker (note 56) pp.119–21.
58. Garber (note 4); Eva Cantarella, *Bisexuality in the Ancient World* (New Haven: Yale University Press 2002); Serena Anderlini-D'Onofrio, *Women and Bisexuality: A Global Perspective* (New York: Haworth Press 2003).
59. Ng (note 37); Ara Wilson, The Intimate Economies of Bangkok: Tomboys, Tycoons, and Avon Ladies in the Global City (Berkeley: University of California Press 2004); Y. Antonia Chao 'Drink, Stories, Penis, and Breasts: Lesbian Tomboys in Taiwan from the 1960s to the 1990s', *Journal of Homosexuality*, Vol.40, No.3/4 (2001), pp.185–209; Swarr and Nagar (note 12).
60. Binnie (note 13).
61. Puar, 'Global Circuits' (note 52); Jackson (note 20).
62. This assurance about Western sexual categories is not only a problem of transnational 'queer' studies, of course. Shelley Budgeon and Sasha Roseneil perform something of the same sleight of hand in their work on British cultures of intimacy, mentioning bisexuals as part of families at one point, but continuing to reinforce the assumption throughout that heterosexual and homosexual desire, identity and behaviour are coextensive and mutually exclusive. Shelley Budgeon and Sasha Roseneil, 'Cultures of Intimacy and Care Beyond the Family: Personal Life and Social Change in the Early Twenty First Century', *Current Sociology*, Vol.52, No.2 (2000), pp.135–59.
63. Jackson (note 20) p.9.
64. See also Alisa Solomon, 'Strike a Pose', *Village Voice*, November (1991), pp.13–19.
65. As Amber Ault (note 3) p.206, notes, queer theory 'rescues lesbianism from [a psychoanalytic] apolitical abyss but leaves bisexuality mired there'.
66. McLelland (note 24) p.463. Chao (note 59) effects a similar gesture, subtitling her article on sexual practices among women 'Lesbian Tomboys in Taiwan', despite none of her informants ever using the term to describe their own behaviour or subjectivity.
67. McLelland (note 24) p.464.
68. Ibid. p.464.
69. Ibid. p.465.
70. Gillian A. Dunne, 'The Lady Vanishes? Reflections on the Experiences of Married and Divorced Non-Heterosexual Fathers', *Sociological Research Online*, Vol.6, No.3 (2001), http://www.socresonline.org.uk/6/3/dunne.html.
71. Boyce, 'Moral Ambivalence' (note 38) p.23.
72. This question of 'the burden of representation' has been raised by numerous theorists, perhaps most canonically by Gayatri Spivak, who cautions against the Western intellectual tendency to expect 'the

other' to do the work of difference. See Gayatri Chakravorty Spivak, *A Critique of Postcolonial Reason: Toward a History of the Vanishing Present* (Cambridge, MA: Harvard University Press 1999); Tobias Hecht, *After Life: an Ethnographic Novel* (Durham, NC: Duke University Press 2006).
73. Gayatri Reddy, 'Geographies of Contagion: Hijras, Kothis, and the Politics of Sexual Marginality in Hyderabad', *Anthropology and Medicine*, Vol.12, No.3 (2005), pp.255–70.
74. While the term MSM would seem to be the ultimate neutral description of behaviour, its use within international public health is now so widespread that it too has been taken up as an identity marker by sexual subjects wanting to access resources. Boyce, PhD Dissertation (note 45).
75. Richard Parker, 'Male Prostitution, Bisexual Behaviour and HIV Transmission in Urban Brazil', in *Sexual Behaviour and Networking: Anthropological and Socio-cultural Studies on the Transmission of HIV* (Liege, Belgium: International Union for the Scientific Study of Population 1992), pp.109–22; Rob Tielman, Manuel Carballo and Aart Hendriks (eds), *Bisexuality and HIV/AIDS: A Global Perspective* (Buffalo, NY: Prometheus Books 1991).
76. Peter Aggleton (ed.), *Bisexualities and AIDS: International Perspectives* (London: Taylor & Francis 1996).
77. Peter Aggleton, 'Introduction', in Aggleton (note 76) pp.1–2.
78. Shivananda Khan, 'Under the Blanket: Bisexualities and AIDS in India', in Aggleton (note 76) pp.161–77; Richard Parker, 'Bisexuality and HIV/AIDS in Brazil', in Aggleton (note 76) p.151.
79. Parker (note 78) p.151.
80. Aggleton, 'Introduction' (note 77) p.1.
81. Parker (note 78).
82. Suiming Pan with Peter Aggleton, 'Male Homosexual Behaviour and HIV Related Risk in China', in Aggleton (note 76) pp.178–90.
83. As Miguel A. Munoz-Laboy suggests in the context of Latino male populations in the United States, 'male bisexuality has been studied for the most part with a focus on men who have sex with men (MSM) and with little attention to sexual desire': Miguel A. Munoz-Laboy, 'Beyond "MSM": Sexual Desire among Bisexually-active Latino Men in New York City', *Sexualities*, Vol.7, No.1 (2004), pp.55–80.
84. Ana Luisa Liguori, M. Gonzalez Bloch and Peter Aggleton, 'Bisexual Communities and Culture in Costa Rica', in Aggleton (note 76) pp.76–98.
85. Green (note 40) p.7.
86. Altman, 'Rupture or Continuity?' (note 30) p.88.
87. For bisexual critiques of this position, see Eadie (note 3); Kaloski (note 3); Stacey Young, 'Bisexuality, Lesbian and Gay Communities, and the Limits of Identity Politics', in Tucker (note 56) pp.219–28.
88. Altman, 'Rupture or Continuity?' (note 30) p.89.
89. In addition to MSM or bisexual behaviour, a common way of seeming to avoid sexual imposition is the anthropological cliché of active/passive engendering. Very often, anthropologists, policy makers and queer theorists describe same-sex behaviour in this gendered way as though this bore no relation to the Western oppositional categories of heterosexual/homosexual. However, theorising behavioural bisexuality in the way I have been doing here as racialised and gendered suggests that active/passive and masculine/feminine oppositions are also central to ideas about the development of modern sexual identities.
90. Eve Kosofsky Sedgwick, *Between Men English Literature and Male Homosocial Desire* (New York: Columbia University Press 1985).
91. This is a similar point to one Amal Treacher and I make in our editorial 'Everyday Struggling': Clare Hemmings and Amal Treacher, 'Everyday Struggling', *Feminist Review*, Vol.82 (2006), pp.1–5.
92. Robyn Wiegman suggests further that we need to challenge the assumption that we know what 'sex' is in the first place, let alone what 'it' means to people, nationally or transnationally: Robyn Wiegman, 'Interchanges: Heteronormativity and the Desire for Gender', *Feminist Theory*, Vol.7, No.1 (2006), pp.89–103.

# Same-Sex Marriage/Constitutionalism and their Centrality to Equality Rights in Hong Kong: A Comparative–Socio-Legal Appraisal

PHIL C. W. CHAN

## I. Introduction

Whether an individual has a right to marry another person of the same sex has garnered tremendous judicial, political and scholarly attention in the past decade, and it certainly will continue to do so in the years to come, for such a right is one which sexual minority rights activists consider to be part and parcel of their struggle for equality whilst opponents of homosexuality and sexual minority rights regard it as the ultimate destruction of the institution of marriage and society.[1] The divisive nature of the debate on whether to recognise such a right was manifest in the run-up to the American presidential election in November 2004, where President George W. Bush exploited the issue to his re-electoral advantage and pushed for a constitutional amendment to the federal United States Constitution which was ultimately rejected by both Houses of Congress. President Bush vowed that such a constitutional amendment would again be pushed forward should he be re-elected, which quite certainly awakened many conservatives to vote in his favour.[2] Since then, it is notable that President Bush's efforts have subsided, to many of his supporters' severe dismay.

Nevertheless, on the same day as the 2004 presidential election, voters in 11 American states[3] approved of various constitutional amendments to their respective state constitutions that thenceforth ban any recognition of same-sex marriage such as those granted in the City of San Francisco which were subsequently nullified by the Supreme Court of California,[4] and those available in the State of Massachusetts through a landmark decision by the Massachusetts Supreme Judicial Court (which continues to be binding)[5] or in the Netherlands, Belgium, Spain, Canada, and South Africa through their respective legislative measures. Some of these constitutional amendments even proscribe civil union or domestic partnership[6] that is currently available in a number of countries[7] and fellow American states.[8] The number of states that have passed such constitutional amendments either by referenda or through state legislatures, as at 14 December 2006, stands at 27.[9] Until the purported Marriage Protection Amendment is eventually passed by both Houses of Congress with two-thirds majorities and then approved by three fourths of the 50 state legislatures,[10] whence the Amendment will preserve the *juridical* heterosexuality of the institution of marriage and remove the issue of same-sex marriage from further oversight by the judiciary including the United States Supreme Court, the issue will definitely continue to be controversial and yet central to American society, as these state constitutional amendments, like the purported Colorado state constitutional amendment in 1991 which sought to prohibit future legislation protecting sexual orientation equality and non-discrimination rights and was ultimately struck down by the United States Supreme Court in *Romer v. Evans*[11] as unconstitutional, will be the subject of numerous sets of judicial proceedings.

In the meantime, in Hong Kong, as the present author has elucidated elsewhere,[12] there is not as yet any legislative measure that protects against sexual orientation discrimination and harassment. Fortunately, the courts in Hong Kong have begun to be attuned to the issue of sexual orientation discrimination in the law, if not also within society, as the Hong Kong Court of First Instance ruled[13] that various provisions of the Crimes Ordinance that stipulate same-sex sexual offences contravened on certain bases without satisfactory justification the guarantee of equality as provided in Article 25 of the Basic Law of Hong Kong,[14] which states unequivocally that '[a]ll Hong Kong residents shall be equal before the law',[15] and Article 22 of the Hong Kong Bill of Rights Ordinance, which, modelled upon and giving effect to Article 26 of the International Covenant on Civil and Political Rights[16] which the Basic Law of Hong Kong has incorporated therein,[17] states that '[a]ll persons are equal before the law and are entitled without any discrimination to the equal protection of the law. In this respect, the law shall prohibit any discrimination and guarantee to all persons equal and effective protection against discrimination on any ground such as race, colour, sex, language, religion, political or other opinion, national or social origin, property, birth or other status.'[18] In September 2006 the Hong Kong Court of Appeal unanimously upheld the decision,[19] and the Hong Kong government has not filed a notice of appeal within the prescribed deadline.

Meanwhile, the government has indicated that it will conduct a public survey, *likely* to be followed by a public consultation[20] which would be the fourth in less than three decades,[21] on the issue of sexual orientation anti-discrimination. Given that '[l]aw emerges not only to *codify* existing customs, morals, or mores, but also to *modify* the behavior and the values presently existing in a particular society',[22] it may therefore be not too optimistic for us to conclude that the time will soon, if it has not already, come where the hetero-normativity of the traditional concept of marriage, which the family court in England decreed in 1865 in *Hyde v. Hyde and Woodmansee*[23] as being 'as understood in Christendom ... the voluntary union for life of one man and one woman, to the exclusion of all others'[24] which in turn was adopted in Hong Kong's Marriage Ordinance,[25] will as in other common law jurisdictions such as the United States, Canada, and South Africa be successfully challenged in Hong Kong.[26]

It is accordingly timely and appropriate for the Hong Kong public to be informed of and to enter the contemporary debate over same-sex marriage, and this paper seeks to assist in serving that cause, so much so that the community in Hong Kong may reflect on any future public consultation(s) on sexual orientation anti-discrimination and on the nature of society at large. As Fields and Narr avow, '[i]f people are not aware of the historical and contextual nature of human rights and are not aware that human rights become realized only by the struggles of real people experiencing real instances of domination, then human rights are all too easily used as symbolic legitimizers for instruments of that very domination.'[27] Given the nature of the same-sex marriage debate, this paper will adopt a comparative and socio-legal approach in its discussion on homosexuality, the protection of sexual minorities and the process and obstacles through which all-inclusive equality may or may not materialise, within Hong Kong and beyond.

## II. Homosexuality: From Sinful Death to (Almost) Equal Recognition

Same-sex sexual conduct between males was first criminalised as a secular offence in 1533 through Henry VIII's Buggery Act, thereby removing jurisdiction from ecclesiastical courts.[28] The Act, which mandated the imposition of death penalty upon conviction, was amended in Great Britain only more than three centuries later through the Offences Against the Person Act 1861, whereby life imprisonment became the maximum penalty for such 'abomination'.[29] Equivalent legislation in the form of the Offences Against the Person Ordinance 1865[30] was enacted by the colonial legislature in Hong Kong. The amended provision was then reinforced by section 11 of the Criminal Law Amendment Act 1885 which proscribed acts of gross indecency between males, carrying a maximum penalty of imprisonment for two years with or without hard labour.[31] Given its pervasive character and vague description, whereby a conviction would succeed even if there were no physical contact between the parties,[32] the Amendment, since repealed in the United Kingdom,[33] has been denounced as a 'Blackmailers' Charter'.[34] Same-sex sexual conduct between females, on the other hand, has never been criminalised, although it is fair to infer that it was heavily censured in Victorian society; Bamforth explains:

> The reasons for the UK's gender-specific approach remain ambiguous, but are probably connected with the fact that when the relevant provisions were drafted,

public acknowledgement of female sexuality would have been unthinkable in English society. Sexual acts between men were unmentionable in polite company, but their existence was at least recognized at the level of public policy, although they were perceived as the product of sinfulness or mental illness rather than a stable sexual orientation; they were therefore legislated against and punished, albeit under oblique names such as 'gross indecency'. Sexual acts between women were simply ignored.[35]

With such outright hostility to sexual minorities in general and gay men in particular, it was hardly surprising that gay men were systematically imprisoned, tortured and murdered during Nazi Germany's undertaking of purifying the Aryan race on the pretext of Paragraph 175 of the German Penal Code as adopted since the unification of Germany in 1871 and subsequently amended in 1935, which was retained after the end of the Second World War with several subsequent amendments, only to be repealed in East Germany in 1989 and in West Germany, and the unified Federal Republic of Germany, in 1994. Plant lucidly describes the sufferings which sexual minorities endured during the Nazi period, as well as the antagonism to which they were subjected by post-war Germany and the international community subsequently;[36] his work is reinforced by that of LaViolette and Whitworth[37] and of Amnesty International.[38]

The Second World War and its horrors, nevertheless, brought forth state and individual awareness that individual rights and freedoms are of fundamental importance to the survival and well-being of individuals and society. The European Convention on Human Rights,[39] signed in 1950 and entered into force in 1953, has become a regional instrument that has given rise to the most elaborate jurisprudence in the field of human rights and fundamental freedoms. However, notwithstanding the United Kingdom's signature of the Convention, state interference through arrests and prosecutions of numerous individuals for same-sex sexual offences mounted in England at the same time.[40] The Wolfenden Committee on Homosexual Offences and Prostitution[41] was eventually created in 1954 and in 1957 recommended that private sexual activity between two consenting males, deemed a felony and unnatural offence under section 12(1) of the Sexual Offences Act 1956,[42] be decriminalised. Decriminalisation, however, did not come into being until 1967 through the Sexual Offences Act 1967[43] (yet even then only in England and Wales).[44] Many of the Commonwealth jurisdictions enacted similar legal reforming legislation thereafter.[45]

On the other side of the Atlantic, notwithstanding a substantial increase in the understanding of sexuality – or, more accurately, sexualities – through the groundbreaking Kinsey studies,[46] which established, *inter alia*, that sexuality is on a fluctuating continuum, advocacy for sexual minority rights came to nought as a result of United States Senator Joseph McCarthy's equation of sexual minorities with communists whom the senator, and the prevailing American administrations, considered threatening to the nation. A witch-hunt of sexual minorities within the administrations and the nation ensued. Such hostility to sexual minorities remained intact until 1969 when patrons of Stonewall, a gay club, became determined to no longer submit to persistent police harassment and decided to stand up for themselves through what are now known as the Stonewall Riots which are regarded as the turning point of the global sexual minority rights movement. The sexual minority community, now no longer underground, consolidated its efforts and successfully lobbied the Board of Trustees of the American Psychiatric

Association to officially vote in 1973 to forthwith declassify homosexuality as a mental illness.[47]

The 1981 decision of the European Court of Human Rights in *Dudgeon v. United Kingdom*[48] was a watershed in sexual minorities' fight for equal recognition and protection. For the first time, decriminalisation of homosexuality in the context of an individual's right to privacy was mandated by a judiciary – one that represents the Council of Europe and its 46 Member States.

Unfortunately, the onset of the HIV/AIDS epidemic in the 1980s, in addition to causing innumerable lives to perish, also brought the sexual minority rights movement to a halt. With HIV/AIDS then (and still) considered a gay plague, sexual minorities became the scapegoat of the epidemic and were severely marginalised and vilified in both the public and private sectors. The hesitation, deliberate or otherwise, of the conservative Reagan administrations to halt the epidemic further contributed to its prevalence and dire consequences. The suppression of sexual minorities was manifest in the United States Supreme Court decision in *Bowers v. Hardwick*,[49] where the state was allowed to continue to interfere with individuals' private lives by banning and criminalising sexual activity between consenting persons of the same sex, and in the purported Colorado state constitutional amendment which, if had been allowed to stand in *Romer v. Evans*, would have the Colorado state government proscribed from protecting sexual minorities and their minority status. Meanwhile, in the United Kingdom, Parliament under the Conservative Thatcher government enacted section 2A of the Local Government Act 1986,[50] applicable in the United Kingdom (save Northern Ireland)[51] and colloquially known as 'Section 28' (as that of the 1988 amendment legislation),[52] which, repealed only in September 2003,[53] forbade the teaching in publicly-funded schools of homosexuality which the provision regarded as a 'pretended family relationship'.[54]

After such dark clouds over the rights and freedoms of sexual minorities, the sexual minority rights movement resurfaced in the following decade with vigour. Most significantly, the United Nations Human Rights Committee, guardian of the International Covenant on Civil and Political Rights, in 1994 in *Toonen v. Australia*[55] decided that criminalisation of homosexuality in the Australian state of Tasmania violated Australia's obligations under Article 17 of the Covenant, which protects an individual's right to privacy.[56] However, the Committee considered that it accordingly was not necessary to examine whether Australia also violated Article 26 of the Covenant, the equality guarantee,[57] even as it noted that 'sex' in the provision and in Article 2 was to be taken as including sexual orientation.[58] In 1996, the European Commission of Human Rights in *Sutherland v. United Kingdom*[59] decided that the then differentiation between the ages of consent for same-sex[60] and different-sex sexual activity[61] violated Article 14 of the European Convention on Human Rights, the equality guarantee,[62] in conjunction with Article 8 of the Convention, which protects an individual's right to privacy.[63] Subsequent decisions by the Strasbourg organs have ruled that laws or policies that discriminate against sexual minorities in respect of such matters as the custody of a child and the armed forces are similarly incompatible with the Convention and the relevant States Parties' obligations thereunder.[64] Finally, in 2000, the Human Rights Committee in *Young v. Australia*[65] concluded that Australia's refusal to provide the applicant with a pension benefit after and by virtue of the death of his same-sex partner on the grounds that their same-sex relationship was not recognised in the relevant legislation as a marriage or a marriage-like relationship entitling him to the pension constituted sexual orientation discrimination in violation of Article 26 of the Covenant[66] and the applicant was thus entitled to an effective remedy, 'if necessary through an amendment of the law'.[67] The issue of whether under the Covenant an individual has a right to same-sex marriage was not at issue and therefore was not addressed by the Committee.

Meanwhile, the Supreme Court of Canada, guardian of the Canadian Charter of Rights and Freedoms,[68] has ruled that sexual orientation discrimination constitutes unlawful discrimination[69] contrary to the equality guarantee embodied in section 15(1) of the Charter[70] and that the state must protect sexual minorities through positive measures, including legislation, where necessary.[71] The previously higher age of consent for anal[72] (as opposed to vaginal)[73] intercourse, which was recognised by the judiciary as the sole avenue through which gay men express their sexual intimacy,[74] was ruled unconstitutional by the Québec and Ontario Courts of Appeal whose decisions[75] the federal government has decided not to appeal.

Similarly, the legislative provisions in South Africa, victim of decades-long apartheid, in respect of sexual activity between consenting males as well as same-sex relationships and immigration rights were held by the South African Constitutional Court in *National Coalition for Gay and Lesbian Equality v. Minister of Justice*[76] and *National Coalition for Gay and Lesbian Equality v. Minister of Home Affairs*,[77] respectively, as unconstitutional, opening the door for the South African Supreme Court of Appeal to recognise and mandate same-sex marriage in *Fourie v. Minister of Home Affairs*[78] as within the protection of equality and dignity guaranteed by South Africa's Constitution, a decision that was subsequently affirmed by the South African Constitutional Court[79] and implemented by legislation.[80] It is noteworthy that the South African Constitution, promulgated in 1996, is the first national constitution in the world that expressly protects against sexual orientation discrimination, in such terms that '[t]he state may not unfairly discriminate directly or indirectly against anyone on one or more grounds, including race, gender, sex, pregnancy, marital status, ethnic or social origin, colour, sexual orientation, age, disability, religion, conscience, belief, culture, language and birth.'[81] Article 9(4) of the South African Constitution goes on to apply the guarantee of equality as between individuals and mandate the enactment of anti-discrimination legislation to that end.[82] Article 10 of the Constitution, in the most unequivocal manner, affirms that '[e]veryone has inherent dignity and the right to have their dignity respected and protected.'[83]

Last, but not least, through the Sexual Offences Act 2003, all same-sex sexual offences in the United Kingdom such as buggery or gross indecency have now been repealed,[84] and the Charter of Fundamental Rights and Freedoms for the European Union,[85] which consists of 27 Member States, expressly protects sexual orientation equality and non-discrimination.[86] In a landmark decision also in 2003, the United States Supreme Court in *Lawrence v. Texas*[87] ruled that criminalisation of homosexuality in the state of Texas was unconstitutional and that its earlier decision in *Bowers v. Hardwick* be thereby overruled.

### III. Legal Developments concerning Homosexuality in Hong Kong

As a Crown Colony of the United Kingdom, Hong Kong adhered to England's legal condemnation of homosexuality in the form of section 50 of the Offences Against the Person Ordinance 1865. However, when legal reform on the matter was brought forth in England and Wales in 1967 and subsequently the rest of the United Kingdom and other Commonwealth jurisdictions, as has been elucidated above, Hong Kong did not follow suit, which Petersen attributes to the conservatism within Chinese society.[88]

Such antagonism to homosexuality intensified in the late 1970s, when a Special Investigation Unit was established in Hong Kong specifically to pursue individual members of sexual minorities especially those who were within law enforcement or the legal profession, which, known as Operation Rockcorry, prompted more than 400 individuals to petition the Hong Kong government for decriminalisation of homosexuality. This the government did not do, and in a police operation on 15 January 1980 that aimed at the arrest of a fellow police inspector named John MacLennan who was allegedly a bisexual suspected of eight counts of gross indecency, the police found the suspect dead in his residence. It was subsequently alleged that MacLennan had been murdered for possessing information on certain high-ranked government officials who were homosexuals. Press coverage was extensive both in Hong Kong and in Scotland where MacLennan originated. An inquiry, however, concluded that the cause of MacLennan's death was suicide.[89]

In response to these two incidents, the Law Reform Commission of Hong Kong was set up in 1980 with a view, as its inaugural task, to investigating whether homosexuality should be decriminalised. The Commission published its findings[90] three years later, declaring that 'it should not be a function of the law to enforce moral judgments in areas where there is no need to protect others'.[91] However, the then colonial administration, due to perceived adverse public sentiment against homosexuality, decided not to implement the Commission's recommendation that consensual sexual activity in private between male adults aged 21 or above be decriminalised.[92] Instead, another consultation paper was produced in 1988,[93] which but recognised similarly that a total ban on homosexuality was incapable of being enforced due to limited police resources[94] and to otherwise 'complete disregard for an individual's right to privacy'.[95] In the light of the lack of public insistence on enforcement, compliance with which would at any rate be impossible, governmental indifference to the need for legal reform on homosexuality was becoming increasingly problematical.

Such overdue legal reform ultimately materialised only as the Tiananmen Massacre in Beijing in June 1989 caused the confidence of the Hong Kong people in their government and the future of Hong Kong sink 'to an all-time low'.[96] In order to alleviate the public's fear about the imminent transfer of sovereignty and potential human rights violations in Hong Kong and to avoid mass emigration from Hong Kong, the Hong Kong colonial legislature assessed the viability of a Bill of Rights modelled upon the International Covenant on Civil and Political Rights – which had already been recognised and given effect by the Basic Law of Hong Kong as promulgated by the National People's Congress of the People's Republic of China in 1990[97] – and ultimately enacted the Hong Kong Bill of Rights Ordinance in July 1991. The Bill of Rights was a watershed in the human rights movement in Hong Kong. It states, *inter alia*, that '[n]o one shall be subjected to arbitrary or unlawful interference with his privacy, home or correspondence, nor to unlawful attacks on his honour and reputation. Everyone has the right to the protection of the law against such interference or attacks.'[98] The administration then put forward a Crimes (Amendment) Bill which aimed at decriminalisation of consensual sexual activity between males[99] as it acknowledged that '[i]t hardly needs saying that the laws of Hong Kong are required, in accordance with our international obligations, to be consistent with those obligations.'[100] After a heated legislative debate,[101] the Crimes (Amendment) Bill was passed in July 1991 (after the enactment of the Bill of Rights Ordinance).[102]

Consensual sexual activity between males was now regulated by section 118C of the Crimes Ordinance in such terms that '[a] man who commits buggery with a man under the age of 21; or being under the age of 21 commits buggery with another man ... shall be liable ... to imprisonment for life.'[103] Despite the lifting of the outright ban on homosexuality, certain but definite inequities remained, which the present author has elucidated in another forum[104] and which the Hong Kong Court of First Instance in an August 2005 judgment declared unconstitutional,[105] which the Hong Kong Court of Appeal in September 2006 unanimously affirmed.[106]

Nevertheless, it is pertinent here to refer to two provisions of the Crimes Ordinance and propositions by the administration to illustrate the government's antagonism to legal reform on homosexuality. Section 118C, as quoted above, stipulates the age of consent for anal intercourse between males at 21, five years higher than that for vaginal intercourse which section 124 of the same Ordinance sets at 16. In a 1988 consultation exercise concerning same-sex sexual offences,[107] the administration elaborated on the issue of the age of consent:

> If homosexual acts were to cease to be criminal offences under certain circumstances (Option 2), it is suggested that the age of consent should be 21 rather than 16 (which is the age of consent for heterosexual intercourse). The reasons are that men between 16 and 21 often have only a limited and possibly distorted knowledge of homosexual activity; they might be curious about and inclined to experiment with new activities and consequently be easily led into committing homosexual acts; and are often dependent both emotionally and financially on others and are therefore vulnerable to temptation by material and other incentives to consent to homosexual acts.[108]

In maintaining this position, the administration contradicted its earlier admission in the same consultation exercise that the cause of homosexuality was – and still remains – unclear,[109] and manifested its bias against homosexuality when *itself* only possessing 'a limited and possibly distorted knowledge' of the subject. Furthermore, it was without foundation to single out young men as the only group prone to emotional and material dependence. Discrimination in the law is obvious and it subsists notwithstanding the reply of Eliza Yau, Principal Assistant Secretary for Security, to the Subcommittee to Study Discrimination on the Ground of Sexual Orientation (hereinafter referred to as the Subcommittee), set up by the Hong Kong Legislative Council's Home Affairs Panel, that '[i]t was unlikely that under normal circumstances proceedings would be taken against a male homosexual under 21 where there were no other aggravating circumstances.'[110] As Lord Reid in his House of Lords opinion in *Knuller v. Director of Public Prosecutions*[111] averred, 'a bad law is not defensible on the ground that it will be judiciously administered.'[112]

Likewise, under section 118C, *both* male parties engaging in anal intercourse are liable to conviction if either or both of them are under 21 years of age. It is, however, stipulated in section 118D by implication that a female person is not guilty of any offence even if she commits anal intercourse with a man when aged below 21. Gay men are thus particularly prejudiced even under the amended legislation. This issue was raised in the legislature, to which the administration gave a most unsatisfactory answer:

> Members question the apparent anomaly between the new sections 118C and 118D in the criminal liability on men and girls under the age of 21 who committed

buggery. *The Administration managed to convince members that homosexual and heterosexual conduct should not always be equated.* The reason for making a male under 21 criminally liable for participating in consensual buggery was to guard against the likelihood of blackmail against the other partner. Members were assured that in normal circumstances it was unlikely that proceedings would be taken against a male under 14.[113]

The fact that the administration managed to so convince members of the legislature, however, does not make its reasoning convincing. As Hepworth discerns, '[q]uestions of whether behaviour is privately or publicly immoral cannot be answered by looking closely at the nature of the conduct in question ... but rather at the pressures constraining certain people at a certain time to interpret these behaviours as threatening to their interests. All vulnerability [to blackmail] is therefore circumstantial vulnerability',[114] to which it is precisely discrimination, both in society and in the law, that gives rise. In addition, it is an offence for a man to have vaginal intercourse with a girl aged under 16.[115] Bearing in mind that '[b]lackmail is possible only when individuals are discreditable',[116] why then should the female participant in such an enterprise be absolved from criminal liability? Furthermore, there is already sufficient legal safeguard against blackmail, as blackmail *per se* is an offence under section 23 of the Theft Ordinance.[117] During a Subcommittee meeting, Ms. Yau maintained that there was no evidence that the provisions on anal intercourse between males were insufficient or ineffective against blackmail.[118] However, there was no evidence that such provisions were sufficient, effective or indeed necessary to that end either. There having been no conviction of anal intercourse between males involving a man aged between 16 and 20,[119] the validity of the blackmail argument is seriously in question. Cyd Ho, Chairperson of the Subcommittee, maintained that '[t]he Administration should have consulted the homosexual community as to whether homosexuals wanted to have such a safeguard in legislation.'[120] In asserting a legal difference between same-sex and different-sex sexual conduct without satisfactory explanation, the government itself has blatantly committed discrimination against its citizens.

In any case, decriminalisation of homosexuality alone cannot eliminate the unrelenting discrimination and harassment members of sexual minorities suffer individually and as a group, contrary to the guarantee of equality embodied in Article 25 of the Basic Law of Hong Kong and Article 22 of the Hong Kong Bill of Rights Ordinance as well as Article 26 of the International Covenant on Civil and Political Rights. With human rights jurisprudence in Hong Kong starting to develop and evolve only since the 1990s, the juridical experience and discourse our common law brethren as well as international bodies have garnered in respect of sexual minority equality, and equality in general, is thus of immense value. As Hong Kong Court of Appeal Vice-President Silke in *R. v. Sin Yau-ming*[121] maintained:

> In my judgment, the glass through which we view the interpretation of the Hong Kong Bill is a glass provided by the [International Covenant on Civil and Political Rights]. We are no longer guided by the ordinary canons of constructions of statutes nor with the dicta of the common law inherent in our training. We must look, in our interpretation of the Hong Kong Bill, at the aims of the Covenant and give 'full recognition and effect' to the statement which commences that Covenant.[122]

His Lordship went on to provide helpful guidance in respect of the sources of law to which Hong Kong courts should refer in the interpretation of the Bill of Rights:

> While this court is, in effect, required to make new Hong Kong law relating to the manner of interpretation of the Hong Kong Bill and consequentially the tests to be applied to those laws now existing and, when asked, those laws yet to be enacted, we are not without guidance in our task. This can be derived from decisions taken in common law jurisdictions which contain a constitutionally entrenched Bill of Rights. We can also be guided by decisions of the European Court of Human Rights ... and the European Human Rights Commission ... Further, we can bear in mind the comments and decisions of the United Nations Human Rights Committee ... I would hold none of these to be binding upon us though in so far as they reflect the interpretation of articles in the Covenant, and are directly related to Hong Kong legislation, I would consider them as of the greatest assistance and give to them considerable weight.[123]

Whilst the Judicial Committee of the Privy Council in *Attorney General v. Lee Kwong-kut*[124] subsequently cast doubt on whether Hong Kong courts should, or indeed may, refer to comparative and international legal material in deciding upon an issue involving or in interpreting the Hong Kong Bill of Rights Ordinance,[125] the issue was put to rest as the Hong Kong Court of Final Appeal, which has replaced the Judicial Committee of the Privy Council as the highest court of Hong Kong as of 1 July 1997, in *Tang Siu Man v. HKSAR*[126] decided that if the reasoning of a particular decision in another common law jurisdiction was cogent then it ought to be followed, as in order to 'develop our own jurisprudence to greatest advantage, it is appropriate for us to tap the best available wisdom of other jurisdictions.'[127]

It is imperative at this stage to define what constitutes discrimination. Reference is had to *Andrews v. Law Society of British Columbia*,[128] where Supreme Court of Canada Justice McIntyre stated:

> discrimination may be described as a distinction, whether intentional or not but based on grounds relating to personal characteristics of the individual or group, which has the effect of imposing burdens, obligations, or disadvantages on such individual or group not imposed upon others, or which withholds or limits access to opportunities, benefits, and advantages available to other members of society. Distinctions based on personal characteristics attributed to an individual solely on the basis of association with a group will rarely escape the charge of discrimination, while those based on an individual's merits and capacities will rarely be so classed.[129]

Similarly, the European Court of Human Rights in the *Belgium Linguistic Case (No.2)*[130] enunciated that

> the principle of equality of treatment is violated if the distinction has no objective and reasonable justification. The existence of such a justification must be assessed in relation to the aim and effects of the measure under consideration, regard being had to the principles which normally prevail in democratic societies. A difference

of treatment in the exercise of a right laid down in the Convention must not only pursue a legitimate aim: Art. 14 is likewise violated when it is clearly established that there is no reasonable [relationship] of proportionality between the means employed and the aim sought to be realised.[131]

It is, then, well established that a discriminatory treatment will not be held unconstitutional if it can be justified. As Hong Kong Court of Appeal Justice Bokhary (as he then was) in *R. v. Man Wai Keung (No.2)*[132] stated:

> Clearly, there is no requirement of literal equality in the sense of unrelentingly identical treatment always. For such rigidity would subvert rather than promote true even-handedness. So that, in certain circumstances, a departure from literal equality would be a legitimate course and, indeed, the only legitimate course. But the starting point is identical treatment. And any departure therefrom must be justified. To justify such a departure it must be shown: one, that sensible and fair-minded people would recognise a genuine need for some difference of treatment; two, that the difference embodied in the particular departure selected to meet that need is itself rational; and three, that such departure is proportionate to such need.[133]

Likewise, Justice McIntyre in *Andrews* indicated that

> [A] complainant under s.15(1) must show not only that he or she is not receiving equal treatment before and under the law or that the law has a differential impact on him or her in the protection or benefit accorded by law but, in addition, must show that the legislative impact of the law is discriminatory ... any consideration of factors which could justify the discrimination and support the constitutionality of the impugned enactment would take place under s.1.[134]

In assessing whether a particular distinction should be held to be justified and therefore not unconstitutional, reference is had to *R. v. Oakes*,[135] where Canadian Supreme Court Chief Justice Dickson stated:

> To establish that a limit is reasonable and demonstrably justified in a free and democratic society, two central criteria must be satisfied. First, the objective, which the measures responsible for a limit on a Charter right or freedom are designed to serve, must be 'of sufficient importance to warrant overriding a constitutionally protected right or freedom'. The standard must be high in order to ensure that objectives which are trivial or discordant with the principles integral to a free and democratic society do not gain s.1 protection. It is necessary, at a minimum, that an objective relate to concerns which are pressing and substantial in a free and democratic society before it can be characterised as sufficiently important.[136]

It is, however, regrettable that the Hong Kong Bill of Rights Ordinance prohibits only discrimination by the government,[137] which limits its value to the protection of equality in all of its manifestations within society at large. Lacey criticises such 'a public/private dichotomy [which] allows government to clean its hands of any responsibility for the state of the "private" world and depoliticises the disadvantages which inevitably spill over the alleged divide by affecting the position of the "privately" disadvantaged in the "public" world.'[138] Nevertheless, subsequent democratic changes in the structure of the Hong Kong legislature,[139] since reversed and a subject of grave controversy in its own right,[140] made possible anti-discrimination legislation directed specifically at the private sector. In 1994, Legislative Councillor Anna Wu presented a comprehensive Equal Opportunities Bill[141] aiming at the prohibition of discrimination on grounds of sex, marital status, pregnancy, family responsibility or family status, race, religious or political conviction, disability, sexuality, spent conviction, age, or union membership or activities, as well as harassment on grounds of sex, race, disability, or sexuality.[142] The Bill was unprecedented in the history of Hong Kong as it was the 'first private member's bill covering an entire area of law'.[143] The Bill encountered enormous resistance from the administration, alongside many of Wu's fellow legislators, who argued that anti-discrimination legislation would hinder Hong Kong's *laissez-faire* economy. Chau, a local economist, observes that

> Human resources and a system of free enterprise are generally considered to be the main impetuses to Hong Kong's economic success. ... It is in the labour market that we can best observe the operation and interaction of these two factors. ... In most other labour markets, the price mechanism is constrained by strong unions and collective bargaining, monopolies, business regulations, labour [legislation], high taxes, and transfer payments. All these impediments to market forces are practically absent in Hong Kong.[144]

Fearing that Wu's Bill might be endorsed, the administration ultimately introduced its own Sex Discrimination Bill[145] and Disability Discrimination Bill,[146] which were much narrower in scope, in order to placate demands for anti-discrimination legislation. Ultimately, the latter two Bills were preferred to Wu's Bill, and pressed upon accordingly,[147] by legislators who argued that Wu's Bill was too comprehensive, and thus inappropriate, before Hong Kong has built up sufficient experience with anti-discrimination legislation.[148] Nevertheless, an Equal Opportunities Commission was created by virtue of the passage of the Sex Discrimination Bill.[149]

The momentum for all-inclusive equality did not subside, however. In 1996, Legislative Councillor Lee Cheuk-Yan sponsored an Equal Opportunities (Family Responsibility, Sexuality and Age) Bill.[150] Unfortunately, the demise of this Bill was brought about by a consultation exercise in the same year, namely *Equal Opportunities: A Study on Discrimination on the Ground of Sexual Orientation: A Consultative Paper*,[151] which concluded that 'public acceptance of homosexuality and bisexuality is on the low side ... [and] scored 3.4 on a rating scale of 0 (totally unacceptable) to 10 (totally acceptable).'[152] The Equal Opportunities (Family Responsibility, Sexuality and Age) Bill therefore was not proceeded upon.[153] It must, however, be pointed out that the consultation exercise contained such material flaws and misconceptions that its validity was seriously in question, as the present author has demonstrated elsewhere.[154] The Hong Kong Legislative Council's Home Affairs Panel then established a Subcommittee to Study Discrimination on the Ground of Sexual Orientation aiming at the exploration of sexual orientation discrimination in specific areas and ultimately reporting its work to the Home Affairs Panel. The Subcommittee has since gone into dormancy with its aim only partially fulfilled, that certain views were brought into open discussion. Some of these views will be discussed here.

## IV. A Right to Same-Sex Marriage in Hong Kong? A Post-Colonial Cultural Schizophrenia Exposed

Opponents of homosexuality and sexual minority rights invariably dismiss the legal developments elsewhere on sexual minority rights as irrelevant to Hong Kong society, claiming sovereignty and cultural relativism – 'Asian values' in particular – in the formation and development of human rights, and news reports have indicated that the Equal Opportunities Commission of Hong Kong, a statutory body acting as guardian of Hong Kong's existing anti-discrimination legislation,[155] has received more than 10,000 letters opposing the enactment of a Sexual Orientation Discrimination Ordinance.[156] The Hong Kong government has so far exulted in their opposition, which it claims to be representative of sentiments in Hong Kong, and has recently objected to civil partnership registration taking place at the British consulate in Hong Kong under the United Kingdom's Civil Partnership Act 2004,[157] whilst continuing to procrastinate over the enactment of sexual orientation anti-discrimination legislation and appealing the Hong Kong Court of First Instance decision in August 2005 that held that various provisions in the Crimes Ordinance were discriminatory against gay men without satisfactory justification and were thus unconstitutional,[158] which decision has since been unanimously affirmed by the Hong Kong Court of Appeal.[159]

This paper will not repeat the vast literature on the universalism–cultural relativism debate in human rights discourse, except for noting that arguments in favour of the universality of human rights have generally triumphed ultimately, especially after the Asian financial crisis in the late 1990s where the alleged correlation between 'Asian values' and Asia's economic boom in the previous decade was disproved. In dismissing sexual minority rights or any other human rights as Western-oriented by relying on state sovereignty as justification, critics, in fact, also are asserting a principle which originated from the 1648 Treaty of Westphalia, a Western treaty peculiar to Western nation-states, and overlooking the historical fact that the notion of state sovereignty was foreign to imperial China as the Middle Kingdom with all neighbouring countries under its tutelage.

Nevertheless, it is important for us to understand cultural values as they pertain to Chinese and Hong Kong society, for the purpose of examining the viability and development or otherwise of sexual orientation equality and non-discrimination rights, and of equality and non-discrimination rights in general, in Hong Kong. Before we do so, however, we need to bear in mind that '[i]dentity is formed through a series of actions and social reactions, and is differently constructed according to different local histories and contexts.'[160] Within a given society, '[p]erception of the same phenomena may vary depending on the culture, class, gender, age, or crisis-experience of the observer',[161] and it is invariably the case that 'powerful individuals and groups tend to monopolize the interpretation of cultural norms and manipulate them to their own advantage.'[162]

As Schwartz maintains, '[t]he commonalities in the intentional and unintentional value socialization to which different members of society are exposed reflect the cultural emphases that support and maintain the social, economic, and political system of the society. The average of the value priorities of societal members reflects these commonalities of enculturation.'[163] Whilst not a religion as such and indeed 'thoroughly secular',[164] Confucianism, embodying the teachings of Confucius, as a philosophy of life is pervasive in the social, political, moral and in many instances juristic fabrics of society and governance in East Asia, and especially amongst the Chinese. Gabrenya and Hwang note that 'Confucian concepts are employed both in an analytical, abstract, philosophical sense and as a useful heuristic for describing the professed values of Chinese people. ... Although Chinese social behaviour is often interpreted as a reflection of Confucian ideological beliefs, historical circumstances and current conditions also shape Chinese behaviour in important ways (as historical circumstances shaped Confucianism itself long ago), providing alternate, albeit often concordant, explanations of observed behaviour patterns.'[165]

The institution of family is central to Confucianism, and thus Chinese and Hong Kong society, with the notion of filial piety controlling all social thoughts and interactions as well as providing moral guidance. In his famous 1994 interview in *Foreign Affairs*,[166] Lee Kuan Yew, then Senior Minister and now Minister Mentor of Singapore, declared that 'the tested norm is the family unit. It is the building brick of society.'[167] Ho indicates that

> Although some of its component ideas (obedience, for example) are shared by other cultures, filial piety surpasses all other ethics in its historical continuity, the proportion of humanity under its governance, and the encompassing and imperative nature of its precepts. The attributes of intergenerational relationships governed by filial piety are structural, enduring, and invariable across situations within Chinese culture. They may be generalized to apply to authority relationships beyond the family, and they are thus potent determinants of not only intergenerational but also superior–subordinate interactions.[168]

The social psychologist points out that

> For centuries, filial piety has served as a guiding principle governing generational Chinese patterns of socialization, as well as specific rules of intergenerational conduct, applicable throughout the length of one's life span. ... It makes stringent demands: that one should provide for the material and mental well-being of one's aged parents, perform ceremonial duties of ancestral worship, take care to avoid harm to one's body, ensure the continuity of the family line, and in general conduct oneself so as to bring honour and avoid disgrace to the family name.[169]

One of the foremost filial obligations is to continue the ancestral line. For a child to disavow such a sacrosanct filial obligation on account of a psychological feeling, in the form of homosexuality, must thus be disallowed; that that psychological feeling is further ostracised by society makes it all the more illicit, and above all its status as a crime renders it an unspeakable disgrace upon the family.

Howard, however, argues that human rights are 'universally applicable in principle' as a corollary of justice.[170] The sociologist reminds us that '[a] far stronger case can be made that human rights are *not* the dominant Western cultural tradition than that they are. The Western philosophical and cultural traditions of social justice include not only liberalism, but also communism, corporatism, racism, and fascism.'[171] For Hong Kong society, and the government, to allude to homosexuality as a crime in its refusal on cultural grounds to recognise sexual minorities as equal members of society deserving of equal recognition and protection is adamantly suspect, when the criminality of homosexuality was not indigenous to Hong Kong but was imported from Great Britain into the then Crown Colony. Historical evidence shows that male homosexuality in mediaeval China 'was considered neither a crime nor immoral behaviour'.[172] Sommer points out that 'it is only in the Qing [dynasty] that lawmakers included such acts in the venerable criminal category of "illicit sexual intercourse" (*jian*).'[173] In republican China, homosexuality has never been explicitly classified as an offence,[174] and the socialist Chinese government, like Queen Victoria in respect of lesbianism, refuses to acknowledge that sexual minorities exist in its territory.[175] In addition, the offence of hooliganism, a law which socialist China used to exploit in the suppression of homosexuality[176] alongside political dissent, was repealed in 1997. Last but not least, the Chinese Psychiatric Association in 2001 followed the footsteps laid in 1974 by the American Psychiatric Association and removed homosexuality from its list of mental disorders.

Furthermore, as Weber points out, the 'Chinese language has no special word for "religion".'[177] Liu notes:

> The Chinese Confucian elite has a long tradition of disregarding local religions; 'gods' and 'ghosts' are considered inappropriate topics for discussion. ... Considered 'feudal superstition' and blamed for China's poverty and backwardness, local religious practices were criticized for not being scientific as they relied on divination to solve problems. Local religions were said to nurture people's selfish and utilitarian attitudes which were now obstacles to the industrialization and modernization of China.
>
> The educated elite in Hong Kong inherited some of this anti-local religious tradition and tend to ignore the existence of local religion. The school curriculum, for example, pushes the anti-local religion tradition, aided and abetted by the prevalence of Christian organizations in Hong Kong's school system. A large number of Hong Kong schools are run by volunteer associations with the government subsidizing their operational costs; many of these organizations are Protestant and Roman Catholic, and because of their own agendas, they are not eager to promote local religion.[178]

It is, thus, disingenuous for those opposed to the development and protection of sexual minority rights in Hong Kong to resort to religion in the name of Christianity as justification for their opposition. In particular, the Society for Truth and Light, the foremost anti-gay and anti-human rights lobby group in Hong Kong, through which the Hong Kong government, relies on 'Victorian readings of the Old Testament Sodom and Gomorrah story'[179] in its condemnation of homosexuality, even as the place of Christian moral teachings is questionable in Hong Kong where less than ten per cent of its more than seven million population consider themselves Christians or holding Christian belief. The prevalence of Christian-denominated primary and secondary schools in Hong Kong reflects not at all any alleged widespread belief in Christianity but Hong Kong's historical colonial status; that the properties of St. John's Cathedral, an Anglican institution, are the only freehold properties in Hong Kong attests again not to the sacredness of Christianity within the population of Hong Kong but Hong Kong's historical colonial subjugation by

Great Britain and subsequently the United Kingdom. Nonetheless, opponents of homosexuality and sexual minority rights will rally with Christian organisations and use the religiosity argument to oppose measures that aim to recognise and protect sexual minority rights, including sexual orientation equality and non-discrimination rights, and contend that the Chinese culture and traditions are necessarily conservative and do not allow such foreign influence as homosexuality, which is only to bring about the Western or 'imported' disease of HIV/AIDS,[180] even as Christianity is foreign and has at times been hostile to the Chinese civilisation as evident in the Boxer Rebellion (1899–1901) which eventually led to the intervention of the Eight-Nation Alliance and the further and final weakening of China at the time. The heatedness of the sexual minority rights debate has conveniently allowed the Society for Truth and Light and similar organisations, as well as the Hong Kong government, to shield such contradictions from general awareness and scrutiny.

Writing in the context of abortion in Ireland, Fletcher reasons that the basis for the Irish's aversion lies in fact in Irish nationalism, and 'as the Irish sought to resist the colonial disenfranchisement of Roman Catholics, Catholicism became a particular marker of Irish nationality. Anti-abortion efforts to make a "pro-life" stance a symbol of Irishness have drawn on and reconstructed this historical association between Catholicism and Irish nationalism',[181] in contrast to Protestant Englishness and in opposition to English colonial legacy. The author maintains that '[s]truggles for political dominance mobilized gender, religious, ethnic, and class divides in the name of consolidating national power. One tactic for justifying the exclusion of "undesirables" from the task of nation-building was to dress them up in colonial clothes.'[182] In post-colonial societies, including Hong Kong, homosexuality, Hemmings discerns, is portrayed as 'a national betrayal ... as a failure of appropriate gendered and sexual citizenship, and as a marker of Western influence.'[183] Speaking of Zimbabwe's ascription of homosexuality to Caucasian males alone, Phillips argues that '[t]his portrayal of such a confluence of racial and sexual degeneration was intended to carry the twin implications that, first, white western European "culture" is depraved as it corrupts other cultures with the "evil" practice of homosexuality; and that, second, homosexuals must be white, as they are, by definition, "depraved".'[184] The gender imbalance enforced against the female, the perceived impenetrability of the human male body, and the uncompromising importance of continuing the ancestral (male) line in Chinese society all render homosexuality to be thus a role which only a 'specialized, despised, and punished'[185] soul would be willing to assume. Along these lines, opponents of homosexuality and sexual minority rights in Hong Kong construct sexual minorities in Hong Kong as foreign to the local population; should they in fact exist, as rare and deserving of infliction of HIV/AIDS, a gay plague which heterosexuals, perforce right-minded, do not suffer. The historical evidence that homosexuality was pervasive in imperial China, and the contemporary evidence that homosexuality exists *everywhere*,[186] is conveniently ignored. The ease and eagerness of these opponents and the Hong Kong government in associating with Chinese traditional culture nevertheless stops when the equality and non-discrimination rights of Mainland Chinese immigrants, the ultimate manifestation of nationalistic integration, call for recognition and protection.[187]

In his study on law and culture in South Korea, which the author regards as generally 'the most Confucian of all Asian cultures',[188] Hahm concludes that '[i]n place of Confucian values like filial piety or ritual propriety, Koreans nowadays prefer to speak in terms of individual rights and describe their country as a "liberal democracy". Whilst the South Korean Constitution makes no reference to Confucianism or Confucian values, it has plenty of provisions protecting individual rights and "free and democratic basic order".'[189] Hahm argues that '[w]hile law must operate in a cultural context and is influenced by the culture, that culture is in turn affected by the operation of law'[190] and that 'culture, which supposedly influences how law operates, should not be seen as static or seamless, and should be understood from a perspective that also allows for its own transformation through the operation of law.'[191] It ought to be borne in mind that at the same time, as Kymlicka emphasises, 'the cultural community continues to exist even when its members are free to modify the character of the culture, should they find its traditional ways of life no longer worth while.'[192]

The same holds true with Hong Kong and the Hong Kong citizenry, who regard the democratisation of Hong Kong as the ultimate bulwark against further Chinese onslaught upon its autonomy and rights and freedoms and have called on the courts to guarantee and protect their rights and freedoms under the Basic Law of Hong Kong and the Hong Kong Bill of Rights Ordinance. In his guest seminar at the Centre for Comparative and Public Law at the University of Hong Kong in September 2006 based on an earlier version of this paper, the present author was asked an interesting question as to whether the eventual materialisation, if there be, of universal suffrage in Hong Kong may *adversely* affect the development and protection of sexual minority rights, as, the participant argued, the majority of the population are opposed to such development and protection, against which they may rally to vote. In reply, the present author explained that universal suffrage and sexual minority rights share one underlying normative root, that is, the self-empowerment of the individual, and we may refer to other democratic and non-democratic jurisdictions to deduce that universal suffrage is the first and essential step to full democracy and the full guarantee and realisation of all rights and freedoms, including sexual orientation equality and non-discrimination rights. It is precisely for this reason that the Chinese and Hong Kong governments are opposed to the materialisation of universal suffrage in Hong Kong, as they do not wish that the citizenry be thereby self-empowered. In another forum[193] the present author has argued that an adolescent has a right to sexual minority identity under the United Nations Convention on the Rights of the Child.[194] Similarly, Katyal states that an individual's right to sexual minority identity is compatible with and mandated by a genuine application of the normative bases underlying state sovereignty and the right of self-determination.[195] Thus, those who desire universal suffrage in Hong Kong may not legitimately deny the normative intrinsicality and validity of sexual minorities' entitlement to equal respect and protection for who they are and their right to autonomy to live freely without discrimination, for otherwise their claim of entitlement to universal suffrage, rooted in the Western right of self-determination which in turn is premised upon self and autonomy and is thus fundamentally adverse to Confucianism, will instantly be contradicted and rendered illegitimate.

Most importantly, we must bear in mind that protection of equality is not a number game but an inherent value of democracy. During the 1991 legislative debate on decriminalisation of homosexuality in Hong Kong, Legislative Councillor Leung Wai-Tung pointed out that *Abide By The Doctrines*, authored by influential Chinese philosopher Han Fei-Zi 2200 years ago, teaches that '[i]t is stipulated in the law that the capable ones should not exploit the incapable ones, the strong ones should not bully the weak ones, and the majority should not jeopardize the interests of the minority.'[196] It is a principle of democratic governance universally acknowledged that the majority must not obstruct enactment of legislation that protects minorities, which include sexual minorities.

As a matter of justice, reason must be held capable of overriding and prevailing over the majority rule:

> The liberal commitment to public reasonableness stands for the view that the mere fact of power – even of overwhelming numerical superiority combined with passionate conviction – is not enough to establish the legitimacy of laws and policies in the face of principled objections. Before limiting important liberties or treating people as less than equal in morally significant ways, the politically powerful need to provide an adequate public justification: reasons that can be openly presented to others, critically defended, and widely shared by reasonable people.[197]

Dworkin gives his explanation thus:

> A legislator who proceeds in this way, who refuses to take popular indignation, intolerance and disgust as the moral conviction of his community, is not guilty of moral elitism. He is not simply setting his own educated views against those of a vast public which rejects them. He is doing his best to enforce a distinct, and fundamentally important, part of his community's morality, a consensus more essential to society's existence in the form we know it than the opinion Lord Devlin bids him follow.
>
> No legislator can afford to ignore the public's outrage. It is a fact he must reckon with. It will set the [boundaries] of what is politically feasible, and it will determine his strategies of persuasion and enforcement within these [boundaries]. But we must not confuse strategy with justice, nor facts of political life with principles of political morality. Lord Devlin understands these distinctions, but his arguments will appeal most, I am afraid, to those who do not.[198]

## V. The Importance of All-Inclusive Equality

In the context of race – specifically the Hong Kong government's recent public consultation on whether race anti-discrimination legislation should be enacted and if so to what extent – the present author has maintained elsewhere that the principle of equality will instantly be defeated if the particular measure or provision that seeks to protect equality is qualified by an exclusion of Mainland Chinese immigrants from protection under an eventual Race Discrimination Ordinance.[199] *Mutatis mutandis*, the guarantee of equality in the Basic Law of Hong Kong and in the Hong Kong Bill of Rights Ordinance will likewise be rendered meaningless if sexual minorities continue to be deprived of their human rights and dignity in equal access to the institution of marriage merely because of their sexual orientation, which the Supreme Court of Canada in *Egan v. Canada*[200] found to be a personal characteristic 'unchangeable or changeable only at unacceptable personal costs'.[201] The notion propounded by opponents of homosexuality and sexual minority rights that gay men and lesbians are *free to marry* persons of the opposite sex was denounced by Justice Ackermann of the South African Constitutional Court in *National Coalition for Gay and Lesbian Equality v. Minister of Home Affairs* as 'a meaningless abstraction'[202] which itself reflects pervasive subjugation both in societal attitudes and in the law. As Massachusetts Supreme Judicial Council Chief Justice Marshall in *Goodridge v. Department of Public Health*[203] maintained, '[a]s both *Perez* [*v. Sharp*][204] and

*Loving* [*v. Virginia*][205] make clear, the right to marry means little if it does not include the right to marry the person of one's choice, subject to appropriate government restrictions in the interests of public health, safety, and welfare.'[206]

The harms attributable to institutionalised or state-sanctioned inequality are enormous, and South Africa's experience from apartheid to progressive liberal democracy is illuminating. The South African Supreme Court of Appeal in *Fourie* pointed out that the pioneering explicit inclusion of sexual orientation in South Africa's constitutional guarantee of equality is precisely a reflection of the recognised need for all-inclusive equality protection. As Judge Cameron elucidated, '[f]or though oppression on the ground of sexual orientation was not paramount in the scheme of historical injustice, it formed part of it, and the negotiating founders deliberately committed our nation to a course that disavowed all forms of legalised oppression and injustice.'[207] Similarly, South African Constitutional Court Justice Goldstone in *President of the Republic of South Africa v. Hugo* [208] stated:

> At the heart of the prohibition of unfair discrimination lies a recognition that the purpose of our new constitutional and democratic order is the establishment of a society in which all human beings will be accorded equal dignity and respect regardless of their membership of particular groups. The achievement of such a society in the context of our deeply inegalitarian past will not be easy, but that that is the goal of the Constitution should not be forgotten or overlooked.[209]

In its scrutiny of sexual orientation discrimination, the South African Constitutional Court in *National Coalition for Gay and Lesbian Equality v. Minister of Home Affairs* categorically maintained:

> The sting of past and continuing discrimination against both gays and lesbians is the clear message that it conveys, namely, that they, whether viewed as individuals or in their same-sex relationships, do not have the inherent dignity and are not worthy of the human respect possessed by and accorded to heterosexuals and their relationships. This discrimination occurs at a deeply intimate level of human existence and relationality. It denies ... gays and lesbians that which is foundational to our Constitution and the concepts of equality and dignity, which at this point are closely intertwined, namely that all persons have the same inherent worth and dignity as human beings, whatever their other differences may be. The denial of equal dignity and worth all too quickly and insidiously degenerates into a denial of humanity and leads to inhuman treatment by the rest of society in many other ways.[210]

Within the narrower confines of whether a person has a right to marry another person of the same sex, the South African court found that denial of such a right conveys the message

> that gays and lesbians lack the inherent humanity to have their families and family lives in such same-sex relationships respected or protected. It serves in addition to perpetuate and reinforce existing prejudices and stereotypes. The impact constitutes a crass, blunt, cruel and serious invasion of their dignity. The discrimination, based

on sexual orientation, is severe because no concern, let alone anything approaching equal concern, is shown for the particular sexual orientation of gays and lesbians.[211]

As human behaviour is not alienable within specific delineations, discrimination on the basis of one personal characteristic is bound to contaminate society and lead to discrimination on the basis of other personal characteristics premised upon stereotypes and prejudices. Here, Canadian Supreme Court Justice Cory's caution in *Vriend v. Alberta*[212] is apposite:

> It is easy to say that everyone who is just like 'us' is entitled to equality. Everyone finds it more difficult to say that those who are 'different' from us in some way should have the same equality rights that we enjoy. Yet so soon as we say any enumerated or analogous group is less deserving and unworthy of equal protection and benefit of the law all minorities and all of Canadian society are demeaned. It is so deceptively simple and so devastatingly injurious to say that those who are handicapped or of a different race, or religion, or colour or sexual orientation are less worthy. Yet, if any enumerated or analogous group is denied the equality provided by s.15 then the equality of every other minority group is threatened. That equality is guaranteed by our Constitution. If equality rights for minorities had been recognized, the all too frequent tragedies of history might have been avoided. It can never be forgotten that discrimination is the antithesis of equality and that it is the recognition of equality which will foster the dignity of every individual.[213]

Whilst a number of national courts have ruled either that sexual orientation is an unchangeable personal characteristic (as in *Egan*) or that it is a suspect ground of unlawful discrimination requiring heightened scrutiny of purported justification,[214] opponents of homosexuality and sexual minority rights argue that sexual orientation is merely a personal choice, if not a deviant lifestyle, and thus should not warrant extra protection or the granting of special rights. On the contrary, peer-reviewed research in fields including psychology, medicine, and sociology has demonstrated that sexual orientation is not a personal choice (save being one's choice to live one's life as it is, freely and fully).[215] Judge Posner of the United States Court of Appeals for the Seventh Circuit, writing extra-judicially, further highlights the anomaly in such a choice argument, that '[g]iven the personal and social disadvantages to which homosexuality subjects a person in our society, the idea that millions of young men and women have chosen it or will choose it in the same fashion in which they might choose a career or a place to live or a political party or even a religious faith seems preposterous.'[216] In another forum on sexual minority identity under the United Nations Convention on the Rights of the Child, the present author discerns that

> heterosexuals who flaunt their heterosexuality whilst at the same time enthusiastically dismissing sexual minority adolescents' (and individuals') sexual orientations by alleging that sexual orientation is merely a choice may ask themselves when *they* chose to become heterosexuals and remind themselves that if such a choice was ever made, their chosen heterosexuality is perforce susceptible to intense volatility. Not surprisingly, this is a foremost reason why those who seek to repress other people's sexual orientations have first to repress their very own.[217]

In its 1996 consultation exercise, the Hong Kong government stated that 'some educational bodies',[218] whose identities and representativeness were not spelled out, maintained that 'the promiscuous behaviour of homosexuals may have an adverse effect on the overall moral standards of society.'[219] As Gert points out, however, 'no one has the authority to settle moral disputes in the way that the United States Supreme Court has the authority to settle legal disputes in the United States or the pope religious disputes among Roman Catholics. Further, no one has some special knowledge of morality not available to others, for everyone who is subject to moral judgment must know what it requires, prohibits, encourages, and allows.'[220] The present author has written elsewhere[221] that instead of propagating irrational hatred, these educational bodies should be at the forefront in teaching the principle of equality to maturing young persons, many of whom already engage in '[h]omophobic performances [as] part of the self-convincing rituals of masculinity',[222] which, Abrams points out, 'may also be a vehicle for extirpating from one's own gender identity tabooed or nonconforming elements, by projecting them onto others who then become the targets of one's abuse.'[223] Such prejudice on the part of these educational bodies squarely contradicted the validity of the government's conclusion in the same consultation exercise that education would be more effective than legislation in eliminating sexual orientation discrimination and harassment.[224] Worse still, the Hong Kong government has recently engaged the Society for Truth and Light, which as aforementioned is an anti-gay, anti-human rights lobby group in Hong Kong, to provide schoolteachers with human rights education, prompting immediate public consternation. The Society has indicated that in its human rights education it will not discuss sexual orientation at all. As Hartman observes, '[t]here is no better way to subjugate human beings than to silence them. There is nothing more oppressive than denying another's reality.'[225] Furthermore, bearing in mind the Society's stance that homosexuality can be cured, in utter defiance of established science,[226] and that human rights education for schoolteachers directly influences their interactions with their students which may then profoundly reinforce the adolescents' view on hetero-normativity, homophobic bullying within schools is an immediate certainty. It is submitted, thus, that the Hong Kong government's decision in this respect contravenes section 7 of the Hong Kong Bill of Rights Ordinance and entails direct as well as vicarious liability under ordinary tort and contract laws for any such homophobic bullying as is to occur.[227]

It is further submitted that the abusive description of sexual minorities as 'promiscuous' is exceedingly inappropriate in the absence of demonstrated supporting evidence; it is even more so in a consultation paper. Petersen points out that '[b]y repeating [the views of these educational bodies] without dispute or disclosure of the lack of supporting evidence ... the government tacitly agreed with these views and gave them credibility. Thus, instead of "consulting" the public on the problem of sexuality discrimination, the government offered justifications for it',[228] which partiality the author laments 'unfortunate'.[229] Kelly states that '[i]mpartiality is a requisite virtue for all public functionaries whether judges, political representatives, bureaucrats, or policemen. Indeed, without the ideal of impartiality the very idea of "corruption" ceases to make sense. ... bureaucrats are expected to be above the ordinary fray of politics, which is shaped by the clash of interests and group claims.'[230] Galloway offers his explanation on the wrongfulness of governmental partiality thus:

> The reason for regarding discriminatory [disadvantage] as wrongful is not that it attacks the social status of the individual but that it attacks the individual's personal

identity. The fact of past and continuing group [disadvantage] will be evidence that powerful groups and individuals within society have not in the past regarded, and do not now regard, the members of the group as worthy of the same respect as others, that they regard them as a lower class of person. If the government further disadvantages members of this group, it participates in the process. The government becomes an accessory to this stereotyping by defining a person in terms of the relevant characteristic, whether it be skin colour, physical disability, gender or some other factor which can be associated with social disadvantage. It collaborates in the powerful attacks perpetrated against those who are defined by a single feature. The pre-existing social [disadvantage] suffered by the group of people who share this characteristic provides strong evidence that this single characteristic is operating as a barrier which is preventing the government from seeing the individual as a full person when the law impacts negatively on those who possess it. The government is reducing an individual's humanity to a single non-essential characteristic. Herein lies the affront.[231]

Accordingly, Canadian Supreme Court Justice Iacobucci in *Egan* observed that '[t]he legislature's reliance upon stereotypical reasoning may very well be an extremely significant factor in determining whether discrimination exists.'[232] Justice L'Heureux-Dubé concurred, stating that '[i]t would be strange, indeed, to permit the government to justify a discriminatory distinction on the basis of presumptions which are, themselves, discriminatory.'[233]

Meanwhile, the popular correlation between homosexuality and promiscuity is unsubstantiated. It is entirely untenable to argue that all members of sexual minorities are promiscuous (just as not all men rape women), as many of them, like different-sex couples, do seek and cherish long-term relationships that would have culminated in marriage but for denial by the state. Furthermore, as Dworkin maintains,

> Even if it is true that most men think homosexuality an abominable vice and cannot tolerate its presence, it remains possible that this common opinion is a compound of prejudice (resting on the assumption that homosexuals are morally inferior creatures because they are effeminate), rationalization (based on assumptions of fact so unsupported that they challenge the community's own standards of rationality), and personal aversion (representing no conviction but merely blind hate rising from unacknowledged self-suspicion). It remains possible that the ordinary man could produce no reason for his view, but would simply parrot his neighbour who in turn parrots him, or that he would produce a reason which presupposes a general moral position he could not sincerely or consistently claim to hold. If so, the principles of democracy we follow do not call for the enforcement of the consensus, for the belief that prejudices, personal aversions and rationalizations do not justify restricting another's freedom itself occupies a critical and fundamental position in our popular morality. Nor would the bulk of the community then be entitled to follow its own lights, for the community does not extend that privilege to one who acts on the basis of prejudice, rationalization, or personal aversion. Indeed, the distinction between these and moral convictions, in the discriminatory sense, exists largely to mark off the former as the sort of positions one is not entitled to pursue.[234]

It is imperative to note that '[o]f the 3,004 cumulative total of HIV infections since 1984 [up to and including the second quarter of 2006 in Hong Kong], around 76% acquired infection through sexual contact. Of them, 67% [resulted] from heterosexual transmission and 140 infections occurred among injection drug users.'[235] Choi Chi-Sum from the Society for Truth and Light in a Subcommittee meeting argued that gay men were six times more likely than heterosexuals to contract the HIV virus.[236] Whether or not his data, based solely on pure arithmetic, were reliable, it is nonetheless the sexual activity, i.e., anal intercourse, to which gay men by nature have to resort for full integrated sexual expression, as recognised by both the Ontario Court of Appeal[237] and the Hong Kong Court of First Instance and Court of Appeal,[238] rather than their sexual minority identity that constitutes a contributing factor to a higher rate of HIV infection. It is a fact that many heterosexuals also engage in anal intercourse, which has explicitly been acknowledged by Hong Kong's legislature in the form of legislation.[239] Indeed, as Anna Wu, then Chairperson of the Equal Opportunities Commission, observed in her meeting with the Subcommittee, 'HIV infection from heterosexual exposure had demonstrated a rising trend ... in 2000. In contrast, transmission through homosexual and bisexual contacts in the same period had dropped.'[240] Thus, considering together the alarming prevalence of HIV/AIDS amongst heterosexuals in Africa, the myth that HIV/AIDS is a gay plague must be rejected outright.

In addition, Ball points out that the unsubstantiated correlation between homosexuality and promiscuity 'contains its own built-in moral disapprobation. A definition that reduces homosexual conduct to the seeking of "orgasmic sexual satisfaction", to the exclusion of all other personal goals and needs, connotes a sexual depravity and a lack of self-control. This definition ignores that homosexual acts, like their heterosexual counterparts, are often based on affectional feelings and on a concept often overlooked in debates about homosexuality, namely, "love".'[241] Likewise, Koppelman maintains that '[f]or at least some same-sex couples, sexual intercourse is valued, not merely as a pleasurable experience unintegrated with the rest of one's life, but as an activity that is an important constituent of one of the primary relationships of one's life, exactly as is the case with heterosexual couples.'[242] Raz goes further and argues that '[t]he existence of a society ... with recognized homosexual marriages is a collective good ... In a society where such opportunities exist and make it possible for individuals to have an autonomous life, their existence is intrinsically invaluable.'[243] It must be unequivocally understood that marriage, in the words of United States Supreme Court Justice Douglas in *Griswold v. Connecticut*,[244] 'is an association that promotes a way of life, not causes; a harmony in living, not political faiths; a bilateral loyalty, not commercial or social projects'.[245] With homosexuality (and bisexuality) considered a less worthwhile form of sexual orientation, of which heterosexuality is the compulsory norm and with which homosexuality is nonetheless synonymous, opponents of homosexuality and sexual minority rights consider that sexual minorities should be content with the fact that many societies in which they live have now decriminalised their 'immoral' behaviour and thus should not ask for any more 'special rights' to which these opponents claim to be fundamentally opposed.

Such an argument is flawed, however. The right of access to the institution of marriage that sexual minorities have been fighting for is a right of equality and not a special or extra right, as opponents of same-sex marriage portray. In fact, emphasis on sexuality is made only, ironically and illustrably by opponents of same-sex marriage. As Lin discerns:

There are two predominant narratives that circulate within American society that help to explain the difficulty that lesbians and gays face in adopting children and establishing families. First, there is the story of lesbians and gays that centers on their sexuality. Whether because of disgust, confusion, or ignorance about homosexuality, lesbian and gay sexuality dominates the discourse of not only same-sex adoption, but all lesbian and gay issues. The classification of lesbians and gays as 'exclusively sexual beings' stands in stark contrast to the perception of heterosexual parents as 'people who, along with many other activities in their lives, occasionally engage in sex'. Through this narrative, lesbians and gays are reduced to one-dimensional creatures, defined by their sex and sexuality.[246]

Herman, furthermore, points out that

*some* rights are 'special' in the sense that they carve out particular bases upon which discriminatory treatment is not acceptable. The inclusion of 'sexual orientation' in civil rights laws, for example, does give sexuality a form of legal protection afforded to recognized categories such as religion, race, sex, and so on, and not, for example, to body size or economic position. If one can be denied housing because one is overweight or on welfare, but not because one is heterosexual or gay, then sexual orientation – including hetero-, homo-, and bi-sexualities – has 'special' status. There is, however, no 'special' status here for lesbians and gay men that is not accorded equally to hetero- and bi-sexualities.[247]

Ultimately, the heterosexual majority argues that sexual minorities should in any case be grateful for its tolerance. On the contrary, the notion of tolerance is vehemently antithetical to the principle of equality, as tolerance perforce implies a hierarchy of acceptability, entailing the implications of power. Legal scholars Morgan and Walker identify that 'tolerance is used as a mechanism of containment. It is portrayed as beneficial to the tolerated subject, but in fact the language of toleration is the language of subordination; it reinforces the subordination already experienced by those it claims to protect.'[248] The authors assert that 'tolerance and privacy, in the context of gay and lesbian rights, are interdependent because lesbian and gay sexual activity, as the abhorred "other" in the sexual hierarchy, is only tolerated if it is unseen.'[249] Theological scholar Nissinen maintains that '[t]he one who tolerates is seen as above the other. The distance and difference between the self and the other remains, because the need to tolerate requires that there is something wrong with the other person. Love, on the other hand, means stepping into another person's shoes, carrying his or her load, suffering together (*sympathein*). Love is not about striving toward objective good but about putting oneself at risk for another human being.'[250] As equality is a right to which every person is normatively entitled, to subjugate such normative entitlement to equality into mere receipt of condescending tolerance fundamentally defeats the principle of equality itself and demonstrates precisely the pervasiveness of inequality in the interplay of domination and subjugation. In the context of same-sex marriage, sociologist Howard-Hassmann is thus adamant that '[t]he truly rights-protective society is one that is "inclusive". These three key words – celebration, diversity, and inclusivity – typify a very recent social attitude that mere tolerance is a type of racism or prejudice, reflecting an unwillingness of the dominant, "tolerant" group to acknowledge that the diverse Other is as morally respectable as the conforming Us.

The rhetoric of diversity insists on more than tolerance. It insists on the moral acceptability of the diverse family.'[251]

Opponents of homosexuality and sexual minority rights, and their governments in many jurisdictions including Hong Kong, then argue that even if sexual minorities are entitled to equality rights, *their* rights should not be rushed through and certainly not by means of legislation but by education. In addition to the fact that it is very often educational authorities that find homosexuality – indeed sexuality itself – troubling, international bodies and national courts have consistently denounced such continual procrastination and called for positive measures to be put in place immediately for the recognition and protection of sexual minorities. As Canadian Supreme Court Justice Iacobucci in *Vriend* maintained:

> the need for governmental incrementalism was an inappropriate justification for *Charter* violations. ... In my opinion, groups that have historically been the target of discrimination cannot be expected to wait patiently for the protection of their human dignity and equal rights while governments move toward reform one step at a time. If the infringement of the rights and freedoms of these groups is permitted to persist while governments fail to pursue equality diligently, then the guarantees of the *Charter* will be reduced to little more than empty words.[252]

The argument for governmental or legislative incrementalism also brings forth the question of whether legal regimes such as civil partnership or civil union between two persons of the same sex such as are available in a number of countries, including the United Kingdom,[253] and American states[254] are sufficient for the effectuation of the guarantee of equality. In July 2006, the Family Division of the High Court of Justice of England and Wales in *Susan Wilkinson v. Celia Kitzinger and The Attorney-General, The Lord Chancellor intervening*[255] ruled that a marriage validly entered into in a foreign jurisdiction between two persons of the same sex, such as that entered into in the Canadian province of British Columbia between the petitioner and the first respondent in the case, cannot be given equal recognition as a marriage in England and Wales. Whilst the issue of foreign recognition of same-sex marriage goes beyond the scope of this paper, it is worth noting that the judgment of the Family Division was, with respect, supported essentially by circular reasoning premised upon stereotypes and errors of law. The Family Division relied, *inter alia*, on its own finding of a longstanding common understanding of the instrumental value of marriage in the procreation of children and their development and nurture in a 'nuclear family', as well as on the present definition of marriage under English laws and recognition under European Convention on Human Rights jurisprudence, in reaching its conclusion that a legally celebrated partnership between two persons of the same sex, such as a same-sex marriage in Canada or a civil partnership in the United Kingdom, was 'indeed different' from a marriage as understood in English laws and European Convention jurisprudence; the difference, according to the court, was thus justified.[256]

On the contrary, the conclusion of the Family Division ran afoul of the judgment of the European Court of Human Rights in *Salgueiro da Silva Mouta v. Portugal*[257] that a distinction made on the basis of the sexual orientation of a parent, a distinction not acceptable under the European Convention on Human Rights, in reaching the conclusion that the best interests of his or her child would *a priori* be adversely affected thereby was of itself not reasonable or proportional and was accordingly a violation of Article 8 taken in conjunction with Article 14.[258] The present author further takes issue with the Family Division's reference to the ambiguity, so found by the court, as to whether feelings of injustice and inequity held by the petitioner and the first respondent in the case were 'shared by a substantial number of same-sex couples content with the status of same-sex partnership'.[259] It must be pointed out that the fact, if there be, that a substantial number of members of a minority resign to unequal treatment does not render the treatment legitimate, reasonable, proportional or justified, and the normative intrinsicality of an individual's right of equality need not pass the hurdle of approval by others including other members of the minority concerned. In fact, their resignation is by and of itself the clearest indication of injustice.

As the majority of the Massachusetts Supreme Judicial Council in its advisory opinion on the constitutionality of a legislative Bill presented by the State Senate that if passed would have civil union recognised and same-sex marriage proscribed by Massachusetts[260] pointed out:

> The bill's absolute prohibition of the use of the word 'marriage' by 'spouses' who are [of] the same sex is more than semantic. The dissimilitude between the terms 'civil marriage' and 'civil union' is not innocuous; it is a considered choice of language that reflects a demonstrable assigning of same-sex, largely homosexual, couples to second-class status. The denomination of this difference by the separate opinion of Justice Sosman as merely a 'squabble over the name to be used' so clearly misses the point that further discussion appears to be useless. If, as the separate opinion posits, the proponents of the bill believe that no message is conveyed by eschewing the word 'marriage' and replacing it with 'civil union' for same-sex 'spouses', we doubt that the attempt to circumvent the court's decision in *Goodridge* would be so purposeful. For no rational reason the marriage laws of the Commonwealth [of Massachusetts] discriminate against a defined class; no amount of tinkering with language will eradicate that stain. The bill would have the effect of maintaining and fostering a stigma of exclusion that the Constitution prohibits. It would deny to same-sex 'spouses' only a status that is specially recognized in society and has significant social and other advantages.[261]

As family law in the United States is an area over which the individual 50 state governments have exclusive jurisdiction, only an amendment to the Massachusetts State Constitution or an amendment to the federal United States Constitution will be able to defeat Massachusetts' highest court's ruling in *Goodridge*. The Massachusetts state legislature in September 2005 in its defeat of the requisite second convention to so amend the State Constitution, which would have same-sex marriage disallowed but civil union remain permissible, by a vote of 157–39 made it adamantly clear that the court's ruling had now been well received by residents of the state.

Meanwhile, in Canada, the provincial courts of appeal of Ontario, British Columbia, Québec, Manitoba, Nova Scotia, Saskatchewan, Newfoundland and Labrador, and New Brunswick as well as the Supreme Court of the Yukon Territory have all provided a similar negative answer, affirming an individual's right to marry another person irrespective of their respective genders.[262] The then minority Liberal government decided not to appeal these judicial decisions; instead, it put forward a legislative Bill giving effect to these rulings and sought advice from the Supreme Court of Canada thereon. The Court since gave its nod in its advisory *Reference re Same-Sex Marriage*,[263] and the Civil Marriage Act 2005, section 2 of which defines marriage as 'for civil purposes ... the lawful union of two persons to the exclusion of all others',[264] was enacted in July 2005 upon a parliamentary vote of conscience. In December 2006, a motion by the minority Conservative government to revisit the issue was defeated upon yet another parliamentary vote of conscience.

### VI. A Right to Same-Sex Marriage? A Great Divide Remains

Opponents of same-sex marriage, including United States President George W. Bush, argue that marriage is the foundation upon which society is built and that it is and must always be heterosexual in nature as consists of one man and one woman to the exclusion of others; to allow and recognise same-sex marriage will open the floodgate for polygamy and eventually destroy the institution of marriage. United States Supreme Court Justice Scalia in his dissenting opinion in *Lawrence v. Texas* further maintained that to decriminalise homosexuality would interfere with the validity and enforcement of state laws that proscribe 'bigamy, same-sex marriage, adult incest, prostitution, masturbation, adultery, fornication, bestiality, and obscenity'.[265] Whilst, as Tushnet points out, a prosecution for masturbation in present-day American, or any, society is unimaginable,[266] Justice Scalia's equation of homosexuality with incest, prostitution, and bestiality is telling of the nature and extent of societal and state hostilities to sexual minorities both as individuals and as a class.

The question of whether marriage is necessarily heterosexual is one of the most significant to be answered in any study, including this one, that concerns whether a right to same-sex marriage exists or ought to exist in law. Opponents of same-sex marriage argue that the *juridical* heterosexuality of *civil* marriage is premised upon *Biblical* teachings which, according to them and their religious teachers, most notably Saint Thomas of Aquinas, vehemently denounce homosexuality and hold that marriage therefore simply cannot be available to a same-sex couple however loving they might be towards each other. The use of the rhetoric 'natural law' here is rather common. According to Finnis, whose restatement of the natural law theory[267] has consistently formed the core of debates between religion and sexual minority rights, sex is impermissible other than for the purpose of procreation and within the confines of a heterosexual marriage.[268] Same-sex relationships, however stable and loving, are, Finnis holds, but an 'illusion of intimacy and self-giving'.[269] The jurist regards same-sex sexual activity as synonymous with 'a prostitute [pleasuring] a client to give him pleasure in return for money, or (say) a man [masturbating] to give himself pleasure and a fantasy of more human relationships after a gruelling day on the assembly line',[270] and he narrowly defines same-sex sexual activity as 'bodily acts, on the body of a person of the same sex, which are engaged in with a view to securing orgasmic sexual satisfaction for one or more of the parties'.[271] As procreation is impossible for a same-sex couple, any sexual activity between them must altogether be condemned. A claim to a right to same-sex marriage, so the argument goes, is simply heretical.

Finnis' premise, in the light of the prevalence of pre-marital and extra-marital sex (oral, vaginal, and anal) amongst heterosexuals, illustrates only 'a double standard of permissiveness toward straights and censoriousness toward gays who engage in acts that are essentially the same'.[272] Bainham points out that 'while it may be cogently argued that fidelity is an ideal for some, perhaps many, who enter marriage, it is equally clearly not an ideal for everyone and, given the evidence of what people actually do rather than the unobtainable evidence of what they think, its normative quality must be seriously doubted.'[273] In respect of the question of whether procreation is a controlling element of marriage, Canadian Supreme Court Justice L'Heureux-Dubé in *Canada (Attorney-General) v. Mossop*[274] maintained:

> The argument is that procreation is somehow necessary to the concept of family and that same-sex couples cannot be families as they are incapable of procreation. Though there is undeniable value in procreation, the Tribunal could not have accepted that the capacity to procreate limits the boundaries of family. If this were so, childless couples and single parents would not constitute families. Further, this logic suggests that adoptive families are not as desirable as natural families. The flaws in this position must have been self-evident. Though procreation is an element in many families, placing the ability to procreate as the inalterable basis of family could result in an impoverished rather than enriched vision.[275]

Likewise, South African Constitutional Court Justice Ackermann in *National Coalition for Gay and Lesbian Equality v. Minister of Home Affairs* stated that

> From a legal and constitutional point of view procreative potential is not a defining characteristic of conjugal relationships. Such a view would be deeply demeaning to couples (whether married or not) who, for whatever reason, are incapable of procreating when they commence such relationship or become so at any time thereafter. It is likewise demeaning to couples who commence such a relationship at an age when they no longer have the desire for sexual relations. It is demeaning to adoptive parents to suggest that their family is any less a family and any less entitled to respect and concern than a family with procreated children. I would even hold it to be demeaning of a couple who voluntarily decide not to have children or sexual relations with one another; this being a decision entirely within their protected sphere of freedom and privacy.[276]

In respect of the correlation or antagonism between religion and homosexuality and sexual minority rights, the political and constitutional experience of the devoutly Catholic Ireland is illuminating. Within the text of the Irish Constitution of 1937, which Chubb credits as a 'Catholic Constitution',[277] God and Jesus Christ are repeatedly explicitly referred to,[278] and successive Irish court decisions have interpreted the Constitution as embodying the teachings of Saint Thomas of Aquinas.[279] The Supreme Court of Ireland, as O'Sullivan and the present author have examined,[280] did on certain occasions interpret the Constitution as subject to a higher norm, namely natural law, on account of the various Christian and natural law references in the Preamble to,[281] in Article 6 of,[282] and in the fundamental rights provisions in the Constitution.[283] Just as it is paradoxical for natural law to claim juridical superiority over positive law, in the form of the Constitution, through positivist application of the Preamble to the Constitution itself, it is equally incongruous for Finnis and others to seek to manipulate positive laws to promote natural law so as to constrain positive laws themselves. In 1994, the Irish Supreme Court rendered a binding reference on the constitutionality of the Irish people's amendment to their Constitution as to the legality of provision of information on abortion obtained by citizens outside the jurisdiction of the state, where the court definitively concluded that natural law is not superior to the Irish Constitution, the ultimate manifestation of positive law of the land.[284]

It is noteworthy that prior to the binding reference the Irish Supreme Court in *The State (Nicolaou) v. An Bord Uchtála*[285] and in *G. v. An Bord Uchtála*[286] held that natural rights as provided for by the Constitution may by one's consent be able to be transferred or dispensed with, holdings that further rid such rights of their alleged divinity. F. F. V. R. von Prondzynski is adamant that '[i]t should be stressed once again that Natural Law in its legal sense as seen by the Constitution has nothing whatever to do with the imposition on us all of a concise set of religious Rules as propounded by the Churches',[287] and the jurist avows that 'Natural Law should be used to strengthen our Constitution, not to replace it.'[288] Clarke, meanwhile, laments that '[t]he question therefore arises: to what extent, if any, might natural law provide guidance to members of the court in deciding constitutional issues? I argue that it provides no valid guidance at all to the courts; rather, natural law is primarily a negative thesis about law which is equally consistent with a variety of mutually incompatible views on any specific issue which the courts may have to decide.'[289] The Supreme Court's holdings in the same two decisions in finding natural rights on the basis of a 'natural' biological or social relationship have only exacerbated the predicament – and confused the metaphysics and legal basis of natural law itself – even further. Last but not least, in *G. v. An Bord Uchtála* Irish Supreme Court Justice Kenny pointed out and warned about the severe ambiguity of the word 'natural' itself.[290]

It ought also to be noted that after the European Court of Human Rights rendered its decision in *Norris v. Ireland*[291] mandating the Irish government to decriminalise homosexuality within its jurisdiction, substantial efforts aiming at the effectuation and protection of sexual minority rights have been undertaken by the Irish government without pressure from either the Strasbourg court or the European Union of which it is a Member State. Indeed, Ireland, a country that only in 1995 legalised divorce by referendum by the narrowest of margins (50.28 per cent), is presently considering recognising civil partnership if not marriage between same-sex couples.

It must be noted that within a democratic society religious freedoms and beliefs, notwithstanding their established place in society and in the law, are not entitled to normative priority over sexual minority rights. Rawls states that '[t]here is no reason why citizen, or association of citizens, should have the right to use state power to decide constitutional essentials as that person's, or that association's, comprehensive doctrine directs.'[292] Massachusetts Supreme Judicial Council Chief Justice Marshall in *Goodridge* discerned the normative parity between sexual minority rights and religious freedoms, stating that

> I do not doubt the sincerity of deeply held moral or religious beliefs that make inconceivable to some the notion that any change in the common-law definition of what constitutes a legal civil marriage is now, or ever would be, warranted. But, as a matter of constitutional law, neither the mantra of tradition, nor individual conviction, can justify the perpetuation of a hierarchy in which couples of the same sex and their families are deemed less worthy of social and legal recognition than couples of the opposite sex and their families.[293]

Irish High Court Justice Budd (as he then was) in his decision in *Educational Company of Ireland v. Fitzpatrick (No.2)* [294] likewise affirmed that

> The Courts will ... assist and uphold a citizen's constitutional rights. Obedience to the law is required of every citizen, and it follows that if one citizen has a right there exists a correlative duty on the part of other citizens to respect that right and not to interfere with it. To say otherwise would be tantamount to saying that a citizen can set the Constitution at nought and that a right solemnly given by our fundamental law is valueless. It follows that the Courts will not so act as to permit any body of citizens to deprive another of his constitutional rights and will in any proceedings before them see that these rights are protected, whether they be assailed under the guise of a statutory right or otherwise.[295]

Indeed, the normative *defect* of using the religiosity argument in suppressing homosexuality and sexual minority rights abounds. Reinig argues that

> The West's religiously-based moral heritage with respect to lesbians and gay men is, at best, disingenuous and, at worst, corrupt. It represents and perpetuates a legacy of intolerance, oppression and hatred which cannot legitimately be invoked against gay people with any consistency and still be characterized as moral. ... Its continuing and pervasive influence over law, policy and politics ... subjugates millions to a hegemonic system of religiously-based morality while disenfranchising them from democratic entitlements which others take for granted.[296]

Whatever the Bible may or may not say about homosexuality is immaterial when what is at stake here is the fundamental right to live fully and freely as a person[297] without discrimination and harassment. As Wintemute opines, '[a] consensus amongst Christian denominations that there is no "moral equivalence" between Judaism and Christianity, or between women and men, would carry little weight in a legislative debate.'[298] By resorting to religion without any objective rationale other than a mere claim of superiority or infallibility of religion or the churches, the anti-gay sector is attempting to unduly influence public policies as it did in medieval times: 'What is new about the antigay crusaders we face now is that they seek to collapse the relatively fragile boundary between church and state. They use the transformative [culture] of homosexuality ... to argue for a fusion of the religious and the secular in order to preserve the status quo. Such a fusion is dangerous to the idea of civil society.'[299] Above all, as the Supreme Court of Canada in its advisory *Reference re Same-Sex Marriage* pointed out, '[t]he mere recognition of the equality rights of one group cannot, in itself, constitute a violation of the rights of another. The promotion of *Charter* rights and values enriches our society as a whole and the furtherance of those rights cannot undermine the very principles the *Charter* was meant to foster.'[300]

Still, given the unquestionable place of the Bible in Christian society, and in secular societies such as Hong Kong amongst those who consider themselves Christians or holding Christian belief, where a Biblical quotation is able to conclude forthwith and definitively any discussion as to life or society,[301] even as Christian fundamentalists lay emphasis on certain Biblical passages over others and at times ignore some passages altogether,[302] it is necessary to address whether the Bible has been correctly interpreted. In his invigorating study on the Bible in relation to homosexuality, Locke concludes that it was xenophobia, in the form of Lot's society rejecting God's messengers, that led to the destruction of Sodom, as indicated in the Bible, and not same-sex acts as is commonly believed.[303] A number of theological scholars have also deduced from the Bible (Romans 1:18–27) that it was idolatry, through worshipping false gods, that God condemns, with homosexuality being the penalty thereof.[304] In this light, homosexuality is the manifestation of a divine penalty, rather than the cause of or for a divine penalty or the manifestation of a divine sin contrary to natural law as propounded by many of the theological and legal scholars such as Finnis. In Helminiak's words, '[t]here is no sense whatever in those words [in Romans 1:18–27] that the practices were wrong or against God or contrary to the divine order of creation or in conflict with universal nature of things.'[305]

Locke also questions the lasting authority of the Bible which many maintain and exploit in condemning homosexuality and sexual minorities. The author refers[306] to Leviticus 18:19, which prescribes that a man be proscribed from carnal knowledge with a woman during her menstruation, and points out that such Biblical injunction is hardly abided by. Similarly, 1 Timothy 2:11–15 states: 'Let a woman learn in silence with full submission. I permit no woman to teach or to have authority over a man; she is to keep silent. For Adam was formed first, then Eve; and Adam was not deceived, but the woman was deceived and became a transgressor. Yet she will be saved through childbearing, provided they continue in faith and love and holiness, with modesty.' This Biblical provision, we should note, became the basis for the centuries-long suppression and disenfranchisement of women in society, which South African Supreme Court of Appeal Judge Farlam in *Fourie* cited as one reason why same-sex marriage had not and could not have been recognised in the jurisdiction, given that 'the principle of legal equality between the spouses was not enshrined in our law there were many rules forming part of our law of matrimonial relations which put the husband in a superior position and the wife in an inferior one. The law could thus not easily accommodate same-sex unions because, unless the partners thereto agreed as to who was to be the "husband" and who the "wife", these rules could not readily be applied to their union.'[307] Social progress has now seen such subjugation fading, as quintessentially illuminated by the fact that Ireland has had its current and two previous presidencies held by two women who were previously law professors at the Catholic country's leading university and who were also instrumental in the founding and work of the Homosexual Law Reform Committee in Ireland. In Hong Kong, the courts now enjoy and exercise jurisdiction under and in accordance with the Matrimonial Causes Ordinance, enacted in 1967, and the Marriage Reform Ordinance, enacted in 1970, to decree divorce, dissolution of marriage and other matrimonial matters, which jurisdiction perforce reverses the outmoded presumption or requirement of such lifelong temporality of 'Christian marriage or the civil equivalent of a Christian marriage' as originating from *Hyde* in 1865 and subsequently sanctioned in the Marriage Ordinance in 1932.[308] We recall that 'Christendom' was explicitly and repeatedly emphasised by the English family court in *Hyde* and was reflected in its pronouncement on the *juridical* definition of *civil* marriage.[309] As the Supreme Court of Canada in its advisory *Reference re Same-Sex Marriage* discerned:

> The reference to 'Christendom' is telling. *Hyde* spoke to a society of shared social values where marriage and religion were thought to be inseparable. This is no longer

the case. Canada is a pluralistic society. Marriage, from the perspective of the state, is a civil institution. The 'frozen concepts' reasoning runs contrary to one of the most fundamental principles of Canadian constitutional interpretation: that our Constitution is a living tree which, by way of progressive interpretation, accommodates and addresses the realities of modern life.[310]

We must then recall that in Hong Kong, Christianity, and the attendant notion of Christian marriage, was but a result of former British colonial rule over the predominantly Chinese and Confucian population. It is therefore apposite to keep in mind that

> Religious 'truths' frequently change as the larger world changes, and as religious organizations adapt their teachings so as not to be out of step with the times. From a sociological point of view, religions are man-made institutions, however much those who partake in debates about religion and human rights might claim that they are relying on the teachings of their various gods. As man made God in his own image, so society makes God's rules in the image of its own.[311]

Nissinen is adamant that the central tenet of the Bible is the principle of Love; the theological scholar maintains:

> The New Testament emphatically asserts, in the mouths of both Jesus and Paul, that the entire law depends on the commandment of love, that love fulfills the whole Law, and that the one who loves has fulfilled the Law (Matt. 22:34–40; Rom. 13:8–10; Gal. 5:14). This applies also to the passages in the Bible that refer to homoeroticism. Making love a priority in applying these texts in real life does not imply all-accepting 'tolerance' or the altering of God's word. To give love priority in biblical interpretation means careful examination of both the Bible and the prevailing reality in which we live with neighbors of flesh and blood.[312]

Meanwhile, from a legal, constitutional and democratic point of view, Canadian Supreme Court Justice Wilson in *Turpin*[313] reasoned that '[t]he argument that s.15 is not violated because departures from its principles have been widely condoned in the past and that the consequences of finding a violation would be novel and disturbing is not, in my respectful view, an acceptable approach to the interpretation of *Charter* provisions.'[314] In *Dagenais v. Canadian Broadcasting Corporation*,[315] Canadian Supreme Court Chief Justice Lamer cautioned that '[a] hierarchical approach to rights, which places some over others, must be avoided, both when interpreting the *Charter* and when developing the common law ... when the protected rights of two individuals come into conflict, ... *Charter* principles require a balance to be achieved that fully respects the importance of both sets of rights.'[316] As Canadian Supreme Court Justice Cory in *Egan* declared, '[s]exual orientation is more than simply a "status" that an individual possesses. It is something that is demonstrated in an individual's conduct by the choice of a partner. The *Charter* protects religious beliefs and religious practice as aspects of religious freedom. So, too, should it be recognized that sexual orientation encompasses aspects of "status" and "conduct" and that both should receive protection.'[317]

## VII. Judicial Activism at Play?

It is commonly understood that the United Kingdom government is generally inclined towards leaving sensitive human rights issues such as sexual minority rights to the European Court of Human Rights to adjudicate upon so that it will not be blamed by the electorate one way or the other for merely complying with the European Convention on Human Rights and the judgments the Strasbourg court issues in accordance therewith. In the battleground of the United States, however, conservative politicians and religious groups have long argued for activist judges (most notably Supreme Court Justice Anthony Kennedy, a Reagan nominee yet author of the majority opinions in *Romer v. Evans*, *Lawrence v. Texas*, and *Roper v. Simmons*)[318] to be removed or impeached. These politicians and religious groups have been particularly outraged at any judges who have ruled in favour of sexual minorities; for them, to rule in favour of a constitutional right to same-sex marriage is tantamount to treachery. Such calls for removal or impeachment of activist judges have intensified tremendously since all courts, including the United States Supreme Court, in the past 15 years that were petitioned by the parents of the severely brain-damaged Terri Schiavo, since deceased, to intervene in artificially prolonging her life against her wishes, as conveyed by her husband and guardian *ad litem*, declined to do so. President Bush's last attempt in artificially prolonging Schiavo's life by signing an emergency *ad hominem* Bill into law[319] was to no avail as all of the courts that were involved in the matter considered the law an intrusion into the judiciary in violation of the established constitutional principle of the separation of powers.[320] An earlier similar attempt by Jeb Bush as Governor of the State of Florida wherein Schiavo was legally resident had likewise been struck down by the Supreme Court of Florida as unconstitutional.[321] It should be noted that religion played a significant role in the matter as Schiavo's parents premised their legal arguments upon *their* freedom of religion as well as that of their daughter as they alleged. Former Republican House Representative Tom DeLay, himself thrice admonished by the House Permanent Select Committee on Ethics and currently facing trial on money-laundering and related charges, has been particularly fervent in his attacks upon the judiciary, repeatedly declaring that those responsible for Schiavo's death would be punished and calling Schiavo's death a 'judicial murder',[322] statements which many regard as incitement of violence towards the relevant judges. Since the United States Supreme Court rendered its decision in *Brown v. Board of Education*[323] in 1954 ruling that segregation on the basis of race was unconstitutional, conservatives and religious groups in the United States have found their judiciary to be unpleasing to their viewpoints, such as through the Supreme Court decisions in *Romer v. Evans* and in the 'murderous' *Roe v. Wade*.[324]

After their first important judicial victory through *Romer v. Evans* – which, one should note, was forced upon them – sexual minorities took their first judicial initiative to challenge the quintessential heterosexual status quo – the definition of marriage. Before the State Supreme Court of Hawaii in *Baehr v. Lewin*,[325] it was successfully argued that the traditional *juridical* definition of marriage mandating a different-sex union was unconstitutional against the Hawaii State Constitution for contravening its guarantee of equality. The state, the court pointed out, failed to show any compelling public interest requiring marriage to be available exclusively to different-sex couples. The court held that the institution of marriage must therefore be open and accessible to same-sex couples, as mandated by Hawaii's constitutional guarantee of equality.

Whilst family law in the United States is a matter for the 50 individual states to formulate and decide, Congress took federal action to counter the Hawaiian decision and passed the Defense of Marriage Act[326] in 1996 allowing a state to refuse recognition of out-of-state marriage licences issued to same-sex couples[327] notwithstanding the Full Faith and Credit Clause of the federal United States Constitution.[328] Legal scholars, however, have since questioned the constitutionality of the 1996 Act.[329] As for Hawaii itself, voters by referendum amended their State Constitution whereby the state legislature is *permitted* to preserve the traditional, namely heterosexual, definition of marriage, which the state legislature has notably refrained from doing. Meanwhile, as noted above, in his efforts to mobilise conservative supporters President George W. Bush exploited the issue of same-sex marriage to his re-electoral advantage. After San Francisco Mayor Gavin Newsom decided to issue marriage licences to same-sex couples who wanted them and the Massachusetts Supreme Judicial Council in *Goodridge* mandated the issuance of marriage licences to desiring in-state same-sex couples,[330] President Bush pushed forward a Marriage Protection Amendment to the United States Constitution that if had been passed would have rendered all same-sex marriages null and void and placed the controversial issue beyond the oversight of the United States Supreme Court. Since the Amendment failed to garner sufficient support in Congress, President Bush has indicated that he would no longer push forward the Amendment unless the federal Defense of Marriage Act 1996 were to be ruled by the judiciary as unconstitutional, a political position by a sitting president of the world's oldest democracy that should be received by those who respect the principle and substance of judicial independence with the severest alarm.

The question of judicial activism and of the role of the judiciary is central to the debate on same-sex marriage. The central allegation by conservatives and religious groups against the judiciary is that the will of the people, as conveyed by their elected Parliament or Congress, and which is paramount, has nonetheless been ignored by various activist benches. It is submitted, however, that whilst the notion of parliamentary supremacy is no doubt valid, the intrinsicality of the fundamental principle of the separation of powers is that it ensures that Parliament or Congress does not transgress the democratic values as embodied in the particular national constitution under the guise of parliamentary supremacy. Judges' independence from politics (and religion, as mandated by the separation of church and state in the First Amendment to the federal United States Constitution)[331] and their blind adherence to the law in upholding the constitution (or constitutions in federations or confederations) are the most alluring and important features of the rule of law and of modern democracy. In *West Virginia Board of Education v. Barnette*,[332] United States Supreme Court Justice Jackson firmly declared that '[t]he very purpose of a Bill of Rights was to withdraw certain subjects from the vicissitudes of political controversy, to place them beyond the reach of majorities and officials and to establish them as legal principles to be applied by the courts. One's ... fundamental rights may not be submitted to vote; they depend on the outcome of no elections.'[333] The adjudication of a particular judicial bench, or benches, one way or the other will perforce prompt dissatisfaction in some quarters, which is yet another testament of a viable and enviable democracy. As Canadian Supreme Court Chief Justice Dickson in *Oakes* maintained, '[t]he court must be guided by the values and principles essential to a free and democratic society which I believe embody, to name but a few, respect for the inherent dignity of the human person, commitment to social justice and equality, accommodation of a wide variety of beliefs, respect for cultural and group identity, and faith in social and political institutions which enhance the participation of individuals and groups in a society.'³³⁴

Thus, Massachusetts Supreme Judicial Council Justice Greaney in *Goodridge* pointed out, '[t]he right to marry is not a privilege conferred by the State, but a fundamental right that is protected against unwarranted State interference.'³³⁵ It must be borne in mind that '[h]uman rights are not gifts made by benevolent administrations. They are part of the essential fabric of a democratic society, and there are few countries which do not at least claim to protect them. But it is the existence of an adequate constitutional procedure which separates us from countries where fundamental rights constitute no more than a hollow phrase in an ineffective document.'³³⁶

## VIII. Hong Kong's International Obligations regarding Same-Sex Marriage

In its *General Comment No.19*³³⁷ in 1990 on Article 23 of the International Covenant on Civil and Political Rights, paragraph 2 of which states that '[t]he right of men and women of marriageable age to marry and to found a family shall be recognized',³³⁸ the United Nations Human Rights Committee refrained from pronouncing on whether there was in or under international law a positive right to same-sex marriage, merely noting that 'the concept of the family may differ in some respects from State to State, and even from region to region within a State, and that it is therefore not possible to give the concept a standard definition.'³³⁹ With the Committee concluding in 1994 in *Toonen v. Australia*³⁴⁰ that 'sex' in Articles 2 and 26 of the Covenant was to be taken as including sexual orientation,³⁴¹ the interpretation the Committee now holds upon the Covenant and its recognition and protection of human rights, including the question of a right to same-sex marriage in or under international law, should therefore be reconsidered. In 2000, the Committee in *Young v. Australia*³⁴² concluded that Australia's refusal to provide the applicant with a pension benefit after and by virtue of the death of his same-sex partner on the grounds that their same-sex relationship was not recognised in the relevant legislation as a marriage or a marriage-like relationship entitling him to the pension constituted sexual orientation discrimination in violation of Article 26 of the Covenant³⁴³ and the applicant was thus entitled to an effective remedy 'if necessary through an amendment of the law'.³⁴⁴ The issue of whether under the Covenant an individual has a right to same-sex marriage was not at issue and thus was not addressed by the Committee.

However, in 2002, the Committee in *Joslin v. New Zealand*³⁴⁵ concluded³⁴⁶ that in the light of Article 23(2), New Zealand's refusal to enable same-sex marriage did not constitute violations of the applicant's rights under Articles 16,³⁴⁷ 17,³⁴⁸ 23(1)³⁴⁹ and (2), and 26 of the Covenant. The Committee reasoned that

> Given the existence of a specific provision in the Covenant on the right to marriage, any claim that this right has been violated must be considered in the light of this provision. Article 23, paragraph 2, of the Covenant is the only substantive provision in the Covenant which defines a right by using the term 'men and women', rather than 'every human being', 'everyone' and 'all persons'. Use of the term 'men and women', rather than the general terms used elsewhere in Part III of the Covenant, has been consistently and uniformly understood as indicating that the treaty obligation of States parties stemming from article 23, paragraph 2, of the Covenant is

to recognize as marriage only the union between a man and a woman wishing to marry each other.[350]

Nonetheless, it should be noted that the wording of Article 23(2), with both genders in plural form, does not necessarily preclude marriage between two persons of the same sex but only recognises and protects the right of all persons of marriageable age, irrespective of their genders, to marry and to found a family. Rishworth stresses that it was the exclusivity of a union of two persons rather than their respective genders that gave rise to and controlled *Hyde v. Hyde and Woodmansee*, a decision which concerned polygamous marriage.[351] As Bala and Bromwich point out, '[s]ignificant concerns about inequality and exploitation emerge in polygamous marriages that do not arise in same-sex relationships.'[352]

At a more fundamental level, the Committee in its concluding observations on Hong Kong[353] criticised the Hong Kong government for its continual failure to enact sexual orientation anti-discrimination legislation and stated that the Committee 'remains concerned that no legislative remedies are available to individuals in respect of discrimination on the grounds of ... sexual orientation'.[354] The Committee requested that Hong Kong enact forthwith '[n]ecessary legislation ... to ensure full compliance with Article 26 of the Covenant.'[355] By virtue of its continual failure to enact such necessary legislation Hong Kong is also in breach of Article 2(1) of the Covenant, which states that '[e]ach State Party to the present Covenant undertakes to respect and to ensure to all individuals within its territory and subject to its jurisdiction the rights recognized in the present Covenant, without distinction of any kind, such as race, colour, sex, language, religion, political or other opinion, national or social origin, property, birth or other status.'[356] Buergenthal explains that

> The obligation 'to ensure' these rights encompasses the duty 'to respect' them, but it is substantially broader. ... the provision implies an affirmative obligation by the state to take whatever measures are necessary to enable individuals to enjoy or exercise the rights guaranteed in the Covenant, including the removal of governmental [such as the common law definition of marriage] and possibly also some private obstacles to the enjoyment of these rights. ... as regards some rights in some circumstances, it may perhaps require the state to adopt laws and other measures against private interference with enjoyment of rights.[357]

The requirements of the Covenant that all necessary steps, including legislation, must be adopted 'to give effect to the rights recognized in the present Covenant'[358] and that 'any persons whose rights or freedoms as herein recognized are violated shall have an effective remedy'[359] are thus of paramount importance in the present context.

It is noteworthy that the United Nations Committee on Economic, Social and Cultural Rights is of the same view, denouncing Hong Kong for its continual 'failure to prohibit discrimination on the basis of sexual orientation'[360] in contravention of Article 7 of the International Covenant on Economic, Social and Cultural Rights[361] that states that '[t]he States Parties to the present Covenant recognize the right of everyone to the enjoyment of just and favourable conditions of work which ensure, in particular: ... (c) Equal opportunity for everyone'.[362] Klerk argues that such 'guarantee' as is required by Article 2(2) of the International Covenant on Economic, Social and Cultural Rights, which states that '[t]he States Parties to the present Covenant undertake to guarantee that the rights enunciated in the present Covenant will be exercised without discrimination of any kind as to race, colour, sex, language, religion, political or other opinion, national or social origin, property, birth or other status',[363] requires enforcement of even more immediacy than does Article 2 of the International Covenant on Civil and Political Rights.[364] In its concluding observations on Hong Kong, the Committee on Economic, Social and Cultural Rights 'urges [Hong Kong] to prohibit discrimination on the basis of sexual orientation'[365] and 'reminds [Hong Kong] that the provisions of the Covenant constitute a legal obligation on the part of the States parties'.[366]

## IX. Conclusion

Whilst marriage may be considered a heterosexist and heterosexualising institution,[367] equal access to the civil institution of marriage is valuable as it affirms that the identity of gay men and lesbians and their relationships is as loving, responsible and morally worthy and valid as that of those who marry another person whose gender differs from his or hers under and in accordance with those same civil laws as which also affect gay men and lesbians as persons desiring to marry. As Massachusetts Supreme Judicial Council Chief Justice Marshall in *Goodridge* discerned:

> Here, the plaintiffs seek only to be married, not to undermine the institution of civil marriage. They do not want marriage abolished. They do not attack the binary nature of marriage, the consanguinity provisions, or any of the other gate-keeping provisions of the marriage licensing law. Recognizing the right of an individual to marry a person of the same sex will not diminish the validity or dignity of opposite-sex marriage, any more than recognizing the right of an individual to marry a person of a different race devalues the marriage of a person who marries someone of her own race. If anything, extending civil marriage to same-sex couples reinforces the importance of marriage to individuals and communities. That same-sex couples are willing to embrace marriage's solemn obligations of exclusivity, mutual support, and commitment to one another is a testament to the enduring place of marriage in our laws and in the human spirit.[368]

It is, however, precisely this sameness of moral worthiness and validity, rather than same-sex marriage, which opponents of homosexuality and sexual minority rights seek to deny, as it is a rule of oppression that the voice of those who are oppressed be forever undermined and unheard.

In the past decade, Hong Kong has faced tremendous political and socio-economic transition and turmoil, from the handover of sovereignty from the United Kingdom to China in which process the Hong Kong people were not at all meaningfully consulted, to the Asian financial crisis in 1997 and the severe acute respiratory syndrome epidemic in 2003. In the light and spirit of the mass demonstrations in July 2003 against passage of national security legislation, it is high time for Hong Kong society to reflect on the importance of individual rights and freedoms, including the guarantee of equality, to all fellow residents and non-residents in Hong Kong.

In proclaiming Hong Kong as a world city, and more importantly in seeking to restore the trust of the people of Hong Kong in their government and in the society in which they live, it is essential that the Hong Kong government fulfil its domestic and international legal, if not also moral, obligations and ensure that equality, including the right to marriage, be available to all individuals within its jurisdiction irrespective of their genders or sexual orientations. Cultural or moral relativism in relation to homosexuality and sexual minority rights, which this paper has refuted, is simply not an option, when what Hong Kong prides and thrives on – and how it differentiates itself from China in its projection to the world – is its constitutional recognition and protection of fundamental rights and freedoms, including its guarantee of equality.

Meanwhile, as this paper has explained, it is, in fact, a grave mistake for the Hong Kong population to rely on arguments premised upon state sovereignty and cultural relativism to oppose the development and protection of sexual minority rights in Hong Kong, as their claim of entitlement to universal suffrage, which continues to be denied and which is rooted in the Western right of self-determination premised upon self and autonomy and thus fundamentally adverse to Confucianism, and sexual minorities' claim of entitlement to equal respect and protection for who they are and their right to live fully without discrimination derive from and draw upon the same normative justifications. Their claim of entitlement to universal suffrage will instantly be contradicted and rendered illegitimate should they deny the normative intrinsicality and validity of sexual minority rights in Hong Kong. Furthermore, for the population to resort to religion in the name of Christianity in condemnation of homosexuality and sexual minority rights disregards Hong Kong's historical, social, cultural and religious backgrounds and merely perpetuates the effects of its colonial subjugation by the United Kingdom whose laws and policies against sexual minorities were simply implanted in Hong Kong without consultation of the local population. As Heinze discerns:

> The notion of minority sexual orientation as 'un-African' or 'un-Asian' is the embodiment of European-style racism, for it does exactly what Europeans were accused of doing: it ignores the histories of thousands of different African and Asian peoples, throughout thousands of years of history, each with their own changing patterns of social and sexual norms. It perpetuates the distinctly colonial idea that Africans or Asians are all alike, that their pre-colonial existence was frozen in time.[369]

It is, thus, merely a disingenuous disservice to the cosmopolitanism of Hong Kong and its residents, upon which Hong Kong's success is built, if the Hong Kong government and population were to argue against the development and protection of sexual minority rights in Hong Kong.

## Acknowledgements

The Author wishes to thank the Gender, Sexuality and Law Research Group at Keele University School of Law, and especially Jane Krishnadas and Nicky Priaulx, for welcoming him as Visiting Fellow during which time this paper was substantially expanded. This paper has benefited greatly from the comments the Author received in his guest seminar at Keele University School of Law (9 May 2006) based on an earlier version. The Author is further grateful to Eric Heinze, Clare Hemmings, and the participants in the Author's guest seminars at the Centre for Comparative and Public Law at the University of Hong Kong (15 September 2006) and the Centre for International and Public Law at the Australian

National University (20 October 2006) for their valuable comments on subsequent versions of this paper, and to Kevin Boreham for correcting him on an important point and Ann Kent for passing on information on a recent development in China. Last but not least, the Author is indebted to Paul Serfaty for all the support and confidence he has given him in his academic endeavours, and for their partnership.

## Notes

1. See Patrick Devlin, *The Enforcement of Morals* (London: Oxford University Press 1965); contrast with Ronald Dworkin, 'Lord Devlin and *The Enforcement of Morals*', *Yale Law Journal*, Vol.75 (1966), p.986; H. L. A. Hart, 'Social Solidarity and the Enforcement of Morality', *University of Chicago Law Review*, Vol.35 (1967), p.1, and H. L. A. Hart, *Liberty and Morality* (London: Oxford University Press 1971). See also Russell Hittinger, 'The Hart–Devlin Debate Revisited', *American Journal of Jurisprudence*, Vol.35 (1990), p.47.
2. For a discussion on negative electoral campaigning, see Richard R. Lau and Gerald M. Pomper, 'Effects of Negative Campaigning on Turnout in U.S. Senate Elections, 1988–1998', *Journal of Politics*, Vol.63 (2001), p.804.
3. They are, namely, Arkansas, Georgia, Kentucky, Michigan, Mississippi, Montana, North Dakota, Ohio, Oklahoma, Oregon, and Utah.
4. *Lockyer v. California*, S122923, 12 August 2004.
5. *Goodridge v. Department of Public Health*, 440 Mass 309 (2003); see also subsequent *In re Opinions of the Justices to the Senate*, 440 Mass 1201 (2004), on the question of whether civil union would be sufficient to satisfy the Council's judgment in *Goodridge*, which the Council answered in the negative.
6. The constitutional amendments to the respective State Constitutions of Arkansas, Georgia, Kentucky, Michigan, North Dakota, and Oklahoma proscribe official recognition also of civil union and domestic partnership, with Ohio prohibiting the state from granting any recognition or benefits to same-sex couples that are attributable to their same-sex relational status.
7. These countries include Denmark (including Greenland), Norway, Sweden, Hungary, Iceland, France, Germany, Portugal, Finland, Croatia, Israel, Luxembourg, New Zealand, the United Kingdom, Andorra, Slovenia, Austria, and Switzerland.
8. The various states include Vermont, California, Oregon, Hawaii, New Jersey, Maine, and Connecticut, as well as the District of Columbia.
9. It must be pointed out, however, that Hawaii in 1998 amended its Constitution only to *permit* the legislature 'to reserve marriage to opposite-sex couples', and the Hawaiian state legislature has since refrained from so acting. The other state jurisdictions that have amended their constitutions to disallow official recognition of same-sex marriage are Alabama, Alaska, Colorado, Idaho, Kansas, Louisiana, Missouri, Nebraska, Nevada, South Carolina, South Dakota, Tennessee, Texas, Virginia, and Wisconsin.
10. Constitution of the United States of America, Art.V.
11. 517 US 620 (1996).
12. Phil C. W. Chan, 'The Lack of Sexual Orientation Anti-Discrimination Legislation in Hong Kong: Breach of International and Domestic Legal Obligations', *International Journal of Human Rights*, Vol.9 (2005), p.69.
13. *Leung T. C. William Roy v. Secretary for Justice* [2005] 3 HKLRD 657.
14. The Basic Law of the Hong Kong Special Administrative Region of the People's Republic of China, 29 ILM 1519 (1990), as adopted by the Seventh National People's Congress at its Third Session on 4 April 1990 in pursuance of the 1984 Joint Declaration of the Government of the United Kingdom of Great Britain and Northern Ireland and the Government of the People's Republic of China on the Question of Hong Kong, 23 ILM 1366 (1984).
15. Basic Law of Hong Kong, Art.25.
16. Adopted and opened for signature, ratification and accession by U.N. G.A. Res. 2200A(XXI) of 16 December 1966 and entered into force on 23 March 1976.
17. Basic Law of Hong Kong, Art.39.
18. Hong Kong Bill of Rights Ordinance (Cap. 383), Art.22.
19. *Secretary for Justice v. Leung T. C. William Roy* [2006] 4 HKLRD 211.

20. See, e.g., Phil Chan, 'Everyone is Equal before the Law', *South China Morning Post*, 10 August 2004, p.A11; Tim Cribb, 'Justice for All: Gay Lobby Groups and Religious Bodies Appear Set for a Showdown as the Government Moves a Step Closer to Formulating Anti-Discrimination Laws', *South China Morning Post*, 27 January 2005, p.A16.
21. Law Reform Commission of Hong Kong, *Report on Laws Governing Homosexual Conduct (Topic 2)* (Hong Kong: Law Reform Commission of Hong Kong 1983); Hong Kong Government, *Homosexual Offences: Should the Law Be Changed? – A Consultation Paper* (Hong Kong: Government Printer 1988); Home Affairs Bureau, *Equal Opportunities: A Study on Discrimination on the Ground of Sexual Orientation: A Consultative Paper* (Hong Kong: Government Printer 1996).
22. William M. Evan, 'Law as an Instrument of Social Change', in Alvin W. Gouldner and S. M. Miller (eds), *Applied Sociology: Opportunities and Problems* (New York: Free Press 1965), pp.285–93 at p.286.
23. (1866) 1 LR P & D 130.
24. Ibid. p.133.
25. Section 40(1) of the Marriage Ordinance (Cap.181) states that '[e]very marriage under this Ordinance shall be a Christian marriage or the civil equivalent of a Christian marriage.' Section 40(2) goes on to elucidate that '[t]he expression "Christian marriage or the civil equivalent of a Christian marriage" implies a formal ceremony recognized by the law as involving the voluntary union for life of one man and one woman to the exclusion of all others.'
26. It is pertinent to note that under Article 158 of the Basic Law of Hong Kong, the power of interpretation of the Basic Law of Hong Kong is vested in the Standing Committee of the National People's Congress of the People's Republic of China ultimately. However, the same provision prescribes that the Standing Committee '*shall* authorise the courts of the Hong Kong Special Administrative Region to interpret on their own, in adjudicating cases, the provisions of this Law which are within the limits of the autonomy of the Region' (emphasis added). It is submitted that the equal recognition and protection of sexual minorities in Hong Kong in general and in relation to the marriage laws of Hong Kong, which does not '[concern] affairs which are the responsibility of the Central People's Government, or [concern] the relationship between the Central Authorities and the Region' (ibid.), falls within the limits of autonomy of the Region, so much so that the Central Authorities are not to intervene. (Indeed, it is worth noting that it is official policy of the Central Authorities that sexual minorities do not exist within their jurisdiction, such that there are no explicit laws concerning homosexuality.) For a discussion on Article 158 and its constitutional, legal and political implications, see Phil C. W. Chan, 'Hong Kong's Political Autonomy and its Continuing Struggle for Universal Suffrage', *Singapore Journal of Legal Studies* [2006].
27. A. Belden Fields and Wolf-Dieter Narr, 'Human Rights as a Holistic Concept', *Human Rights Quarterly*, Vol.14 (1992), p.1 at p.5.
28. 25 Henr. VIII c.6. According to H. Montgomery Hyde, *The Other Love: An Historical and Contemporary Survey of Homosexuality in Britain* (London: Heinemann 1970), p.40, the statute was repealed in 1553, by 1 Mar. c.1; but reinstated intact in 1563, by 5 Eliz. I c.17. Mandatory death penalty was replaced with life imprisonment under section 61 of the Offences Against the Person Act 1861 (c. 100) as the maximum penalty for anal intercourse between males.
29. Offences Against the Person Act 1861, s.61.
30. Offences Against the Person Ordinance 1865, s.50.
31. Criminal Law Amendment Act 1885 (c.69), s.11, since repealed by section 140 of and Schedule 7 to the Sexual Offences Act 2003 (c.42). The equivalent legislative provision in Hong Kong was section 51 of the Offences Against the Person Ordinance (Cap.212), since repealed and replaced by section 118H of the Crimes Ordinance (Cap.200) which provides that '[a] man who (a) commits an act of gross indecency with a man under the age of 21; or (b) being under the age of 21 commits an act of gross indecency with another man, shall be guilty of an offence and shall be liable on conviction on indictment to imprisonment for 2 years.'
32. *R. v. Hornby and Peaple* [1946] 2 All ER 487.
33. Sexual Offences Act 2003, s.140 and Sch.7.
34. Jeffrey Weeks, *Coming Out: Homosexual Politics in Britain from the Nineteenth Century to the Present*, revised ed. (London and New York: Quartet Books 1990), p.22; Donald J. West and Andrea Wöelke, 'England', in Donald J. West and Richard Green (eds), *Sociolegal Control of Homosexuality: A Multi-Nation Comparison* (New York: Plenum Press 1997), pp.197–220 at p.197.
35. Nicholas Bamforth, *Sexuality, Morals and Justice: A Theory of Lesbian and Gay Rights Law* (London: Cassell 1997), p.25.

36. Richard Plant, *The Pink Triangle: The Nazi War Against Homosexuals* (New York: H. Holt 1986).
37. Nicole LaViolette and Sandra Whitworth, 'No Safe Haven: Sexuality as a Universal Human Right and Gay and Lesbian Activism in International Politics', *Millennium: Journal of International Studies*, Vol.23 (1994), p.563.
38. Amnesty International, *Breaking the Silence: Human Rights Violations Based on Sexual Orientation* (London: Amnesty International 1997).
39. Convention for the Protection of Human Rights and Fundamental Freedoms (ETS No.005), opened for signature on 4 November 1950 and entered into force on 3 September 1953. The Convention was amended subsequently by Protocol No.11 (ETS No.155) to the Convention, opened for signature on 11 May 1994 and entered into force on 1 November 1998, to the effect that the then existing supervisory mechanism, consisting of a European Court of Human Rights and a European Commission of Human Rights, be restructured and replaced with a single and permanent European Court of Human Rights. For an account of the theory and practice of the European Convention on Human Rights, see P. van Dijk and G. J. H. van Hoof, *Theory and Practice of the European Convention on Human Rights*, 3rd ed. (The Hague: Kluwer International 1998).
40. West and Wöelke (note 34) pp.197–8.
41. Great Britain Committee on Homosexual Offences and Prostitution, *Report of the Committee on Homosexual Offences and Prostitution*, Cmnd.247 (London: Her Majesty's Stationery Office 1957).
42. Section 12(1) of the Sexual Offences Act 1956 (c.69), since repealed by section 140 of and Schedule 7 to the Sexual Offences Act 2003, states that '[i]t is felony for a person to commit buggery with another person or with an animal.' Although the felony of buggery as stipulated by the provision was not limited by any gender imposition, the history of the offence of buggery as antecedent (as from 1533) and subsequent (up to 2003) to the provision in the 1956 Act, together with the fact that only males and not females were capable of committing gross indecency (or the procurement thereof), a similarly classed unnatural offence originating in section 11 of the Criminal Law Amendment Act 1885 (c.69) and reinforced by section 13 of the same 1956 Act which was repealed *in toto* by the 2003 Act, sufficiently demonstrates that the felony of buggery as stipulated (yet undefined) by section 12(1) exclusively targeted a man who engaged in sexual conduct with another man and not a woman who engaged in sexual conduct with another woman or an individual who engaged in sexual conduct with another individual whose gender differs from his or hers.
43. Sexual Offences Act 1967 (c.60), s.1(1).
44. Homosexuality was decriminalised in Scotland only in 1980 by section 80 of the Criminal Justice (Scotland) Act 1980 (c.62) and in Northern Ireland in 1982 by Article 3 of the Homosexual Offences (Northern Ireland) Order 1982 (S.I.1982/1536 (N.I.19)).
45. Canada, for instance, decriminalised homosexuality in 1969 by section 7 of the Criminal Law Amendment Act 1968–69, S.C.1968–69, c.38. The then Prime Minister Pierre Trudeau was quoted in John Yogis, Randall Duplak and J. Royden Trainor, *Sexual Orientation and Canadian Law: An Assessment of the Law Affecting Lesbian and Gay Persons* (Toronto: Emond Montgomery Publications 1996), p.2, as declaring that 'the criminal law has no place in the bedrooms of the nation'.
46. Alfred Kinsey, Wardell B. Pomeroy and Clyde E. Martin, *Sexual Behavior in the Human Male* (Philadelphia: Saunders 1948); Alfred Kinsey *et al.*, *Sexual Behavior in the Human Female* (Philadelphia: Saunders 1953).
47. See American Psychiatric Association, 'Position Statement on Homosexuality and Civil Rights', *American Journal of Psychiatry*, Vol.131, No.4 (1973), p.497.
48. (1981) 4 EHRR 149.
49. 478 US 186 (1986).
50. Local Government Act 1986 (c.10).
51. Local Government Act 1988 (c.9), s.42(2).
52. Local Government Act 1988.
53. Local Government Act 2003 (c.26), s.127(2) and Sch.8(1), para.1. The Scottish Parliament in July 2000 repealed Section 28 by its Ethical Standards in Public Life etc. (Scotland) Act 2000 (2000 asp 7), s.36(1) and Sch.4, para.1.
54. Local Government Act 1986, s.2A.
55. 1(3) IHRR 97 (1994).
56. Ibid. para.6.8.
57. Article 26 of the International Covenant on Civil and Political Rights states that '[a]ll persons are equal before the law and are entitled without any discrimination to the equal protection of the law. In this respect, the law shall prohibit any discrimination and guarantee to all persons equal and effective protection

against discrimination on any ground such as race, colour, sex, religion, political or other opinion, national or social origin, property, birth or other status.'
58. *Toonen* (note 55) para.8.7.
59. (1997) 24 EHRR CD22.
60. Section 145 of the Criminal Justice and Public Order Act 1994 (c.33), amended in 2000 and subsequently repealed in 2003, stipulated the age of consent for male same-sex sexual activity at 18.
61. Section 6 of the Sexual Offences Act 1956 (c.69) stipulates the age of consent for vaginal intercourse at 16.
62. Article 14 of the European Convention on Human Rights states that '[t]he enjoyment of the rights and freedoms set forth in this Convention shall be secured without discrimination on any ground such as sex, race, colour, language, religion, political or other opinion, national or social origin, association with a national authority, property, birth or other status.' It should be noted that the European Court of Human Rights in *X and Y v. The Netherlands* (1986) 8 EHRR 235, at para.32, ruled that Article 14 'has no independent existence; it constitutes one particular element (non-discrimination) of each of the rights safeguarded by the Convention. The Articles enshrining those rights may be violated alone or in conjunction with Article 14. An examination of the case under Article 14 is not generally required when the Court finds a violation of one of the former Articles taken alone. The position is otherwise if a clear inequality of treatment in the enjoyment of the right in question is a fundamental aspect of the case.' However, in accordance with Protocol 12 to the European Convention on Human Rights (ETS No.177), signed at Rome on 4 November 2000 and entered into force 1 April 2005, it is now no longer necessary to allege and establish breach of a Convention right in order for a claim of discrimination to succeed under the Convention, so long as the right in question is set forth by law (Article 1, taken under Article 3 as additional article to the Convention).
63. Article 8(1) of the European Convention on Human Rights states that '[e]veryone has the right to respect for his private and family life, his home and his correspondence.'
64. *Salgueiro da Silva Mouta v. Portugal* (2001) 31 EHRR 1055; *Smith and Grady v. United Kingdom* (2000) 29 EHRR 493.
65. United Nations Human Rights Committee, Communication No. 941/2000, CCPR/C/78/D/941/2000, 6 August 2003.
66. Ibid. para.10.4.
67. Ibid. para.12.
68. Canadian Charter of Rights and Freedoms (Part I, Constitution Act 1982, S.C.1982, c.79; Canada Act 1982 (United Kingdom), c.11).
69. *Egan v. Canada* (1995), 124 DLR (4th) 609.
70. Section 15(1) of the Canadian Charter of Rights and Freedoms states that '[e]very individual is equal before and under the law and has the right to the equal protection and equal benefit of the law without discrimination and, in particular, without discrimination based on race, national or ethnic origin, colour, religion, sex, age or mental or physical disability.' It should be pointed out that discrimination may be justified under section 1 of the Charter in that '[t]he *Canadian Charter of Rights and Freedoms* guarantees the rights and freedoms set out in it subject only to such reasonable limits prescribed by law as can be demonstrably justified in a free and democratic society.'
71. *Vriend v. Alberta* (1998) 156 DLR (4th) 385.
72. The age of consent for anal intercourse was set at 18 by section 159(2)(b) of the Canadian Criminal Code. Sub-section (2)(a) of the provision provided that an underage married couple, consisting of husband and wife, be exempt from conviction for the offence of anal intercourse. Such marital status defence was denounced by Ontario Court of Appeal Justice Abella (as she then was) in *R. v. M. (C.)*, (1995) 98 CCC (3d) 481, 488: 'The grounds of age and marital status are also engaged, not only because s.159 has a particularly disparate impact on how the consensual sexual choices of adolescent gay men are treated, but also because the exemption for "husband and wife" is clearly illusory for a gay couple. However, these grounds are inextricable from the conclusion that the violation of equality is based primarily on sexual orientation and, in my view, analytically offer no independent grounds upon which to found a s.15 violation. The age and marital status grounds are triggered because they are aspects of how s.159 disproportionately and arbitrarily disadvantages gay men; but absent their relationship to sexual orientation it is difficult to see how, on their own, they are violative of the equality guarantee. I agree, therefore, with the respondent's and interveners' submissions that s.159 of the *Criminal Code* arbitrarily disadvantages gay men and therefore violates s.15 of the Charter on the grounds of sexual orientation.'
73. The age of consent for vaginal intercourse is set at 14 by section 151 of the Canadian Criminal Code.

74. Ontario Court of Appeal Justice Abella (as she then was) in *R. v. M. (C.)* (note 72) maintained, at 488, that '[a]nal intercourse is a basic form of sexual expression for gay men. The prohibition of this form of sexual conduct found in s.159 accordingly has an adverse impact on them. Unmarried, heterosexual adolescents 14 or over can participate in consensual intercourse without criminal penalties; gay adolescents cannot. It perpetuates rather than narrows the gap for an historically disadvantaged group – gay men – it does so arbitrarily and stereotypically and is, therefore, a discriminatory provision which infringes the guarantee of equality.'
75. *R. v. Roy*, (1998) 101 DLR (4th) 148 (Québec Court of Appeal); *R. v. M. (C.)*, ibid. (Ontario Court of Appeal).
76. (1999) 1 SA 6.
77. 39(4) ILM 798 (2000).
78. Case CCT 232/03, 30 November 2004.
79. *Minister of Home Affairs v. Fourie*, Case CCT 60/04, 1 December 2005.
80. Civil Union Act 2006.
81. Final Constitution of the Republic of South Africa of 1996, Art.9(3). Article 9(5) of the Constitution goes on to indicate that discrimination on any of the grounds in Article 9(3) is deemed to be unfair 'unless it is established that the discrimination is fair.'
82. Article 9(4), ibid., states that '[n]o person may unfairly discriminate directly or indirectly against anyone on one or more grounds in terms of subsection (3). National legislation must be enacted to prevent or prohibit unfair discrimination.'
83. Ibid. Art.10.
84. Sexual Offences Act 2003, s.140 and Sch.7.
85. Signed and proclaimed by Presidents of the European Parliament, of the Council of the European Union, and of the European Commission at the European Council meeting in Nice on 7 December 2000.
86. Article 21 of the Charter states that '[a]ny discrimination based on any ground such as sex, race, colour, ethnic or social origin, genetic features, language, religion or belief, political or any other opinion, membership of a national minority, property, birth, disability, age or sexual orientation shall be prohibited.'
87. 539 US 558 (2003).
88. Carole J. Petersen, 'Hong Kong and the Unprecedented Transfer of Sovereignty: Values in Transition: The Development of the Gay and Lesbian Rights Movement in Hong Kong', *Loyola of Los Angeles International and Comparative Law Review*, Vol.19 (1997), p.337 at p.340.
89. For a complete account of the MacLennan Affairs, see Sir T. L. Yang, *Report of the Commission of Inquiry into Inspector MacLennan's Case* (Hong Kong: Government Printer 1981).
90. Law Reform Commission of Hong Kong, *Report on Laws Governing Homosexual Conduct* (Topic 2) (Hong Kong: Law Reform Commission of Hong Kong 1983).
91. Ibid. para.12.11.
92. Ibid. para.12.22. See also Petersen (note 88) p.344.
93. Hong Kong Government, *Homosexual Offence: Should the Law Be Changed? – A Consultation Paper* (Hong Kong: Government Printer 1988).
94. Ibid. para.19.
95. Ibid.
96. Norman J. Miners, *The Government and Politics of Hong Kong*, 5th ed. (Hong Kong: Oxford University Press 1991), p.27.
97. Basic Law of Hong Kong, Art.39.
98. Hong Kong Bill of Rights Ordinance (Cap.383), Art.22.
99. Hong Kong: *Official Report of the Proceedings of the Legislative Council (Hansard)* (1990/11 July 1990), P.2, p.1964.
100. Ibid. *per* Attorney General of Hong Kong Jeremy Mathews, p.1971.
101. Hong Kong, *Official Report of the Proceedings of the Legislative Council (Hansard)* (1991/10 July 1991), P.3, p.2738.
102. Crimes (Amendment) Ordinance 1991.
103. Crimes Ordinance (Cap.200), s.118C.
104. Phil C. W. Chan, 'The Gay Age of Consent in Hong Kong', *Criminal Law Forum*, Vol.15 (2004), p.273.
105. *Leung T. C. William Roy v. Secretary for Justice* [2005] 3 HKLRD 657.
106. *Secretary for Justice v. Leung T. C. William Roy* [2006] 4 HKLRD 211.

107. Hong Kong Government, *Homosexual Offence: Should the Law Be Changed? – A Consultation Paper* (Hong Kong: Government Printer 1988).
108. Ibid. para.43.
109. Ibid. para.5.
110. Subcommittee to Study Discrimination on the Ground of Sexual Orientation, 'Minutes of Meeting of the Subcommittee to Study Discrimination on the Ground of Sexual Orientation held on 8 October 2001': LC Paper No.CB(2)516/01–02, para.6.
111. [1973] AC 435.
112. Ibid. *per* Lord Reid, pp.458–9.
113. Hong Kong (*Hansard*) (note 101) *per* Legislative Councillor Selina Chow Liang Shuk-Yee, p.2741.
114. Mike Hepworth, *Blackmail: Publicity and Secrecy in Everyday Life* (London: Routledge 1975), p.72.
115. Crimes Ordinance, s.124.
116. Laud Humphreys, *Out of the Closets: The Sociology of Homosexual Liberation* (Englewood Cliffs, NJ: Prentice-Hall 1972), p.22.
117. Section 23(3) of the Theft Ordinance (Cap.210) states that '[a]ny person who commits blackmail shall be guilty of an offence and shall be liable on conviction upon indictment to imprisonment for 14 years.'
118. Subcommittee (note 110) para.9.
119. Subcommittee to Study Discrimination on the Ground of Sexual Orientation, 'Minutes of Meeting of the Subcommittee to Study Discrimination on the Ground of Sexual Orientation held on 29 November 2001': LC Paper No.CB(2)2723/01-02, para.27.
120. Subcommittee (note 110) para.15.
121. [1992] 1 HKCLR 127.
122. Ibid. *per* Silke V.-P., p.141.
123. Ibid.
124. (1993) 3 HKPLR 72.
125. In an opt-quoted passage, Lord Woolf, ibid. p.100, maintained that '[w]hile the Hong Kong judiciary should be zealous in upholding an individual's rights under the Hong Kong Bill, it is also necessary to ensure that disputes as to the effect of the Bill are not allowed to get out of hand. The issues involving the Hong Kong Bill should be approached with realism and good sense, and kept in proportion. If this is not done the Bill will become a source of injustice rather than justice and it will be debased in the eyes of the public. In order to maintain the balance between the individual and the society as a whole, rigid and inflexible standards should not be imposed on the legislature's attempts to resolve the difficult and intransigent problems with which society is faced when seeking to deal with serious crime. It must be remembered that questions of policy remain primarily the responsibility of the legislature.'
126. [1998] 1 HKLRD 350.
127. Ibid. *per* Bokhary P.J., p.377.
128. (1989) 56 DLR (4th) 1.
129. Ibid. *per* McIntyre J., p.18.
130. (1968) 1 EHRR 252.
131. Ibid. p.284.
132. [1992] 2 HKCLR 207.
133. Ibid. *per* Bokhary J.A., p.217.
134. *Andrews* (note 128) *per* McIntyre J., p.18.
135. [1986] 1 SCR 103.
136. Ibid. *per* Dickson C.J., pp.138–9, citing *R. v. Big M Drug Mart Limited*, [1985] 1 SCR 295 at 352.
137. Hong Kong Bill of Rights Ordinance, s.7. As has been argued in Chan (note 12), the Hong Kong government's continued refusal to enact a Sexual Orientation Discrimination Ordinance notwithstanding the prevalence of discrimination and harassment in the community against members of sexual minorities amounts to discrimination by the government itself.
138. Nicola Lacey, *Unspeakable Subjects: Feminist Essays in Legal and Social Theory* (Oxford: Hart 1998), p.77.
139. See, e.g., John Flowerdew, *The Final Years of British Hong Kong: The Discourse of Colonial Withdrawal* (Basingstoke: Macmillan 1998).
140. See Chan (note 26).
141. Equal Opportunities Bill 1994, *Legal Supplement No.3 to the Hong Kong Government Gazette*, 1 July 1994, C991–C1275.
142. Ibid. C1012.

143. Kathleen Cheek-Milby, *A Legislature Comes of Age: Hong Kong's Search for Influence and Identity* (Hong Kong: Oxford University Press 1995), p.243.
144. L. C. Chau, 'Labour and the Labour Market', in H. C. Y. Ho and L. C. Chau (eds), *The Economic System of Hong Kong* (Hong Kong: Asian Research Services 1988), pp.169–89 at p.169.
145. Sex Discrimination Bill 1994, *Legal Supplement No.3 to the Hong Kong Government Gazette*, 14 October 1994, C1381–C1535.
146. Disability Discrimination Bill 1995, *Legal Supplement No.3 to the Hong Kong Government Gazette*, 21 April 1995, C965–C1103.
147. The two Bills were passed and enacted as the Sex Discrimination Ordinance (Cap.480) and the Disability Discrimination Ordinance (Cap.487) respectively.
148. Petersen (note 88) p.356.
149. Sex Discrimination Ordinance, s.63
150. Equal Opportunities (Family Responsibility, Sexuality and Age) Bill 1995, *Legal Supplement No.3 to the Hong Kong Government Gazette*, 30 June 1995, C1659–C1767.
151. Home Affairs Bureau, *Equal Opportunities: A Study on Discrimination on the Ground of Sexual Orientation: A Consultative Paper* (Hong Kong: Government Printer, 1996).
152. Ibid., para.51.
153. Nonetheless, there was enacted in 1997 a law that prohibits discrimination on grounds of family status, i.e., the Family Status Discrimination Ordinance (Cap.527).
154. Chan (note 12).
155. The Equal Opportunities Commission, created under section 63 of the Sex Discrimination Ordinance, is empowered to function and to launch formal investigations under sections 64 and 70 of the Sex Discrimination Ordinance; under sections 62 and 66 of the Disability Discrimination Ordinance; and under sections 44 and 48 of the Family Status Discrimination Ordinance. It follows that without a Sexual Orientation Discrimination Ordinance and the corresponding provisions therein the Commission is not capable of handling complaints or indeed enquiries that are based on grounds of sexual orientation. It should be noted, furthermore, that the Commission, due to its consistent success in fighting discrimination by the government, naturally is at odds with the government and its inaugural Chairperson Anna Wu was not offered renewal of her term, notwithstanding the recognition conferred upon the Commission by international bodies such as the United Nations Committee on Economic, Social and Cultural Rights, *Concluding Observations of the Committee on Economic, Social and Cultural Rights (Hong Kong): China*, E/C.12/1/Add.58 (21 May 2001), para.7, that '[t]he Committee notes with satisfaction that the Equal Opportunities Commission established in 1996 is effectively carrying out its mandate without interference from the Government of [Hong Kong].'
156. See Ravina Shamdasani, 'Gays to March for Equality Law', *South China Morning Post*, 13 May 2005, p.A2.
157. For a discussion on the legal implications of the Hong Kong government's objection to civil partnership registration at the British consulate in the territory, see Phil C. W. Chan, 'UK Civil Partnership Registration in Hong Kong under the Vienna Convention on Consular Relations and Strasbourg Jurisprudence', *King's College Law Journal*, Vol.17, No.2 (2006), p.365.
158. *Leung T. C. William Roy v. Secretary for Justice* [2005] 3 HKLRD 657.
159. *Secretary for Justice v. Leung T. C. William Roy* [2006] 4 HKLRD 211.
160. Oliver Phillips, 'Zimbabwean Law and the Production of a White Man's Disease', *Social & Legal Studies*, Vol.6, No.4 (1997) Special Issue: *Legal Perversions* (ed. Leslie J. Moran), p.471 at p.474.
161. W. Michael Reisman, *Law in Brief Encounters* (New Haven, CT: Yale University Press 1999), p.154.
162. Abdullahi Ahmed An-Na'im, 'Toward a Cross-Cultural Approach to Defining International Standards of Human Rights', in Abdullahi Ahmed An-Na'im (ed.), *Human Rights in Cross-Cultural Perspectives: A Quest for Consensus* (Philadelphia: University of Pennsylvania Press 1992), pp.19–43 at pp.27–28.
163. Shalom H. Schwartz, 'Cultural Dimensions of Values: Toward an Understanding of National Differences', in Uichol Kim, Harry C. Triandis, Cigdem Kagitcibasi, Sang-Chin Choi and Gene Yoon (eds), *Individualism and Collectivism: Theory, Method, and Application* (Thousand Oaks, CA: Sage 1994), pp.85–119 at p.92.
164. William K. Gabrenya, Jr. and Kwang-Kuo Hwang, 'Chinese Social Interaction: Harmony and Hierarchy on the Good Earth', in Michael Harris Bond (ed.), *The Handbook of Chinese Psychology* (Hong Kong: Oxford University Press 1996), pp.309–21 at p.310.
165. Ibid. p.309.

166. Fareed Zakaria, 'Culture Is Destiny: A Conversation with Lee Kuan Yew', *Foreign Affairs*, Vol.73, No.2 (1994), p.109.
167. Ibid. p.113.
168. David Y. F. Ho, 'Filial Piety and Its Psychological Consequences', in Bond (note 164) pp.155–65 at p.155.
169. Ibid.
170. Rhoda E. Howard, 'Dignity, Community, and Human Rights', in An-Na'im (note 162) pp.81–101 at p.81.
171. Rhoda Howard, 'Cultural Absolutism and the Nostalgia for Community', *Human Rights Quarterly*, Vol.15 (1993), p.315 at p.335.
172. Fang-fu Ruan, 'China', in West and Green (note 34) pp.57–66 at p.57.
173. Matthew Harvey Sommer, *Sex, Law, and Society in Late Imperial China* (Palo Alto, CA: Stanford University Press 2000), p.114.
174. Ruan (note 172) p.63.
175. Ibid. pp.63–5.
176. Ibid. p.63.
177. Max Weber, *The Religion of China: Confucianism and Taoism*, trans. and ed. Hans H. Gerth (New York: Free Press 1951), p.144.
178. Tik-sang Liu, 'A Nameless but Active Religion: An Anthropologist's View of Local Religion in Hong Kong and Macau', *China Quarterly*, Vol.174 (2003), p.373 at p.390.
179. Eric Heinze, 'Sexual Orientation and International Law: A Study in the Manufacture of Cross-Cultural "Sensitivity"', *Michigan Journal of International Law*, Vol.22 (2001), p.283 at p.306.
180. See, e.g., Mei-Ling Hsu, Wen-Chi Lin and Tsui-Sung Wu, 'Representations of "Us" and "Others" in the AIDS News Discourse: A Taiwanese Experience', in Evelyne Micollier (ed.), *Sexual Cultures in East Asia: The Social Construction of Sexuality and Sexual Risk in a Time of AIDS* (London and New York: RoutledgeCurzon 2004), pp.183–222.
181. Ruth Fletcher, 'Post-colonial Fragments: Representations of Abortion in Irish Law and Politics', *Journal of Law and Society* Vol. 28 (2001), p.568 at p.573.
182. Ibid. p.570.
183. Clare Hemmings, 'What's in a Name? Bisexuality, Transnational Sexuality Studies and Western Colonial Legacies', in this Special Double Issue, p.13 at p.16.
184. Phillips (note 160) p.472.
185. Mary McIntosh, 'The Homosexual Role', in Steven Seidman (ed.), *Queer Theory/Sociology* (Cambridge, MA: Blackwell 1996), pp.33–40 at p.35.
186. See Kinsey, Pomeroy and Martin (note 46); Kinsey *et al.* (note 46).
187. See Phil C. W. Chan, 'Hong Kong's Proposed Race Anti-Discrimination Legislation: A *Discriminatory* Bill Excluding Mainland Chinese Immigrants from Protection', *Chinese Journal of International Law*, Vol.4 (2005), p.599.
188. Chaihark Hahm, 'Law, Culture, and the Politics of Confucianism', *Columbia Journal of Asian Law*, Vol.16 (2003), p.253 at p.257.
189. Ibid. p.269.
190. Ibid. p.279.
191. Ibid.
192. Will Kymlicka, *Liberalism, Community and Culture* (Oxford: Clarendon Press 1989), p.167.
193. Phil C. W. Chan, 'No, it is not just a Phase: An Adolescent's Right to Sexual Minority Identity under the United Nations Convention on the Rights of the Child', *International Journal of Human Rights*, Vol.10 (2006), p.161.
194. Adopted and opened for signature, ratification and accession by U.N. G.A. Res. 44/25 of 20 November 1989 and entered into force on 2 September 1990.
195. Sonia K. Katyal, 'Sexuality and Sovereignty: The Global Limits and Possibilities of *Lawrence*', *William and Mary Bill of Rights Journal*, Vol.14 (2006), p.1429.
196. Hong Kong (*Hansard*) (note 101) *per* Legislative Councillor Leung Wai-Tung, p.2747.
197. Stephen Macedo, 'Homosexuality and the Conservative Mind', *Georgetown Law Journal*, Vol.84 (1995), p.261 at p.299.
198. Dworkin (note 1) p.1002.
199. Chan (note 187).
200. (1995) 124 DLR (4th) 609.
201. Ibid. *per* La Forest J., p.619.

202. *National Coalition for Gay and Lesbian Equality v. Minister of Home Affairs* (note 77) *per* Ackermann J., para.38.
203. 440 Mass 309 (2003).
204. 32 Cal 2d 711 (1948) (Supreme Court of California).
205. 388 US 1 (1967) (Supreme Court of the United States).
206. *Goodridge* (note 203) *per* Marshall C.J.
207. *Fourie* (note 78) *per* Cameron J.A. (with Mthiyane J.A., van Heerden J.A., Ponnan A.J.A. concurring), para.10.
208. 1997 (4) SA 1.
209. Ibid. *per* Goldstone J., para.41.
210. *National Coalition for Gay and Lesbian Equality v. Minister of Home Affairs* (note 77) *per* Ackermann J., para.42.
211. Ibid. para.54.
212. (1998) 156 DLR (4th) 385.
213. Ibid. *per* Cory J., para.69.
214. See Carol Steiker, 'The Constitutional Status of Sexual Orientation: Homosexuality as a Suspect Classification', *Harvard Law Review*, Vol.98 (1985), p.1285.
215. See Chan (note 193).
216. Richard A. Posner, *Sex and Reason* (Cambridge, MA: Harvard University Press 1992), pp.296–7.
217. Chan (note 193) p.170.
218. Home Affairs Bureau, *Consultative Paper* (note 151) para.34.
219. Ibid.
220. Bernard Gert, *Morality: Its Nature and Justification* (New York and Oxford: Oxford University Press 1998), p.11.
221. Chan (note 12) pp.78–9.
222. Anoop Nayak and Mary Jane Kehily, 'Playing It Straight: Masculinities, Homophobias and Schooling', *Journal of Gender Studies*, Vol.5 (1996), p.211 at p.225.
223. Kathryn Abrams, '"Fighting Fire with Fire": Rethinking the Role of Disgust in Hate Crimes', *California Law Review*, Vol.90 (2002), p.1423 at p.1449.
224. Home Affairs Bureau, *Consultative Paper* (note 151) para.51.
225. Ann Hartman, 'Out of the Closet: Revolution and Backlash', *Social Work*, Vol.38 (1993), p.245 at p.245.
226. In December 1998, the Board of Trustees of the American Psychiatric Association condemned the use of reparative therapy for sexual minorities. Its unanimous Position Statement on Psychiatric Treatment and Sexual Orientation states that '[t]he potential risks of reparative therapy are great, including depression, anxiety and self-destructive behavior, since therapist alignment with societal prejudices against homosexuality may reinforce self-hatred already experienced by the patient. Many patients who have undergone reparative therapy relate that they were inaccurately told that homosexuals are lonely, unhappy individuals who never achieve acceptance or satisfaction. The possibility that the person might achieve happiness and satisfying interpersonal relationships as a gay man or lesbian is not presented, nor are alternative approaches to dealing [with] the effects of societal stigmatization discussed. ... Therefore, the American Psychiatric Association opposes any psychiatric treatment, such as reparative or conversion therapy which is based upon the assumption that homosexuality per se is a mental disorder or based upon the *a priori* assumption that the patient should change his/her sexual homosexual orientation.' The American Psychiatric Association's warning was further augmented by its Position Statement on Therapies Focused on Attempts to Change Sexual Orientation (Reparative or Conversion Therapies) adopted in March 2000, which expands and elaborates on the 1998 resolution.
227. Phil C. W. Chan, 'Truth and Light Casts an Unwelcome Shadow', *The Standard*, 6 October 2005, p.A37.
228. Petersen (note 88) p.360.
229. Ibid. p.361.
230. Paul J. Kelly, 'Impartiality: A Philosophical Perspective', in András Sajó (ed.), *Judicial Integrity* (Leiden: Martinus Nijhoff Publishers 2004), pp.17–42 at pp.17–18.
231. J. Donald C. Galloway, 'Three Models of (In)Equality', *McGill Law Journal*, Vol.38 (1993), p.64 at pp.84–5.
232. *Egan* (note 200) *per* Iacobucci J., p.676.
233. Ibid., *per* L'Heureux-Dubé J., p.650.
234. Dworkin (note 1) pp.1000–1.

235. Department of Health, Press Release, 29 August 2006: 'AIDS situation in the second quarter of 2006', http://www.info.gov.hk/aids/english/press/2006/060829.htm (accessed 31 October 2006).
236. Subcommittee (note 110) para.50.
237. *R. v. M. (C.)*, (1995) 98 CCC (3d) 481 at 488.
238. *Leung T. C. William Roy v. Secretary for Justice* [2005] 3 HKLRD 657 at 693–94 (Hong Kong Court of First Instance); *Secretary for Justice v. Leung T. C. William Roy* [2006] 4 HKLRD 211 at 236–37 (Hong Kong Court of Appeal).
239. Crimes Ordinance, s.118D.
240. Subcommittee to Study Discrimination on the Ground of Sexual Orientation, 'Minutes of Meeting of the Subcommittee to Study Discrimination on the Ground of Sexual Orientation held on 19 April 2001': LC Paper No.CB(2)2188/00-01, para.21.
241. Carlos A. Ball, 'Moral Foundations for a Discourse on Same-Sex Marriage: Looking Beyond Political Liberalism', *Georgetown Law Journal*, Vol.85 (1997), p.1871 at pp.1912–3.
242. Andrew Koppelman, 'Is Marriage Inherently Heterosexual?', *American Journal of Jurisprudence*, Vol.42 (1997), p.51 at p.62.
243. Joseph Raz, *The Morality of Freedom* (Oxford: Clarendon Press 1986), p.206.
244. 381 US 479 (1965).
245. Ibid. *per* Douglas J., p.486.
246. Timothy E. Lin, 'Social Norms and Judicial Decisionmaking: Examining the Role of Narratives in Same-Sex Adoption Cases', *Columbia Law Review*, Vol.99 (1999), p.739 at pp.741–2, quoting Julie Shapiro, 'Custody and Conduct: How the Law Fails Lesbian and Gay Parents and Their Children', *Indiana Law Journal*, Vol.71 (1996), p.623 at p.624.
247. Didi Herman, '(Il)legitimate Minorities: The American Christian Right's Anti-Gay-Rights Discourse', *Journal of Law and Society*, Vol.23 (1996), p.346 at p.359.
248. Wayne Morgan and Kristen Walker, 'Tolerance and Homosex: A Policy of Control and Containment', *Melbourne University Law Review*, Vol.20 (1995), p.202 at p.206.
249. Ibid. p.207.
250. Martti Nissinen, *Homoeroticism in the Biblical World: A Historical Perspective* (Minneapolis: Fortress Press 1998), p.139.
251. Rhoda E. Howard-Hassmann, 'Gay Rights and the Right to a Family: Conflicts between Liberal and Illiberal Belief Systems', *Human Rights Quarterly*, Vol.23 (2001), p.73 at p.79.
252. *Vriend* (note 212) *per* Iacobucci J., p.434.
253. Civil Partnership Act 2004 (c.33), s.1.
254. See texts accompanying notes 7–8.
255. [2006] EWHC 2022 (Fam).
256. Ibid. paras.118–21.
257. (2001) 31 EHRR 1055.
258. Ibid. para.36. Article 14 has since reached the status of a substantive right under the European Convention on Human Rights; see text accompanying note 62.
259. *Susan Wilkinson v. Celia Kitzinger and Others* (note 255) para.116.
260. *In re Opinions of the Justices to the Senate*, 440 Mass 1201 (2004).
261. Ibid. *per* Marshall C.J., Greaney, Ireland, and Cowin JJ.
262. For the respective rulings by the courts of appeal of the three most populous Canadian provinces (two of which with substantial Chinese populations), see *Halpern v. Canada (Attorney General)*, (2003) 225 DLR (4th) 529 (Ontario); *Hendricks v. Québec (Procureur general)*, [2002] RJQ 2506 (Québec); *EGALE Canada Inc. v. Canada (Attorney General)*, (2003) 225 DLR (4th) 472 (British Columbia).
263. [2004] 3 SCR 698.
264. Civil Marriage Act 2005, S.C. 2005, c.33, s.2.
265. *Lawrence* (note 87) *per* Scalia J., p.533 (dissenting opinion).
266. Mark Tushnet, *A Court Divided: The Rehnquist Court and the Future of Constitutional Law* (New York: W. W. Norton 2005), pp.171–2.
267. John Finnis, *Natural Law and Natural Rights* (Oxford: Clarendon Press 1980).
268. John Finnis, 'Law, Morality, and "Sexual Orientation"', *Notre Dame Law Review*, Vol.69 (1994), pp.1049 at p.1064.
269. Ibid. p.1068.
270. Ibid. p.1067.

271. Ibid. p.1055.
272. Macedo (note 197) p.277.
273. Andrew Bainham, 'Family Law in a Pluralistic Society', *Journal of Law and Society*, Vol.22 (1995), p.234 at p.238.
274. (1993) 100 DLR (4th) 658.
275. Ibid. *per* L'Heureux-Dubé, p.710 (dissenting opinion).
276. *National Coalition for Gay and Lesbian Equality v. Minister of Home Affairs* (note 77) *per* Ackermann J., para.51.
277. Basil Chubb, *The Politics of the Irish Constitution* (Dublin: Institute of Public Administration 1991), p.39.
278. Constitution of Ireland of 1937, Preamble and Art.6(1).
279. *State (Ryan) v. Lennon*, [1935] IR 170; *Ryan v. Attorney General*, [1965] IR 294; *McGee v. Attorney General and the Revenue Commissioners*, [1974] IR 284.
280. Aisling O'Sullivan and Phil C. W. Chan, 'Judicial Review in Ireland and the Relationship between the Irish Constitution and Natural Law', *Nottingham Law Journal*, Vol.15, No.2 (2006), p.18.
281. The Preamble to Bunreacht na hÉireann, or the Constitution of Ireland as promulgated in 1937 by referendum, emphatically states that '[i]n the Name of the Most Holy Trinity, from Whom is all authority and to Whom, as our final end, all actions both of men and States must be referred, We, the people of Éire, [h]umbly acknowledging all our obligations to our Divine Lord, Jesus Christ, Who sustained our fathers through centuries of trial, [g]ratefully remembering their heroic and unremitting struggle to regain the rightful independence of our Nation, [a]nd seeking to promote the common good, with due observance of Prudence, Justice and Charity, so that the dignity and freedom of the individual may be assured, true social order attained, the unity of our country restored, and concord established with other nations, [d]o hereby adopt, enact, and give to ourselves this Constitution.'
282. Article 6(1), ibid., states that '[a]ll powers of government, legislative, executive and judicial, derive, under God, from the people, whose right it is to designate the rulers of the State and, in final appeal, to decide all questions of national policy, according to the requirements of the common good.'
283. The fundamental rights of an individual are recognised and protected by Articles 40 to 44, ibid., where 'natural law' is repeatedly emphasised. It is important in this respect to note that in *McGee v. Attorney General*, [1974] IR 284, Irish Supreme Court Justice Walsh, at p.310, adamantly adjudged that 'Articles 40, 41, 42 and 44 of the Constitution all fall within that section of the Constitution which is titled "Fundamental Rights". Articles 41, 42 and 43 emphatically reject the theory that there are no rights without laws, no rights contrary to the law and no rights anterior to the law. They indicate that justice is placed above the law and acknowledge that natural rights, or human rights, are not created by law but that the Constitution confirms their existence and gives them protection. The individual has natural and human rights over which the State has no authority; and the family, as the natural primary and fundamental unit group of society, has rights as such which the State cannot control.'
284. *In re Article 26 and the Information (Termination of Pregnancies) Bill, 1995* [1995] 1 IR 1.
285. [1966] IR 567.
286. [1980] IR 32.
287. F. F. V. R. von Prondzynski, 'Natural Law and the Constitution', *Dublin University Law Journal* (1977), p.32 at p.37.
288. Ibid.
289. Desmond M. Clarke, 'The Role of Natural Law in the Irish Constitution', *Irish Jurist*, Vol.17 (1982), p.187 at p.213.
290. *G. v. An Bord Uchtála* (note 286) *per* Kenny J., p.97.
291. (1991) 13 EHRR 186.
292. John Rawls, *Political Liberalism* (New York: Columbia University Press 1993), p.226.
293. *Goodridge* (note 203) *per* Marshall C.J.
294. [1961] IR 345.
295. Ibid. *per* Budd J., p.368.
296. Timothy W. Reinig, 'Sin, Stigma and Society: A Critique of Morality and Values in Democratic Law and Policy', *Buffalo Law Review*, Vol.38 (1990), p.859 at p.878.
297. See, e.g., Article 22 of the Universal Declaration of Human Rights, adopted and proclaimed by United Nations General Assembly Resolution 217A(III) of 10 December 1948, which states that '[e]veryone, as a member of society, has the right to social security and is entitled to realization ... of the economic,

social and cultural rights *indispensable for his dignity and the free development of his personality*' (emphasis added).

298. Robert Wintemute, 'Lesbian and Gay Inequality 2000: The Potential of the Human Rights Act 1998 and the Need for an Equality Act 2002', *European Human Rights Law Review* [2000], p.603 at p.608.
299. Urvashi Vaid, *Virtual Equality: The Mainstreaming of Gay and Lesbian Liberation* (New York: Anchor 1995), p.194.
300. *Reference re Same-Sex Marriage* (note 263) *per* The Court, para.46.
301. Daniel A. Helminiak, *What the Bible Really Says about Homosexuality: Recent Findings by Top Scholars Offer a Radical New View* (San Francisco: Alamo Square Press 1994), p.12.
302. Kenneth A. Locke, 'The Bible on Homosexuality: Exploring Its Meaning and Authority', *Journal of Homosexuality*, Vol.48, No.2 (2004), p.127.
303. Ibid. pp.128–32. See also John Boswell, *Christianity, Social Tolerance and Homosexuality: Gay People in Western Europe from the Beginning of the Christian Era to the Fourteenth Century* (Chicago and London: University of Chicago Press 1980), pp.97–8.
304. Locke (note 302) pp.137–44; James B. Nelson, *Embodiment: An Approach to Sexuality and Christian Theology* (Minneapolis: Augsburg Publishing 1978), pp.186–7; Richard B. Hays, *The Moral Vision of the New Testament: A Contemporary Introduction to New Testament Ethics* (San Francisco: Harper 1996), p.388; L. William Countryman, *Dirt, Greed and Sex: Sexual Ethics in the New Testament and their Implications for Today* (Philadelphia: Fortress Press 1988), pp.115–6; M. L. Soards, *Scripture and Homosexuality: Biblical Authority and the Church Today* (Louisville, KY: Westminster John Knox Press 1995), pp.21–2. In this respect, it is useful to quote Romans 1:18–27 in detail: 'For the wrath of God is revealed from heaven against all ungodliness and wickedness of those who by their wickedness suppress the truth. For what can be known about God is plain to them, because God has shown it to them. ... So they are without excuse; for though they know God, they did not honour him as God or gave thanks to him, but they became futile in their thinking, and their senseless minds were darkened. Claiming to be wise, they became fools; and they exchanged the glory of the immortal God for images resembling a mortal human being or birds or four-footed animals or reptiles. Therefore, God gave them up in the lusts of their hearts to impurity, to the degrading of their bodies among themselves, because they exchanged the truth about God for a lie and worshipped and served the creature rather than the Creator. For this reason God gave them up to degrading passions. Their women exchanged natural intercourse [*ten physiken khresin*] for unnatural [*para physin*], and in the same way also the men giving up natural intercourse [*ten physiken khresin*] with women, were consumed with passion for one another. Men committed shameless acts with men and received in their own persons the due penalty for their error.'
305. Helminiak (note 301) p.64.
306. Locke (note 302) p.148.
307. *Fourie* (note 78) *per* Farlam J.A. (concurring and dissenting opinion), para.121.
308. Marriage Ordinance, s.40(1).
309. *Hyde* (note 23) p.133.
310. *Reference re Same-Sex Marriage* (note 263) *per* The Court, para.22.
311. Howard-Hassmann (note 251) p.82.
312. Nissinen (note 250) p.140.
313. [1989] 1 SCR 1296.
314. Ibid. *per* Wilson J., p.1328.
315. [1994] 3 SCR 835.
316. Ibid. *per* Lamer C.J., p.877.
317. *Egan* (note 200) *per* Cory J., p.675.
318. 543 US 551 (2005). The United States Supreme Court decision, referring to international and Strasbourg decisions, ruled the imposition of death penalty upon juveniles as unconstitutional.
319. An Act for the Relief of the Parents of Theresa Marie Schiavo 2005, http://news.findlaw.com/hdocs/docs/schiavo/bill31905.html (accessed 28 September 2005).
320. See, in particular, *Schiavo* ex rel. *Schindler and Others v. Schiavo*, 358 F.Supp.2d 1161 (2005) (United States Court of Appeals for the Eleventh Circuit).
321. *Bush v. Schiavo*, 885 So.2d 321 (2004).
322. *The Los Angeles Times* in 'In '88, Accident Forced DeLays to Choose between Life, Death', 27 March 2005, reported that DeLay himself had opposed artificially prolonging his father's life through a dialysis machine.
323. 347 US 483 (1954).

324. 410 US 113 (1973). The well-known United States Supreme Court decision recognised a constitutional right to abortion.
325. 74 Haw 530 (1993).
326. 110 Stat 2419 (1996).
327. Section 3, ibid., states that '[n]o State, territory, or possession of the United States, or Indian tribe, shall be required to give effect to any public act, record, or judicial proceeding of any other State, territory, possession, or tribe respecting a relationship between persons of the same sex that is treated as a marriage under the laws of such other State, territory, possession, or tribe, or a right or claim arising from such relationship.'
328. Section 1 of Article IV of the federal United States Constitution states that '[f]ull faith and credit shall be given in each state to the public acts, records, and judicial proceedings of every other state. And the Congress may by general laws prescribe the manner in which such acts, records, and proceedings shall be proved, and the effect thereof.'
329. See, e.g., Paige E. Chabora, 'Congress' Power under the Full Faith and Credit Clause and the Defense of Marriage Act of 1996', *Nebraska Law Review*, Vol.76 (1997), p.604; Nancy J. Feather, 'Defense of Marriage Acts: An Analysis under State Constitutional Law', *Temple Law Review*, Vol.70 (1997), p.1017; Heather Hamilton, 'The Defense of Marriage Act: A Critical Analysis of its Constitutionality under the Full Faith and Credit Clause', *DePaul Law Review*, Vol.47 (1998), p.943; Julie L. B. Johnson, 'The Meaning of "General Laws": The Extent of Congress's Power under the Full Faith and Credit Clause and the Constitutionality of the Defense of Marriage Act', *University of Pennsylvania Law Review*, Vol.145 (1997), p.1611; Andrew Koppelman, 'Dumb and DOMA: Why the Defense of Marriage Act is Unconstitutional', *Iowa Law Review*, Vol.83 (1997), p.351; Scott Ruskay-Kidd, 'The Defense of Marriage Act and the Overextension of Congressional Authority', *Columbia Law Review*, Vol.97 (1997), p.1435; Jeennie R. Shuki-Kunze, 'The "Defenseless" Marriage Act: The Constitutionality of the Defense of Marriage Act as an Extension of Congressional Power under the Full Faith and Credit Clause', *Case Western Reserve Law Review*, Vol.48 (1998), p.351.
330. It should be noted that section 11 of Chapter 207 of the General Laws of Massachusetts states that '[n]o marriage shall be contracted in this commonwealth by a party residing and intending to continue to reside in another jurisdiction if such marriage would be void if contracted in such other jurisdiction, and every marriage contracted in this commonwealth in violation hereof shall be null and void.' The constitutionality of the provision was upheld by the Massachusetts Supreme Judicial Council in *Sandra Cote-Whitacre v. Department of Public Health*, SJC-09436, 30 March 2006.
331. The First Amendment to the United States Constitution states that 'Congress shall make no law respecting an establishment of religion, or prohibiting the free exercise thereof; or abridging the freedom of speech, or of the press; or the right of the people peaceably to assemble, and to petition the Government for a redress of grievances.'
332. 319 US 624 (1943).
333. Ibid. *per* Jackson J., pp.637–8.
334. *Oakes* (note 135) *per* Dickson C.J., p.225.
335. *Goodridge* (note 203) *per* Greaney J. (concurring opinion).
336. F. F. V. R. von Prondzynski, 'The Protection of Constitutional Rights: Comparisons between Ireland and Germany', *Dublin University Law Journal* (1979–80), p.14 at p.28.
337. United Nations Human Rights Committee, *General Comment No.19: Protection of the Family, the Right to Marriage and Equality of the Spouses (Art.23)*, 27 July 1990.
338. International Covenant on Civil and Political Rights, Art.23(2).
339. United Nations Human Rights Committee, *General Comment No.19* (note 337) para.2.
340. 1(3) IHRR 97 (1994).
341. Ibid. para.8.7.
342. United Nations Human Rights Committee, Communication No. 941/2000, CCPR/C/78/D/941/2000, 6 August 2003.
343. Ibid. para.10.4.
344. Ibid. para.12.
345. United Nations Human Rights Committee, Communication No.902/1999, CCPR/C/75/D/902/1999, 17 July 2002.
346. Ibid. para.8.3.

347. Article 16 of the International Covenant on Civil and Political Rights states that '[e]veryone shall have the right to recognition everywhere as a person before the law.'
348. Article 17(1), ibid., states that '[n]o one shall be subjected to arbitrary or unlawful interference with his privacy, family, home or correspondence, nor to unlawful attacks on his honour and reputation.' Article 17(2) of the Covenant goes on to state that '[e]veryone has the right to the protection of the law against such interference or attacks.'
349. Article 23(1), ibid., states that '[t]he family is the natural and fundamental group unit of society and is entitled to protection by society and the State.'
350. *Joslin v. New Zealand* (note 345) para.8.2.
351. Paul Rishworth, 'Changing Times, Changing Minds, Changing Laws – Sexual Orientation and New Zealand Law, 1960 to 2005', in this Special Double Issue, p.85 at p.95.
352. Nicholas Bala and Rebecca Jaremko Bromwich, 'Context and Inclusivity in Canada's Evolving Definition of the Family', *International Journal of Law, Policy and the Family* (2002), p.145 at p.147.
353. United Nations Human Rights Committee, *Concluding Observations of the Human Rights Committee on the Hong Kong Special Administrative Region: Hong Kong (China)*, CCPR/C/79/Add.117, 4 November 1999.
354. Ibid. para.15.
355. Ibid.
356. International Covenant on Civil and Political Rights, Art.2(1).
357. Thomas Buergenthal, 'To Respect and to Ensure: State Obligations and Permissible Derogations', in Louis Henkin (ed.), *The International Bill of Rights: The Covenant on Civil and Political Rights* (New York: Columbia University Press 1981), pp.72–91 at pp.77–8.
358. Ibid. Art.2(2).
359. Ibid. Art.2(3)(a).
360. United Nations Committee on Economic, Social and Cultural Rights, *Concluding Observations of the Committee on Economic, Social and Cultural Rights (Hong Kong): China*, E/C.12/1/Add.58, 21 May 2001, para.15(c).
361. Adopted and opened for signature, ratification and accession by UN GA Res. 2200A(XXI) of 16 December 1966 and entered into force on 3 January 1976.
362. Ibid. Art.7.
363. International Covenant on Economic, Social and Cultural Rights, Art.2(2).
364. Yvonne Klerk, 'Working Paper on Article 2(2) and Article 3 of the International Covenant on Economic, Social and Cultural Rights', *Human Rights Quarterly*, Vol.9 (1987), p.250 at p.260.
365. United Nations Committee on Economic, Social and Cultural Rights, *Concluding Observations on Hong Kong* (note 360) para.31.
366. Ibid. para.27.
367. See, e.g., Kristen Walker, 'The Same-Sex Marriage Debate in Australia', in this Special Double Issue, pp.109–30.
368. *Goodridge* (note 203) *per* Marshall C.J.
369. Heinze (note 179) p.307.

# Changing Times, Changing Minds, Changing Laws – Sexual Orientation and New Zealand Law, 1960 to 2005

PAUL RISHWORTH

**Prologue: Ten Lost Years**

David Balfour held a university degree in psychology. In the early 1970s he taught 'special needs' children in provincial New Zealand. By 1975 he was a secondary school teacher. Then rumours began to circulate that he was 'homosexual'. He resigned. Despite numerous applications, he did not gain another teaching position for ten years.

In 1981 he accepted a position as a social worker in a regional office of the Department of Social Welfare. But principals from local schools did not want him to have contact with school children. They lobbied for his dismissal. The Department asked him to resign even before his commencement date, saying he was 'morally unsuitable'. Balfour refused to resign, but his future employment with the Department was then embarrassingly fettered: he was instructed to stay away from schools. Enduring this humiliation, he continued until the end of 1984. Then he began to apply for teaching positions again. A hundred applications and a year later, he gained a relieving teacher position. A permanent position followed in 1986.

Unhappy about the ten lost years of his professional life as a teacher, Balfour sought and gained access to his personal file held by the Department of Education.[1] There he found a memorandum dated 7 July 1980. A District Senior Inspector of Secondary Schools had been asking for a report on Balfour's suitability to teach handicapped children. On the memorandum was the following note: 'Entirely unsuitable ... A long practising and blatant homosexual – check file to make absolutely sure I have the right person then ring Mrs Brocklesby and inform her.'

Balfour disputed those assertions, and he wanted legal redress. But there were difficulties. Sexual acts between males were illegal in New Zealand in 1980. The file note asserted criminal activity, and even if that were untrue a ready defence of qualified privilege would immunise the author from liability in defamation.[2] Instead, Balfour sued the Department of Education for breach of statutory duty and negligence. The Department, he claimed, had not made reasonable inquiries about his fitness to teach, and had reached an erroneous conclusion as a result. Special damages were sought to compensate for loss of teaching seniority and income, general damages for the harm wrought to his reputation, and punitive damages on the basis that all this was in contumelious disregard of his rights.

Balfour lost at trial[3] and again on appeal to the New Zealand Court of Appeal.[4] There were several reasons for the dismissal of his claims. First, said both courts, there was no causation: rumours about Balfour were rife throughout the whole period, and his employment troubles could not be pinned solely on the Department of Education's objectionable memorandum. Second, and in any event, there was no statutory duty of care: the court rejected Balfour's argument that the offensive file notation was tantamount to a 'deregistration' accomplished without due process. Third, the claim in negligence failed. Neither the incremental approach to the law of negligence[5] nor the policy-based approach[6] supported any common law duty of reasonable care in such a case. Importantly, the court was not prepared to merge the distinct torts of negligence and defamation. As Justice Hardie Boys put it in the Court of Appeal: 'An inability [to bring] a particular case ... within the criteria of a defamation suit is not to be made good by the formulation of a duty of care not to defame.'[7]

Beneath these technical considerations lay the decisive policy factor. Maintaining personal files on individuals was seen as an essential part of the Department of Education's function. Any injustice in denying a remedy for incorrect or prejudicial material was outweighed by the inconvenience and inhibition that would follow if every adverse comment on a teacher had to be painstakingly verified. The following passage from the judgment of Justice Hardie Boys gave the flavour: 'the law must recognise the balance to be preserved between a teacher's rights and the Department's wider responsibilities. Particularly in the case of moral suitability clear proof may be difficult to obtain. Yet to ignore possible warning signals may be irresponsible.'[8]

Note the implications of that last sentence. They were spelled out a little more by Justice Hardie Boys:[9] 'The ... point is one that must not be lost sight of, and it is the great care that educational authorities must exercise when made aware of an allegation, even a rumour, of this kind. Their prime duty must be the protection of the children, if possible to prevent problems rather than await their occurrence.' Balfour's suspected homosexuality was, it seemed, a problem waiting to occur.

Mr Balfour commenced his legal proceedings on 7 July 1986, squeaking in on the last day of the six-year limitation period that commenced with the Departmental memorandum of 7 July 1980. Two days later, on 9 July 1986, the Homosexual Law Reform Bill received its third reading in the New Zealand House of Representatives. Two days later, the Bill received the Royal Assent and became law: sexual activity between consenting males in New Zealand was decriminalised, with the age of consent set at 16.[10]

None of this serendipity availed Balfour, however. Major social changes were looming, but not quickly or powerfully enough to change the past. Balfour's case took another four years to reach its final denouement in the Court of Appeal. Ultimately, the court was keen to acknowledge an injustice done to him. But no remedy was available under New Zealand law.

Even so, no one in New Zealand is likely to suffer a Balfour-like experience again. There are several reasons: times have changed, laws have changed, and minds have changed. This paper seeks to explore the interaction between laws and attitudinal shifts in the arena of homosexuality. The story begins with the decriminalisation of consensual sexual activity between males but, as will be seen, the legal event around which all progress has pivoted was not decriminalisation but the later enactment of anti-discrimination law. Sexual orientation first became a prohibited ground of discrimination under the Human Rights Act 1993, and a corresponding change was made simultaneously to the then-recent New Zealand Bill of Rights Act 1990. This occurred at a time when the international human rights movement was receiving a 'second wind' as a result of the collapse of communist states, and the clarion call of 'human rights' was powerful and evocative. For New Zealand, a domestic by-product of the human rights renaissance was that human rights laws came to be regarded by the citizenry – certainly the elite citizenry – as being 'special'. They were the measure of all other laws. In a country with no formal written constitution, and no constitutional bill of rights, human rights laws provided a quasi-constitutional impetus for legal change. We begin, however, at the beginning – decriminalisation.

**The Decriminalisation Debate, 1960 to 1986**

Sexual acts between consenting males had been illegal since the founding of the New Zealand colony in 1840, as provided for by English criminal law. By the 1960s the prohibition was contained in New Zealand's own Crimes Act 1961.[11] But there was no agitation for reform before the 1960s – New Zealand society was already known for a certain dull homogeneity, with few citizens being prepared to stick their heads above the parapet as reformers. When under-age heterosexual activity had come to light in a New Zealand region in 1954, and the government called for a special committee to investigate, the resulting Mazengarb Report vigorously condemned sexual immorality and affirmed conventional values.[12] As one commentator observed: 'The morals committee had served the National Government well. By spelling out the conventional values it felt New Zealand was abandoning, it fired a warning shot that echoed for the rest of the decade.'[13] That was in the context of heterosexuality; in that era the invisibility of homosexuality was a given.

The impetus for law reform began, slowly, in the mid-1960s as a local response to international developments. The Kinsey Report, from the United States, brought a statistical basis to the idea of diversity in sexual experience, laying a foundation stone upon which much in the law reform movement was built.[14] Biological realities, ultimately, could not be ignored. The Wolfenden Report from the United Kingdom was similarly influential in shaping elite opinion in New Zealand.[15] By persuasively separating the realms of morality and law in the context of homosexual relations, and recommending decriminalisation of homosexual sex, that Report made it possible for high profile reformers to advocate the decriminalisation of homosexual acts without committing themselves to positive approval of homosexuality. Later, in the era of gay pride, this cleavage between toleration and affirmation became problematic. But in the 1960s it was critical for the development of a critical mass of reformers.[16]

In 1967 the New Zealand Homosexual Law Reform Society (NZHLRS) was founded, its mission being, essentially, to implement in New Zealand the objectives of the Wolfenden Report in the United Kingdom. The NZHLRS drew its executive council from academia and the legal and medical professions, and included two bishops in the Anglican Church. Its *modus operandi* was education and persuasion.[17] A petition to Parliament in 1968, with a careful supporting submission urging reform along Wolfenden lines, went to the Parliamentary Petitions Committee but gained no traction there. Even so, by the early 1970s the two principal political parties in New Zealand had each voted, at their annual conferences, to support decriminalisation. The telling figure was the age breakdown of supporters and opponents of decriminalisation: a 1973 poll suggested that 35 per cent of people over 55 supported reform, increasing to 61 per cent of those aged 30–54 and 71 per cent of those aged 18–29.[18] As one commentator subsequently put it: 'A major shift was taking place among the young, and the simple passage of time might well bring NZHLRS nearer to victory.'[19]

But if time can be a reformer, time can also pass slowly. Homosexual law reform treaded an increasingly fractious path. A major stumbling block was the proposed age of consent: general support for reform fractured over whether the age of consent should be 16 years as for participants in heterosexual sex, or 18 or 21 years. Those who supported 16 as the age of consent argued that any higher age would reflect a stigmatising judgment on gay men. For all the apparent support outside of Parliament, decriminalisation was not just around the corner. A private member's decriminalisation Bill introduced in 1975, with the proposed age of consent at 21, was defeated on its second reading (34 to 29, with 24 abstentions).[20] Public tolerance of the idea of decriminalisation was not translating into actual votes in the House.

A second wave of reform impetus came with the advent of gay rights in the 1970s. Whereas the NZHLRS and associated reform initiatives were driven by concerns for tolerance and compassion, the newer gay rights lobby groups adopted the motifs of equality and liberation that by then were associated with race and gender. The gay rights movement had arrived in New Zealand. A National Gay Rights Coalition was formed. Unequivocal demands were made for decriminalisation with 16 as the age of consent. Gay rights activists who were members of NZHLRS used their numbers to make constitutional changes to society so as to make it a more radical advocate of reform. Some founding NZHLRS members resigned, and the NZHLRS' attractiveness waned. The reform movement was now carried on by other groups, and more aggressively.

By 1984 New Zealand's nearest neighbour, the Australian state of New South Wales, had decriminalised consensual sexual activity between males with 18 as the age of consent.[21] Events in New Zealand then moved rapidly. A snap election in July 1984 saw a new Labour government elected in place of the socially conservative National government. Immediately upon taking office the principal parliamentary proponent of reform, Fran Wilde, Member of Parliament representing Wellington, consulted gay rights groups, political support was quietly explored and found to be substantial, and a private member's Bill was introduced in March 1985, easily passing its first reading by 51 votes to 24. The Homosexual Law Reform Bill, co-drafted by University of Auckland law lecturer Don McMorland, comprised a Part I that would decriminalise consensual sexual activity between males with 16 as the age of consent, and a Part II that would prohibit discrimination on the grounds of sexual orientation. Debate over the next 16 months was furious, most of it over the religious dimension of sexual morality.[22]

The New Zealand churches were divided throughout the whole period of reform debates, as indeed they are still. The Methodist Church in New Zealand had endorsed decriminalisation in 1961, for Wolfenden-type reasons, but by the 1980s was accepting of homosexuality *per se*. The Presbyterian Church of New Zealand had similarly endorsed decriminalisation in 1968, but remaining divided on the moral issue (as recently as 2004 it affirmed by a two-thirds vote in its General Assembly that it would not ordain or tolerate as leaders 'any person who is involved in a sexual relationship outside of faithful marriage between a man and a woman').[23] The Anglican Church of New Zealand, through its bishops, was in favour of reform. The Catholic Church issued a statement in opposition, declaring homosexual acts, although not homosexual attraction, to be morally wrong. However, the Catholic Church, in the end, did not make any submission on the Bill.

The principal religious opposition to the Bill was carried by conservative Christians outside mainstream denominations.[24] Particularly prominent was a group called the Coalition of Concerned Citizens, who organised various publications, advertisements and, ultimately, a petition claimed to have 800,000 signatures. Serious doubts were, however, cast upon the authenticity of the 800,000 figure: it appeared that many signed more than once and that children were asked to sign. In the end the petition was a public relations disaster for the Coalition and it was summarily dismissed by the parliamentary committee to which it was referred.

Debate within the House of Representatives was fierce, largely as a result of the 'all or nothing' approach taken by supporters over keeping the age of consent at 16 years. A significant majority of parliamentarians would have compromised at 18 as the age of consent but the supporters' strategy was to maintain a firm line on 16 for fear that, if a higher age were enacted, it would be difficult to change. Part II, the anti-discrimination provision, was, however, defeated at second reading, quite possibly because it suited many politicians who were in favour of decriminalisation to be able to demonstrate to their constituents that they had at least voted against something. Eventually, on 9 July 1986 the Bill was enacted into law by 49 votes to 44.

The substance of the Homosexual Law Reform Act 1986 was as follows. It amended the Crimes Act 1961, repealing legislative provisions on indecency and sodomy between males and replacing them with offences relating particularly to assaults and acts on persons under the age of 16.[25] The nature of the reform was that, once made, little more was heard about it. The absence, thereafter, of prosecutions for consensual sexual activity between males was hardly newsworthy. But the symbolism of the reform was important. That said, it was an ambiguous signal. Decriminalisation had been endorsed by persons with very different opinions about the morality of same-sex sexual activity. It denoted tolerance but not necessarily affirmation. Equality under the criminal law had been achieved, but a much more significant stairway lay ahead – equality under the civil law and, beyond that, public affirmation and acceptance. To anti-discrimination law, which began to bring that about, we now turn.

## Foundations for Change: The Rise and Rise of the Anti-discrimination Principle in New Zealand

As in other common law countries, the default setting in New Zealand law is that all is permitted save that which is expressly forbidden. The Homosexual Law Reform Act 1986 had lifted the prohibition on consensual sexual activity between males, but obviously left various other realms of social interaction – employment, buying and renting houses, trading in goods and services, and so forth – unregulated. In these spheres of ordinary life persons could act according to their own consciences, their liberty rights of free association prevailing over the equality rights of others. With no law providing otherwise, persons might refuse another person employment, accommodation, goods and services, education and so on by reason of that person's race, religion, sex, sexual orientation or, indeed, any characteristic whatsoever. By the mid-twentieth century some judicially created exceptions to the *laissez-faire* principle had emerged: racially restrictive covenants on land sales were held to be unenforceable in Canada[26] and the United States,[27] for example. But no tort of discrimination had evolved. In common law countries it required statutory reform to positively prohibit private sphere discrimination. This type of legislation began to take hold from the 1970s onwards.

New Zealand's first anti-discrimination law was the Race Relations Act 1971, enacted as a prelude to New Zealand's ratification of the United Nations Convention for the Elimination of All Forms of Racial Discrimination (CERD) in 1972.[28] The Act prohibited racial discrimination by private actors as well as the state.[29] It also introduced, as required by article 20 of CERD, a criminal offence of intentionally inciting racial disharmony.[30] A few years later a parallel 'civil' offence was included: publishing of statements that are threatening, abusive or insulting and likely to excite hostility on the grounds of race – but without any requirement of *intention* to incite disharmony.[31] (I mention this because of embryonic moves in New Zealand, discussed below, to expand these provisions to protect groups identified not just by race, but by religion and sexual orientation as well.)

Other forms of discrimination in New Zealand were subsequently outlawed by the Human Rights Commission Act 1977. The Human Rights Commission Act was also in response to anticipated ratification of a human rights treaty, the International Covenant on Civil and Political Rights (ICCPR).[32] The Human Rights Commission Act prohibited discrimination on the basis of sex, marital status, religion, and ethical belief.[33] There was considerable lobbying from gay rights advocacy groups for the inclusion of sexual orientation, but that was a forlorn hope in 1977 given that sexual activity between consenting males was then illegal. We saw above that an anti-discrimination provision had been included in the Homosexual Law Reform Bill of 1985–86, but was omitted from the Bill as enacted.

The early 1990s saw a major review of the Race Relations Act and Human Rights Commission Act, and the result was a new Human Rights Act 1993. The grounds of prohibited discrimination were greatly expanded. Added were age, disability, employment status, political opinion, family status, and sexual orientation.[34] The inclusion of sexual orientation had been vigorously supported by the Human Rights Commission and gay rights organisations, and successfully presented as both a health and equity matter.[35] It was linked, especially, with one particular component of the definition of disability: 'the presence in the body of organisms capable of causing illness', a phrase essentially designed for HIV but capable of wider applications.[36] Protection from discrimination was presented as an essential component of the fight against the spread of HIV and AIDS.[37] Significantly, sexual orientation had not been included in the original Bill introduced into Parliament; it was added by way of a Supplementary Order Paper and moved by a government member other than the sponsor of the principal Bill. The ensuing parliamentary debate over including sexual orientation was intense, but the Bill as a whole gained majority support and was enacted into law.

It is impossible to overstate the impact of the Human Rights Act 1993 on New Zealand law and policy affecting gay men and lesbians. The Act's significance goes well beyond merely making available a process for individuals to complain about discrimination they may suffer. To understand the broader significance of the Human Rights Act, it is necessary to delve into the way the Act was designed to work. As will be seen, it was imbued with a certain quasi-constitutional status, and was to become an important pathway to sexual orientation equality in New Zealand.

The preamble to the Human Rights Act set out its broad purpose: to provide 'better protection of human rights in New Zealand in general accordance with United Nations Covenants or Conventions on Human Rights'. Immediately, then, it can be seen that the Human Rights Act implied an external reference point – international benchmarking to human rights standards. Various statutory functions were then conferred on the Human Rights Commission. Alongside the routine 'complaints' jurisdiction,[38] it was tasked with promoting, through education and publicity, respect for human rights in New Zealand, as well as reporting to and advising the Prime Minister on any matter affecting human rights in New Zealand.[39] These functions had been in the old 1977 Act as well, but the 1993 reform now added a new function: the Commission was required to examine all laws, policies and practices of the New Zealand Government, to identify those that conflicted with the provisions of the Act (or with its 'spirit and intention'), and to report the results of this examination to the Minister of Justice by 31 December 1998.[40]

This was, by any measure, a breathtaking assignment. What it implied was that the Human Rights Act was now a sort of 'super-law': one against which the detailed content of every other law, policy and practice, must be judged. All discriminatory features of law, policy and practice, were to be identified, reviewed and, presumably, removed. This was akin to the role of constitutional law in other jurisdictions, but it was a first in New Zealand which is well-known for having no formal written constitution supporting judicial review of legislation. Of course, in the end the practical significance of the Commission's review of New Zealand law would depend on what the government and Parliament chose to do with the Commission's report. But, for reasons to be explained, the government did not have a completely free hand. The Human Rights Act contained a ticking bomb, set to go off on 1 January 2000.

To explain the nature of the ticking bomb, some further detail is necessary. The starting point is section 151(1) of the Human Rights Act, which directed that any inconsistency between the Human Rights Act and other legislation was to be resolved in favour of the other legislation. This was a carry over from the 1977 Act, designed to ensure that existing and future laws were not read down or held repealed by implication on account of the Human Rights Act. In other words, parliamentary supremacy was explicitly preserved, and any transformative impact of the human rights legislation was explicitly disavowed. Secondly, section 151(2) provided that none of the newly added grounds of discrimination – which included sexual orientation – would apply to the executive branch of government. There was, in other words, an exemption for the state from the very human rights standards which it had proclaimed for private individuals. But – and this is the ticking bomb – these provisions were temporally limited. Under section 152, both the aforementioned provisions would be deemed to be repealed as from 1 January 2000. Thus, an overall coherence now seemed to emerge: (1) the Human Rights Commission had until 31 December 1998 to review legislation and public policies for discriminatory features and report to the government; (2) the government had the calendar year of 1999 to consider the report and amend its policy and law if it saw fit; and (3) from 1 January 2000 the government would be subject to the human rights legislation in its entirety, with inconsistencies between the Human Rights Act and other legislation no longer required to be resolved in favour of the other legislation.

The net result would be something like a half-way house 'Bill of Rights' – after 1 January 2000 it would be possible to argue that the Human Rights Act prevailed over inconsistent legislation, on the grounds that its explicit subordination to other enactments had been removed. There were Canadian precedents for just this sort of result: provincial human rights legislation had by the 1990s been held to be quasi-constitutional and able to control even the application of later legislation.[41] There was also a certain affinity with the approach taken in Canada under its Canadian Charter of Rights and Freedoms,[42] where commencement of the Charter equality provision in section 15 had been delayed for three years after the rest of the Charter became operative, so as to allow time for review of Canadian law for Charter-consistency and the making of any necessary changes.

None of these features of New Zealand's Human Rights Act received much public attention or discussion. Indeed, parliamentary debate had focused almost entirely on the merits of adding sexual orientation to the list of prohibited grounds. But by 1997 the apparent 'quasi-constitutional dimension' of the Act came to be revisited, with some controversy. The Human Rights Commission was by then engrossed in its assigned task of reviewing all laws and policies and practices of the government. Recognising the enormity of its task, it implemented a process whereby government departments were asked to do a 'self-review' of their policies and laws for Human Rights Act-consistency, reporting the results back to the Commission. The Commission had by now adopted the title 'Consistency 2000' for the project, alluding to the apparent goal that by 1 January 2000 all New Zealand laws and policies ought to be consistent with the Human Rights Act. But the Consistency 2000 project became unpopular within the government, which announced its intention to reconsider the project. The government maintained that the main themes of inconsistency had by then been discerned: continued fine-toothed combing of the legislative and policy landscape was needless. In addition, the government wished to reconsider the way in which the Human Rights Act would operate post-2000. It suggested that the government ought not to be bound by the Human Rights Act when acting in its capacity as government – that is, when enacting law or implementing policy. It conceded that the government ought to be bound when acting in a similar capacity as a private individual; for example, as an employer or landlord.[43]

This apparent governmental back-down from the implications of the Consistency 2000 project was unpopular with the human rights community – NGOs and lobby groups – especially in the gay and disability rights sectors. By the mid-1990s the term 'human rights' had become well established in the lexicon of ordinary New Zealanders, especially in the context of appalling 'human rights abuses' perpetrated in foreign lands yet brought into our homes through graphic news reports. Against that background, a claim by one's own government for exemption from its own 'human rights' principles seemed deeply problematic. The Consistency 2000 project had been seen as a foundation for pressing the claims of gay men and lesbians, and those of disabled persons, for law reforms that would end all discriminatory practices in the public sector. In this climate the opposition parties would not agree to amending legislation removing the Human Rights Commission's statutory duty to complete the Consistency 2000 report, and the due date for the report – 31 December 1998 – came. The report, filed that day, comprised a general thematic commentary to which was added a table of identified 'instances' of conflicts between laws and policies and the Human Rights Act. The report was far from complete, the Commission having ceased to put much work into it once the government's desire to end the project was made known. However, the Report demonstrated the broad themes. One such theme was the different recognition accorded *de facto* and same-sex couples, compared to married couples, in numerous areas of law and policy. The Commission recommended that a 'comprehensive review of the legal recognition of same sex relationships be carried out'.[44]

Eventually the political wrangle over how the Human Rights Act should relate to other laws and governmental policies was resolved. Amending legislation was enacted in 2001. To appreciate the solution, and the reasons for it, background information is need on the impact of the New Zealand Bill of Rights Act 1990, which has not so far been discussed.

**The New Zealand Bill of Rights Act 1990**

Back in 1985 the then Labour government proposed a 'higher law' Bill of Rights for New Zealand, one that would be adopted by referendum and control all laws in much the same way that the United States Bill of Rights[45] and Canadian Charter controlled those countries' laws. After a period of public consultation the government accepted there was little public support for such a measure – the consensus was that New Zealand's citizenry was comfortable with contentious policy issues being resolved by elected representatives in Parliament rather than by judges. But the New Zealand Bill of Rights Act 1990 was enacted, nonetheless, as a sort of compromise. It was a statutory Bill of Rights, purporting to influence the interpretation of other legislation but not to affect its validity. In its form and wording it seemed little different from a constitutional Bill of Rights – listing a set of rights and freedoms and stating they could be subject only to such 'reasonable limits as may be demonstrably justified in a free and democratic society'.[46] But a special provision, in section 4, was added to make it clear that if legislation were found by a court to be inconsistent with the Bill of Rights, then that court had to apply it despite the inconsistency.[47]

As a sort of quid pro quo for the explicit retention of parliamentary supremacy, section 7 of the Bill of Rights introduced a procedure whereby the Attorney-General is required to bring to the attention of the House of Representatives, on introduction of a parliamentary Bill, any provision of that Bill which he or she believes is inconsistent with the Bill of Rights. This has subsequently occurred on more than 30 occasions, and at least half these occasions have concerned government-sponsored Bills. Fulfilment of this function requires, therefore, that there be a legal 'vetting' of all legislative proposals, and this is performed by a dedicated 'Bill of Rights vetting team' in the Ministry of Justice, as well as by lawyers in the Crown Law Office. In practice, the Bill of Rights vetting procedure translates into explicit requirements that the human rights dimensions of proposed legislation be considered at the policy development and drafting stages.[48]

In the early days, New Zealand judges and lawyers found the Bill of Rights somewhat perplexing. It worked tolerably well when it was police or executive-branch *conduct* that was in issue. But when rights appeared to be limited by legislation, it was far from clear what profit lay in deciding whether those limits were reasonable and thus met the Bill of Rights standards. After all, the message in section 4 was that the legislation must be duly applied whatever the court may decide. Eventually – and the *Quilter* case in 1998 on same-sex marriage,[49] discussed below, was a turning point – the logical structure of the New Zealand Bill of Rights became apparent.[50] The Bill of Rights really *did* envisage the giving of judicial opinions on whether legislation met Bill of Rights standards. Only then could a court obey the injunction, in section 6 of the Bill of Rights, to interpret other legislation consistently with those standards where possible. Indeed, even the injunction to apply legislation despite the inconsistency, if no interpretive solution was to be found, implied a prior conclusion that inconsistency existed. Thus, the New Zealand Bill of Rights envisaged judicial review leading to declarations of incompatibility, and this meant that it had obvious affinity with the United Kingdom's then newly-minted Human Rights Act 1998, wherein declarations of incompatibility were a centrepiece. In an important Bill of Rights case in late 1999 the New Zealand Court of Appeal unequivocally affirmed the responsibility of a New Zealand court to make a declaration of inconsistency if it identified a statutory provision that infringed the Bill of Rights.[51]

Returning, then, to the saga of the Human Rights Act and the Consistency 2000 project, it had become clear by 2001 that it was the Bill of Rights that should serve as the benchmark against which all New Zealand law, policy and executive action must be measured. It was seen as wrong that the Human Rights Act had been pushed into that role. That Act addressed only rights from discrimination, whereas the Bill of Rights contained not only the right of non-discrimination but also the full panoply of civil and political rights. Amending legislation in 2001 made a raft of changes to the Human Rights Act: thenceforth all complaints brought against the government to the Human Rights Commission were to be measured against the anti-discrimination provision in section 19 of the Bill of Rights. The Human Rights Review Tribunal – the first-instance forum for discrimination complaints – was expressly empowered to make a formal declaration if it found legislation inconsistent with section 19 of the Bill of Rights.[52] Such declarations, if affirmed on appeal, must be brought to the attention of Parliament by the minister responsible. The minister must also state what, if anything, it is intended to do in response. But the inconsistent legislation would remain effective and enforceable. In short, the position is much the same as under the United Kingdom's Human Rights Act 1998, which similarly permits declarations of incompatibility. But the New Zealand legislation stops short of conferring a power of executive amendment of legislation.[53]

A by-product of this saga was that, by now, political will had been generated to deal with the inconsistencies in the treatment of *de facto* and same-sex couples compared to married couples.[54] In September 2001 the government agreed in principle that neutral laws on relationships, whether married, *de facto* or same-sex, should be applied across the whole field of legislation and policy.[55] The Ministry of Justice was subsequently asked to report on the required law changes and it identified 657 provisions in New Zealand statutes that appeared to be unjustifiably discriminatory against same-sex and opposite-sex *de facto* couples.[56] The vast majority of these were subsequently amended by the Relationships (Statutory References) Act 2005 and associated legislation. This task was done as part of the legislative package that introduced civil union in

New Zealand, to which we shall come below. But, to conclude the present section on anti-discrimination law, enough has been said to show that the addition of sexual orientation into the Human Rights Act was the single biggest driver of sexual orientation equality in New Zealand. This was not only because it enabled gay men and lesbians to complain about private sector discrimination, but also because the Human Rights Act and, following the amendments described above, the New Zealand Bill of Rights were aimed at making a 'top-down' reform of New Zealand law in light of equality principles. In the field of gay rights they have largely succeeded.

It is significant to note, for example, that the reform won by litigation in other jurisdictions, particularly Canada,[57] came about in New Zealand through legislative reform in the wake of the Consistency 2000 saga just described. New Zealand's experience in this regard illustrates the truism that a human rights *culture* is the best protection of rights from infringement. True, constitutional guarantees will offer an alternative (judicial) forum for groups contending that legislatures and governments have not properly dealt with their rights claims. But no recourse to judges is required if the primary actors – legislature and executive – are perceived to act in accordance with those claims. In short, the proclamation of constitutional standards, even when proclaimed in ordinary legislation, can have a powerful impact. They become the reason for re-examination of state practice, and are an impetus for appropriate reform. Political debate takes place in the context of human rights standards that have been publicly proclaimed, even if they are ultimately not judicially enforceable.

**The Same-Sex Marriage Debate in New Zealand**

Once sexual orientation was added to the Human Rights Act 1993 and to the New Zealand Bill of Rights as a prohibited ground of discrimination it became possible to challenge the orthodox conception of marriage.[58] Such a challenge soon came. In 1997 three lesbian couples sought marriage licences, which the Registrar of Marriages refused on the grounds that the Marriage Act 1955 permitted licences for different-sex marriages only. In common with legislation in some other jurisdictions,[59] New Zealand's Marriage Act did not include any definition of 'marriage', no doubt because in 1955 the meaning was seen as so obvious as to require no definition. To the extent 'marriage' was defined anywhere, it was in the common law. The well known nineteenth century case of *Hyde v. Hyde and Woodmansee*[60] had proclaimed marriage as between one man and one woman, although having regard to the dispute in that case (validity of a polygamous marriage) it was the word 'one' rather than the words 'male' and 'female' that was important.

The three couples commenced proceedings in the High Court for a declaration that they were entitled to marriage certificates. They invoked their right under section 19 of the Bill of Rights: to be free from discrimination on all of the grounds set out in the Human Rights Act 1993, particularly sex and sexual orientation. The presiding High Court judge raced speedily to the anticipated conclusions.[61] He held that the Marriage Act anticipated different-sex unions only, that the Registrar of Marriages could not have acted other than he did, and that the plaintiffs therefore could not obtain licences and could not marry. He referred to section 4 of the New Zealand Bill of Rights: the section that says no enactment is unenforceable, ineffective or invalid solely by reason of its inconsistency with the Bill of Rights. What the judge's reasoning failed to reckon with, however, was that his reliance on section 4 might have been seen as an implicit concession that same-sex marriage was actually required to be permitted by the Bill of Rights. If same-sex marriage were *not* required, then the Marriage Act was not inconsistent with the Bill of Rights at all. In short, although the plaintiffs had lost there had been an inadvertent judicial declaration of inconsistency! Nobody noticed this at the time. The plaintiffs appealed.

In the Court of Appeal the plaintiffs' argument was advanced in a more sophisticated manner, designed to elicit an unequivocal judgment on the merits. The case was put this way: (1) nothing in the Marriage Act actually precluded same-sex marriages, and the Act could and should be read to accommodate them; (2) what needed to change, therefore, was the common law definition, to include same-sex 'marriages'; (3) the common law should be so changed, for otherwise it remained discriminatory; and (4) the Bill of Rights positively compelled such change.[62]

The change in strategy drew the Court of Appeal judges down a path they had not before taken in Bill of Rights litigation. While the plaintiffs lost their appeal, with all five judges agreeing that the Marriage Act 1955 clearly contemplated only different-sex marriage and that it would be illegitimate to read it as permitting same-sex marriages, four judicial opinions were nonetheless elicited on whether the inability of same-sex couples to marry was discriminatory. Three held it was not. For Justice Gault, the operative reasoning was that differentiation was discriminatory only if it was unjustified, and that justification may lie in 'social policy resting on community values'.[63] While somewhat Delphic, this appeared to be a similar approach to that taken in the Supreme Court of Canada by Justice La Forest, whereby legislative distinctions were acceptable so long as 'relevant' to social policy choices made in the legislature by elected representatives.[64] That approach also had affinity with the 'rational basis' scrutiny in the United States.[65] A second judge, Sir Kenneth Keith, a highly respected international lawyer, reached a similar conclusion on different grounds. For him the prohibition on discrimination in the Bill of Rights was not intended to 'reach' the question of same-sex marriage. He pointed to the progressive conferral by the legislature on same-sex couples of many of the incidents of marriage, and asserted that continuation of this process was the way in which the aspirations of same-sex couples could be fulfilled. Parliament's intention in enacting the Bill of Rights did not, he affirmed, include redefining marriage itself. Court President Richardson agreed with both these judges.

Justice Thomas dissented on this point, holding that the different-sex definition of marriage was indeed discriminatory and ought to be changed. Anticipating much that was to come in the later Canadian[66] and Massachusetts[67] cases, Justice Thomas concluded that the essence of marriage was not procreation but commitment, intimacy and financial interdependence. Once capacity for procreation was excluded as an essential feature of marriage, the limiting of marriage eligibility to different-sex couples was wrong because it treated same-sex couples as less worthy of concern and respect. Justice Thomas' judgment was the first, and remains the only, judgment in New Zealand to explore in any detail the legal test for what counts as discrimination under section 19 of the Bill of Rights.

The fifth judge, Justice Tipping, only went as far as to say that the Marriage Act clearly contemplated different-sex marriage and that it was thus not necessary to decide whether it was, as a result, discriminatory. Overall, then, a 5–0 loss for the plaintiffs, but only a 3–1 loss on the ultimate question whether the lack of ability for same-sex couples to marry was discriminatory. Gaining the support of Justice Thomas for same-sex marriage was significant. His was the first judicial declaration of inconsistency in New Zealand, albeit in a dissenting opinion.[68]

No appeal was brought by the *Quilter* plaintiffs, but four of them took their complaint to the Human Rights Committee of the United Nations under the Optional Protocol to the ICCPR. In *Joslin v. New Zealand*[69] the Committee delivered its views, rejecting the complaint on the basis that the ICCPR's affirmation in article 23 of the right to marry envisaged different-sex marriages only. The plaintiffs therefore lost for the same reasons as they had in the New Zealand courts: the ICCPR (like New Zealand's Marriage Act) affirmed a heterosexual conception of marriage. On that basis the true merits of the question were not reached in *Joslin*.

**Civil Unions**

Litigation did not produce recognition of same-sex marriage in New Zealand, but the legislature has since enacted a civil union regime. Introduced into Parliament in June 2004 on a government-sponsored Bill, members of Parliament were allowed to exercise conscience votes. Public opinion on the Bill was divided, but the tone of public debate was more measured and respectful than in the era of decriminalisation, 1985–86. The passage of 20 years was noticeable. And, needless to say, the fact that it was a civil union proposal rather than a Bill for same-sex marriage was significant. Opponents of civil union took the position that civil union was tantamount to marriage and was thus objectionable. For a majority of citizens, it seemed, this was not persuasive: opinion polls indicated a comfortable majority in favour of civil union. Amongst those opposed to the Civil Union Bill the prevalent ground of opposition remained, of course, a morality-based rejection of the legitimacy of homosexuality. A smaller set of opponents took a different view: that the Bill was objectionable because it did not unequivocally extend the status of marriage to same-sex couples. But the 'marriage or nothing' viewpoint was a minority one and the Civil Union Act 2004 was enacted in December 2004 by a majority of 65 to 55 votes. It allows any couple, same-sex or different-sex, to enter into a civil union.[70] A registrar or civil union celebrant is required to solemnise the union.[71] They may be dissolved in accordance with the same general procedures as for marriage.[72] Persons in a marriage can convert the marriage to a civil union, and a different-sex civil union can be converted into a marriage.[73] The Relationships (Statutory References) Bill accompanied the Civil Union Bill through Parliament and, though the former was enacted a few months after the latter, their combined effect is now to remove most of the discriminatory distinctions between marriages and same-sex or *de facto* couples. The expressions 'civil union' and 'civil union partner' are introduced into other relevant legislation alongside references to marriage and *de facto* partner, where appropriate. Some differences between married couples and civil union partnerships remain, however. In particular, differences continue to subsist in relation to adoption of children: while there is no restriction on individuals seeking adoption orders in respect of a child, the ability of a couple to seek a joint adoption order is limited to couples who are 'spouses'.[74]

It is conceivable that the inability of same-sex couples to marry could again be litigated. While the *Quilter* case was still recent, it has to be said that it was unevenly decided, with differing views amongst the judges as to how important it really was to explore the overall merits of the question (the concept of judicial declarations of inconsistency had not then been articulated). In 1998 the most telling feature against the plaintiffs was that the Marriage Act 1955 simply did not contemplate same-sex marriage. In 2006 the exclusion of same-sex marriage would be the very starting point of a given case, with the critical question being whether the Marriage Act is thereby invidiously discriminatory. A judicial declaration of inconsistency could be sought, for such moral suasion as that may then bring to bear on Parliament. No claim of this type has yet been brought for several possible reasons. Since the *Quilter* case there has been reform to the New Zealand court structure: appeals to the Judicial Committee of the Privy Council in London were abolished with effect from July 2004, with the 'Supreme Court of New Zealand' established to serve as the nation's highest court in lieu.[75] Given that the *Quilter* case was a decision of the New Zealand Court of Appeal, the new Supreme Court of New Zealand would in no sense be bound by it. But the founding members of the Supreme Court (which comprises five judges) were the five most senior judges of the Court of Appeal, and this included three of the five judges who decided *Quilter*.[76] No different result could have been expected. But two of those judges retired in late 2005 and by February 2007 only one *Quilter* judge remains on the Supreme Court. Re-litigation of the same-sex marriage question is therefore a distinct possibility.

### The Hate Speech Debate

Between decriminalisation in 1986 and the introduction of civil union in 2004, the single biggest controversy concerning the legitimacy of homosexuality swirled around the subject of 'hate speech'. The issue came to prominence in an unusual way, through censorship law.

The story begins with the Films, Videos and Publications Classification Act 1993, which wrought a major reform of censorship law ostensibly based on the 'harm' principle as opposed to older notions of morality. The Act revolves around the concept of 'objectionable publications'.[77] It states (in words that were later to become crucial in litigation) that a publication is objectionable if it deals with matters 'such as sex, horror, crime, cruelty or violence in such a manner that the availability of the publication is likely to be injurious to the public good'.[78] There then follows a list of various factors to which the censorship body either must, or may, have regard when deciding if a publication is objectionable.[79] Section 3(3)(e) of the Act states that '[i]n determining, for the purposes of this Act, whether or not any publication ... is objectionable ... particular weight shall be given to the extent and degree to which, and the manner in which, the publication represents (whether directly or by implication) that members of any particular class of the public are inherently inferior to other members of the public by reason of any characteristic of members of that class, being a characteristic that is a prohibited ground of discrimination by reason of section 21(1) of the Human Rights Act 1993.'

In 1997 a gay rights advocacy group known as the Human Rights Action Group referred to the Office of Film and Literature Classification two United States-made videos: 'AIDS: What You Haven't Been Told' and 'Gay Rights/Special Rights: Inside the Homosexual Agenda'. The message of the first video was that the gay rights lobby had captured United States public policy on AIDS when the better response to the crisis (the video was made in 1989) was the counselling of sexual abstinence. The 'Gay Rights/Special Rights' video was essentially a sustained critique of the idea that sexual orientation be added to the list of prohibited grounds of discrimination in the United States. It came from the era of *Romer v. Evans*,[80] the United States Supreme Court case in which

Colorado's citizen-initiated constitutional amendment precluding the banning of sexual orientation discrimination in Colorado was held unconstitutional.

The Office of Film and Literature Classification ruled that the two videos should be classified as 'restricted', which meant they were objectionable except in the hands of persons aged 18 years or above. The Human Rights Action Group was dissatisfied with this ruling and appealed it to the Film and Literature Board of Review. The Board held the videos to be 'objectionable', meaning that they were effectively banned (it being an offence to possess objectionable material).[81] The Board relied on the section quoted above, holding that the videos depicted gay men and lesbians as 'inherently inferior'. Amongst its reasons, the Board pointed to material that it deemed inaccurate, such as assertions of condom failure and criticisms of the 'safe sex' message being delivered in the US by public health authorities. But its main objection was to the tone of the videos, which essentially carried a conservative or fundamentalist Christian objection to the legitimacy of homosexuality. The Board was satisfied that any concern about the inroad into freedom of expression was met by recognising that the censorship regime existed to protect the equally important right of a lesbian or gay man to equality and freedom from discrimination. It rested that conclusion on the viewpoints associated with critical race theory in the North American jurisdictions.[82]

The importer of the videos appealed these censorship decisions to the High Court and ultimately (and successfully) to the Court of Appeal.[83] First, ruled the Court of Appeal, the censorship legislation was restricted to publications that depicted matters 'such as' sex, horror and so forth. But, the court pointed out, there was no sex at all in the videos: they simply made assertions of opinion about homosexuality. Nor could it be said that they involved any matters 'such as' sex. The Board's error, then, was to assume a free-ranging censorship power over any material that ascribed inferiority to sexual minorities, regardless of whether or not that material contained sex, horror, crime, cruelty or violence. In short, the court affirmed that censorship law was essentially about sex and the like, and not about matters of opinion or attitude. The Court of Appeal also accepted the appellant's submission that the Board was wrong in holding that the right against discrimination trumped the freedom of expression. The Board ought to have had regard to the video importer's freedom of expression when determining whether or not the availability of the videos was injurious to the public good.

The Court of Appeal decision in the case landed on the front pages of Auckland's daily newspapers and led to considerable debate throughout the country.[84] Some considered that the video importers had won on a technicality. Others considered, quite the reverse, that the decision had closed a dangerous loophole that the Film and Literature Board of Review were beginning to exploit – censoring ideas and viewpoints beyond the traditional realms of sexual prurience and violence. The debate prompted a parliamentary committee to undertake two separate inquiries. First, in 2001, the Government Administration Committee undertook an inquiry into whether the Court of Appeal decision ought to be overturned by legislation. The Office of Film and Literature Classification claimed that the court's interpretation of 'matters such as sex' was problematic: if 'sex' must exist in a publication for it to be labelled 'objectionable', what about images of naked persons not engaged in sex? What about naked children and child pornography? The Government Administration Committee was persuaded by this and argued vigorously for a statutory amendment to remove any requirement that a publication be about any particular matter – be it sex, horror or anything else – before it became amenable to censorship. In particular, it believed that the amendment would allow videos such as the ones in the *Videos Case* to be banned.[85] The government's response was to acknowledge the underlying concern about 'hate speech', but to question whether it was 'an appropriate matter for censorship or [instead for] human rights reform'.[86] (The 'nudity is not sex' point was dealt with sometime later, in 2005, by way of an amendment that expressly included nudity as a matter for censorship.)[87] Subsequently the Government Administration Committee announced a second inquiry, an 'Inquiry into Hate Speech', and called for public submissions.[88] Many submissions were made, and public hearings held in early 2005, but the Committee has not reported back. With a parliamentary election forthcoming in October 2005, any further steps are up to the successor committee in the new Parliament.

Support for a 'hate speech' law for the protection of religious and sexual minorities has been far from unanimous. Many find difficulty in preserving a freedom to make controversial and even offensive statements in the face of 'hate speech' laws which necessarily cannot be worded with precision and the enforcement of which will be left to the discretion of police or, more likely, the Human Rights Commission. The debate has not, however, been intense: this may be a field where the passage of time makes a 'hate speech' law less vigorously sought than in the past, partly because general attitudinal changes in society have eroded the perceived need for it. As a general matter, and over time, freedom of expression is equality's ally rather than its opponent.[89]

In the fields of radio and television broadcasting, control of offensive and denigrating speech is accomplished through developing and enforcing 'broadcasting standards'. The Broadcasting Act 1989 constituted a Broadcasting Tribunal that hears complaints under various codes of practice. There are different codes for different genres of broadcasting. The Free-to-Air Television Code of Broadcasting Practice includes, for example, a 'guideline' which requires that broadcasters avoid portraying persons in a 'manner that encourages denigration of, or discrimination against, sections of the community on account of sex, sexual orientation, race, age disability or occupational status'.[90] There have been a number of decisions premised on the sexual orientation ground. A community television station aired a 'Voice of Islam' programme that was extremely condemnatory of homosexual persons, saying for example that the Islamic position on homosexuality was 'death'. The station was ordered to broadcast the upholding of the complaint, and an apology.[91] In another decision the Tribunal dismissed a complaint about an American Christian religious programme, holding that the viewpoint expressed – that homosexual relations were immoral and wrong – was a religiously-derived opinion which the speaker (and broadcaster) was permitted to express. It did not reach the threshold of denigration, and was not an 'incitement to hatred' as argued by the complainant.[92] These cases do turn on their facts.

These codes of practice are but a part of a community consciousness that has emerged, where offensive remarks about persons on account of race, religion or sexual orientation are generally regarded as unacceptable. The same standards are likely to be advanced through professional codes of conduct, as well as school and university codes of conduct. While there will always be departures from these standards, the position has been reached where the standards themselves are generally in place. In the case of the teaching profession, for example, it is unthinkable that homosexuality would be seen as problematic: the anti-discrimination provisions in the Human Rights Act inform the standards for teacher registration and education.[93]

## Sexual Orientation and Religion

Over the last two decades a debate has been simmering in mainstream Christian denominations over the ordination of clergymen and pastors who are gay. While this debate need not involve the state and its laws, the introduction of sexual orientation into the list of prohibited grounds in 1993 added a new dimension. First, the fact that the state had itself frowned upon sexual orientation discrimination added some support to those who took the view that churches were out of step. But second, and more significantly, the wording of the Human Rights Act led some to contend that the Act positively *required* changes in those religious institutions who do not allow gay and lesbian leaders. The true position was a little more complex. Essentially, the Human Rights Act seeks to exempt religious institutions from its operation, but does so in a manner that has produced an apparently unintended effect: it has required some denominations to clearly articulate their position. So religious institutions are not entirely unaffected. The following explains why.

The Human Rights Act prohibits discrimination in employment *and* in the conferral of 'authorisations' or 'qualifications' that facilitate a profession or calling.[94] An exemption is provided for religious institutions, in obvious recognition of the value of institutional religious freedom as well as the separation of church and state.[95] But the wording of the exemption is problematic – or perhaps it was just carefully crafted! The exemption is available where an authorisation or qualification is needed for engagement in organised religion 'and is limited to one sex or to persons of that religious belief so as to comply with the doctrines, rules or established customs of that religion'.[96] The intent seems clear: a religious institution that has a definite position on the matter of gay clergymen or pastors is allowed to maintain that position without falling afoul of the Human Rights Act. The difficulty lies in applying the exemption. First, one has to transmute the sexual orientation issue into a *religious* difference – after all, a gay candidate is not so much turned down because he or she is gay, it is more likely to be because he or she has a religious belief that it is acceptable to be a gay minister. That belief will clash with the belief of the institution, and so the exemption will apply – but only so long as the refusal is based on doctrines, rules or established customs.

This leads to the second complication. Not all mainstream denominations find it easy to point to doctrines, rules or established customs on the subject of ordaining gay candidates. Then there is debate about the meaning of the silence: if nothing is said does it mean that ordaining gay priests is permitted, or that it is precluded? Protagonists on either side of the debate then tend to deduce their positions from more general doctrines, rules or established customs, including those about scriptural interpretation and authority. From the point of view of the Human Rights Commission it is problematic as it is unclear as to what a church's doctrines, rules or established customs actually are. Simply asking the church's highest authority would not resolve the matter when the denomination itself is wracked by internal debate over whether it has a position on the issue, and if it has one what that position is.[97] The notion of 'established customs' suggests that unwritten practices may suffice, but the record shows that some denominations will not reach internal agreement about their customs. The matter has recently come to the fore within the Presbyterian Church of New Zealand whose Judicial Commission ruled in 2003, in the context of the particular gay candidate's contested application for ministry training, that as the Church had no specific doctrines, rules or established customs on the subject it was required to permit the application to proceed.[98] Subsequently, at its General Assembly in 2004, the Church countermanded that decision by resolving that no one 'involved in a sexual relationship outside of faithful marriage between a man and a woman' can be a leader.[99] This leaves future debate to take place within the Church; its articulation of a rule has saved the matter from proceeding as a Human Rights Act complaint. Internal resolution of these conflicts does seem best, for it would be difficult for the Human Rights Commission to impose an adverse judgment on an unwilling religious denomination. The Commission, no doubt recognising this, has trod warily in this area. However, the latent effect of the Human Rights Act has been to prompt a clear statement of position by a prominent religious denomination. Some might see this as problematic: some religious denominations have made an art out of keeping their position on such matters benignly vague, for fear of needlessly excluding people. Seen in this way, the need to declare a position in response to a Human Rights Act complaint can lead to controversy and potential schism. It seems to be an unintended effect of the legislation; the drafters appear to have assumed that it would be simple to determine a religious institution's position on ordaining gay leaders.

## Conclusion: Human Rights, Public Values, Changing Times

It has been said that, in a secular age, Bills of Rights and human rights instruments come to serve as a statement of secular ethics.[100] While traditionally seen as negative prohibitions – what governments ought not to do to their citizenry – much attention is now focused on the 'horizontal' impact of human rights instruments and how they might be brought to bear on law and policy affecting private relations.[101] But sexual orientation discrimination in New Zealand is, by the combination of the Bill of Rights and Human Rights Acts, explicitly made unlawful in both public and private spheres (at least in the realms of employment, goods and services, accommodation and related areas). It is highly likely, but not easy to prove, that this has had an educative and mind-changing effect on New Zealanders. One field in which there is a reasonably direct link between the statement of public values and the formation of opinions is, of course, public education. It is now well recognised that schools must offer their students a safe educational environment, in which students do not suffer disadvantage (by, for example, bullying) on account of a characteristic that is listed in the Human Rights Act as a prohibited ground of discrimination.[102] Typically schools would have policies that affirm their intention to comply with human rights legislation, and they will be alert to negative stereotyping and signs of discrimination. It is, at the present time, unthinkable that a teacher would be regarded as unemployable on account of the ascription of homosexuality, as occurred in the case of Mr Balfour.

Was it the legal changes described in this paper that brought about this shift in attitudes and perceptions? Or were those legal changes merely a result of that shift? Evidence appears to point to the latter proposition, as Mr Balfour re-entered the teaching profession in 1986, well before sexual orientation discrimination was legally prohibited and even before decriminalisation.[103] The winds of change that brought fresh teaching employment to Mr Balfour were, in all probability, the very winds that led to decriminalisation and, subsequently, to majority support for anti-discrimination legislation. However, decriminalisation and especially anti-discrimination legislation served, as this essay has suggested, as a platform for further and more detailed reforms in the sphere of relationship recognition. In that sense, anti-discrimination law has done much of its work already. The grand prize of sexual orientation equality has been, in other western nations, the opening up of marriage to same-sex couples. In the wake of the recent Civil Union Act there is little or no pressure for that sort of reform in New Zealand and one senses that no approach will be made to the courts unless it is judged that the time is right, by which time judicial assistance by way of a declaration is likely to be less important in any case. The New Zealand record has been one of legislative rather than judicial change, and public opinion has broadly supported change at each step on the path. Outside the sphere of relationship recognition, the next battleground seems likely to be fought in the arena of freedom of expression, and will concern whether the state ought to enact laws that penalise expressions of adverse opinion about the morality of homosexuality. The merits of that controversy are a topic for another, one hopes long-distant, day. Public opinion appears to be against speech-restrictive laws. Indeed, if the story just told has any significance, it is that freedom of expression makes it possible for people's minds to be changed, laws to be changed, and times to change.

## Notes

1. Balfour's ability to request copies of information on a personal file came about as a result of passage of the Official Information Act 1981. This important legislation heralded a new era governed by the principle that information held by governmental agencies was to be made available to those who requested it, unless a statutory exception applied.
2. Qualified privilege operates as a defence to an action in defamation on occasions where the allegedly defamatory statement was made by a person who had an interest or a duty – whether legal, social or moral – to make that statement to the person to whom it is made, and the person to whom it was made had a corresponding interest or duty to receive it (*Adam v. Ward* [1917] AC 309, 344 per Lord Atkinson). The defence differs from absolute privilege insofar as it can be defeated on proof of malice.
3. *Balfour v. Attorney-General* (22 May 1989), unreported, High Court of New Zealand, Wellington, Grieg J, CP 266–86.
4. *Balfour v. Attorney-General* [1991] 1 NZLR 519 (CA). The Attorney-General instead of the Department of Education was the named defendant because the latter had no formal legal capacity to sue or be sued.
5. *Sutherland Shire Council v. Heyman* (1985) 60 ALR 1.
6. *Anns v. Merton London Borough Council* [1978] AC 728.
7. *Balfour v. Attorney-General* (CA) (note 4) p.522.
8. Ibid. p.529.
9. Ibid. p.524.
10. While the Homosexual Law Reform Act 1986 became law on 11 July 1986, it was expressed to take effect 28 days later. So the true date of the reform was 8 August 1986.
11. The provisions that criminalised homosexual acts between consenting males were contained in sections 140 to 142 of the Crimes Act 1961.
12. *Special Committee on Moral Delinquency in Children and Adolescents (Mazengarb Report)* (Wellington: Government Printer 1954).
13. R. Yska, *All Shook Up: The Flash Bodgie and the Rise of the New Zealand Teenager in the Fifties* (Auckland: Penguin 1993), p.82, cited in L. Guy, *Worlds in Collision: The Gay Debate in New Zealand, 1960–1986* (Wellington: Victoria University Press 2002), p.31. I record here my general indebtedness to the latter work throughout the brief account of the history of decriminalisation in New Zealand given in this section.
14. A. Kinsey, *Sexual Behavior in the Human Male* (Philadelphia: W. B. Saunders & Co 1948).
15. Sir John Wolfenden, *Report of the Committee on Homosexual Offences and Prostitution* (London: Her Majesty's Stationery Office 1957).
16. The Wolfenden Report sparked a famous jurisprudential debate between Patrick Devlin and Herbert Hart, which became a staple in New Zealand legal education as elsewhere in the world. Generations of law students were influenced. See P. Devlin, *The Enforcement of Morals* (London: Oxford University Press 1959), and H. Hart, *Law Liberty and Morality* (Stanford, CA: Stanford University Press 1963).

17. A prominent lawyer and committee member of NZHRLS, D. L. Mathieson, wrote in the New Zealand *Listener* magazine in 1969, urging decriminalisation ('Homosexuals and the Law', *Listener*, Vol.61, 1 August 1969, p.1555), and again in the *New Zealand Law Journal* in 1972 that homosexual acts harmed no-one, while criminalisation of them wrought substantial harm ('Homosexual Acts – Why the Law Must be Changed', *New Zealand Law Journal* (1972), pp.1–2). This prompted a reply (J. S. O'Neill, 'Homosexual Acts – Why the Law Must Not be Changed', *New Zealand Law Journal* (1972), pp.241–2) and response (D. L. Mathieson, 'Homosexual Law Reform: A Reply to Mr O'Neill', *New Zealand Law Journal* (1972), pp.322–3).
18. Guy (note 13) p.82.
19. Ibid.
20. Ibid. pp.83–4.
21. See Crimes (Amendment) Act 1984, which inserted section 78K into the Crimes Act 1900 (NSW).
22. The New Zealand Human Rights Commission, established by statute in 1977 to promote human rights and receive complaints of discrimination on grounds of sex, marital status, race, colour, national origin, and religious and ethical belief, contributed to the debate by the release of a discussion paper prepared by University of Auckland legal academic William C. Hodge, 'Homosexual Law Reform: Questions and Answers concerning the Legality of Homosexual Male conduct in New Zealand' (Auckland: Human Rights Commission 1985) and a public statement: 'Public Statement on the Homosexual Law Reform Bill' (Auckland: Human Rights Commission 1985).
23. See text on pp.101–2 of this paper (under 'Sexual Orientation and Religion').
24. A representative sample is C. James Bacon (ed.), *The Social Effects of Homosexuality in New Zealand* (Christchurch: Coalition of Concerned Citizens 1985).
25. The Act repealed section 140 of the Crimes Act 1961 replacing it with new sections 140 and 140A. Sections 141 and 142 were repealed and replaced and s.146 was repealed. Section 147(2) was amended, with the term 'woman' replaced by 'person'.
26. *Re Drummond Wren* [1945] OR 778 (Ont SC).
27. *Shelley v. Kraemer* 334 US 1 (1948).
28. International Convention for the Elimination of All Forms of Racial Discrimination, GA res 2106 (XX), Annex 20 UN GAOR Supp (No 14) at 47, UN Doc A/6014 (1966), 660 UNTS 195, entry into force 4 January 1969 in accordance with article 19, ratified in New Zealand 22 December 1972.
29. Sections 3 to 8 of the Race Relations Act 1971, now repealed and replaced by the Human Rights Act 1993.
30. Race Relations Act 1971, section 25, repealed and replaced by Human Rights Act 1993, section 131.
31. Originally section 9A of the Race Relations Act 1971, now section 61 of the Human Rights Act 1993. This, as noted in the text, is a 'civil' matter, for which the publisher of impugned statements may be held liable by proceedings taken before the Human Rights Review Tribunal, which has the power to impose an award of damages: see section 92I of the Human Rights Act 1993. It is not a criminal offence.
32. International Covenant on Civil and Political Rights, GA Res 2200A (XXI), 21 UN GAOR Supp (No 16) at 52, UN Doc A/6316 (1966) 999 UNTS 171, entry into force 23 March 1976, ratified in New Zealand 28 December 1978.
33. Human Rights Commission Act 1977, sections 15, 22–4, repealed and replaced by the Human Rights Act 1993.
34. The grounds of discrimination are found in section 21(1) paragraphs (a) to (m); the grounds added in 1993 for the first time are in paragraphs (i) to (m).
35. New Zealand Human Rights Commission, *Discrimination on the Ground of Sexual Orientation: A Discussion Paper* (Auckland: Human Rights Commission 1992).
36. Human Rights Act 1993, s.28(1)(h)(vii).
37. See R. Paterson, '"Softly, Softly": New Zealand Law Responds to AIDS', in P. Davis (ed.), *Intimate Details and Vital Statistics: AIDS, Sexuality and the Social Order in New Zealand* (Auckland: Auckland University Press 1994).
38. The 'complaints jurisdiction' denotes the Commission's function of receiving and dealing with individual complaints of discrimination in employment, accommodation goods and services, and so on.
39. Human Rights Act 1993, section 5(1), paras (a) to (h).
40. Human Rights Act 1993, s.5(1) paras.(i), (j), and (k).
41. *Winnipeg School Division No. 1 v. Craton* [1985] 2 SCR 150.
42. Canadian Charter of Rights and Freedoms, Part I of the Constitution Act 1982; Schedule B to Canada Act 1982 (UK).

43. For an account and discussion of the Consistency 2000 project, see P. Rishworth, 'Human Rights', *New Zealand Law Review* (2001), pp.217–38.
44. Human Rights Commission, *Report to the Minister of Justice pursuant to section 5(1)(k) of the Human Rights Act 1993 ('Consistency 2000')*, 31 December 1998, p.70.
45. Constitution of the United States of America, Amendments I to X.
46. New Zealand Bill of Rights Act 1990, s.5.
47. For a summary of the history of the enactment of the New Zealand Bill of Rights Act 1990, see P. Rishworth, 'The Birth and Rebirth of the Bill of Rights', in G. Huscroft and P. Rishworth, *Rights and Freedom* (Wellington: Brookers 1995), pp.1–35.
48. See, for a general discussion of section 7 of the Bill of Rights and its impact, P. Rishworth, G. Huscroft, S. Optican and R. Mahoney, *The New Zealand Bill of Rights* (Oxford: Oxford University Press 2003) ch. 6.
49. *Quilter v. Attorney-General* [1998] 1 NZLR 523 (NZCA).
50. The *Quilter* case and its implications for the idea of declaring a statute's incompatibility with the Bill of Rights are explored in P. Rishworth, 'Reflections on the Bill of Rights after *Quilter v Attorney-General*', *New Zealand Law Review*, Vol.1 (1998), pp.683–99.
51. *Moonen v. Film and Literature Board of Review* [2000] 2 NZLR 9.
52. The effect of this reform is that the Human Rights Act now relates almost entirely to private sector discrimination. For public sector discrimination, only that arising out of employment practices remains covered by the substantive provisions of the Human Rights Act. However, procedural provisions apply (as to mediation, with reference of unmediated complaints to the Office of Human Rights Proceedings for possible litigation before the Human Rights Review Tribunal).
53. The key provisions in the Human Rights Act 1993, introduced by the 2001 amendment, are sections 92J and 92K, empowering declarations of inconsistency and setting out the consequences of such a declaration.
54. In 2001 there had been a series of 'section 7 reports' by the Attorney-General advising that in her view proposed legislation dealing with social security benefits was inconsistent with the anti-discrimination right in the New Zealand Bill of Rights because it treated same-sex couples, in certain cases, less favourably than opposite-sex couples. In some instances there was financial advantage for lesbian and gay couples, since they were treated as two individuals rather than as a married or *de facto* couple. But the stigmatising effect of exclusion was pointed to by the Attorney-General. For discussion see Rishworth *et al.* (note 48) p.213. See also *Report of the Attorney-General under the New Zealand Bill of Rights Act 1990 on the War Pensions Amendment Bill (No 2) 2001* (Wellington: House of Representatives 2001), E.63. The relevant legislation in each case was enacted by Parliament despite the noted inconsistency. In each case the Attorney-General reported also that the whole subject of same sex couples was under review and that a comprehensive reform was in the offing, albeit that this did not excuse the inconsistency in the bill on which she was reporting.
55. Cabinet Policy Committee Minutes, September 2001, CABMin(01)27/14.
56. Cabinet Policy Committee Minutes, 10 November 2003, CABMin(03)29/10.
57. See, e.g., *M. & H. v. Attorney-General of Ontario* [1999] 2 SCR 3, which held that the Ontario Family Law Act was constitutionally under-inclusive in that it did not permit access by same-sex couples to the legislative regime for dealing with the breakdown of relationships. In New Zealand that situation was resolved by a 2001 amendment to the Matrimonial Property Act 1976, which renamed the legislation as the Property (Relationships) Act 1976 and extended it to cover same-sex relationships as well as *de facto* relationships (irrespective of the genders of the partners).
58. The case could have been brought as far back as 1977, when the Human Rights Commission Act 1977 first prohibited sex discrimination. After all, if two persons of the same sex cannot marry each other it is the *sex* of one of them, and not their sexual orientation, that is the operative factor. That said, it was beyond argument that courts in New Zealand would never have entertained such a claim, and the sex discrimination complaint would have been easily, if superficially, answered: both sexes are treated the same because same-sex marriage is precluded for both men and women.
59. In Australia and Canada, the different-sex 'requirement', as in New Zealand, was imposed not by legislation but by common law.
60. (1866) 1 L R P & D 130.
61. *Quilter v. Attorney-General* [1996] NZFLR 481.
62. *Quilter v. Attorney-General* [1998] 1 NZLR 523.
63. Ibid. p.527.

64. See the general discussion on the approach of the Supreme Court of Canada to equality cases by Justice Binnie, 'Equality Rights in Canada', in G. Huscroft and P. Rishworth, *Litigating Rights: Perspectives from International and Domestic Law* (Oxford: Hart Publishing 2002), p.101.
65. This refers to the principle that, to comply with the Equal Protection Clause in the Fourteenth Amendment to the United States Constitution, distinctions drawn in legislation need only have a rational basis unless they involve distinctions of race or sex, in which case the distinctions are subjected to heightened or strict scrutiny. See generally J. Nowak and R. Rotunda, *Constitutional Law* (St Paul: West Publishing 1995), 14.3.
66. *Halpern v. Attorney-General (Ontario)* (2003) 65 OR (3d) 161 (Ont CA).
67. *Goodridge v. Department of Public Health* 440 Mass 309 (2003).
68. This can be debated. At one point in his judgment Justice Thomas appeared to concede that the discrimination he found would be cured by the enactment of a civil union regime. If that were so, then the Marriage Act 1955 was not itself inconsistent with the Bill of Rights for excluding same-sex couples. The passage is at page 548.
69. Comm 902/1999, 30 July 2002.
70. Section 4(1).
71. Sections 14 and 15.
72. Section 44, providing for amendments to the Family Proceedings Act 1980, so as to permit dissolutions of civil unions as well as marriages.
73. Section 18.
74. Adoption Act 1955, s.3.
75. See the Supreme Court Act 2003, s.5 (establishing the Supreme Court of New Zealand) and s.42 (ending appeals to the Judicial Committee of the Privy Council).
76. Further, the three judges elevated to the Supreme Court included two (Justices Gault and Keith) who held in *Quilter* that the orthodox definition of marriage was not discriminatory. The third judge to be elevated, Justice Tipping, did not examine the question and his views were thus unknown. Justice Thomas had retired by 2004.
77. Section 3.
78. Section 3(1).
79. Sections 3(2) to (4) and Section 4.
80. 517 US 620 (1996).
81. Re. Gay Rights/Special Rights: Inside the Homosexual Agenda (1997) 4 HRNZ 422.
82. See the seminal article by Mari Matsuda, 'Public Response to Racist Speech: Considering the Victim's Story', *Michigan Law Review*, Vol.87 (1989), pp.2320–81 was cited. Critical race theory is a school of legal and social philosophy that points to, and proposes the displacement of, dominant narratives in society by alternative visions that reflect the reality of individual or minority group perspectives. So, for example, the value of 'free speech' may be critiqued for its implicit protection of established social hierarchies, and its capacity for subordinating racial (and other) minorities who may not in practice have equal access to the benefits of free speech.
83. *Living Word Distributors Ltd v. Human Rights Action Group* [2000] 3 NZLR 570. The author discloses that he was counsel for Living Word.
84. 'Court Okays Anti-Gay Videos', *The New Zealand Herald*, 1 September 2000, p.1.
85. *Government Administration Committee Report on Its Inquiry into the Operation of the Films, Videos and Publications Classification Act 1993 and Related Issues*, March 2003, p.23.
86. *Government Response to Government Administration Committee Report on Its Inquiry into the Operation of the Films, Videos and Publications Classification Act 1993 and Related Issues*, para.[8].
87. See new section 3 (1A) and (1B) of the Films Videos and Publications Act introduced by amendment in 2005.
88. Media Release, Government Administration Committee, 5 August 2004.
89. This viewpoint was vigorously pressed by Professor Nadine Strossen of the American Civil Liberties Union when she addressed a New Zealand audience. Her remarks may be found in her 'Liberty and Equality: Complementary, Not Competing, Constitutional Commitments' in *Litigating Rights* (note 64) pp.149–85.
90. Free-to-air Television Code of Broadcasting Practice, reg. 6 g.
91. Broadcasting Standards Authority, Decision No 2004-001, 26 February 2004.
92. Broadcasting Standards Authority, Decision No 2004-128, 21 December 2004.

93. An unexplored question in respect of New Zealand is whether a strident disposition against the legitimacy of homosexual acts would be a disqualifying factor, for an individual or a teacher training institution. No question such as that involved in *British Columbia College of Teachers v. Trinity Western University* [2001] 1 SCR 772 has arisen in New Zealand (whether the College of Teachers could withhold certification of teacher training programme by the University on the grounds that students at that University were asked to promise to abstain from same-sex sexual activity).
94. Human Rights Act 1993, s.38.
95. Ibid. s.39.
96. Human Rights Act 1993, Section 39.
97. While a number of complaints to the Human Rights Commission have been made in the context of church employment and ordination, no formal ruling has yet been called for. A related debate is whether church ministers are 'employed' for the purposes of the part of the Act that deals with employment discrimination. Although there is an extended definition of 'employment' in section 2 of the Human Rights Act, the better view is that it does not extend to clergy where their position is held by a court to constitute a 'calling' or an appointment to an office. A Methodist minister's appointment was so classified by the Court of Appeal in *Mabon v. Methodist Church of New Zealand* [1998] 3 NZLR 513 (following United Kingdom cases including *Davies v. Presbyterian Church of Wales* [1986] 1 All ER 705).
98. Decision of the Judicial Commission, Presbyterian Church of Aotearoa New Zealand, October 2003.
99. Minutes of the 2004 General Assembly of the Presbyterian Church of Aotearoa New Zealand, Session 10, decision 69, Thursday 23 September 2004. That decision was of immediate interim effect but under the Barrier Act 1697 of the Church of Scotland, cannot be enacted as legislation within the Church without the approval of a majority of Presbyteries. In 2005 a majority of Presbyteries approved the rule 'that those involved in a sexual relationship outside of faithful marriage cannot be trained, licensed, ordained or inducted for leadership within the Presbyterian Church of Aotearoa New Zealand'. This rule was affirmed at the General Assembly on 29 September 2006 by a vote of 230 votes to 124.
100. See, for example, F. Klug, 'A Bill of Rights as Secular Ethics', in R. Gordon and R. Wilmot-Smith (eds), *Human Rights in the United Kingdom* (Oxford: Oxford University Press 1996), pp.37–57.
101. The expression 'horizontal application of human rights' is used to denote the phenomenon whereby, in addition to regulating state-citizen interaction ('vertical'), human rights imperatives influence relations between citizens. See M. Hunt, 'Human Rights Review and the Public-Private Distinction', in Huscroft and Rishworth (note 64) pp.73–88.
102. Section 57 of the Human Rights Act 1993 makes it unlawful to treat students differently in a school by reason of a prohibited ground of discrimination, and it has been accepted that, in principle, the failure of a school to adequately deal with student bullying will be a breach of this section. See *D. v. J., G. and H.*, Human Rights Commission Complaints Division C250/97, reported in *Human Rights Law and Practice*, Vol.3 (1998), p.298.
103. It bears repeating here that Mr Balfour's case was that he was not a gay man and that everything said about him to that effect was untrue. One obvious change since the time of the events in Balfour's case is that now there would be no need to disavow homosexuality in order to have a case before the courts or before the Human Rights Commission. This is not meant to suggest that Mr Balfour's disavowal was untrue, only that the Human Rights Act now makes it irrelevant whether or not the ascription of a prohibited ground of discrimination is untrue. Section 21(2) provides that '[e]ach of the grounds specified in subsection (1) of this section is a prohibited ground of discrimination, for the purposes of this Act, if (a) it pertains to a person or to a relative or associate of a person; and (b) it either (i) currently exists or has in the past existed; or is suspected or assumed or believed to exist or to have existed by the person alleged to have discriminated.'

# The Same-Sex Marriage Debate in Australia

KRISTEN WALKER

## I. Introduction

Same-sex marriage[1] was, for many years, not on the legal or political agenda in Australia, either for 'defenders' of traditional marriage or for lesbian and gay rights activists. Historically, the Australian gay and lesbian communities have not indicated a great deal of interest in marriage.[2] As recently as 2001, Jenni Millbank and Wayne Morgan wrote that 'the notion of "same-sex marriage" is quite alien to Australia'.[3] Indeed, there has been much criticism of marriage from queer scholars and activists.[4] Also, in Australia, lesbian and gay rights activists have generally been successful in obtaining many (though not all) of the benefits associated with marriage through recognition of unmarried relationships (in parity with unmarried different-sex couples).[5]

Further, because marriage is an area currently regulated by the federal level of government, which has been hostile to equality claims by lesbian and gay rights activists, it was thought that seeking recognition of same-sex marriage would not be a successful strategy. In the absence of any push for recognition of same-sex marriage, there was no real need for those who oppose such unions to take action or even discuss the issue. However, following the recognition of same-sex marriage by the Canadian courts,[6] and the possibility that such marriages may be recognised in Australia under the Australian Marriage Act 1961 (Cth), there began a flurry of interest on both sides of the debate. Reflecting this change in the legal landscape, a survey of lesbians and gay men in Victoria in 2001 indicated that only 23 per cent of respondents wanted to be able to marry. By 2005 this number had almost doubled, to 45 per cent.[7] And in 2004 a new activist movement, Australian Marriage Equality, was launched to campaign for recognition of same-sex marriage.[8]

Canadian recognition of same-sex marriage followed some two years after the Netherlands became the first country in the world to recognise same-sex marriage. However, as Dutch law requires that one of the partners be a Dutch citizen or resident, it has had a limited impact on the Australian legal and political landscape.[9] Canadian marriage laws, on the other hand, contain no such restriction, thus raising the prospect of Australians travelling to Canada to marry — 'marriage tourism' — a prospect that eventuated in 2003. That year, two Australian same-sex couples travelled to Canada, married, returned to Australia and initiated proceedings in the Family Court to have their marriages recognised in Australia.[10] One was a gay male couple with no legal or social connections with Canada; the other was a lesbian couple, one of whom had legal and social connections with Canada, namely citizenship as a result of birth and extended family in Canada.

After the Family Court proceedings were initiated, the Australian federal Parliament amended the Marriage Act 1961 (Cth) so as to preclude recognition of a foreign marriage between two persons of the same sex.[11] While this swiftly terminated the legal proceedings, it did not terminate the debate that had begun in Australia on same-sex marriage. In this paper, I explore the parameters of the legal and social debate on same-sex marriage in Australia. In the next section, I outline the legal issues in relation to same-sex marriage. These range from recognition of foreign same-sex marriages to constitutional questions concerning the power of the different levels of government, state, territory and federal, to legislate in relation to same-sex marriage. In section three, I consider the political aspects of the marriage debate in Australia. In section four, I briefly consider the question of whether same-sex marriage is worth fighting for.

## II. The Legal Debate over Same-Sex Marriage

*The legal benefits of marriage*

It is important, in understanding the same-sex marriage debate in Australia, to understand the recognition of unmarried couples, as this forms the background to the debate. In Australia there has been extensive recognition of unmarried different-sex relationships at both state or territory and federal levels, starting in the 1970s. This occurred initially at state or territory level, through the enactment of legislation recognising what were known as '*de facto* marriages'.[12] Such legislation generally specified a certain time for which a different-sex couple must have lived together (usually two years) before recognition would occur.[13] Once it did occur, however, such couples were treated in a manner virtually identical to married different-sex couples (although the extent of recognition varied somewhat from state to state or territory). At federal level, recognition was ad hoc, but on the whole unmarried different-sex couples were (and still are) treated substantially in the same way as married couples.[14]

The existence of such recognition of unmarried different-sex relationships offered a relatively easy avenue for recognition of same-sex relationships. Rather than pursuing the politically and legally difficult goal of recognition of same-sex marriage, recognition of unmarried same-sex couples was sought, generally by parity with the legal position of different-sex couples. This has been achieved in all states and territories bar one (South Australia),[15] albeit in relatively recent times (the first recognition of same-sex couples being in 1994 in the Australian Capital Territory[16] and the most recent in

Tasmania in 2003),[17] thus giving same-sex couples substantially the same rights as unmarried different-sex couples and, in most states and territories, substantially the same rights as married different-sex couples.[18]

At federal level, however, there has been only limited recognition of same-sex couples. Thus, as a result of exclusion from the institution of marriage, same-sex couples suffer both material and symbolic injustice. Immigration benefits that are available to married different-sex couples, for example, are denied same-sex couples, as are benefits granted to different-sex couples under tax law and, until recently, superannuation law.[19] Further, recognition through 'domestic partner' regimes at state or territory level, while a positive step, can still produce material inequality because of the requirement that couples live together for a minimum period — a requirement that can be bypassed by different-sex couples simply by marrying. Finally, exclusion from the institution of marriage also perpetuates an important symbolic injustice: exclusion from an institution that remains important in the way in which our society recognises significant relationships reinforces the fact that lesbians and gay men are not equal members of the Australian community and sends a message about the (devalued) nature of same-sex relationships. For these reasons, recognition of same-sex marriage is sought by some in the lesbian and gay communities, and opposed by significant sectors of the community in Australia.

*Recognition of foreign marriages*

It appeared (and still appears) unlikely that there will be legislative recognition of same-sex marriage in Australia. However, once same-sex marriage began to be recognised in Canada, it was only a matter of time before Australian couples began to marry in Canada and seek recognition of their marriages at home. This was possible because of the provisions of the federal Marriage Act dealing with recognition of foreign marriages, section 88D of which provided as follows:

(1) Subject to this section, a marriage to which this Part applies shall be recognised in Australia as valid.
(2) A marriage to which this Part applies shall not be recognised as valid in accordance with subsection (1) if:
   (a) either of the parties was, at the time of the marriage, a party to a marriage with some other person and the last-mentioned marriage was, at that time, recognised in Australia as valid;
   (b) where one of the parties was, at the time of the marriage, domiciled in Australia — either of the parties was not of marriageable age within the meaning of Part II;
   (c) the parties are within a prohibited relationship within the meaning of section 23B [this section concerned consanguinity]; or
   (d) the consent of either of the parties was not a real consent for a reason set out in subparagraph 23B(1)(d)(i), (ii) or (iii).

On the face of the legislation, a marriage that was validly celebrated in another country is recognised in Australia, unless it falls within one of the listed exceptions. None of the listed exceptions mentioned same-sex marriage. Thus, on its face, a valid Canadian same-sex marriage would have been capable of recognition in Australia pursuant to the Marriage Act as it stood in 2003.

The issue, however, was not as straightforward as it seemed. There was an argument that when the Marriage Act provided for recognition of foreign marriages, the term 'marriage' included only different-sex marriage; it did not provide for recognition of same-sex marriage as such a union was not a 'marriage' within the meaning of that term in the Marriage Act. Certainly it appeared that the term 'marriage', when used in the Act to regulate the celebration of Australian marriages, contemplated different-sex marriage only.[20] However, there was scope for arguing that when it was used in Part IV of the Marriage Act, dealing with recognition of foreign marriages, the term 'marriage' needed to be interpreted in light of the Hague Convention on Celebration and Recognition of the Validity of Marriages, which Part IV was explicitly intended to implement.[21] Thus the interpretive question shifted to a question about the meaning of 'marriage' in the Convention.

On this question, the answer was unclear. At the time the Hague Convention was adopted in 1978 there was no country that recognised same-sex marriage and no immediate prospect of any country doing so. Yet the drafters of the Convention were aware of the possibility of future recognition of same-sex marriage; and it appears that they intended the term 'marriage' to be interpreted in its 'broadest, international sense'[22] and not to be confined to a Western, Judeo-Christian concept.[23] Indeed, a suggestion that the Convention be expressly limited to 'marriages between persons of different sexes' was considered and rejected by the drafters (including Australia).[24] Further, one point of the Convention was to encourage recognition between nations that might not share the same religious and cultural traditions. If the term 'marriage' in the Convention was intended to include same-sex marriage if such marriages were to be recognised in the future, then it could be argued that the term 'marriage' in Part IV of the Act, which gives effect to the Convention, must also include foreign same-sex marriage.[25]

The question, however, was never judicially resolved, as shortly after the two couples instituted proceedings seeking declarations of validity of their marriages the federal Parliament passed the Marriage Amendment Act 2004 (Cth). This amending legislation was introduced in response to the proceedings, in order to preclude recognition of foreign same-sex marriage in Australia.[26] The Marriage Amendment Act amended the Marriage Act to insert several new provisions. Section 88B(4) provided that '[t]o avoid doubt, in this Part (including section 88E) marriage has the meaning given by subsection 5(1)'. Section 5(1) defines marriage as 'the union of a man and a woman to the exclusion of all others, voluntarily entered into for life'. And, in what must surely be overkill, section 88EA provides that '[a] union solemnised in a foreign country between: (a) a man and another man; or (b) a woman and another woman; must not be recognised as a marriage in Australia'. Together, these provisions operate to preclude not only recognition of the particular foreign same-sex marriages in issue in the proceedings, but also of all Canadian, Dutch, Belgian, American (the state of Massachusetts only), Spanish, and South African same-sex marriages.

*Marriage and the Australian Constitution*

One cannot consider the legal status of same-sex marriage in Australia without adverting to the constitutional aspects of the issue. These arise as Australia is a federal system under which the federal level of government ('Commonwealth') has only enumerated legislative powers (listed principally in section 51 of the Australian Constitution and known as 'heads of power'); states and territories retain plenary legislative powers, including power over the powers allocated to the Commonwealth by section 51. If there is an inconsistency between a valid Commonwealth law and a valid state or territory law, then the Commonwealth law prevails to the extent of the inconsistency.[27]

Section 51(21) gives the Commonwealth Parliament power to make laws 'with respect to ... marriage'. This raises two questions:

- Does this head of power extend to authorising Commonwealth legislation dealing with same-sex marriage?
- Can states and territories legislate in respect of same-sex marriage?

*The Commonwealth Parliament's power over same-sex marriage.* The High Court of Australia has not been called upon to decide whether the term 'marriage' in the Constitution extends to same-sex marriage.[28] Nonetheless, there have been *obiter dicta* comments by the High Court on the meaning of marriage over the years, some potentially supporting a broad approach to the term and some supporting the 'traditional' definition of marriage. For example, in *The Queen v. L*, Justice Brennan commented that the traditional definition of marriage in *Hyde v. Hyde and Woodmansee*,[29] an English court decision in 1866, 'has been followed in this country and by this Court'.[30] In contrast, in 1908 in *Attorney-General for New South Wales v. Brewery Employees Union of New South Wales*, Justice Higgins stated that 'under the power to make laws with respect to marriage, I should say that the parliament could prescribe what unions are to be regarded as marriages'.[31] More recently, in *Re Wakim, ex parte McNally*, Justice McHugh stated that 'in 1901 "marriage" was seen as meaning a voluntary union for life between one man and one woman to the exclusion of all others. If that level of abstraction were now accepted, it would deny the Parliament of the Commonwealth the power to legislate for same sex marriages, although arguably "marriage" now means, or in the near future may mean, a voluntary union for life between two *people* to the exclusion of others'.[32] Thus, the issue remains unresolved, although I am of the view that the High Court would likely take the broader rather than the narrower view of the marriage power, in line with its general approach to the Commonwealth's legislative powers.[33]

When the topic of federal power to regulate same-sex marriage is discussed in Australia, it is often done in the context of an ongoing debate between originalists and non-originalists[34] about the appropriate way to interpret the Constitution.[35] The question of the Commonwealth Parliament's ability to use the marriage power in the Constitution (section 51(21)) to provide for same-sex marriage provides a classic (but to date hypothetical) illustration of this debate, often on the assumption that originalists would conclude that the Commonwealth Parliament has no power to provide for same-sex marriage, whereas progressivists would reach the opposite conclusion.

'Originalism' in constitutional interpretation can be broadly defined as a theory which places significant weight on foundational authority or the intention of the framers of the Constitution.[36] As such, it is distinguished from non-originalism, or progressivism, which holds that constitutional interpretation should as far as possible reflect contemporary concerns and values.[37] The term 'originalism' is an import from the United States, where there is immense and controversial literature on the subject. In Australia, the debate has been rather more muted, though recently there has been something of a resurgence of academic interest in these two interpretive approaches. I do not intend to revisit this general debate in detail here.[38] I will, however, discuss the debate in the specific context of same-sex marriage and will explain that superficial assumptions about the position of originalists and progressivists on the question of same-sex marriage are misleading. In fact originalism may support a Commonwealth power over same-sex marriage, and progressivism may well oppose such a power.

*Originalism and same-sex marriage.* At first glance, it would appear that an originalist would deny the Commonwealth Parliament power over same-sex marriage. In 1900, a legally recognised marriage encompassed only the union of a man and a woman to the exclusion of others, and there appears to be little scope for extending this to encompass same-sex marriage. Mirko Bagaric, for example, concludes that 'one can be reasonably confident that the framers did not intend for the Commonwealth's marriage power to extend to same-sex marriages'.[39]

There are two ways, however, in which an originalist may permit Commonwealth regulation of same-sex marriage. The first is by the use of the connotation/denotation distinction. The second is by focusing not on the framers' understanding of the meaning of the term 'marriage', but on their purpose in giving the Commonwealth power over marriage – that is, on the 'mischief' at which the section was aimed.

*Connotation and denotation.* Although the connotation/denotation distinction has been criticised,[40] it is still used from time to time in constitutional interpretation. Put simply, the connotation is the essential or core meaning of the term, as at 1900. This core meaning cannot change. The denotation, on the other hand, is the set of things covered by that core meaning, and this can change. From an originalist perspective, this allows the Constitution to adapt to changing circumstances without breaking with the framers' intentions.[41]

Whether the connotation/denotation distinction offers some scope for originalists to permit recognition of same-sex marriage under section 51(21) depends, as Justice McHugh noted in *Wakim*, on the level of abstraction at which one defines the connotation:

> In 1901 "marriage" was seen as meaning a voluntary union for life between one man and one woman to the exclusion of all others. If that level of abstraction were now accepted, it would deny the Parliament of the Commonwealth the power to legislate for same sex marriage, although arguably "marriage" now means, or in the near future may mean, a voluntary union for life between two *people* to the exclusion of others.[42]

Of course, an originalist would prefer a connotation that accords with the understandings of the framers. Thus, Geoffrey Goldsworthy argues that 'in 1900 the word 'marriage' meant a union of a man and a woman — and this would almost certainly have been regarded as an essential part of the connotation, and not merely the denotation, of the word'.[43]

Certainly, if an element of heterosexuality is included within the connotation, so that the connotation is the same as the traditional common law definition, then there is no scope to argue that the denotation includes same-sex marriage, as the denotation cannot be inconsistent with the connotation. If, however, the connotation was defined more broadly as 'an intimate union between two people', so that different-sex unions were simply an example of this central type (albeit the only such example in 1900), then the denotation could expand to include same-sex unions.

For an originalist, it would appear that the connotation ought to include the element of heterosexuality, given that the framers understood marriage in this way at 1900 and did not contemplate same-sex marriage. However, several points may be noted. The first is that the question of same-sex marriage is not one to which the framers actually turned their minds and decided to reject. Rather, same-sex marriage simply was not in their minds as a matter that needed addressing. In this sense, same-sex marriage may be analogised to a technological advance – and the High Court has had little difficulty in accepting that the Constitution may be interpreted so as to encompass technological advances.[44] Alternatively, an analogy may be drawn with the majority's approach to the interpretation of 'foreign power' in *Sue v. Hill*.[45] Although the connotation of foreign power in 1900 was, arguably, 'any sovereign state other than the United Kingdom',[46] that was not the formulation adopted by the High Court. Rather, the majority interpreted foreign power as meaning 'any sovereign state other than the state for whose purposes the question of the other's status is raised'[47] and concluded that, although the United Kingdom did not previously answer that description, it did today.[48] The connotation adopted by the majority is one that clearly could describe the framers' understanding of the term 'foreign power' at a relatively high level of abstraction. It does not misrepresent the concept of foreign power. Similarly, in the marriage context, the framers can be said to have understood marriage as 'the intimate union of two people' – this would not misrepresent the notion of marriage; it simply states it at a higher level of abstraction – but they had a different understanding of who were included in the term 'people' as we do today.

*A purposive approach to the framers' intent.* Goldsworthy has offered an alternative originalist approach that would permit the Commonwealth Parliament to provide for same-sex marriage. His argument is premised on the purpose of the marriage power. He argues that section 51(21) was included in the Constitution to avoid the 'mischief' of fragmented marriage laws, as was (and is) the situation of marriage law in the United States, where marriage was a state matter and there was therefore a patchwork of marriage laws across the nation.[49] In Australia, at least some of the framers intended that the Commonwealth Parliament should be able to provide for the uniform, national regulation of marriage,[50] and Goldsworthy argues that this purpose would be undermined if same-sex marriage is excluded from the marriage power, as this would leave the states and territories able to recognise such marriage, thus leading potentially to the very fragmentation of marriage law the founders sought to avoid.[51] The author states:

> The founders did not anticipate the possibility of same-sex marriage. ... [T]he important question is surely not whether the unanticipated phenomenon comes within the precise literal meaning of the word chosen by the founders to give effect to their purpose in allocating legislative power to the national legislature. It is whether the phenomenon comes within that purpose, and is so closely related to the word's original meaning that it can be included by a simple and obvious expansion of that meaning consistent with contemporary conceptions. ... [T]here is a powerful argument that it does.[52]

Of course, not everyone would agree that including same-sex marriage within the meaning of the term 'marriage' is a 'simple and obvious expansion' of the meaning of marriage. But the argument is clearly a plausible one.

*Other originalist approaches.* Jeremy Kirk, a self-described 'evolutionary originalist', also supports the extension of the marriage power to include same-sex marriage, on the basis that 'changes in values, preferences, standards or expectations are relevant' in interpreting a Constitution that communicates 'broad ideas and concepts, the width of which allows evolutionary changes in how particular subjects have been, can be or should be understood'.[53] Also, Dan Meagher in his comprehensive article about the marriage power proposes an interpretive approach premised on the argument that many terms in the Constitution are 'constitutionalised legal terms of art' that can and ought to be interpreted so as to 'reflect developments in the common law and statute law and to accommodate, where the text and structure of the Constitution permits, innovative Parliamentary responses to new and unforeseen social, technological and economic circumstances'.[54] While not entirely an originalist approach, Meagher argues that this approach to at least some terms in the Constitution 'remains faithful to intentions of the framers who included these terms in the Constitution never intending that their meaning were to be frozen in 1900'.[55] Whilst an extended analysis of Kirk and Meagher is beyond the scope of this paper, it suffices to note that although many originalists may indeed oppose interpreting the marriage power to include same-sex marriage,[56] there is no necessary correlation between originalism (at least in its more moderate forms) and a narrow construction of the marriage power.

*Non-originalism and same-sex marriage.* If one is a non-originalist, one is (relatively) uninterested in the views of the framers. Thus the meaning of marriage in 1900 would not be particularly relevant to the inquiry as to the extent of the marriage power. Rather, as a non-originalist, one is seeking the contemporary understanding of marriage — what does the term 'marriage' mean in contemporary Australia?

At one level, the answer to that question would surely be that 'marriage' in Australia today means 'the union of a man and a woman ...', just as it did in 1900. After all, no state or territory has recognised same-sex marriage. The Commonwealth has not done so (and if it did, surely the existence of Commonwealth legislation cannot of itself demonstrate its own validity). Most mainstream Australian churches will not perform marriage or similar ceremonies for same-sex couples. If one consults a contemporary dictionary, a habit of Australian judges, one finds the definition replete with heterosexuality,[57] although the Macquarie dictionary has as its third definition (after the first two definitions which refer only to different-sex marriage) 'the intimate union of two people'. And if a court were able to commission a survey (or if such information were provided to a court), the likelihood is, I suggest, that most Australians would say that marriage is the union of a man and a woman.[58]

Some non-originalists will allow the use of international law to influence the interpretation of the Constitution,[59] although this is controversial.[60] But here, too, little help is to be gained for a non-originalist who seeks to interpret marriage broadly. The International Covenant on Civil and Political Rights (ICCPR), to which Australia is State Party, contains three relevant articles:

- Article 23 ('the right of men and women of marriageable age to marry');
- Article 2 (non-discrimination in enjoyment of the rights protected by the ICCPR); and
- Article 26 (all persons are 'equal before the law' and receive 'equal protection of the law').

Together, or even separately, these provisions may be construed as requiring that the right to marry under international law extend to all persons equally, irrespective of their genders or sexual orientations. If this were the correct interpretation of the ICCPR, then this would provide a basis for interpreting marriage to include same-sex marriage.

Unfortunately (or fortunately, depending on one's perspective), this is not the interpretation of the ICCPR that has been adopted by the United Nations Human Rights Committee in its consideration of the issue. In *Joslin v. New Zealand*, the Committee held that New Zealand's refusal to enable same-sex couples to marry did not violate the ICCPR. The Committee's reasoning was brief:

> Given the existence of a specific provision in the Covenant on the right to marriage, any claim that this right has been violated must be considered in the light of this provision. Article 23, paragraph 2, of the Covenant is the only substantive provision in the Covenant which defines a right by using the term 'men and women', rather than 'every human being', 'everyone' and 'all persons'. Use of the term 'men and women', rather than the general terms used elsewhere in Part III of the Covenant, has been consistently and uniformly understood as indicating that the treaty obligation of States parties stemming from article 23, paragraph 2, of the Covenant is to recognize as marriage only the union between a man and a woman wishing to marry each other.[61]

The Committee thus concluded that New Zealand's 'mere refusal to provide for marriage between homosexual couples' did not amount to a violation of articles 16, 17, 23, or 26 of the Covenant.[62]

While the Committee's views are not binding, its interpretation of the ICCPR is regarded as highly persuasive.[63] Thus the views in *Joslin* effectively preclude (or at least make very difficult) the use of the ICCPR as a basis for interpreting marriage in section 51(21) of the Australian Constitution to include same-sex marriage, at least until international law evolves to such an extent as to recognise a right to same-sex marriage; there are no other relevant treaties that impose obligations that may be used to provide a basis for legislation.[64]

A non-originalist might instead look to foreign rather than international law. One might argue that six nations thus far have recognised same-sex marriage, and that the term thus can evolve[65] and a non-originalist can interpret the term broadly. This is particularly so in relation to common law terms used in the Constitution, as the High Court has acknowledged that such terms were not intended to be frozen to their common law meaning in 1900 given the dynamic nature of the common law and the role of the courts in its development.[66] There are, however, some difficulties with this approach. First, it is hard to see why attention should be paid to foreign law (as opposed to international law)[67] in interpreting the Australian Constitution. Second, this is particularly so when some of the countries that recognise same-sex marriage have done so on the basis of their national bill of rights, which Australia does not have. Third, if we are to pay attention to foreign law, why select those half-dozen nations that have recognised same-sex marriage? Why not pay attention to the 186-odd that have not?[68]

Finally, one may have recourse to values such as equality and dignity, values that are recognised in international law[69] and in domestic law,[70] as the basis for a broad interpretation of marriage. This is the strongest argument for the non-originalist who seeks to recognise same-sex marriage. However, such recourse raises the question of legitimacy as it is so explicitly value-laden, and in Australia there are some who consider value-judgments to be within the confines of politics and not law. Thus, the non-originalist is left with little to support an interpretation of 'marriage' that includes same-sex marriage, if he or she is faithful to the pursuit of the contemporary understanding of marriage in Australia, counter-intuitive though this may seem.

*Can the states and territories legislate for same-sex marriage?* For many years, the question of state or territory laws recognising same-sex marriage was thought to be a hypothetical matter, considered only by constitutional theorists and having no relevance to the real world. In 2004, however, a bill was introduced into the Tasmanian Parliament providing for same-sex marriage in Tasmania: the Same Sex Marriage Bill 2004 (Tas). Although the bill was not passed, it nonetheless revealed the possibility that a state or territory might legislate for state or territory recognition of same-sex marriage.[71] While there is no real doubt as to the power of the state and territory legislatures to enact such a law, there is nonetheless doubt as to its constitutional validity if enacted, as the Commonwealth has used its power under section 51(21) to enact the Marriage Act – the question is then whether there is an inconsistency between the state or territory law and the Commonwealth law; if there is, the Commonwealth law will prevail.

In order to answer this question, a short explanation of the concept of 'inconsistency' in Australian constitutional law is necessary. There are three ways such an inconsistency may arise. First, it may be impossible for a person to obey both the state or territory law and the federal law, in which case there is a direct inconsistency and the state or territory law is invalid to the extent of the inconsistency.[72] Second, it may be that one law grants a right and the other law takes away or interferes with the enjoyment of that right – again there is a direct inconsistency (known as a rights inconsistency) and the state or territory law is invalid to the extent of the inconsistency.[73] Finally, the two laws may both operate in the same way, by creating the same rights and duties. In this case, there appears on the face of the laws to be no inconsistency – they are seeking to achieve the same goal. But, if the Commonwealth Parliament intended the Commonwealth law to be an exhaustive statement of the law in the field that it regulates, then there will be an inconsistency and again the state or territory law is invalid to the extent of such.[74]

If we assume, as a starting point, that under section 51(21) the Commonwealth has the power to legislate in relation to same-sex marriage, then it is clearly possible that the Commonwealth legislation may render the state or territory legislation on the same subject law to be invalid. This may occur in one of two ways. First, there may be a direct inconsistency, for example if the Commonwealth explicitly precluded recognition of same-sex marriage by the states and territories and a state or territory nonetheless purported to recognise or provide for such a marriage. This would amount to a rights inconsistency: the state or territory law would provide for a right to marry, and the Commonwealth law would remove that right (notably, however, there would be no impossibility of simultaneous obedience, as both laws could be obeyed by two persons of the same sex simply not marrying).

Alternatively, it could be argued that the Marriage Act as it now stands operates to render state or territory legislation recognising same-sex marriage invalid, as it is intended to cover the field of marriage, thus precluding any state or territory legislation on the subject, even if there is no direct inconsistency. Whether this is so depends on the field that the Marriage Act covers. It is at least arguable that, given the terms of the Marriage Act, which now applies only to different-sex marriage,[75] the relevant field on which it operates is that of different-sex marriage. If that is so, then a state or territory law providing for same-sex marriage does not operate on the same field and thus is not inconsistent with the Marriage Act. If, however, the relevant field is marriage generally, then a state or territory law purporting to provide for same-sex marriage would enter the field regulated by the Commonwealth and be rendered inoperative while the Commonwealth continues to regulate the field.

If the Commonwealth's legislative power under section 51(21) does not encompass same-sex marriage, then it could be argued that the field for the purposes of an inconsistency analysis would need to be more narrowly defined, as the Commonwealth cannot purport to cover a field going beyond its legislative power. This more narrowly defined field would be different-sex marriage. In this scenario, state or territory legislation recognising same-sex marriage would not intrude into the field and thus would not be invalid.

Yet even if the scope of the Commonwealth's legislative power is defined more narrowly, such that no inconsistency covering the field can be generated, there remains an argument as to whether the Commonwealth could generate a direct inconsistency by passing 'defence of marriage' legislation. Such legislation would of course require a head of power, which may not be found in section 51(21). But it may well be that the 'incidental power' (whether express or implied)[76] may extend to permitting the enactment of legislation intended to defend the institution of marriage, and it is likely that the courts would defer to Parliament as to the necessity of such legislation.

Ultimately, it remains unclear whether the states and territories can, at present, pass legislation that will effectively provide for same-sex marriage. The answer depends on questions of interpretation of the Commonwealth Constitution and of the federal Marriage Act. These questions are unlikely to be resolved until a state or territory passes legislation providing for same-sex marriage — yet this is unlikely to occur while the legal issues remain unresolved.

Finally, it should be observed that it is unclear what effect state or territory legislation providing for same-sex marriage would have. Such legislation would operate to provide access to the rights and benefits associated with marriage under the laws of the state or territory in question.[77] However, the effect of a state or territory same-sex marriage in other states and territories and federally is uncertain. Notably, section 118 of the Constitution provides that '[f]ull faith and credit shall be given, throughout the Commonwealth to the laws, the public Acts and records, and the judicial proceedings of every State'. It is at least arguable that either as a result of this section, or as a result of principles of conflict of laws, states and territories would be required to recognise a same-sex marriage solemnised in one state if the couple in question moved or travelled interstate, although there is scope for debate as to whether a 'public policy' exception may apply to permit non-recognition.[78] Similarly, the Commonwealth may be required to recognise a validly solemnised state same-sex marriage, subject to the operation of section 109. It is also unclear as to whether other nations would recognise a state- or territory-celebrated same-sex marriage; nonetheless, it seems likely that at least those nations that themselves provide for same-sex marriage would recognise a validly celebrated state or territory same-sex marriage.[79]

*The Constitution and non-marriage recognition of same-sex relationships.* One final question that arises in a discussion of the constitutional aspects of same-sex marriage in Australia is whether the Commonwealth and/or the states or territories could enact a recognition regime other than marriage: a registration system, or a regime for 'civil unions', as has occurred in the United Kingdom[80] and New Zealand.[81] Indeed, Tasmania has already enacted a regime for the registration of (amongst others) same-sex relationships.[82]

*Registration of same-sex relationships: the Commonwealth.* It is likely that the Commonwealth Parliament has the power to legislate for a non-marriage registration system for same-sex relationships. This is because whenever the Commonwealth exercises any of its heads of power, it may need to provide for recognition of various relationships; and its power to do so stems from the substantive head of power in question. Thus, for example, when the Commonwealth legislates in relation to immigration, it recognises an unmarried different-sex couple, even though it has no separate head of power in relation to such a couple. Similarly, it recognises, for some limited purposes, an unmarried same-sex couple. Assuming that such recognition is valid, then the Commonwealth may also establish the conditions for proving the existence of such a relationship, one of which may be registration with a Commonwealth agency under a registration system.

Further, the Commonwealth could in my view provide for registration of same-sex relationships using the external affairs power (section 51(xxix) of the Constitution) or the reference power (section 51(xxxviii)). The latter allows the Commonwealth to legislate on matters referred to it by the states or territories; its utility is thus dependent on state or territory action, and while such action is possible, it seems unlikely at present. Thus I will not discuss the reference power in any detail.

The external affairs power offers the potential for the enactment of a registration system for same-sex relationships because it permits the implementation of Australia's treaty obligations. It is at least arguable that the obligations in the ICCPR concerning equality and non-discrimination (discussed briefly above) would authorise Commonwealth legislation providing for recognition of same-sex relationships. Given that different-sex relationships are recognised through the Marriage Act and same-sex relationships are not, there is clear discrimination between persons on the basis of their sexual orientation. The jurisprudence of the United Nations Human Rights Committee indicates that the ICCPR, either in its reference to 'other status' or its reference to 'sex', includes within its equality and non-discrimination provisions the requirement that States Parties to the ICCPR not discriminate on the basis of sexual orientation.[83] Australia thus has an international legal obligation to protect against sexual orientation discrimination, and to provide for relationship recognition that gives citizens substantive rights and obligations on par with those attached to marriage is one way to achieve this. This is so notwithstanding that the ICCPR imposes no obligation to provide for same-sex marriage;[84] the argument is that to do so is simply one way to ensure equality and thus to implement the equality and non-discrimination provisions of the ICCPR. It need not be the only, or the required, way to do so in order to enliven the external affairs power of the Commonwealth Parliament.

*Registration of same-sex relationships: the states and territories.* The constitutional validity of the Tasmanian registration regime has not yet been tested, but it is likely to survive any challenge. This is because the power of the state or territory legislatures, as discussed above, is plenary — that is, it is not constrained by reference to a list of topics over which the Parliament has power. Thus, *prima facie* the states and territories have power to enact laws to provide for the registration of same-sex relationships. The only limit on this power is that legislation that is inconsistent with a Commonwealth law is invalid under section 109 of the Constitution (or, in the case of territories, under the Act granting legislative power). There are two possible ways in which such an inconsistency could arise. The first is if, at some point in the future, the Commonwealth Parliament were to enact a valid non-marriage registration system, then there could be an inconsistency between the state or territory law and the Commonwealth law. Whether an inconsistency existed would depend on the provisions of the two laws in question and cannot be determined in abstract. The second possible inconsistency would be between a state or territory registration system and the Marriage Act as it now stands. That is, it could be argued that the Marriage Act intends to cover the field for all forms of registration of relationships. This seems unlikely – there is nothing in the Marriage Act to suggest such an intention. Furthermore, the Marriage Act was enacted pursuant to the marriage power (section 51(xxi) of the Constitution) and arguably cannot cover a field that is greater than the power under which it was enacted; thus it cannot cover a field that includes all forms of relationship registration; it can only cover the field of marriage. Thus it is unlikely that state or territory legislation providing for the registration of same-sex relationships, such as the Tasmanian system, will be constitutionally invalid.

A remaining question is what operation, if any, will state or territory same-sex relationship registration laws have in other states and territories and federally. The answer is most likely that such systems will not be formally recognised outside of the state or territory where they are provided for. However, in states and territories that recognise a *de facto* same-sex relationship, an interstate registration of the relationship would at least provide strong evidence of the existence of the relationship should that be disputed by one party to it or by a party's biological family upon death or incapacity. Furthermore, international recognition of registered relationships is also possible; indeed, the United Kingdom now recognises Tasmanian registered relationships as civil partnerships.[85] Thus, the utility of state or territory registration systems ought not to be minimised.

## III. The Political Debate over Same-Sex Marriage in Australia

Leaving to one side the legal difficulties associated with recognition of same-sex marriage, it is instructive to consider the political debate over same-sex marriage in Australia. As indicated in the introduction, there was very little debate on the issue in Australia prior to the Commonwealth Parliament's amendment to the Marriage Act. This is notably different from the situation in the United States and Canada, where same-sex marriage has been an important issue for all sides of politics for many years. The reasons for the lack of interest in Australia are not entirely clear, but I suggest several reasons.[86]

First, legislative change in relation to lesbian and gay rights claims has historically been easier to achieve in Australia at the state or territory level of politics rather than at the federal level. As marriage was regarded as a federal issue,[87] but recognition of unmarried couples a state or territory issue, it was seen as easier to seek to achieve substantive outcomes for same-sex couples through state or territory legislative change in the recognition of unmarried couples.[88] Indeed, as noted in above, this has in large part been achieved.

Second, the very fact that most Australian states and territories (and certainly those with large and politically active lesbian and gay communities) have had a tradition of extensive recognition of unmarried different-sex couples (unlike most states in the United States, for example) renders the prospect of achieving substantive outcomes for same-sex couples through state or territory legislative change more realistic. In Australia, for instance it is not (and has not been for around 30 years) necessary for a person to be married to be recognised as next of kin upon the death of her or his partner or to receive a property distribution on the breakdown of their relationship — although it used to be necessary that the relationship be a different-sex one. Nor is access to health insurance connected to marriage, as

Australia has a comprehensive publicly-funded medical insurance system. Thus marriage was not the only way to achieve substantive rights, as it is in some other countries.[89] On a related note, it has been suggested that presumptive or *de facto* relationship recognition is a more equitable way to achieve substantive rights.[90]

Third, Australia has no constitutional or legislative bill of rights, so seeking change to marriage through the courts was not an option. Judicial change is often seen as an easier option than the time-consuming and difficult process of lobbying politicians for legislative change – as illustrated by the successful court cases in the United States[91] and in Canada[92] (although this strategy has not been successful in New Zealand, which has a statutory bill of rights).[93] Although the denial of marriage to same-sex couples is discriminatory, that fact is simply irrelevant in the Australian constitutional system. It provides no basis for a challenge to the validity of the Marriage Act. Similarly, issues of equality and discrimination would be irrelevant if the Commonwealth decided to institute an anti-miscegenation rule precluding marriage between different races. There is nothing in the Australian Constitution to prevent such a step; no basis on which a court could strike down such legislation.

Fourth, marriage is seen by some lesbian and gay rights activist groups as a much more difficult area of reform, politically. That is, there is a perception that, while the broader community may be willing to recognise a same-sex relationship on the death of a partner or the breakdown of the relationship, they will not be willing to give up the exclusive nature of marriage.[94] Indeed, the broader community is prepared, in some jurisdictions, to give same-sex couples all the same substantive rights as married couples – but not to give them the name 'marriage'.[95] That is, the symbolism of marriage, which is so important for some in the lesbian and gay communities, is equally important for some in the broader society in which we live, although for different reasons, of course. While the symbolism of marriage for lesbians and gay men is about equality and dignity, the symbolism of marriage in the broader community centres on its exclusionary nature. Marriage is *and can only ever be* the union of a man and a woman. Marriage will be diminished if same-sex marriage is permitted. Marriage is for procreating and raising children, which same-sex couples cannot do (or cannot do properly).[96] Underlying all of these arguments against same-sex marriage is, I argue, a deep-seated homophobia: a view that lesbian and gay couples are simply not as good as different-sex couples and not deserving of access to a revered institution. And it is, I think, in part a recognition of this deep-seated homophobia that prompts some activist groups to eschew pursuing same-sex marriage. After all, why devote significant time and resources to a battle that seems unwinnable — particularly if it also seems that positive outcomes can be obtained in other ways.

Finally, it seems that many lesbians and gay men in Australia are simply not much interested in marriage. While they want substantive equality, a significant number[97] do not seem to care much about the symbolic nature of being allowed to marry.[98] And a number of lesbians and gay men in Australia are quite critical of marriage as an institution. It is to this aspect of the debate that I shall now turn: why marriage as an institution is not worth fighting for.

## IV. Same-Sex Marriage in Australia: Not Worth Fighting For?

Ultimately, it is my view – though I acknowledge that it is not a view universally shared — that lesbian and gay rights activists in Australia should not be fighting for same-sex marriage. I hold this view not because of the legal and political obstacles to same-sex marriage (although they are significant and do raise the question of best allocation of political energy), but because I consider marriage a problematic institution and one which would have negative effects on the lesbian and gay communities in Australia; negative effects that would outweigh the positive effects of same-sex marriage.

*'Treat me as a person, see me fully as a human being, as fully your equal, without condescension'* [99]

Let me start by reiterating that the denial of same-sex marriage perpetuates the continued inequality of lesbians and gay men in Australian society. Being denied access to a fundamental social institution sends a powerful message about the value we accord (or do not accord) same-sex relationships, and indeed lesbian and gay lives – regardless of the conferral of substantive rights elsewhere.[100] As Raymond Gaita puts it, far better than I can:

> Firstly the demand that the law should permit same sex marriage is not at all like the demand for equal access to goods and opportunities. If it were, then some generous version of civil union would be acceptable. To many gays and lesbians, however, to demand the right to marry is not like demanding yet more of something that exists on the same continuum as, say, the right to inherit property. It is in a different dimension. It is, to be sure, a demand for justice, but like the demand that it should be acknowledged that Australia was not *terra nullius* at the time of settlement was not a demand for justice as fairness, so the demand to have the right to marry is not a demand for justice as fairness. It is the demand for justice conceived as equality of respect. It is, I think, absurd to think that the demand to be acknowledged as fully human is of the same kind as the demand for equal access to good and opportunities. Is it hyperbole to say that when gays and lesbians demand the right to marry, they demand acknowledgment of their full humanity? I believe it is not. Recall my earlier claim that to acknowledge someone as a fellow human being is to see him or her as capable of rising fully, in full responsiveness, to the meaning of the defining facts of the human condition. One of those defining facts is our sexuality and the way it goes deep with us – so deep as to be fundamental to our sense of identity.[101]

Why, then, would I be opposed to extending marriage to same-sex couples? The reason is that I think that the normative impact of marriage will be such that it will ultimately diminish, not enhance, the choices available to lesbians and gay men concerning their relationships. I have written about this elsewhere,[102] as have others,[103] so I shall not repeat the argument in depth. But it is important, in my view, to keep in mind the negative impact of marriage when considering whether legal recognition is appropriate and worth fighting for.

*'An optimum to which one must move'* [104]

Briefly stated, in my view opening marriage to same-sex couples would have a number of problematic effects related to its normative impact. For some, it would operate as 'the norm to which we must move' — that is, there would be pressure on same-sex couples to marry, just as there is pressure on different-sex couples to marry. Not only would there be overt pressure, eventually (perhaps immediately), marriage would become the 'natural' way to express commitment. Same-sex couples would want to marry (regardless of pressure), simply because marriage would be *the* way to celebrate a relationship. The freedom lesbians and gay men currently have in defining their own relationships would be diminished.

For others, the choice would be not to marry. However, the extension of marriage to same-sex couples would mean that unmarried same-sex relationships would be seen as something less valuable than marriage. If marriage is *the* socially sanctioned method for recognising significant intimate relationships, then those who choose not to marry would see their relationships downgraded, viewed as less worthy and less committed. Thus I am not persuaded by those who frame the argument as one of choice, not mandatory marriage; in my view, even if not legally mandated, the very option of such an institution for recognition of relationships has disciplinary effects.

Thus my concern is that ultimately the extension of marriage to same-sex couples would simply push same-sex couples into a heterosexual model — and one that has been the subject of critique by feminists in its heterosexual form for many years.[105] Rather than fight for same-sex marriage, I would fight for the removal of marriage from our legal system. Not its removal from life — that I see as impossible — but the removal of the state from the institution of marriage. While we need state recognition of significant relationships for a variety of reasons (death, relationship breakdown, the rights of children, and so forth), such recognition does not require marriage — indeed, arguably a more tailored system of recognition, with a combination of presumptive recognition and a registration system for various purposes, allowing for recognition of a more diverse range of relationship forms, will be more appropriate.[106]

## V. Conclusion: Some Questions about Marriage

In reflecting on same-sex marriage in Australia, one ought to start by asking what 'marriage' *is*. Is it an 'intimate union between two people' or is it an 'intimate union for life between one man and one woman to the exclusion of others',[107] the definition derived from nineteenth century English common law? The question is important in the Australian constitutional context as the Commonwealth Parliament has power to legislate in relation to marriage.[108] Does the term 'marriage' in the Constitution include same-sex marriage? There is considerable debate and not yet a definite answer.

However, one ought also to question whether the constitutional notion of marriage also requires a union 'for life' and 'to the exclusion of all others', aspects of the traditional definition which are yet not fully reflected in contemporary Australian marriage law.[109] If marriage no longer includes the requirement of 'for life' and 'to the exclusion of all others', even thought it arguably included such requirements in 1900, then need marriage still require 'one man and one woman'? If so, why is this seen as more essential than other aspects of the definition? If some aspects of the definition can change, why not others? Does Australia's continued adherence to the heterosexual aspect of marriage reflect deep levels of homophobia (or at least of heterosexism) in our society? Or does the relative lack of interest in same-sex marriage with the lesbian and gay communities indicate that marriage is an institution not worth fighting for?

At base, these questions reflect an ultimate question about what marriage is for – and what it should be for. Is it simply a relationship registration system, used to determine who may access certain basic social goods? Is it a social institution deliberately intended to elevate and privilege some relationships over others? Is it simply a way to recognise adult sexual relationships? Or is it a way to foster procreation and provide benefits to children? Is it a way to privatise care and responsibility for those who cannot care for themselves?[110] People are deeply divided over these questions, but the answer to them will often determine a person's attitude to same-sex marriage.

## Addendum

Since this paper was written, the parliament of the Australian Capital Territory (ACT) passed the Civil Unions Act 2006, providing for civil unions between both same-sex and different-sex couples. Territories are, unlike the Australian states, creatures of and subject to the direct control of the Commonwealth government. Section 35 of the Australian Capital Territory (Self-Government) Act 1988 (Cth) provides that the Governor-General (the monarch's representative in Australia and titular head of the Commonwealth executive, who acts on the advice of his or her Ministers) may disallow any Act passed by the ACT parliament within 6 months of its enactment. On 6 June, some few weeks after the Civil Unions Act was passed, the federal cabinet decided that the Act should be disallowed and it was formally disallowed on 13 June 2006.[111] There is no doubt that, although undemocratic, federal executive disallowance of a territory law is constitutionally permissible.

In December 2006 the Civil Partnerships Bill 2006 was introduced into the ACT parliament, in an attempt to enact a law that is sufficiently different from marriage to satisfy the federal government. However, on 7 February 2007 the Federal Attorney-General indicated that he will advise the Governor-general to disallow this Act too, should it be passed.

## Acknowledgements

This paper was completed while the Author was Visiting Fellow at the Gilbert and Tobin Centre of Public Law at the University of New South Wales. I wish to acknowledge the research assistance of Jennifer Anderson on an earlier version of this paper, the comments of Justice Michael Kirby on a draft version, and the continued support of Miranda Stewart in all my endeavours.

## Notes

1. The focus of this paper is on same-sex marriage, and not on transgender or inter-sex marriage which raise different legal and political issues and are beyond the scope of this paper.
2. Jenni Millbank and Kathy Sant, 'The Bride in Her Everyday Clothes', *Sydney Law Review*, Vol.22 (1999), pp.181–219; Equal Opportunity Commission of Victoria, *Discussion Paper on Same-Sex Relationships and the Law* (Melbourne: Equal Opportunity Commission of Victoria 1997), p.5; Cynthia Banham, 'A Lot More Than a Piece of Paper', *Sydney Morning Herald* (Sydney), 5 June 2004.
3. Jenni Millbank and Wayne Morgan, 'Let Them Eat Cake and Ice Cream: Wanting Something More from the Relationship Recognition Menu', in Robert Wintemute and Mads Andenaes (eds), *Legal Recognition of Same-Sex Partnerships: A Study of National, European and International Law* (London: Hart 2001), p.296.
4. See, e.g., Kristen Walker, 'UN Human Rights Law and Same-Sex Relationships: Where to from Here?', in Wintemute and Andenaes (note 3) p.743; Nancy D. Polikoff, 'We Will Get What We Ask For: Why Legalizing Gay and Lesbian Marriage will not "Dismantle the Legal Structure of Gender in Every Marriage"', *Virginia Law Review*, Vol.79 (1993), p.1535–50; Paula L. Ettelbrick, 'Since When is Marriage a Path to Liberation?', in Suzanne Sherman (ed.), *Lesbian and Gay Marriage: Private Commitments, Public Ceremonies* (Philadelphia: Temple University Press 1992), p.20; Janet E. Halley, 'Recognition, Rights, Regulation, Normalisation: Rhetorics of Justification in the Same-Sex Marriage Debate', in Wintemute and Andenaes (note 3) p.97; Davina Cooper, 'Like Counting Stars? Re-Structuring Equality and the Socio-Legal Space of Same-Sex Marriage', in Wintemute and Andenaes (note 3) p.75.
5. See below.
6. *Barbeau v. Attorney-General (British Columbia)* [2003] BCCA 251; *Henricks v. Quebec (Attorney-General)* [2002] JQ 3816; *Halpern v. Canada (Attorney-General)* (Ontario Court of Appeal), http://www.ontariocourts.on.ca/decisions/2003/june/halpernC39172.htm (accessed 6 February 2007). Unlike the orders in the first two cases, which were suspended in operation for two years, the orders of the Court in *Halpern* took immediate effect and since then many same-sex couples have married. The Ontario government

announced that it would not appeal the decision. Two non-party religious organisations attempted to appeal the case to the Supreme Court of Canada, but their application was rejected by the Court. Since these decisions, the Supreme Court of Canada decided that the Canadian federal Parliament had constitutional power to provide for same-sex marriage: see *Reference re Same-Sex Marriage* [2004] 3 SCR 698, and in 2005 the Canadian Parliament legislated for national recognition of same-sex marriage: Civil Marriage Act 2005 (Can).
7. Victorian Gay and Lesbian Rights Lobby, *Not Yet Equal: Report of the VGLRL Same-Sex Relationships Survey 2005* (Melbourne: Victorian Gay and Lesbian Rights Lobby 2005), p.40, http://www.vglrl.org.au/files/VGLRL%202005%20-%20SSRS%20Report.pdf (accessed 6 February 2007).
8. See http://www.australianmarriageequality.com/ (accessed 6 February 2007).
9. See Kees Waaldijk, 'Others May Follow: The Introduction of Marriage, Quasi-Marriage, and Semi-Marriage for Same-Sex Couples in European Countries', *New England Law Review*, Vol.38 (2004), p.569.
10. Jacqueline Tomlins, 'When I Do Becomes I Don't', *The Age* (Melbourne), 3 September 2004; Farah Farouque, 'Gay "Husbands" to Test their Marriage in Court', *The Age* (Melbourne), 4 February 2004.
11. Marriage Amendment Act 2004 (Cth).
12. See, e.g., Property (Relationships) Act 1984 (NSW); Property Law Act 1974 (Qld); Family Relationships Act 1975 (SA)(limited recognition only); De Facto Relationships Act 1996 (SA); Family Court Act 1997 (WA); De Facto Relationships Act 1999 (Tas)(now replaced by the Domestic Relationships Act 2003 (Tas); Domestic Relationships Act 1994 (ACT); De Facto Relationships Act 1991 (NT). For an extensive discussion of the New South Wales regime, see Reg Graycar and Jenni Millbank, 'The Bride Wore Pink ... To the Property (Relationship) Legislation Act 1999: Relationship Law Reform in New South Wales', *Canadian Journal of Family Law*, Vol.17 (2000), p.227.
13. In particular, a cohabitation period is required for certain areas of law, such as division of property and inheritance.
14. In most Commonwealth legislation, both married and *de facto* different-sex relationships are recognised. See, e.g., Social Security Act 1991 (Cth), s.4; Superannuation Act 1976 (Cth), s.8A; Income Tax Assessment Act 1936 (Cth), s.6 (definition of 'spouse').
15. Bills have been introduced into the South Australian Parliament for the recognition of same-sex relationships, but have not yet passed: see, e.g., Statutes Amendment (Relationship) Bill 2004 (SA) and the report thereon by the Social Development Committee of the South Australian Parliament, http://www.parliament.sa. gov.au/committees/lccdocuments/SD/public_documents/Tabled%20Reports/21st%20Report%20Statutes %20Amendments%20(Relationships)%20Bill%202004.pdf (accessed 6 February 2007).
16. Domestic Relationships Act 1994 (ACT).
17. Domestic Relationships Act 2003 (Tas).
18. The precise rights granted vary from state to state or territory, and in some states and territories rights in certain areas of law such as adoption and access to assisted reproductive services remain unavailable to same-sex couples. Adoption, for example, is only open to different-sex couples and single persons in New South Wales and Victoria.
19. For a general discussion of federal discrimination against same-sex couples, see Jenni Millbank, 'If Australian Law Opened its Eyes to Lesbian and Gay Families, What would it See?', *Australian Journal of Family Law*, Vol.12 (1998), pp.99–139; Millbank and Morgan (note 3); New South Wales Gay and Lesbian Rights Lobby, *Fact Sheet: Federal Discrimination*, http://www.glrl.org.au/publications/fact_sheets/Federal_discrimination.html (accessed 6 February 2007). Although federal superannuation law was recently amended to give some recognition to same-sex couples, through the recognition of 'interdependent relationships', full equality has not yet been achieved in this area: Miranda Stewart and Michael Flynn, *Death and Taxes: Tax Effective Estate Planning* (Melbourne: Thomson 2004), p.87.
20. Section 46 of the Marriage Act 1961 (Cth) requires that a marriage celebrant explain the nature of marriage with words that include 'marriage according to the law of Australia, is the union of a man and a woman to the exclusion of all others voluntarily entered into for life ... or words to that effect'. Further, at the time when the Act was enacted, there was no discussion of same-sex marriage and it is implausible to argue that the legislators had in mind anything other than 'traditional' marriage.
21. Section 88A states that '[t]he object of this Part is to give effect to Chapter II of the Convention on Celebration and Recognition of the Validity of Marriages signed at The Hague on 14 March 1978'.
22. See Peter Nygh, 'The Consequences for Australia of the New Netherlands Law Permitting Same Gender Marriages', *Australian Journal of Family Law*, Vol.16 (2002), pp.139–45.
23. A. Malmstrom, *Explanatory Report on the Hague Marriage Convention* (1978), cited in Nygh (note 22) p.142.

24. Nygh (note 22) p.142.
25. See Jennifer Norberry, 'Marriage Legislation Amendment Bill 2004', *Commonwealth Parliamentary Library Bills Digest No. 155 2003–2004*; Nygh (note 22).
26. See Commonwealth of Australia, Parliamentary Debates, House of Representatives, *Official Hansard*, No 11, Thursday 24 June 2004, p.31460.
27. Constitution, s.109.
28. I note that if some or all of the states and territories were to refer power over same-sex marriage to the Commonwealth pursuant to section 51(xxxviii) of the Constitution then the debate over the Commonwealth's power would become moot. However, such a reference seems unlikely at present. Thus, this possibility will not be discussed in detail.
29. (1886) 1 LR P & D 130, 133.
30. (1991) 174 CLR 379, 392.
31. (1908) 6 CLR 469, 610.
32. (1999) 198 CLR 511, 553.
33. It has been observed many times by the High Court of Australia that 'it must always be remembered that we are interpreting a Constitution broad and general in its terms, intended to apply to the varying conditions which the development of our community must involve. For that reason, where the question is whether the Constitution has used an expression in the wider or in the narrower sense, the Court should ... always lean to the broader interpretation unless there is something in the context or in the rest of the Constitution to indicate that the narrower interpretation will best carry out its object and purpose': *Jumbunna Coal Mine v. Victorian Coal Miners' Association* (1908) 6 CLR 309, 367; cited, e.g., in *Bank of New South Wales v. Commonwealth Bank* (1948) 76 CLR 1, 332; *Re Patterson, ex parte Taylor* (2001) 182 ALR 657, 678.
34. Sometimes non-originalism is referred to as 'progressivism', however it has been suggested that this term involves a value judgment about the interpretive approach; a claiming of the moral high ground perhaps. Thus I use the term non-originalism.
35. See, e.g., Jeffrey Goldsworthy, 'Interpreting the Constitution in its Second Century' *Melbourne University Law Review*, Vol.24 (2000), pp.677–710; Dan Meagher, '"The Times are they a-changin"? – Can the Commonwealth Parliament Legislate for Same-Sex Marriages?', *Australian Journal of Family Law*, Vol.17 (2003), pp.134–54.
36. Jeremy Kirk, 'Constitutional Interpretation and a Theory of Evolutionary Originalism', *Federal Law Review*, Vol.27 (1999), pp.323–66, part 1.1; Jeffrey Goldsworthy, 'Originalism in Constitutional Interpretation', *Federal Law Review*, Vol.25 (1997), pp.1–50.
37. Michael Kirby, 'Constitutional Interpretation and Original Intent: A Form of Ancestor Worship?', *Melbourne University Law Review*, Vol.24 (2000), pp.1–14; Goldsworthy (note 35) p.78. There has been sufficient disagreement amongst theorists for the term 'originalism' now to embrace a number of different approaches (see for example the difference between Goldsworthy (note 35); Kirk (note 35); Greg Craven, 'Heresy as Orthodoxy: Were the Founders Progressivists?', *Federal Law Review*, Vol.31 (2003), pp.87–129; and Mirko Bagaric, 'Originalism: Why Some Things should Never Change – Or at Least not Too Quickly', *University of Tasmania Law Review*, Vol.19 (2002), pp.173–204). For the purposes of the present argument, I will not distinguish between the variants of originalism. The resulting analysis is therefore somewhat superficial, but the resolution of this debate is not the focus of this paper.
38. Of course, one may note that no one is an absolute originalist or an absolute non-originalist. All theories of interpretation in play in Australia offer some scope for 'updating' the Constitution to suit the needs of the present. There seem to be few judges or commentators who would doubt, for example, the Commonwealth's power to provide for an airforce or the issue of plastic money, notwithstanding the text of sections 51(6) ('*naval and military* defence') and 51(xxii) ('the issue of *paper* money') respectively. The label 'originalist' is therefore not to be read in an absolute sense as indicating that no departure from the meaning of 1900 or the intentions of the framers is permitted. Rather, as Craven has pointed out, there is really a continuum of non-originalism, with originalists permitting less updating of the Constitution and placing greater emphasis on the intentions of the framers than non-originalists: Greg Craven, 'Original Intent and the Australian Constitution: Coming Soon to a Court Near You', *Public Law Review*, Vol.1 (1990), pp.166–85). Similarly, there is no one who is completely non-originalist, either. We all start with the constitutional text as the basis for the rules that enable and constrain the Commonwealth Parliament in the exercise of its legislative power. The words of section 51 were, of course, chosen by the framers of the Constitution, not by present-day Australians. And those words convey to us some meaning. Thus, in the context of the term 'marriage', it clearly includes the

intimate union of one man and one woman; no one is likely to dispute that. It, also, equally clearly excludes fish. That is, Parliament cannot deem fish to be marriage and thus gain legislative power over fish; likewise, Parliament cannot deem commercial partnership to be marriage and thus gain power over commercial partnership which it does not otherwise have under the Constitution. Even the staunchest 'non-originalist' is an originalist in accepting that the words chosen by the framers to delimit the Commonwealth Parliament's power should be given some effect and enforced by the courts. Debates about interpretation thus occur in the intermediate ground, where plausible arguments may be made on each side of the debate.

39. Bagaric (note 37) p.190.
40. See, e.g., Dan Meagher, 'Guided By Voices? – Constitutional Interpretation on the Gleeson Court', *Deakin Law Review*, Vol.7 (2002), pp.261–93; Anthony Mason, 'Constitutional Interpretation: Some Thoughts', *Adelaide Law Review*, Vol.20 (1998), pp.49–55; *Re Wakim, ex parte McNally* (1999) 198 CLR 511, 551–2 (McHugh J.); Goldsworthy (note 35); Kirby (note 37).
41. Goldsworthy (note 35) p.678. Meagher, '"The Times are they a-changin"?' (note 35) p.137.
42. (1999) 198 CLR 511, 553.
43. Goldsworthy (note 35), p.699.
44. See, e.g., *Grain Pool of Western Australia v. Commonwealth* (2000) 202 CLR 479, 500–501.
45. (1999) 199 CLR 462.
46. Meagher, 'Guided By Voices?' (note 40) pp.267–9.
47. *Sue v. Hill* (1999) 199 CLR 462, para.161 (Gaudron J.).
48. I note that the judgment in *Sue v. Hill* did not use the language of connotation and denotation, but arguably this distinction within the core meaning of a term and the set of things falling within the core meaning underlies the reasoning of the majority. See *Eastman v. The Queen* (2000) 203 CLR 1, 45 (McHugh J.). See Meagher 'Guided By Voices?' (note 40) pp.267–8.
49. Goldsworthy (note 35) pp.699–701. See, also, *Debates of the Australasian Constitutional Convention*, 22 September 1897 (Sydney), 1080–81, http://parlinfoweb.aph.gov.au/piweb/view_document.aspx?ID=459&TABLE=CONCON (accessed 6 February 2007).
50. Ibid. Goldsworthy
51. Goldsworthy (note 35) p.700.
52. Ibid.
53. Kirk (note 36) Part 5.6.
54. Meagher, '"The Times are they a-changin"?' (note 35) p.150.
55. Ibid. But see Craven, *Heresy as Orthodoxy* (note 37), where it is argued that there is little evidence to suggest that the framers were progressivists.
56. Bagaric appears to be of this view: Bagaric (note 37) pp.189–90.
57. See, e.g., *Macquarie Dictionary* (2001); *Australian Oxford Dictionary* (2004). It is noted that *Encarta*, the Microsoft online dictionary (of American derivation), contains an entirely sex- and gender-neutral definition, referring only to the union of two persons.
58. I acknowledge, however, that this conclusion is based on impression rather than hard data. It may well be that attitudes to marriage in Australia are changing.
59. High Court of Australia Justice Kirby has been the principal proponent of the use of international law in recent times, though historically various judges have used international law in constitutional interpretation. See Kristen Walker, 'International Law as a Tool of Constitutional Interpretation', *Monash University Law Review*, Vol.28 (2002), p.85.
60. In recent times High Court Justices Gummow and Hayne have been critical of the use of international law in this way: see Walker, ibid.
61. *Joslin v. New Zealand*, Communication No 902/1999, 30 July 2002, para.8.2, http://66.36.242.93/./html/newzealand_t5_iccpr_902_1999.php (accessed 6 February 2007).
62. Ibid. para.8.3. The more recent decision of the United Nations Human Rights Committee in *Young v Australia* (Communication No 941/2000: Australia. 18/09/2003, CCPR/C/78/D/941/2000), which found that denying same-sex couples benefits available to *unmarried* different-sex couples violated the right of equality, does nothing to challenge the Committee's decision about marriage in *Joslin*.
63. Henry Steiner and Philip Alston, *International Human Rights in Context: Law, Politics, Morals* (Oxford: Oxford University Press 2000), pp.739–40.
64. This also precludes the use of the 'external affairs' power (section 51(29)), which permits the Commonwealth to legislate to give effect to Australia's treaty obligations, to support legislation providing for same-sex marriage.
65. The South African Supreme Court of Appeal recently held that the common law meaning of marriage in South African had evolved so as to recognise same-sex marriage: see *Fourie v. Minister of Home*

*Affairs*, Case no 232/2003, 30 November 2004, http://wwwserver.law.wits.ac.za/sca/files/2322003/2322003.pdf (accessed 6 February 2007). The Canadian Supreme Court held that the term 'marriage' in the Canadian Constitution was not frozen in 1867 (when the British North America Act was enacted), but had evolved so as to now include same-sex marriage thus giving the Canadian Parliament power to provide for the same: see *Reference re Same-Sex Marriage* (note 6). Notably, both these decisions depended on the constitutional bill of rights in place in the two countries.

66. See, e.g., *Re Refugee Tribunal, ex parte Aala* (2000) 204 CLR 82, 97; Meagher, '"The Times are they a-changin"?' (note 35) pp.149–51.
67. See Walker, 'International Law' (note 59), where I argue that customary international law is a legitimate influence on constitutional interpretation because it reflects values held by the international community. In contrast, foreign law simply reflects the values of a particular nation; values that may or may not reflect widely held views.
68. An answer to this question may be that our legal system has more in common with those that have recognised same-sex marriage than with those that have not, but this founders somewhat on the shoal of Australia's lack of a bill of rights.
69. The Preamble to the ICCPR, for example, states that 'recognition of the inherent dignity and of the equal and inalienable rights of all members of the human family is the foundation of freedom, justice and peace in the world' and that human rights 'derive from the inherent dignity of the human person'. Further, the ICCPR expressly provides for the right of equality and non-discrimination (articles 2 and 26).
70. In Australia, all states and territories have anti-discrimination laws that prohibit discrimination on the basis of sexual orientation.
71. The government of the Australian Capital Territory is presently considering how best to recognise same-sex relationships and has included marriage as an option in its discussion paper on the issue: see Department of Justice and Community Safety (ACT), *The Recognition of Same Sex Relationships in the ACT: Discussion Paper* (2005), p.11, http://www.jcs.act.gov.au/eLibrary/papers/RecognitionofSameSexRelationships-discussionpaper.pdf (accessed 6 February 2007).
72. See, e.g., *R v. Brisbane Licensing Court, ex parte Daniell* (1920) 28 CLR 23.
73. See, e.g., *Colvin v. Bradley Brothers Pty Ltd* (1943) 68 CLR 1.
74. See, e.g., *Viskauskas v. Niland* (1983) 153 CLR 280.
75. See note 26 above and accompanying text.
76. Section 51(39) of the Constitution gives the Commonwealth Parliament power to legislate in respect of matters incidental to the execution of its legislative powers. It is also accepted by the High Court that each grant of substantive power in section 51 carries with it an implied power to legislate on matters necessary to make the grant of power effective: see, e.g., *D'Emden v. Pedder* (1904) 1 CLR 91.
77. It is, however, noted that such rights and obligations are largely already available through recognition of same-sex relationships through a presumptive or *de facto* regime, as discussed above.
78. This issue is untested and complex, a full discussion of which is beyond the scope of this paper. The issue has arisen in the United States and has not yet been judicially resolved: see, e.g., Andrew Koppelman, 'Interstate Recognition of Same-Sex Marriages and Civil Unions: A Handbook for Judges' *University of Pennsylvania Law Review*, Vol.153 (2005), pp.2143–94. Notably, both conflict of laws principles and the full faith and credit clause in the United States Constitution allow for a public policy exception, so that the 50 individual states may refuse to recognise an out-of-state marriage that offend a substantial public policy of the forum: see, e.g., Larry Kramer, 'Same-Sex Marriage, Conflict of Laws and the Unconstitutional Public Policy Exception', *Yale Law Journal*, Vol.106 (1997), pp.1965–2008.
79. Sections 212 to 218 of and Schedule 20 to the Civil Partnership Act 2004 (UK) provide for recognition of foreign same-sex marriages in the United Kingdom as civil partnerships.
80. Civil Partnership Act 2004 (UK).
81. Civil Union Act 2004 (NZ).
82. Relationships Act 2003 (Tas), Part 2.
83. *Toonen v. Australia*, Communication No. 488/1992, U.N. Doc CCPR/C/50/D/488/1992 (1994), http://www1.umn.edu/humanrts/undocs/html/vws488.htm (accessed 6 February 2007); *Young v. Australia*, Communication No 941/2000, UN Doc CCPR/C/78/D/941/2000 (2003), http://www1.umn.edu/humanrts/undocs/941-2000.html (accessed 6 February 2007).
84. See *Joslin v. New Zealand* (note 61).
85. Civil Partnership Act 2004 (UK), ss.212–18 and Sch. 20, as amended by the Civil Partnership Act 2004 (Overseas Relationships) Order 2005/3135 (UK).

86. The Lesbian and Gay Legal Rights Service provides a useful list of the pros and cons of marriage in its discussion paper on relationship recognition: Lesbian and Gay Legal Rights Service, *The Bride Wore Pink: Legal Recognition of Our Relationships: A Discussion Paper*, 2nd ed. (Sydney: LGLRS 1994), Part 8.4.
87. As I argue above, this is by no means constitutionally certain. Yet it was received wisdom in the lesbian and gay rights activist movement for many years. See, e.g., LGLRS (note 86) Part 8.4.
88. See, e.g., Miranda Stewart, 'It's a Queer Thing: Campaigning for Equality and Social Justice for Lesbians and Gay Men', *Alternative Law Journal*, Vol.29 (2004), pp.75–80; LGLRS (note 86) Part 4.2.
89. See New South Wales Gay and Lesbian Rights Lobby, Press Release, *GLRL Position on Same-Sex Marriage*, 28 August 2003, http://www.glrl.org.au/publications/press_releases/2003/01Sep2003_Marriage.htm (accessed 6 February 2007).
90. See, e.g., Jenni Milbank, 'The De Facto Relationships Amendment Bill 1998 (NSW): The Rationale for Law Reform', *The Australasian Gay and Lesbian Law Journal*, Vol.8 (1999), pp.1–26.
91. See, e.g., *Goodridge v. Department of Public Health* 440 Mass. 309, 798 NE2d 941 (2003).
92. See note 6.
93. *Quilter v. Attorney-General* [1998] 1 NZLR 523.
94. See, e.g., New South Wales Gay and Lesbian Rights Lobby (note 86), in which same-sex marriage was described as an 'impossible dream'. But see Stewart (note 88) p.80.
95. For example, in Western Australia all substantive legislative provisions pregnant with discrimination against same-sex couples have been removed, but the meaning of marriage has not been altered (although that may be for reasons of constitutional law, as discussed above). In the United Kingdom, same-sex couples are not granted all of the substantive rights and obligations as different-sex married couples, and are denied the right to enter into 'marriage': see Civil Partnership Act 2004 (UK).
96. For an example of a rebuttal of these arguments, see Dale Carpenter, 'Bad Arguments Against Gay Marriage', in Greg Wharton and Ian Phillips (eds), *I Do/I Don't: Queers on Marriage* (San Francisco: Suspect Thoughts Press 2004).
97. It is impossible to be precise about numbers, as there are no national up-to-date data available. A state-based survey of 670 people by the Victorian Gay and Lesbian Rights Lobby indicated that 55 per cent of the respondents did not wish to marry, but that close to 80 per cent of the respondents conceived that marriage should be available as an option for same-sex couples: see Victoria Gay and Lesbian Rights Lobby (note 7) pp.39–40. And see New South Wales Gay and Lesbian Rights Lobby (note 89).
98. But see Stewart (note 88) p.80.
99. Raymond Gaita, 'Same-Sex Marriage: A Philosophical Perspective', http://www.law.monash.edu.au/castancentre/public-edu/gaita-ssm.html (accessed 6 February 2007).
100. See, also, Susan Boyd and Claire Young, '"From Same-Sex to No Sex"?: Trends Towards Recognition of (Same-Sex) Relationships in Canada', *Seattle Journal for Social Justice*, Vol.1 (2003), pp.757–87.
101. Ibid.
102. Walker, 'UN Human Rights Law' (note 4).
103. See the sources cited in note 4.
104. Michel Foucault, *Discipline and Punish* (London: Penguin 1995), pp.182–3.
105. See, e.g., Martha Albertson Fineman, 'Our Sacred Institution: The Ideal of the Family in American Law and Society', *Utah Law Review*, Vol.2 (1993), pp.387–405.
106. I have made this argument in more detail elsewhere: see Kristen Walker, 'Same-Sex Relationships and the Law: Comments on the Victorian Equal Opportunity Commission's Discussion Paper', *Alternative Law Journal*, Vol.22 (1997), pp.293–7.
107. *Hyde v. Hyde* (note 29).
108. Constitution, s.51(21).
109. Divorce, of course, is possible and relatively easy, and it is not a criminal offence to engage in sexual activity outside marriage although it is a criminal offence to marry more than one person. Furthermore, Australian law recognises polygamous unions entered into outside Australia for certain limited purposes: see J. H. Wade, 'Void and De Facto Marriages', *Sydney Law Review*, Vol.9 (1981), pp.356–401.
110. See Boyd and Young (note 100) pp.783–5.
111. See 'Explanatory Statement Issued by the Authority of the Attorney General for the Minister for Local Governments, Territories and Roads', *Australian Capital Territory (Self-Government Act) 1988, Instrument of Disallowance, ComLaw*, http://www.comlaw.gov.au/ComLaw/Legislation/LegislativeInstrument1.nsf/0/9B231E99E8803105CA25718C0017E065/$file/Amended+Civil+Unions+E+Statement.pdf (accessed 6 February 2007).

# Non-Governmental Organising for Gender Equality in China – Joining a Global Emancipatory Epistemic Community

CECILIA MILWERTZ AND WEI BU

At the United Nations World Conference on Human Rights held in Vienna in 1993, feminists succeeded in reconstructing the dominant human rights discourse and in so doing they brought women's human rights concerns into the framework of international human rights.[1] The international emphasis on women's rights as human rights was further developed at the United Nations Fourth World Women's Conference in 1995. The convening of this conference and the accompanying NGO (non-governmental organisation) Forum in Beijing provided a unique opportunity for both newly established feminist NGOs and the older party-state All-China Women's Federation to link their work to internationally defined gender equality issues and to adopt modes of action applied by women's movements globally.[2] Of the three major groups under the direct control of the Communist Party through their respective organisations – youth, workers and women – only women have formed independent organisations and had this kind of direct contact with organisations outside China.[3] In fact, the 'unintended consequence' of the Women's Conference being held in China was that external influences became an integral part of the Chinese women's movement.[4] One subsequent result has been a recasting of gender inequality issues as human rights issues by some Chinese activists.

Not only the conference held in China, but also earlier women's conferences under the auspices of the United Nations and NGO forums have played an important role in mobilising women's movement participants in many countries. They have achieved this by providing alternative structures for networking and organising and they have focused the efforts of both organised and non-institutionalised marginalised groups upon changing national and international political processes.[5] However, the 1995 conference has also been criticised. Gayatri Spivak, for example, regards it as a 'repressive ideological apparatus' that fails to consider the poorest women of the South as self-conscious critical agents.[6] Spivak, who is not against United Nations conferences in principle but believes less time and effort should be spent on them, notes that more and more serious activists are staying away from such events. Recognising that not only the Women's Conference but also projects funded by non-Chinese donor organisations have played a significant role in facilitating the interactions between the emerging Chinese women's NGOs and women's movements in other parts of the world, Tani Barlow has criticised the inclusion of the Chinese women's movement into what she calls 'international U.S. feminism'.[7] Barlow defines this version of feminism as an ideological package comprising a 'well-financed, resurgent, neo-liberal, United States-focused effort to establish common ground for feminism', and she contends that this comes hand in hand with institutions that have the economic power to enforce their agendas.[8] Similarly, Nicola Spakowski has argued that the financial power and discursive dominance of Western donor organizations has shaped the development of women's and gender studies in China.[9]

We do not contest these critical interpretations of the objectives and power of a neo-liberal elitist feminism as one of several global feminisms. In an article on feminist bioethics and the language of human rights in China, Jing-bao Nie notes that criticism of the transfer of so-called Western values to non-Western cultures should be taken seriously when they are imposed regardless of the wills and wishes of people in these societies. However, the author adds, 'it is an entirely different matter if people in non-Western societies *want* to use Western values in their own struggles against injustice and inequality'.[10] Alena Heitlinger notes of the case of Western support to Czech women's groups since 1989 that while Anglo-American feminist litterature is critical of the dominance by the West, for the Czech women's activists, Western connections and funds enabled the development of political spaces that would otherwise not exist.[11] Thus, it is important to recognise that for many activists in Beijing, participation in preparations for the Women's Conference and the Women's Conference NGO Forum was an eye-opening experience. In several cases this provided the very catalyst to critical reflections about prior understandings of gender relations and the basis for developing transformatory activism for gender equality. In order to understand both the homogenising effects of macro-level globalisation and the heterogeneity of micro-level globalisation Manisha Desai distinguishes between two levels of women's agency in the global political economy.[12] Activity at these two levels of globalisation are reflected in the distance between neo-liberal 'international U.S. feminism', as defined by Barlow, and Beijing activists' experiences of engaging with international and global feminisms.[13] The situation is complicated not only by the global/local distinction, but also the different forms of feminisms that exist both globally and locally, as well as the possibilities for transnational collaboration. Making the point that following the Women's Conference 'it is no longer possible to talk of women's needs [in China] in purely local terms' Zhang Naihua argues that Chinese activists' interactions with feminisms outside China transcend a binary international-local model.[14] A similar point is made by the contributors to the volume *Human Rights and Gender Politics: Asia-Pacific Perspectives*. They ask whether 'we are seeing a return to an apparently universalizing discourse of human rights, just when many feminist intellectuals and activists alike had become acutely aware of the complexities of women's politics of difference?' In response they argue that many human rights claims in Asia are better understood 'as highly specific products of local social movements'.[15] Our approach in this paper falls within such a perspective while recognising that local organising in China has developed through interaction with the global women's movements and international organisations.

Here we present a case study of the emergence and development of activism against domestic violence (violence perpetrated by men against women within existing relationships and following separation). Through this we show how some Chinese activists' engagement with women's movements outside China has prompted the generation of knowledge and sites of action for enacting new political and cultural practices concerned with gender equality issues. International relations studies uses the concept of epistemic networks or communities in order to understand the transfer of norms and ideas originating in one system to another system, nation or region.[16] Jennifer Chan-Tiberghien conducted a study of how international law, which defines women's rights as human rights, is diffused locally in Japan. On the basis of this, she argues that even in countries where the state is believed to be dominant, civil society weak, and the political participation of women limited, effective change can be brought about through the mobilisation of global human rights discourses by a local 'epistemic network'.[17] Chan-Tiberghien contends that the local diffusion of global human rights norms is essentially an educational process involving a network of local civil society actors and supportive politicians. The questions we address are: How is new knowledge in such a local network established? How do local actors go about adopting and adapting the international rendition of domestic violence as a human rights issue? We argue that the transformation and dissemination of knowledge about domestic violence by Chinese non-govenmental feminist organisations is taking place as a learning process.

Popular women's organisations address a wide range of gender inequality issues and use a variety of activities to target different social levels and groups. In Beijing, organising was initially concerned with issues such as unemployment, prostitution, and so-called 'marriage and family' problems.[18] In the course of addressing these issues, some activists and organisations began addressing domestic violence. Activists involved in popular organising constitute one relatively small group among many other groups that are currently contributing to changes of attitudes, practices and legislation regarding domestic violence in China.[19] Despite the relatively small size of this group of activists, it is playing a role in introducing new ways of rights-based thinking about domestic violence in China.

This paper is based on a study of non-governmental organising to address gender inequality issues in Beijing in the 1990s and early 2000s.[20] After a brief introduction to attitudes and legislation regarding domestic violence in China, we describe the process by which new knowledge about domestic violence can be generated. We are concerned with the micro-level of globally engaged feminism in the form of the specific activities of activists in Beijing. Using interviews with activists from six NGOs – the Domestic

Violence Network, which was established in 2000, and five organisations involved in addressing domestic violence in the 1990s (the Women's Research Institute/Maple Women's Psychological Counselling Centre, the Women's Media Watch Network, the Legal Advice Service Centre, the Centre for Women's Law Studies and Legal Services, and the *Rural Women* magazine) – we seek to show how addressing domestic violence has been a process of changing knowledge and modes of action.[21] We propose to enhance understanding of the way in which the activists come to challenge the discriminatory practices embedded in the dominant gender order, in part by adopting a discourse that defines women's rights as human rights. To do this, we argue that it is necessary to explore the agency of women's movement activists in their interactions with global feminisms and donor organisations. We show that when they were confronted with the issue of domestic violence in China and simultaneously inspired by new ways of understanding such violence, activists began questioning taken-for-granted assumptions. Thus, they initiated a process of constructing new knowledge that challenges dominant views of this form of violence in their society. They developed gender-aware understandings of domestic violence, defining it now as a public issue that requires legal intervention. In this way, they entered a global epistemic community that sees domestic violence as a human rights issue. We have elsewhere argued that transformations of knowledge among activists in China, as are the case elsewhere, take place in the context of international interactions.[22] We have also proposed that activists are engaged in what Eyerman and Jamison define as the social movement 'cognitive praxis' of producing new knowledge.[23] In this paper, we develop these arguments further by showing that the construction of new knowledge has not been imposed from without as a top-down education process but has instead been shaped by the activists themselves in the context of international interactions. They have engaged in what Jean Lave and Etienne Wenger generally regard as a situated learning process within a global community of practice, and by engaging in such processes activists have joined a global emancipatory epistemic community.[24]

**Domestic Violence in China**

The sociological literature on China in the nineteenth and early twentieth century indicates that wife-beating was an institutionalised form of male domination.[25] Christina Gilmartin notes that beatings served as a constant reminder of women's inferior position in the family and 'constitued an almost ritualised display of male domination that ultimately inhibited women from asserting themselves or trying to claim their officially sanctioned rights to equality'. She suggests that the common occurrence of wife-beating in the past may have led authorities in the reform period (from 1978) to overlook the continuing function of the practice in contemporary society.[26]

The early 1980s saw increased coverage of violence against women in the Chinese media as a consequence of the new emphasis on legality following the promulgation of the Criminal Law in 1980.[27] Since its establishment in 1984, the All-China Women's Federation newspaper *China Women's News* has been addressing violence against women as one form of violations of women's rights. After 1992, when the newspaper lost its state funding and became self-funded, the newspaper became increasingly oriented towards the market. Nonetheless, the overall focus on women's rights has continued.[28] In contrast, a survey of newspaper reporting of domestic violence during 1991–98 concluded that the mainstream mass media in China in the 1990s were either silent on the issue of domestic violence or generated misunderstandings about the problem by exaggerating or sensationalising incidents of domestic violence. Moreover, the media tended to blame the victims.[29]

As an institutionalised form of male domination, wife-beating has been viewed by Chinese society in general largely as an acceptable form of social behaviour towards women who were seen to be breaking prescribed gender norms.[30] Wife-beating has long been generally considered by the Chinese to be a form of marital dispute, and therefore a private family matter. However, authorities such as the Women's Federation then began intervening in marital disputes and helping to find non-violent means of resolving them. Several notable changes in such intervention are now taking place. First, Women's Federation intervention tended initially to be carried out within a framework that supported the existing gender order. Wife-beating was viewed through an evolutionary lens that rendered violators as backward, insufficiently 'developed' or educated or unable to keep up with the pace of reforms. Within this evolutionary scheme it is women (rather than their male abusers) who may end up being blamed for the violence they have endured.[31] The framework of understanding that is currently being introduced, however, is based on an understanding of domestic violence as an issue of rights and of gendered power relations. Second, Women's Federation intervention did not at first fully shift violence out of the private family domain into the public sphere of society where it merits legislation and intervention. Violence was addressed within the semi-private, semi-public sphere of the Federation. This situation is currently changing as the issue is increasingly being brought into the public sphere. Third, popular organising has joined the Women's Federation in addressing the issue. Fourth, the earlier focus primarily on physical wife-beating is being broadened to include also mental abuse and rape within marriage as forms of domestic violence. More recently date rape is beginning to be addressed as a form of violence against women. The Sex/Gender Education Forum at Zhongshan University has played a role in focusing attention on date rape in connection with the case of Huang Jing.[32]

The 1995 Women's Conference, including the two years of preparations for the conference, was a watershed event in terms of drawing attention to violence against women, including domestic violence, in China. Activism addressing domestic violence was legitimised by the conference Platform for Action and an individual rights perspective and gendered interpretations of such violence have been introduced in China.[33] The main change that has taken place since the 1990s is a gradual shift in the interpretation of, and thereby also the action taken against, wife-beating. Wife-beating is now beginning to be viewed from the standpoint of challenging rather than maintaining the existing gender order. Although a whole series of Chinese laws include paragraphs that could be seen as addressing domestic violence, it was not until the revised Marriage Law was adopted in 2001 that actual 'domestic violence' wording became included as a legal matter at the national level. Most forms of 'wife-beating' were defined as 'light injuries' and only 'serious injury' was defined as a crime under the Criminal Law.[34]

This very brief overview of domestic violence in Chinese society cannot do justice to the extensive literature on the issue published over the past decade by Chinese scholars and activists.[35] The main point we aim to make is that while male violence against women continues to be an institutionalised form of male domination, significant changes in attitudes, practices and legislation have taken place over the past 20 years.

## Challenging an Institutionalised Form of Male Domination

Activists themselves shared the general understanding in China of wife-beating as a non-issue until they began to engage in a process of generating new knowledge and altering interpretations. They more or less 'accidentally' discovered wife-beating in the course of addressing other gender inequality issues. They then started investigating the characteristics and extent of wife-beating. This in turn led to their re-interpretation of wife-beating as a women's movement issue and the re-naming of the phenomenon as domestic violence. Finally, some activists defined domestic violence as an issue involving gendered power relations and as a human rights issue. In the following we outline these stages of generation of new knowledge.

### *Discovering wife-beating*

Activists who were dealing with gender equality issues through their employment in the 1980s, before they became involved in popular organising, did not then consider domestic violence to be a women's movement issue. Looking back on that time, one activist who had worked as a journalist for *China Women's News* and had therefore dealt with gender equality issues said: 'I did not consider domestic violence, it just did not enter my field of vision.' This activist did in fact hear about domestic violence but noted that 'it did not enter my heart, it just seemed to blow over me' and 'it did not enter my head'.

For two Women's Federation employees in Beijing it was their encounters with wife-beating through their work that served as a starting point for their later engagement in non-governmental organising. The lawyer Pi Xiaoming encountered women who had been severely beaten when she was working for a city district Women's Federation in central Beijing in the 1980s. Women with battered faces, broken arms, as well as blood-stained clothes and bedclothes were shown to her in her office. Also in the 1980s, an editor of the Marriage and Family Section of *China Women's News* met beaten women both among her colleagues but also women who came to the newspaper to seek help. As the editor explained,

> This was all near to me, but at that time I did not think of this as domestic violence. I thought of this as a couple not getting along. We had not linked this thing with the women's movement, we all thought that this was probably a normal conflict between spouses that developed to a certain stage and escalated. We also somehow thought that women who were beaten probably all had something wrong with them, something that made violence understandable.[36]

Similarly, wife-beating was brought to the attention of the Women's Hotline, set up in 1992 by the Women's Research Institute, when callers would ring asking for advice with regard to their husbands' violence. The *Rural Women* magazine's editorial office also received letters from readers describing their experiences of domestic violence. In its early years, the Hotline would advise its callers to improve their behaviour in order not to provoke the anger of their husbands, in keeping with the assumption that they themselves were to blame for being beaten.[37] At the *Rural Women* editorial office the initial reaction to rural women's experiences of domestic violence was to assume that there was a huge difference between urban and rural Chinese and that only rural, uneducated women without their own incomes could be the victims of such violence.

Some activists had encountered domestic violence in their own homes or in the homes of neighbours during and after their childhood, while others had no knowledge of such practices in society until they were confronted with victims of violence seeking their assistance. They shared their experiences of having first encountered wife-beating 'accidentally' as a women's movement issue, as wife-beating was not one of the issues they had originally planned to address through their non-governmental organising. Either they were not aware of the problem and/or they did not view it as a women's movement issue. Once they had become aware of the issue, activists' interaction with transnational women's organising prompted them to begin challenging understandings of such violence. Reflecting on this, one activist recounted:

> When I was a child ... our neighbour used to beat his wife but we did not think anything of it. In reality this is how Chinese see it. I thought it was a very common thing, nothing special. If you don't pay attention then you don't see it, even though it is there in people's attitudes and in practice. But I didn't feel it was a particular issue. Even though I had listened to so many stories from rural women. When other people alert you to the fact that this is domestic violence, slowly you begin to think of it as a problem.[38]

Similarly a lawyer who took part in the 1995 Women's Conference NGO Forum noted the effects of international interactions:

> Taking part in the women lawyers' workshop made an impression on me – I think it was a US delegate – she asked us about China: does China have NGOs? And how does China handle domestic violence cases? I had read some materials, but I had not been very conscious of the issue and I had not really thought it was important. At that time I thought that China did not have this problem and the Chinese delegates basically did not answer the question.[39]

## Exploring Wife-beating

Once they had noticed and begun to acknowledge the existence of the problem, activists began to explore the extent and characteristics of wife-beating. In 1989 lawyer Pi Xiaoming received 260 people at the letters and visits department of the city district Women's Federation in Beijing where she was working. Because the annual report of these cases submitted to higher levels of the Women's Federation system did not have a category into which one could slot cases of wife-beating, she decided to establish a new set of categories in order to register these cases. The result was that about three-quarters of the cases she had handled that year related to domestic violence.[40] Pi Xiaoming explains how she gradually changed her view of these cases: 'these facts accumulated before me and developed from a sense that there was a serious problem into definite knowledge that this was the case. First you see with your own eyes, and then gradually you feel that this is an issue. ... I realised that this would not work, that this was a phenomenon. In fact, by the end of the 1980s, I made this problem into an issue.'[41]

At the Women's Hotline wife-beating was also beginning to be noticed and explored during 1993–94. Calls from domestic violence victims led activists to carry out a study of cases of domestic violence in both urban and rural regions. They were astonished to find that well-educated university professors, journalists, and company directors beat their wives. Prior to setting up the Hotline and undertaking the study they had thought that it was uncommon for a woman to be beaten in her home by her husband, particularly in urban China.

After the Women's Conference other organisations that had come across wife-beating in the course of their work began to systematise their data in order to examine factors such as social class, urban/rural differences, age and the educational level of perpetrators and victims, and the extent of the violence. In 1997, a study of the media coverage of domestic violence was conducted by journalist members of the Media Watch Network. In 1998, an investigation among readers was initiated by the magazine *Rural Women* and the Women's Centre for Law Studies and Legal Services began in 1998 to systematise and register cases of domestic violence. In February 1995 the Women's Centre for Law Studies and Legal Services opened a nationwide legal hotline. In its first three years of operation, 58 per cent of the calls received were concerned with marriage and family issues, but there were very few reports of domestic violence. This was most likely not a reflection of the incidence of domestic violence, but was probably because victims would not define violence as the problem they needed assistance for and also because the activists themselves were not registering the cases as such. The investigation of wife-beating, however, meant that a form of violence previously viewed as a non-issue was now being registered and studied. A *Rural Women* magazine activist explains how the focusing on the issue made it visible and identifiable as a social problem: '[t]he [understanding of the] word domestic violence gradually deepened. From being an occasional experiential thing at that time, it became a general phenomenon – it became a social phenomenon.'[42]

*Making wife-beating into a women's movement issue*

Before the Women's Conference both Women's Federation lawyer Pi Xiaoming and activists at the Women's Hotline had proceeded to a third stage of activism. They began making the previously invisible and private issue public. Pi Xiaoming compiled a set of material based on the cases she had handled and started preparing to publish them in the media because she felt that the violence she was witnessing was a serious issue. She wanted to make society aware of this and increase concern for the problem. In December 1991 the All-China Women's Federation magazine *China Women*, and also the magazine *Developing District News* (*Kaifaqu daobao*), published her article 'Whitebook on Domestic Violence' based on the cases from the local Women's Federation letters and visits department.[43] Strictly speaking Pi Xiaoming did not present her findings as an activist representative of an NGO as she had not yet become involved in the establishment of the Legal Advice Service Centre at the time. She was acting as what we would define as a women's movement activist, rather than in her capacity as a Women's Federation employee. As in this case, while the new NGOs are playing an important role in changing attitudes, practices and legislation regarding domestic violence, in practice the boundaries between the work done by the Women's Federation (either formally or by Federation employees in other contexts) and the new NGOs are often fluid. Pi Xiaoming used the new term 'domestic violence' to describe 'a husband who beats his wife' because all the victims who turned up at her office to seek assistance were women and the violators were their husbands. Pi Xiaoming thought she was doing something important and that the publication of the documentation she had collected would cause a sensation. In fact her publication prompted absolutely no reaction either from the public or within the Women's Federation system. Only the All-China Women Federation newspaper *China Women's News* printed an extract of the article under the title 'Woman Lawyer Bitterly Attacks Husbands Who Beat Their Wives'. Nonetheless, activists often refer to this article as one of the first examples of how they began to engage the media to address domestic violence in a manner designed to disrupt the dominant discourse. Before the convening of the Women's Conference, the Women's Hotline began to publish the results of their urban–rural study and, despite a series of obstacles, they were able to present their work at a workshop at the Women's Conference NGO Forum. Viewing domestic violence as a women's movement issue meant seeing the issue from many different perspectives. One activist explained how she at first had no 'clear concept' of domestic violence. Then gradually she came to understand the problem as a public and a legal issue and later on, after reading certain reports and attended a meeting in Manila, also as a health issue.[44] These changes were accompanied by a shift in terminology from 'wife-beating' to the new globally current term 'domestic violence'.

### *Defining domestic violence as a gender and human rights issue*

Some activists and organisations have taken a further step in the process of changing their interpretations of wife-beating. These have come to view domestic violence as a reflection of unequal gender relations in society.[45] In the words of an activist:

> I believe that domestic violence is definitely related to gender relations and relations of power between the two sexes, that men always believe that they are the controllers of power, that their wife is their property. In feudal society wives were bought into families to ensure their survival. Her financial situation was completely dependent on him and it was equivalent to a woman being bought by a man as a piece of merchandise. Whoever wanted to beat or abuse could just do so. There were also the three subjections and four virtues – these Confucian ethical codes tied up women. This culture permeates Chinese society. I think many people still follow these cultural codes of patriarchy and clan authority. This is a very deep oppression of women – a power relationship.[46]

This quote reflects the introduction of the analytical category of 'gender' to China. Among activists a shift has taken place from viewing sexual divisions of labour and power as biologically determined to being socially, culturally and historically constructed. This has had important consequences for women's movement activism, as the implication of interpreting gender relations as constructed is that they can also be changed. Some activists have also come to view domestic violence, and violence against women in general, as a human rights issue. One activist explained that in Chinese society the rights of citizens are not emphasised and the rights of women even less so. Another noted that it is extremely difficult to change deep-rooted ways of understanding such matters:

> In my country patriarchal thinking is very deep-rooted. Drinking and beating your wife are things a man is supposed to do. The shocking thing is that we still

believe this, even after the reforms that have been made. We have not placed this [domestic violence] in a human rights perspective in order to view women as human beings who should not encounter such violence. Even though I have worked at a Women's Federation school for many years and have been engaged in women's issues for ages, my mind has not been liberated. I have not seen this as a violation – as women's rights that should not be violated. For Americans this is not a taboo. They often say that they protect women from a human rights perspective. Women are also human beings. Other matters can be viewed as human rights issues, so why not domestic violence?[47]

Understanding gendered power relations and domestic violence as human rights issues has implied that male violence against women is seen by activists as an unacceptable aberration. In this way such understanding challenges gender order-maintaining understandings.

## The Learning Process of Generating New Knowledge

Through these stages of generating new knowledge activists have shifted position from one of ignorance or denial of the existence of wife-beating to acknowledgment that women were in fact being beaten by their husbands in their homes. Subsequently, they began to view such behaviour as unacceptable and as meriting recognition as a gender equality issue by the women's movement.

Chan-Tiberghien, as mentioned above, defines the transfer of an epistemic community from one context to another as an educational process.[48] We have mapped out the above four stages in changing understandings of the issue of domestic violence from the private and invisible sphere to the public sphere of the women's movement. In this way we have shown how Chinese activists' engagement with global norms has taken shape as a gradual learning process. Here we employ the concept of situated learning, by which is meant that learning is 'a process of changing understanding in practice' through participation in everyday life.[49] This means that activists have not simply adopted a body of knowledge through their engagement with women's movements outside China. On the contrary, they have engaged in what Lave and Wenger define as an active process of knowledge creation – constructing knowledge that resonates with their experiences.[50] Activists tend to point to one or several incidents that were decisive in changing their knowledge. However, although particular catalysts of change may be identified, the overall knowledge-generating process takes place gradually in the context of interactions with both the Chinese and the global women's movement communities. In other words, particular catalysts of change occur within an overall context of learning through social co-participation. Activists are well aware of the nature of this learning process, as reflected in the following comment:

What is the [domestic violence] foundation? What is the theoretical foundation? In social terms what is it? For example if we talk about the power structure, well, I have come to see it as such through personal experience and investigations. That it is a control mechanism. I have not reached this understanding through books. It is a process. Like the Manila meeting where violence was presented as a health issue. Well, it was only then that I realised that it is a health issue.

The meeting was a revelation for me. I had seen the Women's Conference documents that China had signed, but for me this was a gradual, deepening process.[51]

By delineating four stages of knowledge creation we have tried to capture knowledge generation as a learning process. However, this process is not straightforwardly sequential or linear. Activists do not simply move directly from one of the four stages to the next, nor do they necessarily move through all stages. We see a parallel here to the continuous nature of changes in awareness described by Patti Lather in her study of students' resistance to a liberatory curriculum.[52] Lather uses a chart to identify the stages of feminist conciousness-raising through which awareness of the politics of knowledge is brought about. Discussing the chart gave the students an opportunity to put names to their various reactions to an introductory women's studies course. The chart depicts changes in knowledge, first, from 'ignorance' to rejecting or accepting 'oppositional knowledge'. And, second, in the case of acceptance of new knowledge, from experiencing acceptance as either liberating or burdensome. It also makes it clear that such changes of knowledge are not linear processes.[53]

The stages of knowledge generation are not, moreover, necessarily tied to particular time periods. Some activists went through the first stage – encountering wife-beating – in the 1980s, while others did so later. Nor does an encounter with domestic violence necessarily imply a direct confrontation with an act of violence and/or a victim of such violence. One activist explained how she became aware of domestic violence when the poet Gu Cheng killed his wife and then committed suicide. She was stunned by the fact that the media subsequently expressed great sorrow over the loss of a great poet while there was little mention of his murder of his wife. This episode sensitised her to the way in which male violence against women can be invisible and it led her to question whether the advocacy of human rights among male intellectuals also included women. She began to reflect on why the Chinese literary intelligentsia, who were writing numerous articles in renowned newspapers in praise of this excellent poet and who should have knowledge of human rights, appeared totally oblivious to the plight of his wife whose rights had persistently been violated. She suddenly saw them as very superficial in their understanding of human rights. These were the people who promoted democracy, freedom and human rights and they were totally ignoring that Gu Cheng was also a murderer.[54]

The Women's Conference provided a major impetus to change in addressing gender issues for activists as well as for Chinese society in general. However, there have been many other catalysts of change since then and not all of these are necessarily linked directly to the conference. We have mentioned participation in conferences as important catalysts of change, and this is most likely because attending conferences, and also taking part in study tours to other countries, provide opportunities to stop and reflect on one's own experiences and practices in the light of other perspectives and contexts. A series of such prompts to reflection have given rise to a learning process and the generation of new interpretations, insights and knowledge. On one hand, there has been the encounter with the phenomenon of wife-beating in Chinese society and, on the other hand, the interaction with a global epistemic community that sees domestic violence as a women's movement and human rights issue. Alison Assiter argues that knowledge-building processes are co-operative, constructive endeavours that enable experiences and values to be illuminated in a way that isolation does not.[55] Alternative ways of understanding domestic violence have resonated with encounters with such violence in Chinese society and in so doing they have brought activists into the realms of what Assiter defines as a feminist global epistemic community of 'emancipatory values'.

Assiter defines an epistemic community as 'a group of individuals who share certain fundamental interests, values and beliefs in common, for example, that sexism is wrong, that racism is wrong, and who work on consequences of these presuppositions'.[56] Building on Benedict Anderson's 'imagined' communities, Assiter's notion of community includes people who may share no physical, social or cultural ties.[57] The nature of an epistemic community is such that it undermines claims made by other communities. Activists in China do this by criticising wife-beating as an institutionalised form of male domination in Chinese society and by making challenging claims about reality. The epistemic community that the activists have joined is emancipatory, in Assiter's sense, by dint of being committed to values that oppose oppressive power relations. According to Assiter, commitment to emancipatory values can lead to the advancement of knowledge by revealing information that is hidden from view. Activists have altered their interpretation of wife-beating, as something that the victim bore the blame for by failing to adhere to the norms of the dominant gender order, to an interpretation that challenges the gendered power relations of the dominant gender order and views violence against women as a human rights issue. In other words, they have moved away from the dominant discourse on wife-beating in Chinese society by generating new, counter-hegemonic knowledge.

## Changing Modes of Action and a Continuum of Domestic Violence Knowledge

The transformative learning process of social movements involves an ongoing interaction between different kinds of new knowledge leading to new forms of action.[58] For example, following the Women's Conference NGO Forum and her realisation that mental abuse is also a form of domestic violence, a lawyer activist rewrote an earlier report of a case she had handled prior to the conference. The case concerned a professor whose wife committed suicide following many years of mental abuse by her husband. He had not hit her, he had not shouted at her, but he had quietly mentally and verbally abused her. Before attending the Women's Conference and being introduced to new ways of defining such behaviour, this lawyer had not thought of the case as a criminal offence. Following the conference she reframed the husband's behaviour as a form of domestic violence that ought to be addressed by law. The purpose of rewriting the report was to submit it to both the Women's Federation and the People's Congress Interior Affairs and Justice Committee in order to inform them of this plausible interpretation of behaviour.

New knowledge has led to several new forms of collective action. The counselling provided by all the organisations involved has shifted in style from tending to maintain the status quo towards challenging the extant gender order. This involves informing victims that what they are experiencing is unacceptable and offering them assistance in accessing available support. At present, however, there are inadequate support possibilities. In the mid-1990s there were attempts to set up shelters for battered women in both Beijing and Shanghai but the efforts failed, and to our knowledge there were by mid-2005 no such facilities in either of the two major cities. However, in recent years shelters have been set up in several places outside of the large cities. For example in both Liaoning and Hebei provinces local Women's Federations have set up shelters. Importantly, initial steps have been made to amend legislation. What was previously understood as light wounds, which were not covered by legislation, are now in principle included in the

Marriage Law definition of domestic violence and police and other authorities are obliged to act accordingly. On a long term basis the Domestic Violence Network is working for the passing of a Law on Domestic Violence. A draft law was submitted to the National People's Congress and the People's Political Consultative Conference in 2003. Activists estimate that it will take at least ten years to get the proposal through the legislative process.

As domestic violence is beginning to be viewed as a rights-based issue, a major shift in modes of action is being promoted by popular feminist organisations in collaboration with local Women's Federations. This is based upon a model of comprehensive intervention, which emphasises the public nature of intervention. It means that a range of authorities, including the police, the local community, the medical and legal systems, the media, and the educational system, are all being encouraged to intervene in domestic violence cases. Schools are encouraged to teach children about and against domestic violence; the medical system is being trained to identify domestic violence cases and treat victims appropriately; the police are being trained in intervention, and in several places the police can be reached on the special 110 domestic violence number.

The Domestic Violence Network is developing this model in Beijing and the Maple Women's Psychological Counselling Centre has run a project in Tianjin. Both organisations have used the method of gender training to spread knowledge of domestic violence as a human rights issue. The objective of gender training is to actively engage participants in learning processes. The method was introduced to a group of activists engaged in popular organising in Beijing in 1998 when they took part in a United Nations Development Programme training course and subsequently compiled a gender training manual. The methodology furnishes a framework for understanding and transforming gender relations. It was initiated by women's movements and has been adopted by governments, donor organisations, NGOs and United Nations bodies as an important tool to enhance gender awareness at all societal levels. The generic aim of gender training is 'to consciously introduce gender as a category of analysis (as opposed to description), to point to the differing needs and interests of women and men and their unequal representation, and to increase awareness and reduce gender-bias which informs the actions of individuals and institutions'.[59] A fundamental goal of gender-transformative training programmes is to sensitise participants to the need for a gender-relations perspective, and to demystify the social construction of gender. The Domestic Violence Network has incorporated gender training into its activities in several ways. Firstly, all activists and Network partners employed in party-state institutions are requested to take part in gender training undertaken by the Beijing-Tianjin Facilitators Team on Gender and Development, a non-governmental group that was established following the training course. Secondly, tailored gender training courses are designed for specific professional groups such as the judiciary, medical personnel, the media, and the police to be involved in Network projects. The activists' conviction of the usefulness of gender training for disseminating critical understandings of gender is reflected in their suggestion that all police officers, throughout the country, should undergo gender training. This suggestion formed part of a proposal on action against rape submitted to the People's Political Consultative Conference and the National People's Congress in March 2004 by a group of about 30 academics, and supported (at least informally) by the All-China Women's Federation. Non-governmental women's organisations benefit from the fact that there is a tradition for and institutional system of women's organising in China. The Domestic Violence Network works closely with the All-China Women's Federation, the Women's Federation system is in Beijing as well as in provinces across the country. Likewise, the Maple Women's Psychological Counselling Centre project in Tianjin was implemented in collaboration with the Tianjin Women's Federation. Both non-governmental women's organisations and the Women's Federation benefit from this form of collaboration, which is based on a mutual interest in working to address gender inequality. Women's Federations gain access through the NGOs to funding and knowledge resources, while the NGOs gain access to the various professional groups they are aiming to involve in their work, as well as to party-state institutions.

This beginning of a dramatic change in values that is taking place in China is reflected in the existence by the early 2000s of a broad continuum of knowledge regarding domestic violence. At one end of the continuum we find the view of wife-beating as an acceptable way of maintaining the dominant gender order. At the other end, we have the newly developed understanding of domestic violence as a question of gendered power relations and as a human rights issue. The revised Marriage Law, which reflects the ongoing changes in knowledge and aims at changing practices, could be placed somewhere in the middle of the continuum. On one hand, the law criminalises domestic violence; on the other hand, activists criticise it for being gender-blind and not recognising that domestic violence is predominantly an issue of male violence against women. By generating new knowledge, activists engaged in domestic violence activism have moved from one end of the continuum to various points towards the other end. The process of changing knowledge is ongoing and although leaders and core activists in several organisations define domestic violence as a question of gendered power relations, not all activists agree with them. In our survey 37.4 per cent of 155 Beijing activists stated that male domestic violence against women is rooted in unequal gendered power relations, with whom only 33.5 per cent were in partial agreement.[60]

Moreover, among activists who view domestic violence as a women's movement and human rights issue there is disagreement about the relative importance of addressing this particular issue compared to other gender equality issues. Some activists contend that resources – including both activist time and energy and donor funds – should primarily be concentrated on problems such as gender inequality in education and employment. In 2001, Pi Xiaoming, who was among the first activists to address domestic violence and who in 1997 co-organised one of the first conferences held by an NGO on the issue of domestic violence, was of the opinion that sufficient attention had been focused on domestic violence and that issues such as literacy and employment should now be prioritised. Conversely, others, notably the Domestic Violence Network, argue that domestic violence can detrimentally affect women's ability to gain an education, earn a livelihood, develop personal relationships and fully enjoy the human rights to which they are entitled as equal citizens. Thus, addressing domestic violence functions as an entry point towards alleviating a wide range of gender inequalities in all spheres of women's lives. Another point of contention among activists concerns the intervention into the 'private' sphere of the family in domestic violence cases that is now being advocated by some NGOs and Women's Federations. The argument against intervention is that at a time when the state is reducing its penetration into many spheres of people's lives, it is not desirable to advocate new forms of penetration into the realm of the family.

## Conclusion

Of all the activists we interviewed who considered domestic violence a public issue meriting legislation, who subscribed to a gendered power relations interpretation and who viewed domestic violence as a human rights violation, none had held such a view when they first became aware of and began to address the issue of wife-beating. Domestic violence activism has developed, and is continuously developing, through stages of discovery, exploration, re-interpretation and re-definition as a complex issue that can ultimately be viewed as a human rights issue. Non-governmental feminist activism is grounded in a situated learning process that started within the Women's Federation system and in popular organising before the 1995 Women's Conference. The Women's Conference legitimised activism against the issue of domestic violence. Subsequently, interpretations that were already being explored were further developed by activists in popular organising and through a process of transnational interactions. Activists encountered a global emancipatory epistemic community and they developed their knowledge in interactions with this community. Some of these activists then joined an emancipatory epistemic community that clearly defines domestic violence as a human rights issue.

At present those who operate at the core of Beijing's non-governmental organising against domestic violence firmly subscribe to interpretations that see such violence as a human rights issue. By adopting the terminologies and interpretations of a global epistemic community involved in the defining of women's rights as human rights, including United Nations declarations, they actively promote the development of domestic violence legislation in China and challenge unjust gender discourse and practices. In this paper we have shown how one particular group of activists from popular organising in Beijing has generated new knowledge on the issue. By continuing and further developing collaboration with party-state institutions, primarily the Women's Federation system, these activists are working to reach out to various professional groups such as the police, the judiciary, and the medical establishment. In so doing they hope to promote changes of attitudes and practices in Chinese society and gradually shift the general attitude to domestic violence towards the human rights end of the current continuum of understanding. The process of questioning taken-for-granted assumptions related to domestic violence and building up new knowledge has been systematised through the use of gender training. This training aims to disseminate to policy-makers and professionals a gender transformative perspective for understanding and addressing domestic violence widely in society. Gender training has become a tool with which to guide individuals and groups through the various stages of knowledge acquisition: from challenging notions that hold wife-beating to be acceptable practice towards recognising domestic violence as a public and gendered issue. The latter position is based upon an international recognition of domestic violence as situated within a social and structural context of unequal power relations between men and women. Through a process of knowledge construction, a relatively small group of well-educated, urban activists have joined a global emancipatory epistemic community. In collaboration with the Women's Federation their aim is to extend that community throughout China to party-state institutions and to citizens in both urban and rural regions.

## Acknowledgements

This paper is a radically revised version of earlier papers. It first appeared under the title 'NGO Activism – Changing Domestic Violence Knowledge', a paper presented at the

Danish Institute of Human Rights Workshop on Law Implementation in China in May 2004. Parts of it subsequently reappeared in a paper entitled 'Popular Organizing to Combat Domestic Violence – Gender Analysis and Media Interaction', presented at the International Conference on Feminism in China since the Women's Bell, held at Fudan University in Shanghai, in July 2004; a Chinese version of this paper has been published in *Shehui Xingbie (Gender Studies)*. Some of the material discussed here was also presented in a paper entitled 'Organizing for Gender Equality in China – a Process of Cultural and Political Change' at the 36th World Congress of Sociology in Beijing in July 2004. We are most grateful to the audiences and to Michael Jacobsen, Mads Holst Jensen, Marina Svensson, and Hatla Thelle for their comments and suggestions. We also thank Erik Baark for special advice, Alexandra Kent for language revision, the NIAS–Linc librarians for their help, and the anonymous reviewers for valuable suggestions. Research for this article was made possible by a grant from the Danish Council for Development Research.

## Notes

1. C. Bunch, 'Tranforming Human Rights from a Feminist Perspective', in J. Peters and A. Wolper (eds), *Women's Rights – Human Rights. International Femnist Perspectives* (New York and London: Routledge 1995), pp.11–17, and J. Joachim, 'Shaping the Human Rights Agenda: The Case of Violence against Women', in M. K. Meyer and E. Prügl (eds), *Gender Politics in Global Governance* (Lanham, MD: Rowman & Littlefield 1999), pp.142–60.
2. In this paper we use the term 'non-governmental organisation' (NGO) synonymously with the Chinese term 'popular organisation' (*minjian zuzhi*). We define 'popular', meaning 'of the people', as bottom-up organising initiated by activists themselves with activities also determined mainly from below by activists. For an elaboration on the definition and use of the term popular organising, see C. Milwertz, *Beijing Women Organizing for Change – A New Wave of the Chinese Women's Movement* (Copenhagen: Nordic Institute of Asian Studies 2002), pp.23–5. For a discussion of the definition of women's NGOs in China see N. Sausmikat, 'NGO, Frauen und China', *Asien – Deutsche Zeitschrift für Politik, Wirtschaft und Kultur*, No.80 (July 2001), pp.81–92. For a brief overview of the establishment of popular organising in Beijing see C. Milwertz, 'Activism Against Domestic Violence in the People's Republic of China', *Violence Against Women*, Vol.9, No.6 (June 2003), pp.630–55. We define popular/non-governmental organising as feminist in the sense that the activists and their organisations engage in political and cultural processes of critically examining, challenging and transforming taken-for-granted social discourse and practices. They do so from the position of protest against unjust gender relations.
3. N. Zhang, 'Unintended Consequences of Hosting a Women's Conference: Beijing and Beyond', in H. R. Christensen, B. Halsaa and A. Saarinen (eds), *Crossing Borders: Re-mapping Women's Movements at the Turn of the 21st Century* (Odense, Denmark: University Press of Southern Denmark 2004), pp.171–87. See P. Hsiung, M. Jaschok and C. Milwertz, with R. Chan (eds), *Chinese Women Organizing – Cadres, Feminists, Muslims, Queers* (Oxford: Berg 2001), and J. Howell, 'Women's Organizations and Civil Society in China', *International Feminist Journal of Politics*, Vol.5, No.2, (2003), pp.191–215 on the emergence and development of popular/non-governmental women's organising in China.
4. Zhang (note 3). See also J. Howell 'Post-Beijing Reflections: Creating Ripples, but not Waves in China', *Women's Studies International Forum*, Vol.20, No.2 (1997), pp.235–52.
5. L. A. West, 'The United Nations Women's Conferences and Feminist Politics', in Meyer and Prügl (note 1) pp.177–272 (p.178).
6. G. C. Spivak, '"Woman" as Theatre: United Nations Conference on Women, Beijing 1995', *Radical Philosophy*, No.75 (January–February 1996), pp.2–4.
7. T. Barlow, 'International Feminism of the Future', *Signs*, Vol.25, No.4 (2000), pp.1099–105 (p.1100).
8. Ibid., p.1099.
9. N. Spakowski, 'The Internationalization of China's Women's Studies', *Berliner China Hefte*, Vol.20 (May 2001), pp.79–100.

10. J. Nie, 'Feminist Bioethics and the Language of Human Rights in the Chinese Context', in R. Tong, A. Donchin and S. Dodds (eds), *Linking Visions: Feminist Bioethics, Human Rights and the Developing World* (Lanham, MD: Rowman & Littlefield 2004), pp.73–88, p.78.
11. A. Heitlinger, 'Cross-border Connections of Czech Women's Groups: The Role of Foreign Funding', in Christensen *et al.* (note 3) pp.189–204.
12. M. Desai, 'Transnational Solidarity. Women's Agency, Structural Adjustment and Globalization', in N. A. Naples and M. Desai (eds), *Women's Activism and Globalization* (New York and London: Routledge 2002), pp.15–33.
13. The encounter between the new NGOs in China and this type of neo-liberal feminism is still more complex. The meetings between Hillary Rodham Clinton (then First Lady of the United States; described by Barlow (note 7) as exemplifying an 'international U.S. feminism' that presents no fundamental challenge to gender and global inequalities) with activists in Beijing and her visits to women's organisations were valued by activists. These meetings, as well as visits by United States Secretary of State Madelaine Albright, served to demonstrate to the Chinese government that high-level, non-Chinese politicians were awarding these women's organisations recognition as important social actors.
14. Zhang, p.182 (note 3).
15. M. Stivens, 'Introduction: Gender Politics and the Reimagining of Human Rights in the Asia-Pacific', in A. Hilsdon, M. Macintyre, V. Mackie and M. Stivens (eds), *Human Rights and Gender Politics. Asia-Pacific Perspectives* (London and New York: Routledge 2000), pp.1–36 (p.2).
16. P. Haas, 'Epistemic Communities and International Policy Coordination', *International Organization*, Vol.46, No.1 (1992), pp.1–35.
17. J. Chan-Tiberghien, 'The Rise of a Women's Human Rights Epistemic Network in the 1990s: Global Norms, Gender Politics and Civil Society', in E. P. Mendes and A. Lalonde-Roussy (eds), *Bridging the Global Divide on Human Rights* (Aldershot: Ashgate 2003), pp.195–219. Chan-Tiberghien's concept of epistemic community was developed within international relations constructivist theory by Peter Haas (note 16). An epistemic community is defined as 'a network of professionals with recognised expertise and competence in a particular domain and authoritative claim to policy-relevant knowledge within that domain or issue-area'. S. Hsu, 'International Linkage and China's Environmental Policies', *Issues and Studies*, Vol.36, No.3 (May–June 2000), pp.61–102 provides an introduction to the concepts of 'epistemic community' and 'epistemic learning' in constructive theory in international relations. See also the TransLECS project, which studies the influence of Western legal and judicial co-operation on the development of the legal and judicial system in China, http://www.chinapolitik.de/trans/index.htm (accessed 24 September 2003).
18. Milwertz (note 2) and S. Wesoky, *Chinese Feminism Faces Globalization* (New York and London: Routledge 2002).
19. According to figures provided by each of the 22 Beijing organisations in our study, a total of 717 activists were active in these organisations up to the year 2000. Of these, 482 were reported to be active in 2000. This figure is approximate as the organisations cannot provide exact numbers. The 180 activists we interviewed were active in an average of three organisations. If we assume that all of 482 then active activists were active in an average of three organisations, then the total number of activists would be 160. We have not been able to include all activists and it is likely that the numbers of activists reported is somewhat low. According to the organisations' reporting, it appears that there may in fact have been some 500 activists who were active in 2000. However, these should also be broken down into those activists that are placed at the core of organising and others who have looser links to organising. See W. Bu and C. Milwertz, *Beijing minjian funü zuzhi shizheng yanjiu*. (Research Report on Popular Women's Organisations in Beijing), Unpublished report prepared for a workshop held in Beijing, November 2002.
20. Building on earlier work by Milwertz (Note 2), this study, which was conducted in 2000 and 2002, of 22 informal groups, registered organisations, and women's studies centres in Beijing includes interviews with 180 activists from these organisations and case studies of six organisations engaged in addressing domestic violence. Five of these organisations addressed domestic violence in the 1990s. One organisation was established in 2000 based on and bringing together experiences from 1990s' activism. We carried out interviews with core and/or leading activists in each of these organisations.
21. The Women's Research Institute was established in 1988. In 1996 it changed its name to the Maple Women's Psychological Counselling Centre.
22. C. Milwertz and W. Bu, 'Creating and Disseminating Gender Knowledge in China', in W. Burghoorn, K. Iwanaga, C. Milwertz and Q. Wang (eds), *Gender Politics in Asia – Processes of Change and Empowerment* (Copenhagen: NIAS Press forthcoming).

23. R. Eyerman and A. Jamison, *Social Movements. A Cognitive Approach* (Oxford: Polity Press 1991) and R. Eyerman and A. Jamison, *Music and Social Movements* (Cambridge: Cambridge University Press 1998) in Milwertz 2003 (note 2).
24. J. Lave, 'The Practice of Learning', in S. Chaiklin and J. Lave (eds), *Understanding Practice. Perspectives on Activity and Context* (Cambridge: Cambridge University Press 1993), pp.3–32, and J. Lave and E. Wenger, *Situated Learning. Legitimate Peripheral Participation* (Cambridge: Cambridge University Press 1991).
25. C. Gilmartin, 'Violence Against Women in Contemporary China', in J. N. Lipman and S. Harrell (eds), *Violence in China* (New York: State University of New York Press 1991), pp.203–21.
26. Ibid. For results of investigations on the extent of domestic violence in Chinese society, see for example A. Guo, *Jiating baoli* (Domestic Violence) (Beijing: Zhongguo gongren chubanshe 2000), pp.109–21, and L. Zhang Lixi and M. Meng, *Zhongguo jiating baoli yanjiu* (Research on Domestic Violence in China) (Beijing: Zhongguo shehui kexue chubanshe 2004).
27. Gilmartin, p.204 (note 25).
28. W. Bu, 'Tantao Zhongguo Funübao ershi nian' (Exploring Twenty Years of China Women's News), Speech at the twentieth anniversary of *China Women's News*, 12 September 2004, and W. Bu and X. Mi (C. Milwertz), 'Minjian funü zuzhi yu dazhong meijie de hudong – Jiating baoli chengwei gonggong wenti de guocheng' (Interaction Between Popular Women's Organisations and the Mass Media – The Process of Making Domestic Violence into a Public Issue), (*Yazhou Chuanmei Yanjiu* (Asian Communication and Media Studies) 2004), pp.61–71.
29. Y. Guo and Y. Cai, 'Xiaochu jiating baoli – xinwen meijie ruhe jingzhong changming' (Eradication of Domestic Violence – How the News Media Can Be Aware of the Issue), in Y. Guo and Y. Feng (eds), *Shui shi bawang, shui shi ji* (Who is the Conqueror and Who is the Concubine) (Beijing: China Women's Publishing House 2000), pp.168–74.
30. C. S. Tang, D. Wong and F. M. Cheung, 'Social Construction of Women as Legitimate Victims of Violence in Chinese Societies', *Violence Against Women*, Vol.8, No.8 (August 2002), pp.968–96, and X. Tong, 'The Production and Reproduction of Unequal Gender Relations – An Analysis of Domestic Violence in China', in L. Stearns (ed.), *Chinese Women's Rights*, Working Paper No.10 (Oslo: Institutt for Mennskerettigheter/ Norwegian Institute of Human Rights 1999), pp.42–56.
31. M. Hester, 'Domestic Violence in China', in J. Radford, M. Friedberg and L. Harne (eds), *Women, Violence and Strategies for Action: Feminist Research, Policy and Practice* (Buckingham: Open University Press 2000), pp.149–66.
32. The Sex/Gender Education Forum has documented the Huang Jing case and the engagement of activists in supporting the case in the documentary 'Garden in Heaven' directed by X. Ai and J. Hu (2005).
33. United Nations, *The Beijing Declaration and Platform for Action* (New York: UN 1996).
34. Tong (note 30), and N. Xue *Revision of the Chinese Marriage Law in 2001*, Working paper (Oslo: Norwegian Institute of Human Rights 2002). See also Guo (note 26) p.5 for a short overview of the three degrees of bodily injuries in the law.
35. For a recent review of research on women and domestic violence see X. Wang, 'Funü yu jiating baoli yanjiu zongshu' (Review of Research on Women and Domestic Violence), in Quanguo fulian funü yanjiusuo (All-China Women's Federation Women's Studies Institute) (ed.), *Zhongguo funü yanjiu nianjian 1996–2000* (Almanac of Chinese Women's Studies 1996–2000) (Beijing: Zhongguo funü chubanshe 2004), pp.56–65.
36. Interview 29 April 2001, transcript 2.4.
37. Milwertz (note 2), and X. Wang, 'Domestic Violence in China', in F. Cheung, M. Karlekar, A. De Dios, J. Vichit-Vadakan and L. R. Quisumbing (eds), *Breaking the Silence: Violence Against Women in Asia*. (Hong Kong: Equal Opportunities Commission 1999), pp.13–37.
38. Interview 3 May 2001, transcript 7.1.
39. Interview 28 April 2001, transcript 6.1.
40. The Women's Federation has since begun to register domestic violence cases. Out of a total of 128,900 complaints registered in 1995 by the All-China Women's Federation in Beijing about one-third related to domestic violence, see Guo (note 26) p.2.
41. Interview 8 May 2001.
42. Interview 3 May 2001, transcript 5.
43. X. Pi, 'Jiating baoli – baipishu' (Domistic Violence – Whitebook), *Zhongguo funü* (Chinese Women), No.12 (1991), pp.20–2. See also Y. Cai, Y. Feng and Y. Guo, 'The Women's Media Watch Network', in P. Hsiung,

M. Jaschok and C. Milwertz with R. Chan (eds), *Chinese Women Organizing – Cadres, Feminists, Muslims, Queers* (Oxford: Berg 2001), pp.209–26 for an account of the difficult process of Pi Xiaoming's efforts to publish.
44. Interview 3 May 2001, transcript 3.1–3.3.
45. See also Tong (note 30).
46. Interview 5 November 2000, transcript 33.
47. Interview 2 May 2001, transcript 3.
48. Chan-Tiberghien (note 17).
49. Lave (note 24) p.6.
50. Lave and Wenger (note 24).
51. Interview 29 April 2001, transcript 7.3 and 70.1.
52. P. Lather, *Getting Smart. Feminist Research and Pedagogy With/in the Postmodern* (New York and London: Routledge 1991).
53. Ibid.
54. Interview 5 November 2000, transcript 2.2, 2.3 and 7.2.
55. A. Assiter, *Enlightened Women* (London: Routledge 1996).
56. Ibid. p.82.
57. B. Anderson, *Imagined Communities: Reflections on the Origins and Rise of Nationalism* (London: Verso 1982).
58. Eyerman and Jamison (note 23).
59. M. Mukhopadhyay and M. Appel, 'Introduction: Gender Training and Social Transformation: An Agenda for Change', in S. Cummings, H. van Dam and M. Valk (eds), *Gender Training: The Source Book* (Amsterdam: Royal Tropical Institute 1998), pp.13–25, p.16.
60. Bu and Milwertz (note 190).

# On China's Slow Boat to Women's Rights: Revisions to the Women's Protection Law, 2005

MICHAEL PALMER

## 1. Introduction

A very significant dimension of the policies on social inequality in post-Mao China has been a shift in concern from social class to social disadvantage. Under Mao, class differences in China were highlighted and class injustices treated – and to some extent corrected – through political mobilisation. In the post-Mao era, however, the concern has been to identify vulnerable socially disadvantaged categories of person and to offer special protection through law to those characterised as socially vulnerable. As a result, a distinctive area of Chinese human rights law has emerged in the past two decades or so. This is characterised as 'social protection law' (*shehui baozhang fa*) or 'social law' (*shehui fa*), that is, legislation designed to protect socially vulnerable categories of citizens (*teshu qunti*, literally 'special groupings') who, in one way or another, are in danger of suffering unfair treatment because of their distinctive social characteristics.[1] This type of rights law is a combination of civil, administrative and criminal law, underpinned by broad principles of constitutional law.

The range of categories seen to be in need of such protection is now very wide. It includes private households and entrepreneurs, handicapped persons, overseas Chinese, and consumers.[2] The three main areas of social vulnerability given such attention, however, are youth, old age, and gender. In the system for the protection of the young we see a strongly controlling framework of rules and policies, seemingly directed at creating the model Chinese socialist citizen. In contrast, in the legal support offered to the elderly, there is a robust and seemingly more genuine attempt to protect and assist the elderly to deal with difficulties of age discrimination.[3] In the legal framework for protecting women's rights and interests – the subject of this paper – we see a continuation of many old problems, with new rules introduced in 2005 in order to try to deal with some of the more intractable difficulties of women's status and discrimination against women. While the revised Women's Protection Law is a significant attempt to deal with these problems, it is still seriously weak in many ways.

As the three categories of person seen as being in greatest need of protection are the young, the elderly, and women, social protection law is also connected closely with family law. Indeed, it was these three categories that were particularly promised 'liberation' from the patriarchal family by Mao Zedong prior to Liberation in 1949. As a result, since 1950, family law has offered special protection for the rights and interests of these categories of 'disadvantaged' persons. Article 1 of the 1950 Marriage Law promised protection for the 'lawful interests of women and children'. In the 1980 Marriage Law this was expanded in several ways. Article 2 (also in the 2001 revised version of the 1980 Law) thus promised that 'the lawful rights and interests of women, children and the elderly shall be protected' – with 'rights' and 'the elderly' being added to the original 1950 wording, indicating a significant expansion in the scope of such protection.

In some respects, the current corpus of protective legislation is primarily a conscious and positive attempt by the Chinese party-state leadership to respond through law to some of the harsh social consequences of China's post-Mao changes – more specifically, it is an attempt to address some of the worst systematic injustices created by traditional prejudices and new, post-Mao, processes of economic change and re-integration with the outside world. However, there is more to the official response than this. For, in reality, the party-state also controls the system of social protection in such a way as to prevent key actors in China's emerging civil society – especially non-governmental organisations – from gaining too much autonomy and capacity for protest. This control is achieved through the distinctive manner in which social protection policy is being implemented – in particular, through mass organisations such as the All-China Women's Federation, which was specifically set up to protect and promote the rights and interests of women. In addition, the social protection policies are located in an environment in which the state seeks to assume fewer social responsibilities but has yet to provide the comprehensive system of social welfare that it has promised in legislation such as the 1994 Labour Law.[4] Thus, within the corpus of special protection legislation, the onus is often placed on the role of the family in dealing with the three key disadvantaged groups' distinctive problems. The stream of protective legislation is also very much the product of traditional paternalistic state attitudes. It is reminiscent of the imperial Chinese legal protection – based on Confucian notions of benevolence[5] – extending special treatment to children, the elderly, and women.[6] This benevolence served to 'balance' or 'compensate' for the generally punitive and authoritarian nature of the imperial code. In contemporary China, too, the emergence of 'modern' protective legislation over the past decade has been accompanied by an intensification of the punitive nature of the criminal law through a series of important amendments to the 1979 Criminal Law – amendments written into the revised code of 1997. As a result, there are now approximately 70 offences carrying the death penalty.[7] The 'protection' legislation, then, also bears the imprint of some traditional thinking – it extends a 'compensatory' protection to categories of person severely disadvantaged by the prevailing political and governmental system and by social attitudes. In offering this protection, China's authoritarian state lays claims to, and 'demonstrates', its inherent benevolence, despite imposing at the same time a very draconian system of criminal justice. Finally, the need for such specific legislation arises because of the failure of Chapter II of the 1982 Constitution of the People's Republic of China to protect adequately the rights of citizens. The purpose of the provisions in that chapter should be seen as exhortatory and programmatic, rather than as concrete expressions of the state's concern with the welfare of its citizens.[8] However, at the same time China has signed and sometimes acceded to various international human rights instruments, thereby assuming various obligations under international law. Thus, something additional has often been needed in order to provide more legally meaningful provisions in domestic law.[9]

The 2005 revisions to the Women's Protection Law[10] represent the first major reform of the various social protection laws that have been steadily introduced in the post-Mao period, although they do also build on a number of relevant changes affecting the legal position of women introduced through a refurbishment of the Marriage Law in 2001.[11] This paper examines the nature and significance of the latest attempt to promote women's rights and interests, and to discourage discrimination against women, by means of legal provisions. It considers the revisions to the Law and their likely impact in the light of what is known about problems of gender discrimination and inequality in China. This paper sees the revision of the Women's Protection Law as reflecting a continuing concern with the problems of realising the official policy of equality between men and women and, more specifically, with protecting women's rights and interests. Nevertheless, on closer examination, the 2005 reforms may be seen to be relatively limited in extent, indicating that rather slow progress is being made in the direction of the declared robust official policy on the need for gender equality and the protection of women's rights and interests. In this paper, the section that follows provides a very compressed historical account of the unfolding efforts to enhance the position of women in Chinese society. Sections three to eight will then each deal with particular chapters, or groupings of related chapters, of the revised Women's Protection Law. The most important provisions in the General Principles chapter are considered, together with an examination of the key general issue of enforcement, in section three. The section that follows deals with efforts to promote the socio-economic position of women, and considers issues of education, employment and property. The rights of person are then examined in section five, with particular attention being given to problems of sexual harassment and violence against women. The two succeeding sections will look at the position of women in the family, and is concerned primarily with questions of divorce, domestic violence and family planning. Section eight examines the issue of women's participation in the system of political representation in China, a key issue that need to be addressed successfully if China's policy commitment to gender equality is to be transformed into effective practice. There then follows a concluding section which draws together and discusses the findings.

## 2. Women in Chinese Society and Efforts at Reform

When it was established in 1949, the People's Republic of China inherited a long-standing and persistent problem of gender inequality.[12] Traditional values and norms – predominantly Confucian inspired – emphasised the importance of inequalities of gender and age, both in society in general and within the fundamental social unit, the family. Men, especially older men, were dominant; women, especially younger women, were subordinate. This was reflected in imperial statutory law as well as local customary norms; men were accorded a privileged status with the status of women rigorously subordinated to that of men. Not surprisingly, reforms in the position of women were a recurrent theme in more general efforts to transform Chinese society. Such reformist efforts were found in the mid-nineteenth century Boxer Rebellion, Western missionary teachings, the May Fourth Movement, the Nationalist Government Family reforms especially as expressed in Books IV and V on 'Family' and 'Succession', respectively, of the Civil Code 1931,[13] and the experimental policies pursued (albeit inconsistently) in areas 'liberated' by the Chinese Communist Party.[14] The marriage law-based reforms of the early 1950s introduced shortly after 'liberation' by the Communist party-state were also important in promoting the legal and social position of women. Alongside policies designed to encourage greater female participation in the workforce, the legal reforms of the early 1950s were in particular intended to promote the position of women so that they might be able to contribute more effectively to the construction of a socialist society in China. However, as Evans has emphasised, while there were indeed major improvements to the position of women after 'liberation', the post-1949 reforms were invariably qualified: 'the subordination of gender to the supposedly more substantial matters of economic development and political power has been a recurring feature of the party-state's approach to woman-work since the early days of communist control'.[15] As a result, while laws were enacted as part of a general policy to release women from marriages in which their primary roles were the production of a son and domestic service, and the party-state consistently promoted the idea and practice of women working outside the home, as well as providing education that would facilitate women's participation in a new, socialist community, the impact of these reforms was rather more limited than many had hoped – an outcome characterised by some scholars as the 'unfinished liberation' of Chinese women.[16]

Moreover, the gains that women did make in the period under Mao have been put in jeopardy by some of the negative consequences of the post-Mao economic reforms. In particular, as market-orientated and private-sector-focused policies increasingly replaced the old emphasis on the public sector and macro-economic management of the economy by means of state planning, so the collective institutions developed in the first three decades of socialist rule, such as the state-owned enterprise and the rural commune, have been supplanted to a significant extent by newer and somewhat less protective and welfare-orientated institutions including the joint-stock company, township government, and privatised agriculture. These and other significant changes and difficulties – for example, a greater degree of personal freedom and therefore more social space for the operation of re-emergent patriarchal popular attitudes – have made inroads into the position of women, leaving them exposed to the risk of discriminatory and oppressive conduct in a range of areas. Among the most serious of such difficulties are reduced access to educational opportunities – including university entrance;[17] gender stratification in the workplace – including within the ranks of the unemployed;[18] reduced access to the public health services;[19] unlawful purchase or kidnapping of women for sale as wives or for the purpose of coerced prostitution; forced marriage; sexual exploitation; as well as greater burdens on women in respect of birth limitation;[20] infringement and lack of awareness of women's property rights;[21] heavier domestic duties for women;[22] and reduced female political participation.[23] One noted analyst concludes that the difficulties have been most serious in the countryside and observes that even today many rural women endure lives of extreme brutality: 'if they survive birth, abandonment and poor medical care, they may find themselves abducted and sold into prostitution or marriage, or coerced into making decisions about fertility and reproduction with devastating effects on themselves and their offspring'.[24] From the early 1980s onwards, sustained attempts were made to address some of these difficulties – attempts that included in particular the introduction in 1992 of a Law for the Protection of Women's Rights and Interests. Unfortunately, this Law has struggled to combat discrimination against women, in part because 'in the drafting process the government backed away from passing a truly revolutionary document and finally adopted a draft that reaffirmed its existing sexist policies'.[25]

## 3. Policy, Enforcement and Duties

In the post-Mao period, the development of legislation specifically designed to promote and protect women's rights and interests began in 1980, when China became a party to the 1979 United Nations Convention on the Elimination of All Forms of Discrimination Against Women (CEDAW, which entered into force on 26 November 1982). Following this, a number of provincial codes of women's protection were introduced,[26] these efforts culminating in the promulgation on 3 April 1992 of the Law of the People's Republic of China for the Protection of Women's Rights and Interests (which entered into force on 1 October 1992). This Law was a significant effort to promote a higher status for women in Chinese society.[27] However, as we have suggested, the Law is not considered to have been a success – the generally conservative thinking that underpinned it limited its effectiveness. After more than a decade of experience with this Law, the party-state leadership moved to substantially modify it through a revised version promulgated on 28 August 2005.

The General Principles chapter of the revised Law lays out important dimensions of China's policies on women. The basic principle of gender equality is emphasised in Article 1: 'this law is enacted to [1] safeguard women's lawful rights and interests (and) [2] to promote equality between man and women'. Indicative of the party-state's felt need to strengthen its commitment to gender equality, Article 2 now contains a provision not found in the 1992 version of the Law: 'it is a basic policy of the State to implement equality between men and women'. In addition, a new Article 3 requires that the State Council and local governments enact programmes for women's development. The decision to require governmental bodies specifically to include women's rights and interests in their planning is a step forward. It is significant because – as emphasised in the preceding section – the policies of the party-state leadership, in promoting a more market-orientated and private-property-based programme of economic development, have not included an appropriate vision of the contributions that women might make in this area of social life. Nor has the party-state thought through how women might be best protected against the social pressure steadily mounting against them. Post-Mao development strategies have emphasised 'consumerism, capital accumulation, massive lay offs and centrally located, export-orientated, foreign-funded industries',[28] and these goals have not worked to the benefit of the economic or social position of women.

Articles 6, 7, and 9 in this chapter repeat earlier provisions (Articles 4, 5, and 7 in the 1992 version of the Law) encouraging governmental bodies and relevant mass organisations such as the All-China Women's Federation and trade unions to protect women's rights and interests. Thus, the 'mass organisation' approach[29] to the issue of gender equality is persisted with – indeed, a revised provision in Article 10 (formerly Article 9) strengthens this approach. Women's organisations such as the All-China Women's Federation now have the right to be consulted in the drafting of all new laws. Of course, the extent to which this has a beneficial impact on gender equality will depend in part on the policies of the Women's Federation, and this is a matter considered later in this paper.

In order to enhance the prospects for effective implementation of women's rights, the Law has a special section on 'Legal Responsibility'. This provides opportunities for women to obtain relief against discriminatory conduct. Thus, Article 52 (formerly, Article 48) gives women the right to demand that the relevant government department remedy the problem or to bring suit in a people's court. Moreover, Article 50 specifies that administrative discipline (*xingzheng chufen*) may be taken against state officials who bear responsibility for discriminatory conduct against women in the following specific areas: first, in dealing with complaints of infringement of women's rights; secondly, in employment matters; thirdly, in allocations of land and housing in rural areas; and, finally, in educational matters. In addition, Article 56 stipulates that not only is there the prospect that administrative discipline will be imposed on state functionaries who take retaliatory action against those who lodge complaints against them, but also threatens a more serious response: 'if the reprisal is criminal, [the functionary] shall be dealt with in accordance with the criminal law'.

Nevertheless, a preference persists here to push women into administrative processes to resolve their grievances rather than to encourage greater use of the courts. Especially in rural areas, women will continue to find it difficult to secure gender justice. Despite the strengthening of the system of enforcement through these amendments to the Women's Protection Law and by institutional changes such as the creation of special chambers for women's rights in the people's courts, the law remains vague in the area of remedies and the manner in which such remedies might best be secured and enforced. A key problem here is that the revised Law again fails to provide a clear and adequate definition of 'discrimination against women' – one that would involve both direct and indirect aspects of such conduct. Moreover, elsewhere in the General Principles section there are also indications that the party-state's commitment to equality of status continues to be less than whole-hearted. Thus, Article 1 also states that gender equality in China is valued not only for its own sake but also because it will assist women to contribute more effectively to China's 'socialist modernisation' (*shehui zhuyi xiandaihua*). The retention from the 1992 version of the Law of this functional justification of an enhancement of the role of women in China's socialist development may well serve to perpetuate inequality. It continues to encourage the view that in circumstances in which the protection of women's rights and the promotion of equality between men and women do not obviously contribute to economic advances there is less need to take action against discrimination. This qualified view is reinforced by the provisions of Article 6 which suggest that women are to some extent responsible for the discrimination that they suffer, for women are now urged to 'have self-respect, self-confidence, to stand on their own feet, to improve themselves [*ziqiang*], and to use the law [*falü*] to defend their own lawful rights and interests'.

Moreover, in the Chapter on Educational and Cultural Rights, the revised Law merely continues to provide in Article 21, in respect of cultural rights, that women should 'enjoy equal rights with men in their participation in scientific, technological, literary, artistic and other cultural activities'. This ignores the real need in China to deal with many of the traditional and cultural stereotypes about women and gender differences – labels that have been important factors encouraging the persistence of gender discrimination. Stereotypes that men are superior to women in terms of academic abilities, suitability for the world of employment, and aptitude for leadership continue to prevail, and this failure to confront such stereotypes in the section on cultural rights is especially regrettable in a society in which state control of the media is so pronounced. It reflects the fact that the party-state still views women in instrumental terms, to be valued not in their own right but instead for what they can do to meet China's developmental needs.[30]

In addition, there is China's important philosophical/jurisprudential principle that in the family and other areas of social life there should be a balance of rights and duties. In a manner consistent with this principle, women are still advised, in the second paragraph of Article 5, to 'observe the laws of the state, respect social ethics and fulfil the obligations prescribed by law'. More generally, the continuing concern with social ethics is important because it not only again indicates that women's rights are contingent rather than absolute. It also suggests that women have a particular responsibility to bear for the decline in moral standards that the party-state leadership feels has taken place in the post-Mao era. Elsewhere in the Law, concern with duties is manifested in relation to matters of family planning. Article 51 of the revised Law continues to place disproportionate responsibility on women for contraception and other forms of birth control, which encourages violence and other forms of coercive conduct against women, leaving them vulnerable to forced methods of birth control such as abortions, non-consensual sterilisation, and imposed contraception (for example, a covertly fitted intrauterine device), as well as discrimination at work. The problem of the unfair burden placed on women in the name of the policy goal of population control is another key issue to which this paper will return.

## 4. Education, Employment and Property Rights

Chapter III of the 2005 revised Women's Protection Law deals primarily with educational matters and, *inter alia*, declares gender equality to be a basic feature of education in China (Article 14). Here, as elsewhere in this chapter, the provisions in the 1992 version and those in the 2005 version are in most respects the same. The chapter reminds parents and guardians of their duty to ensure that their daughters receive compulsory education (Article 19). It also encourages the state to continue the good fight against female illiteracy (Article 18). This, however, is an area of the revised Law that is given a small but potentially very significant additional measure. Article 16, replacing Article 15, now attempts to secure greater equality of access to educational institutions: 'when enrolling students, schools shall not reject female students nor raise the standards for admission of female students on grounds of gender except for special subjects (*teshu zhuanye*)'. Any enhancement of gender equality in this area is potentially very significant because, of course, social status in China – old and new – has been and still is very much a reflection of command of language, especially the written script.[31] That is, Chinese society has always placed great emphasis on language competence – the 'technology of the intellect' – and without special support there is always a danger that young girls will be given second-class treatment and denied access to this important social resource.[32]

In subsequent chapters, too, significant efforts are made to respond to the disadvantaged position of women in post-Mao society. Two especially important areas that the 1992 Law addressed were property and employment, and these concerns are also stressed in the revised Law.

Thus, the revised Law continues to affirm legal equality for women in respect of property (Article 30, formerly Article 28). The revised Law also continues to offer protection to women's lawful property rights within the web of family property relations (*jiating gongyou caichan guanxi*) (Article 31, replicating Article 29 of the 1992, unrevised, version of the Law). Article 32 repeats the provisions in Article 30 of the 1992 Law, giving women equal rights to farm land under the rural responsibility or *chengbao* contract system.[33] Meanwhile, there is some strengthening of women's property rights in the 2005 revisions as Article 32 goes beyond its predecessor to insist that women enjoy equal rights of compensation for land which has been resumed by the state – thereby implementing the revised constitutional provision on the vexed question of land grabbing by local governments and others: 'the State may, in the public interest and in accordance with the provisions of law, expropriate or requisition land for its use and shall make compensation for the land expropriated or requisitioned' (Constitution, Article 10, as amended in 2004). In addition, the provisions of Article 33 – absent in the 1992 version of the Law – strengthen women's economic rights at the local level, and also encourage uxorilocal marriage. Thus, on one hand the new provisions prohibit discrimination against women in their involvement in the local collective economy by virtue of a particular marital status – such as being divorced or otherwise without a spouse; on the other hand, a man who marries uxorilocally is also to enjoy equal rights in the local collective economy – that is, a man who moves in with his wife's family should enjoy equal rights and interests in local collective economic organisations as other local men. And the uxorilocally married man's children are to be similarly protected by Article 33. Thus, there is in the new measures a significant attempt to promote an alternative to patrilocal post-marital residence – a traditional norm that has continued in the Chinese countryside through to the present day and which often places young married women in a difficult and sometimes dangerous position *vis-à-vis* her husband and his family.

The succession rights of widows continue to be given special protection but even in the 2005 revised version of the Women's Protection Law the provisions offer little more than that already provided in the Inheritance Law 1985. Emphasis continues to be given to the rights of the dutiful daughter-in-law – the succession rights of the widow who has been a particularly dutiful daughter-in-law are expressed in terms significantly stronger than those used in the Inheritance Law itself. Article 35 (formerly Article 32) of the revised Women's Protection Law insists that there be no infringement of the inheritance rights of a married woman who has taken principal responsibility for providing care for her mother-in-law or father-in-law. She is a first-order heir and benefits equally with the children of the deceased. Given the continued importance in the Chinese countryside of traditional attitudes on widow's rights – attitudes which in social practice severely restrict the enjoyment of such rights – it is likely that the widow who intends to remarry will continue to be barred in practice from retaining possession of the property which she is entitled in law to inherit. For this reason, Article 34 (previously, Article 31) of the revised Women's Protection Law emphasises the widow's right to dispose freely of the share of the estate which she has inherited and 'no one is permitted to interfere with the disposal'. Articles 34 and 35 do, however, appear to continue to reflect not so much the state's concern with women's rights as its policy that the household should function effectively as a unit of care. That is to say, women's rights are here given special protection because they contribute to China's social welfare policies.

Discrimination against females in employment matters is another major concern for Chinese women's protection law. Building on legislation introduced in the late 1980s, the 1992 Law attempted to address the problem of unequal treatment of women at work. It stipulated that there be equality in the right to work and in matters of hiring, pay, housing and other material benefits, and promotion (Articles 21 to 24, now Articles 22 to 25). In general, the employment position of women has not improved since the early 1990s, with strong evidence of continued inequality – even in urban areas – in respect of educational attainments and their effects on employment history, seniority and salary, job flexibility in the growing market sector, and so forth.[34]

However, in the revised Law, a clause has been added to the current Article 22 giving women not only the equal right to work but now also the equal right to social security. This is an important extension of the basic principle of gender equality in employment matters, as the lay-off of workers from state-owned enterprises in particular has differentially and adversely impacted on women. Thus, the Law now acknowledges that women too need assistance when laid-off or suffering from similar problems. More might have been done to protect women from the problem of lay-offs from state-owned enterprises, but this is at least a step in the right direction.

In the revised Law there is also been a generalisation to all women of the provisions on the welfare needs of physically disadvantaged women – these were given special attention in Article 27 of the 1992 version of the Law: 'the state should develop social insurance, social relief and medical welfare systems to provide material assistance for old, sick or disabled women'. In the replacement provision – Article 28 – such assistance is extended to women in general: 'The state shall develop social insurance, social relief, social welfare and health care ... so as to ensure women enjoy the rights and interests in the aspects of social insurance, social relief, social welfare and health care.... The state promotes and encourages the public welfare activities aiming to help women.' At the moment, this remains little more than a set of paper promises but, again, it is a small step in the right direction.

The 1992 Law also addressed the issue of discrimination against women in relation to the bearing of children. Along with a prohibition in Article 26 on dismissal of a female worker because of her marriage, pregnancy and childbirth, specific safeguards were provided in Article 25 for women during pregnancy and for a period after childbirth. These forms of protection are confirmed in Articles 27 and 26 of the revised Law. However, Article 27 of the revised Law provides additional safeguards: lowering women's salary – not just dismissal – on gender grounds and discriminating against women in implementing the national retirement system are now also forbidden. Thus, women's salaries and pension rights are given greater protection in law.

A major problem persists, however, with the provision formerly contained in paragraph 1 of Article 25 and now repeated in Article 26, which may well serve to reinforce traditional gender stereotypes in the world of work. For it speaks of 'women's special needs' (*funü tedian*) as a basis for limiting access to certain kinds of work – a unit 'should not assign women any work or labour that is unsuitable for them'. Moreover, the specific safeguards afforded women in relation to pregnancy and associated matters may also have unintended consequences inimical to the employment position of women. In particular, they will continue to make the employment prospects of women in the private sector more difficult as the law makes women more expensive to recruit and retain. Article 27 of the revised Law states:

> No unit shall reduce salaries of women staff, dismiss women staff, or unilaterally terminate employment contracts or service agreements with them by reason of marriage, pregnancy, maternity leave or breast feeding unless the female staff requests termination of the employment contract or service agreement.
>
> No unit shall discriminate against women by reason of gender when implementing the national retirement system.

In addition, the 2005 revised Law contains a provision on family planning and women's employment absent from the 1992 version, in Article 29:

> The state implements the child-bearing insurance system and shall establish other sound guarantee systems relating to child-bearing.
>
> The local people's governments at all levels and the relevant departments shall provide poor women with necessary child-bearing assistance in pursuance of the pertinent provisions.

Thus, there is here an explicit linking of work and reproduction. On one hand, financial assistance in the form of insurance is to be given to women who give birth, designed to deal with the troubles often found in families in which the first child is a girl. On the other hand, special assistance is to be given to women from poorer families in their reproduction. This reflects the fact that the party-state is concerned about the correlation between childbirth and poverty; it tends to be the case that poorer families tend to be the ones that have a comparatively higher number of births as well as births of children suffering from some form of disability. Poor people prize large families as a way of overcoming labour shortages, and also often suffer from poor environmental conditions – which are thought to increase the likelihood of children being born disabled.[35]

Finally, the revised Law addresses issues in relation to the employment of young girls. The provisions in Article 23 stipulate that a female under the age of 16 may not be employed, unless there are special circumstances so permitting. Interestingly, the equivalent provisions in Article 22 of the 1992 Law did not have this 'get-out' clause: 'unless there are special provisions permitting this'. Thus, it appears that the revised Law is actually a little softer on the employment of young girls – this more relaxed approach is explained in terms of the need to deal with the particular circumstances of acrobats and other performers among which young girls are stars.[36]

## 5. Rights of Person

Chapter VI of the 2005 revised Law of the People's Republic of China on the Protection of Women's Rights and Interests is concerned with the rights of person and reaffirms provisions in the Criminal Law 1997 and the General Principles of the Civil Law 1985 that protect women's rights to life, representation, and reputation. We have already briefly noted the reforms regarding protection of women from domestic violence that have been introduced by the Marriage Law as revised in 2001 and Article 46 of the revised Women's Protection Law. These will be considered at greater length in the following section. In addition, reflecting some of the other problems of abuse that women have suffered in recent years, a number of important provisions were introduced into the revised Women's Protection Law.

Thus, Article 42 of the revised Women's Protection Law brings together the provisions in Articles 38 and 39 of the 1992 Law to give better consideration to safeguarding women's rights of portrait, reputation, privacy and honour. This is intended to protect women and young girls against media intrusion and distortion, false rumours about sexual honour, and unauthorised use of a photographic image: 'without a woman's [express] permission, it is prohibited to use her portrait in advertisements, trademarks, window display, newspapers, periodicals, books, audio-visual products, electronic publications, internet, and so on'.[37]

In addition, Article 42 prohibits not only discrimination (*qishi*) against women but also abuse (*nüedai*) and injury (*canhai*). The revised Law adds a category of maltreatment not found in its 1992 predecessor, namely, *yiqi* or abandonment. While this is an important reform, it is not necessarily one in which the sole or even prime motive is the protection of women's rights and interests, for this also represents the strengthening of the family as a unit of care. It is fully consistent with general policies in which welfare burdens that are carried by the state in many other jurisdictions have been made the responsibility of the family in China, especially since 1978.

Article 36 reaffirms the provision that women enjoy equal rights to person as men do. Article 38, reiterating the provisions in Article 35 of the 1992 Law, provides for women's rights to life and health, but further adds that women who are suffering illness or are disabled or who are elderly deserve special protection. The concern with physical abuse of women as manifested in Article 38 is important, as it points to the need to deal with continuing injustices suffered by women in contemporary China – some of which, indeed, have emerged as serious problems as a result of China's post-1978 changed developmental direction. Article 38 thus states:

> Women's right of life and health shall be inviolable. Drowning, abandoning or infanticide in any manner of female babies shall be prohibited; discrimination against or maltreatment of women who gave birth to female babies or who are barren shall be prohibited; cruel treatment causing injury even death of women by superstition or violence shall be prohibited; maltreatment or abandonment of sick, disabled and aged women are prohibited.

An amendment to Article 39 (formerly Article 36) strengthens the position of abducted women in two respects. First, efforts to assist such women are given greater protection, because any attempt to resist such assistance is prohibited. Secondly, the All-China Women's Federation is now given a role, alongside government departments and the police, in providing such assistance and in helping women cope with the after-effects of their abduction. In addition, Article 59 of the revised Law bans discrimination against women who have been abducted and trafficked, or kidnapped. Also, as we have seen, the revised Marriage Law gives women forced into marriage the right to secure an annulment of the forced marriage. These are important reforms, although the problem they address – the kidnapping of women for the purpose of marriage or trafficking – is a serious social difficulty in rural China, and given that the women victimised by such kidnapping are often very poor, have gained very little education and hail from remote areas, it is likely that much greater attention to the problem and institutional support for oppressed women will be necessary before significant improvement can be secured in reality.[38]

In a major breakthrough, a prohibition is placed in Article 40 on sexual harassment or *xingsaorao*. Thus, women who suffer sexual harassment may now make a complaint to their work unit or other relevant authorities. Also, under Article 58, in case of sexual harassment or domestic violence a woman can ask the Public Security Bureau to intervene. Sexual harassment is an issue to which increasing attention has been paid since the mid-1990s. Initial worries focused on the treatment of women migrant workers and on male physicians' misconduct in respect of their female patients. In due course a wider concern emerged, giving rise to demands among some of China's people's deputies for the introduction of an anti-sexual harassment law. Indeed, the issue was first raised in the National People's Congress in 1998, when China's parliamentarians were considering a draft law on licensed doctors. However, progress has been slow. Victims who spoke out often found themselves jeopardised in terms of employment, career prospects, and personal reputation. The first attempt to bring suit on this issue, which took place in a local court in Xian City, failed because the plaintiff was deemed not to have provided sufficient evidence. The plaintiff, Mrs. Tong, and her lawyer were both very dissatisfied with the outcome, arguing that evidence of sexual harassment by the General Manager of the company where she worked was extremely strong.[39] This case, however, resulted in calls for clearer legal definitions of such misconduct, as the provisions in China's civil law on infringement of a citizen's personal rights and interests did not provide sufficient guidance for a court to handle such suits effectively. A series of cases followed, some of which were successful, and in the refurbishment of the Women's Protection Law some of China's foremost family law specialists – in particular, Professors Yang Dawen and Wu Changzhen – pushed hard for the inclusion of an anti-sexual harassment provision. Although the prohibition is expressed in broad terms as a matter of principle, it is expected that Supreme People's Court interpretations will provide more specific detail, and that codes such as the Labour Law, the Teachers Law and the Doctors Law will be amended in order to deal with sexual harassment in the near future.[40]

Finally, as noted above, Article 41 strengthens the language prohibiting organised prostitution or forced participation in obscene activities. Article 41, which now not only prohibits the organisation of prostitution and the forcing or enticing of women into prostitution and other 'obscene activities' but also forbids forcing or enticing women into 'obscene performances' or *yinhui biaoyin huodong* – which, we may assume, include striptease and suchlike. However, this provision on striptease also reflects rather paternalistic and patriarchal values. In addition, it is not clear in what ways, if any, these provisions afford greater protection than those already available in the Criminal Law 1997. Moreover, as emphasised above, the stress in the Legal Responsibility section is still placed on administrative rather than judicial redress of discriminatory conduct, and in practice this will mean that many disputes are handled through mediation and compromise – processes which are not necessarily advantageous for women.

## 6. Marriage and Family

The promulgation of a revised Women's Protection Law in 2005 was preceded by an important and major modification of the 1980 Marriage Law in 2001, designed to address such problems as a high incidence of unregistered marriage and a rising divorce rate. The revised Marriage Law, introduced in April 2001 after a surprisingly robust, but ultimately party-state controlled, public debate, also provided a number of reforms intended in whole or in part to enhance the position of women.[41] Thus, in order to enhance the principle of gender equality, a new provision was added to the General Principles section of the revised Marriage Law: 'husband and wife shall be faithful to and respect each other. Members of the family shall respect the old and take good care of the young, and assist each other so as to maintain equal, harmonious and civilised matrimonial and family relations' (Article 4, Marriage Law, as revised in 2001). The intention here is to encourage a style of family life in which mutual care and respect are fundamental so that, *inter alia*, the wife occupies a secure and protected position. To the extent that this ideal of the harmonious family involves an emphasis on traditional authority norms between family members, and a preference for suppressing rather than expressing grievances within the family, the likelihood is that it will undermine rather than promote gender equality in the domestic context.

In addition, domestic violence is explicitly prohibited in national legislation for the first time.[42] Building on a series of local-level initiatives, Article 3 in the General Principles section of the revised Marriage Law declares: 'domestic violence is prohibited. Within the family, maltreatment or desertion of one family member by another is prohibited.' Procedures for dealing with incidents and complaints of domestic violence and desertion are provided in Articles 43 to 46. The inclusion of these provisions in the revised Marriage Law is a response not only to pressures from within China – it also reflects the party-state leadership's concern about adverse findings by the United Nations Committee on the Elimination of Discrimination Against Women on the state of implementation of China's obligations under CEDAW. In its observations on China's third and fourth periodic reports, the Committee emphasised its concern with a range of types of violence against women including violence in custody; violence within the household; sexual violence; sexual abuse; workplace sexual harassment; and other forms of maltreatment. The Chinese government was advised to reconcile its laws and policies on these issues with CEDAW standards.[43]

Further, the reviving traditional practice of taking a concubine (*bao'er nai*) is explicitly forbidden. Article 3 of the revised Law now declares not only that bigamy is unlawful but also that 'no one who has a spouse may cohabit with any other person'. This reform was directed not only at counteracting the resurgence of a traditional aspect of matrimonial relations demeaning to women but also at the domestic violence that is often thought to be the result of concubinage.[44] In addition, the 2001 revisions introduced a clearer distinction in China's family law between void and voidable marriages, and added a provision on the processes to be followed in seeking a ruling on the matter, as well as the basic principles to be applied where a marriage is declared void (Articles 10, 11, and 12). In particular, the problem of forced marriage is now dealt with in Article 11, which enables a woman forced into marriage to seek dissolution of the union within one year of the forced marriage or one year after her release from captivity. Also important for the protection of women are provisions in Article 8 which allow for remedial marriage registrations in many cases in which one spouse (or both) is underage at the time when the union commenced; I have shown elsewhere that in the absence of such remedial registration, women who marry underage may be discriminated against by the courts.[45] The possibility of remedial registration of marriage removes in some cases the legal disadvantages which a woman may suffer where a couple have commenced cohabitation as if they had registered their relationship as one of lawful marriage but, in fact, have failed to register their union as required by law.

Another important change introduced by the 2001 revision of the Marriage Law concerns women's rights in the system of matrimonial property. The 1980 Marriage Law, promulgated at the very beginning of post-Mao economic reforms, provided only an elementary provision on property relations between spouses: 'the property acquired by the husband and wife during the period in which they are under contract of marriage shall be in their joint [possession] unless they have agreed otherwise husband and wife enjoy equal rights in the disposition of their jointly [possessed] property'. The 2001 revisions, in Article 17, provide a much clearer distinction of what property may be considered as jointly (possessed) matrimonial property. Article 18 defines more effectively the scope of the individually owned property of each spouse and Article 19 encourages the use of clearly expressed, written pre-nuptial agreements between the spouses in cases where they wished to define their own matrimonial property relationships. Among other things, the hope is that the enhanced certainty which these provisions bring will assist women in securing a more equitable division of the matrimonial estate, especially where the husband attempts to defraud his wife by concealing, transferring, selling off or destroying the spousal property or creates a false debt in order to convert their joint property. Finally, the 2001 revisions provide for a system of compensation in which the legislators clearly expect the principal beneficiaries to be maltreated wives. Article 46 allows for the compensation of a spouse against whom the other party has behaved badly; provided that the spouse is without fault, she or he may seek compensation if the other party has committed bigamy, cohabited with a third party (concubinage), inflicted domestic violence or otherwise maltreated or abandoned her or him.

The revised Marriage Law has also introduced specific processes for responding to incidents of domestic violence and other forms of intra-familial abuse, building on experiments that had been taking place at the local level since the late 1990s. Thus, Article 32 provides an abused wife with an exit route from her domestic torment by recourse to divorce – a divorce may be granted if domestic violence, maltreatment or desertion has occurred and divorce mediation has failed. In addition, victims of domestic violence are empowered by Article 43 to seek assistance from a local unit of semi-official ('grassroots') government – that is, an urban neighbourhood residents' or a villagers' committee. The latter bodies are expected to persuade the offender to cease his or her abusive conduct, and to mediate differences between the parties. In addition, the public security bureau may impose an administrative penalty in order to correct and punish the deviant conduct. Thus, domestic violence is no longer a private matter to be dealt with inside the family, and public bodies are expected to play a much more interventionist role in the local responses to incidents and complaints of domestic violence. Article 44 extends similar provisions to those who have been deserted by their spouse, and Article 45 empowers those who have suffered domestic violence, bigamy or other forms of abuse to bring a private prosecution in a people's court. Public security officials are then to investigate the case and if there is sufficient evidence against the perpetrator then the procuracy is to initiate a public prosecution. Although law enforcement officials are known to be reluctant to intervene in such situations, Article 45 leaves them less room to avoid their responsibilities.

I have elsewhere analysed these changes introduced by the revisions to the Marriage Law in some detail.[46] It suffices to say here that while they certainly enhance the legal position of women in a number of important respects, the law continues to carry some of the characteristic weaknesses of Chinese legislation. These include reliance on exhortatory and sometimes ambiguous language, lack of attention to detail in its enforcement processes, a lack of clarity in allocating responsibility and a conservative moral assumption that fault can be readily ascertained when a marriage breaks down.

The effort to enhance the position of women within the family is continued in Chapter VII of the 2005 revised Women's Protection Law, which deals with marriage and family rights (*hunyin jiating quanyi*). Some of the provisions merely reaffirm existing principles and rights – in particular, Article 43 reiterates the declaration made in Article 40 of the 1992 Law that within the family women and men enjoy equal rights. Other areas of protection provided in Chapter VII, too, replicate provisions found elsewhere in the broader corpus of Chinese law. Thus, for example, the stipulation in the revised Law in Article 44 (formerly Article 41) protecting a woman's right to marry a partner of her choice is already legally guaranteed by Article 49 of the 1982 Constitution, the Marriage Law 1980 as revised in 2001 (Articles 2 and 3), and the General Principles of Civil Law 1986 (Article 103). Nevertheless, the revised Law has made some significant changes in the direction of enhanced legal safeguards. Women's property rights in the domestic context are strengthened. In addition, Article 46 deals with the difficult issue of domestic violence and, as noted above, continues the efforts to deal with the problem found in the 2001 revisions to the Marriage Law – which, however, still tend to push abused women into people's mediation and the administrative punishment system (Marriage Law as revised in 2001, Articles 43, 44, and 45). These issues are dealt with below.

The revised Law attempts to protect the position of women in respect of domestic property. Article 47 (formerly Article 43) reaffirms the equality of rights of women in the matrimonial estate. The revised Law deals with two main aspects of the matrimonial estate: first, finance and other property, and, secondly, the matrimonial home. These represent a further contribution to the strengthening of women's property rights noted above.

*Finance and other property*

In the 2005 revised Women's Protection Law, Article 47 is extended with a paragraph added to take into account the officially encouraged practice of pre-nuptial property agreements – officially encouraged in order to reduce disputes over property division at time of divorce. Thus, the new provisions in Article 47 state that in circumstances where the wife and the husband have agreed in writing that each will own their properties during the marriage, but the wife has made greater contributions to key aspects of their marriage, then she is entitled to compensation from the husband at the time of divorce. What are these contributions? Well, they include raising the children of the marriage, taking care of parents (given the continuing norm of patrilocal post-marriage residence in practice this means in particular the husband's parents), and supporting the work of the husband.

### The matrimonial home

The matrimonial home is the second area for which the revised Women's Protection Law provides specific rules for safeguarding women's rights and interests in matrimonial property. The issue of housing rights of women at the time of divorce was complicated in the era of the planned economy and state ownership of the urban housing stock as it was ordinarily the husband's work unit that provided a married couple with their housing. Thus, separation or divorce meant that the woman had to remove herself from the family home. In rural areas, too, there were (and still are) problems – the norm of post-marriage patrilocal residence meant that in many cases the wife lived in the home of her husband's family. Again, separation or divorce meant that the woman had to remove herself from the family home. Thus, albeit for slightly different reasons, an unhappy wife, whether urban or rural, was put in a difficult position. The possibility of expulsion from the family home puts pressure on her to tolerate conduct from her husband that she otherwise would not accept, and even to refrain from bringing a divorce suit.

The revised Law attempts to address the problem of housing at the time of divorce in Article 48 (formerly Article 44). In the revised Law the first paragraph of the old Article 44 – 'the state protects women's ownership of housing' – has been removed. It is submitted that this is a step backwards, that this broad, supportive assurance has been removed. However, commentaries on the revised Law suggest otherwise. If the matrimonial home is *jointly owned*, the presumption is that favourable consideration will be given to the rights and interests of the wife and children if the parties are unable to negotiate their own agreement. Greater consideration is given to the parties' own understandings and compromises, and the court will only make a ruling should the parties fail to settle their differences. This is consistent with the provisions in the revised Marriage Law noted above encouraging intending spouses to enter into pre-nuptial agreements. But if the matrimonial home is *jointly rented*, favourable consideration is to be given to the rights and interests of the wife and children, without any allowance for negotiations between the divorcing spouses. In the 1992 version of the Law a third situation was envisaged: where the property belongs to the husband's work unit. The Law in Article 44 afforded some relief by urging the husband 'to do all he can to help the wife solve her housing problem'. Such exhortation was clearly less than inadequate as a protective mechanism. In the 2005 revised version of the Law, however, Article 48 in replacing Article 44 has removed this requirement. This is because housing is less and less allocated by work units as a result of the 'commoditisation' – or privatisation – of the housing stock.

### Domestic violence

As we have seen, there were no provisions in the Marriage and Family section of the 1992 Women's Protection Law dealing with the issue of domestic violence. This issue was addressed indirectly in Chapter VI 'Rights of Person'. As noted, Article 33 (now Article 35) declares that the state protects the rights of person, which women enjoy in equality with men. Article 35 (now Article 38) insists that 'women's rights to life and health brook no infringement'. Some detail was (and still is) added by Article 35, which reaffirms the prohibitions on maltreatment of baby girls (including female infanticide), and forbids maltreatment of a woman in a number of specific circumstances where she might be especially vulnerable: if she seeks to exercise her right not to bear children, if she gives birth to a female child, if she is elderly, or if there is use of 'superstitious' or 'violent' methods to injure her. The latter provision, especially in the social context of rural China, was an important step in the moves to ban the often tolerated physical abuse of women, with social opinion in the countryside allowing a husband to routinely abuse his wife.

In practice, as is well-known, many incidents of domestic violence in China were dealt with by people's mediation rather than by the police and the courts. As noted above, there are now quite specific provisions on the issue in the revised Women's Protection Law, extending the changes introduced in the Marriage Law as revised in 2001. Article 46 of the Women's Protection Law as revised in 2005 specifies:

> Domestic violence against women is prohibited.
> The state shall take measures to prevent and stop family violence.
> The Public Security Bureau, civil affairs, judicial administrative departments, the urban and rural grassroots self-governing organisations, and social organisations shall, according to their respective functions, prevent and stop family violence and help the women victims.

As a matter of general principle, this is an important step forward. But, in the absence of more detailed provisions we must assume that the grand statements made in Article 46 essentially serve to confirm the advances made in the 2001 revisions to the Marriage Law. This means that the policy preference for dealing with problems of domestic violence through mediation and administrative measures will persist. While this is a worry, it may not be quite so conservative an approach as it might seem at first sight, given the very evaluative and relatively coercive nature of mediation and the system of administrative penalties in China.

## 7. Family Planning

As we have noted, a further key aspect of the role of women and the family was also subject to major legislative developments in 2001, namely, the Population and Birth Planning Law (promulgated on 28 December 2001 and entered into force on 1 September 2002). This contains a number of important provisions affecting women, but is at heart very conservative in its approach to gender discrimination and women's rights. For although the general position in Chinese Law is that 'both husband and wife bear the obligation to practise family planning' (revised Marriage Law 2001, Article 16; Population and Birth Planning Law 2001, Article 17; 1982 Constitution, Article 49), in reality the principal responsibility is borne by women, so much so that the earlier law on the human reproduction process was called the Law for the Protection of the Health of Mothers and Children (1994). It is women's fertility that is controlled: for example, after the birth of a married couple's child, it is the woman who is fitted with an IUD, and when a birth outside the plan is terminated it is the women on whom the abortion is carried out. The entrenched preference for sons has encouraged the development of a seriously imbalanced sex ratio, contributed to by sex-selective abortion, child abandonment, and female infanticide. The 2001 Law of Population and Birth Planning does little to alleviate the gender-discriminating nature of the family planning system, and arguably worsens the situation by insisting that citizens not only 'bear responsibility for practising family planning according to law' but also 'possess the right to reproduction'.[47] In a society in which all human reproduction is meant to take place within marriage, this may be seen as a significant limitation on a woman's right not to bear children. More generally, the continuing preference for sons undermines efforts to enhance the status of women. Especially in the rural areas of post-Mao China, the party-state's economic policies have combined with the practice of uxorilocal post-marriage residence to intensify the need for families to rely on sons for their old-age security. Women are often trapped between the demands from their husband and his parents for sons and still more sons, and the party-state's policies designed to severely limit their fertility. Not surprisingly, this has also been a major cause of domestic violence.[48]

In the 1992 Women's Protection Law, the relationship between women's rights and reproduction had begun to be given some specific legislative attention. Article 51 of the 2005 revised Law (formerly Article 47) deals with issues of reproduction. It is an attempt to significantly improve the position of married women by declaring not only that women have the right to bear children[49] but also that they may choose not to have children. The former provision – the right to bear children – is designed, *inter alia*, to assist women who give birth to daughters. The latter – the right not to bear children – is a right introduced in order to empower a wife to resist child-bearing pressures from her husband and his family, especially when the first-born child is a daughter. But the right of a woman not to bear children is one for which it is difficult to secure popular acceptance, given that the traditional female role in China renders the women's reproductive and nurturing functions central. Moreover, as suggested above, it now rests uneasily with provisions in Article 17 of the Population and Birth Planning Law 2001 which declare that: 'citizens have the right to reproduction'. Some commentators in China argue that Article 17 may even be characterised as encouraging marital rape.[50]

A further paragraph is found in Article 51 of the Women's Protection Law as revised in 2005: 'The state administers the pre-marriage, pregnancy and confinement health care system and shall develop the ... health care of infants and mothers. The people's governments at all levels shall take measures to guarantee that the women enjoy the family planning technologies and services so as to enhance the women's procreative health level.' This reiterates the provisions of the Law for the Protection of the Health of Mothers and Children 1994, subjecting women to the technology and administration of the birth planning system, and Article 30 of the Population and Birth Planning Law 2001.[51] Far from protecting Chinese women's rights and interests, it is discriminatory, placing disproportionate responsibility on women to comply with the demands of the rigorous family planning system. Thus, Article 51, like its predecessor, in its second paragraph 'balances' the woman's right to give or not give birth with a duty placed on couples to 'practise family planning in accordance with the relevant provisions of the state'. In social practice this duty falls primarily on women; thus, for example, the following paragraph imposes on relevant government departments a duty not only to provide proper contraception facilities but also to 'protect the health and safety of *women* having birth control surgery' (emphasis added).

Nevertheless, the revised Women's Protection Law does contain some useful reforms, even in the area of family planning. Article 45, like its 1992 predecessor (Article 42), assists a woman who has agreed to undergo an abortion but then finds herself being divorced, by forbidding her husband to seek divorce within a period of six months after her abortion. It broadens the protection by extending the period to include the duration of the pregnancy itself and a term of one year after the wife has given birth. Thus: 'During the period of pregnancy, within one year after childbearing or within 6 months after termination of pregnancy of a woman, her husband shall not apply for divorce. If the woman applies for divorce or if the people's court deems necessary to accept the divorce application of the husband, the case shall not be subject to this restriction.'

China's population policies and practice have been subject to international criticisms since the early 1980s, with initial concerns focusing on coerced abortions. Other problems that have emerged in the ensuing 20 years include the socialisation of children in single-child families, rural social welfare (with the smaller family still expected to provide care for its elderly members),[52] attitudes to law[53] and – especially important from the point of view of this paper – issues in relation to gender.

In regard to gender issues generally, it is clear that the population control system continues to impact negatively on women in a number of ways. In particular, it is women's bodies that are subjected to many of the demands of the system, including abuses in the system such as forced abortion. The birth limitation programme is inconsistent with the spirit of Article 16 of CEDAW, which provides that women should have the right to determine 'truly and responsibly on the number and spacing of their children, and to have access to the information, education and means to enable their exercise of these rights in all matters relating to marriage and family relations'. It may also be inconsistent with the requirement that governments must eliminate discrimination against women in the field of health-care in order to ensure 'access to health care services, including those related to family planning' (Article 12). For, in practice, it is women who bear the bulk of responsibility to conform to the norms of the family planning system in China.

The 2005 revisions to the Women's Protection Law may come to help the position of women in several respects. The anti-domestic violence provisions may assist a woman in dealing with the abuse that is closely associated with the birth limitation programme as the husband puts pressure on the wife. Secondly, the expanded role given to the All-China Women's Federation in law drafting may result in a more effective representation of women's interests in the drafting of new population control regulations.

However, a particular problem in the population control system that has emerged over the years has its origins in the continuing preference in many Chinese families for male children. China now has the most severe shortage of girls compared to boys of any country in the world. Even before the founding of the People's Republic of China in 1949, sex ratios in China were skewed in the direction of a surplus of boys, but during the last two decades the relative dearth of girls has become pronounced.[54] The principal causes are sex-selective abortions, excessive female infant mortality, and maltreatment of girls up to the age of three. Until recently, the dearth of girls was confined to second or higher-order births, as various provincial regulations permit a second pregnancy if the first results in the birth of a daughter. However, it seems that couples are now using sex-selective abortions for first births as well.

As a result, as of the late 1990s provincial regulations and from 2001 the Population and Birth Planning Law explicitly proscribe the use of pre-birth testing to determine the sex of a foetus, especially as a prelude to sex-selective abortion. However, the Women's Protection Law as revised in 2005 is silent on the issue. Moreover, in the same year, the Standing Committee of the National People's Congress, China's highest legislative organ, withdrew a proposal to make sex-selective abortions illegal in an important revision to the criminal law. Some lawmakers and family planning officials wanted to change the law because of the serious gender imbalance in the population. The proposed amendment would have made it an offence punishable by up to three years' fixed term imprisonment to perform or assist an abortion based on the gender of the foetus. However, other lawmakers argued that it would not be appropriate to criminalise such practice because a pregnant woman should enjoy the right to know the gender of her foetus.[55]

## 8. Political Representation

The 2005 revised Women's Protection Law in its chapter on political rights contains only little encouragement to women and relevant governmental and legislative bodies to improve the position of women in public life. In Article 14 (formerly, Article 13) the authorities are obliged to ensure that complaints about the infringement of women's rights and interests are dealt with properly. However, beyond this, there is little direct support for giving women in China an expanded political role. The history of the limited involvement of women in China's socialist movement and system indicates that this is a serious omission.[56]

From the very beginnings of the Chinese Communist Party in 1921, the party's Politburo has allowed only a handful of women to be full members. And it was only in the radical days of the Cultural Revolution (1966–76) that as much as 10 per cent of the members of the Party's Central Committee were women. In the post-Mao era, there has been little advance in women's involvement in the leadership of the party. There also appears to have been little change in terms of basic membership: Shu and Bian report that 'among the 15% to 20% of working adults recruited into the Communist Party, the male–female ratio was 2:1 in the 1990s and 1990s' – a continuing gender gap of considerable importance because 'party members have been significantly more likely than non-members to be promoted to positions of authority, to receive party sponsorship for further education and job training' and so forth.[57] Most women who are in leading positions in the party-state leadership have been pressed into doing 'woman-work', regardless of their own particular area of expertise. Women on the Standing Committee of the National People's Congress tend to be both underrepresented and pressed into positions of responsibility for matters considered primarily of concern only to women. The situation is characterised in China as 'one low and three small' (*yi di san shao*), alluding to the fact that the proportion of women in politics is low, and that the number of women in key positions and what are regarded as key sectors is small. At the local ('grassroots') level, many official studies have confirmed that the large majority of women engaged in politics are primarily involved in 'woman-work'. The limited degree of democratisation of the political system at the local level, with the introduction of competitive elections to bodies such as the Villagers' Committees, has tended to work against the political position of women as female candidates suffer from both traditional male prejudices and the legacy of their governmental experience in 'soft' jobs in educational and cultural matters or in unpopular sectors such as population control. More generally, women who challenge the status quo are unlikely to ascend very far in the political system. And the emerging corpus of genuinely autonomous women's groups that has emerged in China since the Fourth World Conference on Women in 1995 have found it difficult to get the Chinese party-state leadership to listen to their more ambitious and imaginative agendas.[58] Neither problem is surprising, given the party-state leadership's central goal of maintaining political order and social stability.

Instead of directly advancing the political position of women, the 2005 revisions to the Law persist in Article 13 in following an indirect route – one of giving the All-China Women's Federation and local women's federations a greater role in promoting women's interests in the political system and in wider society. First, the All-China Women's Federation and local women's federations are required to participate actively in the political process on behalf of women, especially in the areas of 'democratic decision-making', management and supervision of the state and social affairs. Secondly, women's federations are encouraged to recommend female cadres to state organs, public organisations, enterprises and institutions. The extent to which this is seen as a positive reform will depend on the view taken of the role of women's federation in representing and promoting women's rights and interests.

It is important to stress here that the Women's Protection Law is intended to function in such a way that not only women's rights but also the individual women's interests are to be protected and promoted. Interests is a more political concept than rights, and concerns groups having recognised interests that require special treatment in order to achieve social justice in China's socialist system. Also, interests, unlike rights, are not burdened by correlative duties. The party-state recognises that women have a stake in the changing social system, a stake that needs protecting. The All-China Women's Federation is the body that is meant to promote those interests actively. The problem, however, is that the history of the Federation suggests that there are real limits to its ability to challenge the government on many key issues. The Federation is a quasi-governmental body that attempts to fulfil its mission of representing women by acting as a bridge between the party-state and society. Unfortunately, it is a bridge in which the flow of information and power is predominantly one-way. And while the revised Women's Protection Law does encourage individual litigants who bring suit to seek support from the Federation, it tends to act for women as a whole in a way that means individual women's interests are often overlooked. Moreover, its approach does not challenge the party-state's understanding of the nature of women's interests. This has manifested itself in many ways. For example, the Federation continues to define its role not in terms of promoting gender equality *per se* but, rather, in terms of promoting 'equality between men and women' (*nan-nü pingdeng*) – thereby encouraging the view that it is men and their position in society that are the appropriate standards, and that women's disadvantages are the result of deviation from these standards. In addition, as we have stressed, as a large, nation-wide representative body, with close links to the party-state leadership, the Federation tends to operate in a top-down manner. Its endeavours at the grass-roots level and its responsiveness to the local community are limited and its activities and campaigns tend to prioritise the party-state's axiomatic goals of economic development rather than women's welfare. The Federation also 'continues to call upon women to contribute more in social, moral and family affairs. From the point of view of the party-state leadership, an important role of the Federation is to safeguard moral purity and stability'.[59] Thus, while the Federation has made considerable ground in some areas at the national level, securing revisions to the Marriage Law in 2001 and to the Women's Protection Law in 2005, strengthening women's rights to contracted land, gaining for women greater protection against domestic violence, and so forth, its ability to operate outside the political parameters set for it by the party-state leadership and to challenge the patriarchal thinking that often underpins government policy is relatively limited.

## 9. Conclusion

In September 2005, the People's Republic of China introduced a revised version of its 1992 Women's Protection Law. The revisions were introduced for a variety of reasons: as a belated honouring of Mao Zedong's promises that socialism would liberate Chinese women; as a domestic implementation of China's obligations under the United Nations Convention on the Elimination of All Forms of Discrimination Against Women; as a response to the adverse impact of post-Mao economic reforms on the position of women; and because of a felt need on the part of the Chinese party-state leadership to deal more effectively with a longstanding and persistent problem of women's subordinate position in society. The revised Women's Protection Law 2005 is a serious attempt to address the continuing problems of gender stratification and discrimination in socialist China. The revised Law identifies many of the more intractable difficulties which Chinese women face today, and introduces important changes in the statutory framework for the legal protection of women in China. Positive changes can be found in a range of areas including the incorporation of women into state development plans; strengthened educational rights; protection against sexual harassment; new rules against domestic violence; better protection of women who are pregnant or who have recently given birth; greater support for uxorilocal marriage; greater rights to social security; and better responses by state organs to women who bring complaints of gender discrimination. Nevertheless, the law remains much stronger on exhortatory language than it is on concrete, effective measures to enhance the status of women and to protect the rights and interests of women.[60] Thus, while there has undoubtedly been a significant overhaul of the legal framework for protecting women's rights and interests in Chinese society, the substantive revisions to the Women's Protection Law are relatively limited and, ultimately, should be seen as only very incremental in nature. Moreover, the very fact of such a Law may have unintended consequences that work against the intention of the law. By identifying women as a socially disadvantaged category in need of special protection there is the danger that the law will strengthen social definitions of women as being less than the equal of men and thereby perpetuate inequality between the sexes. In addition, in defining women in a certain ultimately subordinate manner, according to which they need special protection, the revised Law may be seen also as a form of social control, subtly reflecting an ideology of male dominance. This is also linked to a continuing general emphasis in China on 'harmony ideology',[61] with women whose rights and interests have been infringed still encouraged to channel their grievances into mediatory and administrative processes rather than through the courts. In my view, the revised Law deals with the symptoms rather than the causes of gender discrimination; insufficient attention is given in the Law to the role of family, education, the media, the single-child policy, and so forth in the *creation* of injustice for women. The revised Law tends to mandate people on what not to do, rather than to lay the foundations for positive conduct and thinking by, for example, providing detailed actionable provisions, ensuring women a much greater role in public life, and enthusiastically promoting the rights of women to educational benefits.

Women's protection is part of a more general system of social protection in China, with two other key components are being protection for children and for the elderly. Gender and age are the two most entrenched inequalities in traditional Chinese society, and are the two areas of inequality to which most official attention has been given in post-Mao China.

They continue to be especially significant social problems in rural China. The party-state reserves its best and most effective protective legislation for the elderly, and is most limited in its protection of young people. This should be seen as an indication of the social control impulse that underpins such legislation. In addition, this is a special kind of law which combines both the public and private and which encourages a personal morality within the individual that is strongly reflective of traditional Chinese family values. Through such law, the party-state seeks to protect vulnerable individuals and to maintain social order and control. Its ability to provide effective protection, however, is to a significant extent limited by its retreat from a state-owned economy. The move to a more market-based system intensifies the need for such legislation, and yet simultaneously undermines the ability of the state to ensure that such legislation is meaningful. Thus, it places a great deal of responsibility on the family for delivery of this social protection. Yet, within the family as defined in Chinese law, there is often a world of traditional patriarchal values that continue to work against the interests of women. The political and cultural influences on the social protection legislation are strong, and in the case of women this can be seen not only in the role assigned to the family but also in the reliance on government-dominated 'mass organisations'. Unfortunately, in the approach of the key women's mass organisation – the All-China Women's Federation – there are inherent problems arising from the Federation's close association with the party-state and its organisational style, which will continue to limit its ability to positively influence understandings of gender equality and to enhance the position of women in Chinese society, especially in the absence of any serious attempt in the revised Law to enhance the participation of women in China's political and governmental systems.

## Acknowledgements

The Author wishes to thank the anonymous reviewer, Zhang Xiaoping, and Xi Chao for their most helpful comments on an earlier draft of this paper, as well as Phil C. W. Chan for his editorial kindness and patience. Responsibility for the views expressed, as well as any errors remaining, rests entirely with the Author.

## Notes

1. See, e.g., Ronald C. Keith and Lin Zhiqiu, *Law and Justice in China's New Market Place* (Basingstoke and New York: Palgrave 2001), pp.49–92 ('Special Groupings of Human Rights').
2. See, e.g., Michael Palmer, 'The Emergence of Consumer Rights: Consumer Protection Law in the People's Republic of China', in K. Latham, S. Thompson and J. Klein (eds), *Consuming China* (London: Routledge-Curzon 2006), pp.56–81.
3. Michael Palmer, 'Minors to the Fore: Juvenile Protection Legislation in the PRC', in M. Freeman (ed.), *Annual Survey of Family Law: 1991*, Vol.15 (London: International Society on Family Law 1993), pp.299–308; and Michael Palmer, 'Caring for Young and Old: Developments in the Family Law of the People's Republic of China, 1996–8', in A. Bainham (ed.), *International Survey of Family Law, 2000* (Dordrecht, The Netherlands: Kluwer 2000), pp.95–107. Taken together, the two approaches to age-based discrimination law appear to go a long way towards preserving a system of gerontocracy.
4. Thus, the Labour Law 1994 promises in Article 70 that 'the state shall develop social insurance undertakings, establish a social insurance system, and set up social insurance funds so that labourers may receive assistance and compensation in such circumstances as old age, illness, work-related injury, unemployment and childbirth'. However, the Law immediately qualifies this promise by declaring that 'the level of social insurance shall be in proportion to the level of social and economic development and social affordability'.

5. For an extended discussion of the relationship between such benevolence and special treatment in imperial Chinese statutory law see Derk Bodde, 'Age, Youth and Infirmity in the Law of Ch'ing China', in Jerome A. Cohen, R. Randle Edwards and Fu-mei Chang Chen (eds), *Essays on China's Legal Tradition* (Princeton NJ: Princeton University Press 1980).
6. Protected in China's current legal system by the 1990 Law for the Protection of Disabled Persons.
7. See Michael Palmer 'The Death Penalty in the People's Republic of China', in Andrew Rutherford and Peter Hodgkinson (eds), *Capital Punishment: Global Issues and Prospects* (London: Waterside Press 1996), pp.105–41.
8. An observation stressed in Ann Jordan, 'Women's Rights in the People's Republic of China', *Journal of Chinese Law*, Vol.8 (1994), pp.47–104.
9. In particular, China's decision to accede to the United Nations Convention on the Rights of the Child was an important impetus for the promulgation of the 1991 Minors' Protection Law, and accession to the United Nations Convention on the Elimination of All Forms of Discrimination Against Women was a major factor informing the promulgation of the 1992 Women's Protection Law. The Minors' Protection Law is now under revision, in part as a result of China's increasing commitments to the welfare of children under various international conventions. In 2002 China ratified the Convention concerning the Prohibition and Immediate Action for the Elimination of the Worst Forms of Child Labour, as well as the Optional Protocol to the Convention on the Rights of the Child on the Sale of Children, Child Prostitution and Child Pornography. In April 2005, China ratified the Hague Convention on Protection of Children and Cooperation in respect of Inter-Country Adoption. At the same time, the current Minors' Protection Law makes no provision for situations that have developed since the mid-1990s, and amendments are being considered by the Standing Committee of the National People's Congress in order to bring the Law up-to-date – particularly important changes currently under consideration are the introduction of new rules that would deal with problems of minors' Internet addiction and their patronage of insalubrious internet cafes, both of which are perceived to be widespread behavioural difficulties.
10. Zhonghua Renmin Gongheguo Funü Quanyi Baozhang Fa (Law of the People's Republic of China on the Protection of Women's Rights and Interests) promulgated on 28 August 2005 and entered into force on 1 December 2005, revising the Law of 1992.
11. Michael Palmer, 'Marriage Reform and Population Control: Changing Family Law in Contemporary China', in A. Bainham (ed.), *International Survey of Family Law: 2005* (Bristol: Jordon 2005), pp.173–201.
12. For an interesting account of the creation and intensification of ideologies and practices of gender inequality in traditional Chinese society see the insightful but neglected essay: Chiao Chien, 'Involution and Revolution in Gender Inequality', in the Christian Academy (ed.), *Changing Families in the World Perspective*, Volume 1 (Soeul: Wooseok Publishing 1989), pp.138–53.
13. This goal was robustly asserted in the Introduction to Books IV and V: 'The reform of the Chinese family system constitutes one of the most important items in the Kuomintang programme for the political and social rehabilitation of China ... and to enable the citizens to make use of their personal abilities to the best interest of their country ... the excessive grip of the old family tier over the individuals should be loosened ... The enfranchisement of the woman ... is now placed on the same footing as men'. Foo Ping-sheung, 'Introduction', in Ching-lin Hsia and James L. E. Chow (trans.), *The Civil Code of the Republic of China, Book IV Family, Book V Succession* (Shanghai: Kelly and Walsh 1931), pp.v–x.
14. Judith Stacey, *Patriarchy and Socialist Revolution in China* (Berkeley and Los Angeles: University of California Press 1983), pp.108–57.
15. Harriet Evans, *Women and Sexuality in China* (Cambridge, Polity Press 1997), p.31. For a classic statement of the concept and practice of 'woman-work' and its relationship to Communist Party policy, see Delia Davin, *Woman-Work: Women and the Party in Revolutionary China* (Oxford: Clarendon Press 1976), especially p.17, where the author writes: 'I use the term woman-work for the Chinese *funü gongzuo* ... The term covers all sorts of activities among women, including mobilizing them for revolutionary struggle, production, literacy and hygiene campaigns, social reform and so on.'
16. Phyllis Andors, *The Unfinished Liberation of Chinese Women, 1949–1980* (Bloomington: Indiana University Press; Brighton, Sussex: Wheatsheaf Books 1983). See also, for example, Norma Diamond, 'Collectivization, Kinship and the Status of Women in Rural China', in Rayna R. Reiter (ed.), *Towards an Anthropology of Women* (New York and London: Monthly Review Press 1975), pp.372–95.
17. See, e.g., Martin King Whyte and William L. Parish, *Urban Life in Contemporary China* (Chicago and London: Chicago University Press 1984), p.199.

18. See, e.g., John Bauer, Wang Feng, Nancy E. Riley, and Zhao Xiaohua, 'Gender Inequality in Urban China: Education and Employment', *Modern China*, Vol.18, No.2 (1992), pp.333–70.
19. Joan Kaufman, 'China: The Intersections between Poverty, Health Inequity, Reproductive Health, and HIV/AIDS', *Development*, Vol.48, No.4 (2005), pp.113–19.
20. See, e.g., Jordan (note 8).
21. See, e.g., Brian Schwarzwalder, Roy Prosterman, Ye Jianping, Jeffrey Reidinger and Li Ping, 'An Update on China's Rural Reforms: Analysis and Recommendations Based on a Seventeen-Province Survey', *Columbia Journal of Asian Law*, Vol.16 (2002–3), pp.141–225.
22. See, e.g., Jennifer Duncan and Li Ping, 'Women's Land Tenure in China: A Study of Women's Land Rights in Dongfang County, Hainan Province' (Seattle: Rural Development Institute, April 2001), p.13.
23. See, e.g., Stanley Rosen, 'Women and Political Representation in China', *Pacific Affairs*, Vol.68, No.3 (1995), pp.315–41.
24. Evans (note 15) p.31.
25. Jordan (note 8) p.95. Of course, there is another side to this story. The general absence of clearly defined and enforceable human rights for the individual Chinese citizen was a significant aspect of socialist rule in pre-1979 China. For women there was less deprivation relative to men, but overall there was a widespread burden on both women and men from the system of authoritarian and often repressive rule that had been put in place under the leadership of the party. Moreover, the almost complete absence of a free press during the Maoist era means that the fact of numerous news reports detailing abuse of and discrimination against women in contemporary China may tend to give a somewhat exaggerated picture of post-Mao deterioration in the position of women in Chinese society.
26. See, for example, Richard Siao and Yuanling Chao (eds) and Yan Kong (trans.), 'Provincial Laws on the Protection of Women and Children', *Chinese Law and Government*, Vol.27, No.1 (January–February 1994), pp.3–105.
27. Michael Palmer, 'Women to the Fore: Developments in the Family Law of the PRC', in A. Bainham (ed.), *Annual Survey of Family Law: 1994* (Dordrecht, The Netherlands: Kluwer 1996), pp.155–79.
28. Ann D. Jordan, 'Human Rights, Violence Against Women, and Economic Development (The People's Republic of China Experience)', *Columbia Journal of Gender and Law*, Vol.8 (1994), pp.216–72, at p.267.
29. For a somewhat dated but nevertheless insightful characterisation of the system of 'mass organisations' see James R. Townsend, *Political Participation in Communist China* (Berkeley and Los Angeles: University of California Press 1967), pp.150–58.
30. On state and market manipulation of some of these stereotypes, and the emergence of more complex images of women, see Harriet Evans, 'Fashions and Feminine Consumption', in Latham *et al.* (note 2), pp.173–89.
31. On the importance of literacy as a male preserve, and local female responses to conditions of illiteracy, including the development of a special female-specific script known as *nüshu* ('female writing') in Jiangyong County of southern Hunan, see Liu Fei-wen, 'Literacy, Gender and Class: Nüshu and Sisterhood Communities in Southern Rural Hunan', *Nan Nü*, Vol.6, No.1 (2004), pp.241–82.
32. In addition, the 1986 Compulsory Education Law has recently been revised in order to implement a number of important reforms. Entered into force on 1 September 2006, the revised Law attempts to promote greater equality in access to education by, for example, abolishing so-called 'key schools'; reducing the charges that schools have increasingly imposed even during the period of compulsory education; and sharing competent teachers between schools so that children in poorer areas are not disproportionately taught by unqualified teachers. These reforms, if fully implemented, will undoubtedly significantly assist female students.
33. For current developments in China's system of rural land contracts see Schwarzwalder *et al.* (note 21).
34. See, for example, Shu Xiaoling and Bian Yanjie, 'Market Transition and Gender Gap in Earnings in Urban China', *Social Forces*, Vol.81, No.4 (June 2003), pp.107–45. Shu and Bian conclude that the persistent gender gap in employment in post-Mao China reflects 'a consistent gender difference in human capital, political capital, and labor-force placement that remains largely unchanged over the years. Women [have] had less education, had fewer years of seniority, were less likely to be Communist Party members, less likely to be in the state sector ... less likely to be cadres and managers in sate agencies and enterprises ... Moreover, women were more likely to be workers and to work in service and education ... Market forces [have not necessarily eliminated] the practice of discrimination, and its numerous mechanisms of self-maintenance, including gender-based occupational segregation, sex-typed career orientations, and institutional and attitudinal biases' (pp.1136–7).
35. Michael Palmer, 'The Re-emergence of Family Law in Post-Mao China: Marriage, Divorce and Reproduction', in Stanley Lubman (ed.), 'Law in China Under Reform', Special Issue of *The China*

*Quarterly*, Vol.141 (March 1995), pp.110–34; republished in Stanley B. Lubman (ed.), *China's Legal Reforms* (Oxford: Oxford University Press 1996), pp.127–8; Michael Palmer, 'The People's Republic of China: More Rules but Less Law', in M. D. A. Freeman (ed.), *Annual Survey of Family Law: 1989* (London: International Society on Family Law 1991), pp.325–42, at pp.337–9.

36. Quanguo Renmin Daibiao Dahui Changwuhui Fazhi Gongzuo Weiyuanhui Xingzheng Fashi (Administrative Office of the Law Committee of the Standing Committee of the National People's Congress) (ed.), *Funü Quanyi Baozhang Fa* (The Law on the Protection of Women's Rights and Interests) (Beijing: Guojia Xingzheng Xueyuan Chubanshe 2005), p.68. See also Wang Qiongzhi (ed.), *Funü Quanyi Baozhang Fa* (The Law on the Protection of Women's Rights and Interests) (Beijing: Renmin Fayuan Chubanshe 2006), p.175.
37. See Quanguo Renmin (note 36) p.122.
38. On the development of provisions in the criminal law dealing with these kinds of offences, see Palmer, 'Caring for Young and Old' (note 3) pp.96–9.
39. 'China's First Sexual Harassment Case Rejected', *People's Daily* (online edition), 25 December 2001, http://english.peopledaily.com.cn/200112/25/eng20011225_87414.shtml.
40. See, e.g., 'An Epic Struggle Against Sexual Harassment', *China Daily* (online edition), 29 August 2005, http://www.china.org.cn/english/china/140117.htm.
41. Palmer, 'Marriage Reform and Population Control' (note 11).
42. Michael Palmer, 'Patriarchy, Privacy and Protection: Slowly Conceptualising Domestic Violence in Chinese Law', in N. Iu. Erpyleva, J. Henderson, and M. Butler (eds), *Forging a Common Legal Destiny: Liber Amicorum in Honour of Professor W. E. Butler* (London and New York: Wildy, Simmonds and Hill 2005), pp.786–812.
43. CEDAW A/54/38/Rev.1 (1999). The Committee on the Elimination of Discrimination Against Women in addition to the specific criticisms noted above observed that China's approach was misplaced: 'The Committee is concerned that the Government's approach to the implementation of the Convention has an apparent focus on the protection of women rather than on their empowerment. Thus, the central machinery responsible for government policy is the National Working Committee on Women and Children, perpetuating the identification of women with children. Similarly, in the area of women's health, there is a focus on mother-child health, limited to women's reproductive function. Likewise, labour laws and regulations overemphasise the protection of women' (para.280). The Committee, at para.281, recommended 'that the Government re-examine its approach to realising gender equality, with an emphasis on the human rights framework of the Convention and the empowerment of women. The Government should encourage a country-wide social dialogue that advocates equality between women and men, and a comprehensive public campaign aimed at changing traditional attitudes.' Also, at para.282, the Committee recommended 'that the Government examine and enhance the structure, authority and resources of the national machinery for the advancement of women'.
44. Palmer, 'Marriage Reform and Population Control' (note 11); and Palmer, 'Patriarchy, Privacy and Protection' (note 42).
45. Palmer, 'The People's Republic of China' (note 35).
46. Palmer, 'Marriage Reform and Population Control' (note 11); and Palmer, 'Patriarchy, Privacy and Protection' (note 42).
47. 2001 Population and Birth Planning Law, Article 17. For text of this Law and related legislation see: *Funü Quanyi Baozhang Fa: Peitao Guiding* (Law on the Protection of Women's Rights and Interests and Supporting Regulations) (Beijing: Zhongguo Fazhi Chubanshe 2005).
48. See, e.g., the matrimonial case analysed at length in Anthony Clayre, 'Mediating: Caring and Control', in Anthony Clayre (ed.), *Heart of the Dragon* (Boston: Houghton, Mifflin 1988), pp.91–109.
49. The actual text reads, 'women have the right to bear children in accordance with the relevant principles of the state'. That is, women do not have the right either to bear children outside marriage or to give birth in violation of the provincial regulations which implement the single-child policy. See Palmer, 'The Re-Emergence of Family Law in Post-Mao China' (note 35).
50. The issue of marital rape is one of considerable controversy within Chinese legal circles, with the possibility that a husband could be considered to have raped his spouse having been accepted in principle as an offence, but dealt with very conservatively as a matter of judicial practice so that very few prosecutions have actually convicted a husband of the rape of his wife.
51. Article 30 of the 2001 Population and Birth Planning Law states: 'The State shall establish premarital health care and maternal health care systems to prevent or reduce the incidence of birth defects and improve the health of newborn children.'

52. See Palmer, 'The Re-Emergence of Family Law in Post-Mao China' (note 35), and Palmer, 'Caring for Young and Old' (note 3).
53. In the sense that this is an area of government regulation where policy rather than law has played the key normative defining role, and judicial review of administrative action has sometimes proved very difficult and even dangerous for plaintiffs seeking redress for official misconduct. See, e.g., Josephine Ma, 'Four Years in Jail for Blind Activist', *South China Morning Post*, 25 August 2006, p.A7, cols.3–5; and John Pomfret, 'China's Bumpy Path to Justice; Victim of Birth Control Policy Sues, Wins, Has Yet to Collect', *The Washington Post*, 27 March 2001, Section A.
54. See, in particular, Judith Banister, 'Shortage of Girls in China today', *Journal of Population Research*, Vol.21, No.1 (2004), pp.19–45, and Liu Sisi, 'Where Have All the Young Girls Gone?', *China Rights Forum*, No.4 (2004), pp.50–55. China has 119 male births for every 100 female, significantly higher than the global ratio of 103–107:100: see 'Abortion Law Amendment to be Abolished', *China Daily* (online edition), http://www.china.org.cn/english/government/172719.htm.
55. Josie Liu, 'Changes to Criminal Law under NPC Review', *South China Morning Post*, 26 December 2005, p.A-4, cols.2–3, and Sun (note 54).
56. Rosen (note 23). Rosen's insightful analysis demonstrates that in both party and state sectors, women have persistently been underrepresented in leading positions, and that those women who have achieved some degree of success have also experienced the 'glass ceiling' of limited promotion prospects and been appointed often specifically because of their responsibilities for women, and have also often been expected to fulfil other 'minority' criteria (for example, to be a member of a minority nationality, or one of the democratic parties). Although there was something of a breakthrough in women's political roles during the Cultural Revolution, this was but a temporary development; moreover, the most important of the women who attained leading positions during this radical period did so with the aid of significantly powerful husbands: for example, Jiang Qing (wife of Mao Zedong), Ye Qun (wife of Mao's designated successor, Lin Biao), and Deng Yingchao (wife of Zhou Enlai).
57. Shu and Bian (note 34) p.1112.
58. Du Jie, 'Gender and Governance: The Rise of New Women's Organisations', in Jude Howell (ed.), *Governance in China* (Lanham and Oxford: Rowman & Littlefield 2004), pp.172–92.
59. Ibid. p.183.
60. Indeed, the Law has already been unofficially criticised in China for such failings. Perhaps the most trenchant criticism to date comes form Zhang Zhicheng, who complains that the refurbished Law remains essentially 'declaratory-type law-making' (*xuanshixing lifa*). The revised Law proclaims general political and ideological principles; fails to provide meaningful and enforceable legal remedies; imposes broad duties on government that may well not be capable of implementation; incorporates grand moral standards; is inappropriate even in its efforts to encourage greater political participation for women (better for China to have free and fair elections); and lacks key definitions (for example, for the term 'sexual harasssment'): see Zhang Zhicheng, 'Tanlun < Zhonghua Renmin Gongheguo Funü Baozhang Fa > de Ruogan Quexian', (A Discussion of A Number of Weaknesses in the Women's Protection Law of the PRC), 2006, at Beida Law Information Network, http://article.chinlawinfo.com/article/user/article_display.asp?ArticleID=30524 (accessed 1 November 2006).
61. On the concept of harmony ideology, see Laura Nader, *Harmony Ideology: Justice and Social Control in Zapotec Mountain Villages* (Stanford, CA: Stanford University Press 1990), and Laurel L. Rose, *The Politics of Harmony: Land Dispute Strategies in Swaziland*, (Cambridge: Cambridge University Press 1992), pp.79–85.

# Inequality of Educational Opportunity in Korea by Gender, Socio-Economic Background, and Family Structure

HYUNJOON PARK

**Introduction**

Considering the critical role of educational qualifications for life chances in contemporary industrial societies, sociologists have long investigated factors that affect individuals' educational opportunities. They have been particularly interested in assessing the extent to which socio-economic origins of individuals and other ascribed characteristics such as sex and race influence their educational outcomes, attempting to measure the degree of inequality of educational opportunity.[1] During the twentieth century, in almost all industrial countries younger generations have continued their educational careers much longer than previous generations. How has this growing pie of education been sliced into pieces for people from different socio-economic origins? How do countries differ in how they divide the educational pie? What factors may explain cross-national and temporal variation in educational inequality?

Probably the most astonishing feature of educational development in South Korea during the past few decades has been the remarkable increase in educational attainment within the South Korean population. Although educational expansion, more or less, has occurred in many industrial countries as well, the degree of South Korea's educational expansion has been so dramatic that few other countries have achieved a comparable increase in the past 30 years. The remarkable degree of educational expansion, along with its distinctive features of educational policies as will be described later, makes South Korea an interesting case study for examining the magnitude of and trend in inequality of educational opportunity.

Because socio-economic background and other ascribed characteristics to some extent relate to individuals' education in all contemporary societies, it is necessary to assess a country's degree of educational inequality in cross-national comparative perspective: how great is educational inequality in South Korea compared to that in other industrial countries? Similarly, the degree of educational inequality at one point within a society should be assessed in temporal comparative perspective: how has educational inequality changed over time in South Korea? In this paper, I will summarise findings from previous studies that have addressed educational inequality in contemporary South Korean society in comparative perspective, mostly derived from sociological research. I do not intend this review to be extensive but rather focus on some selected studies of educational inequality related to three social factors: gender, socio-economic background, and family structure; full and extensive coverage of existing literature on the issue is beyond the scope of this paper.

I will first review empirical findings related to gender differences in educational outcomes. Although it has improved over time, gender inequality is still salient in contemporary South Korea in many respects such as the division of household labour, wages and employment, and welfare.[2] However, recent evidence of educational differences between females and males in some advanced industrial countries shows significant gains for women over recent decades, which have resulted in a reversed pattern of gender differences (i.e., females outperform males) in some indicators of education, especially educational attainment (such as dropping out of secondary school and college enrolment and completion). Of course, gender differences still remain in other respects such as the fields of study in post-secondary education.[3] How have contemporary South Korean women fared in various indicators of educational outcomes compared to men?

I will then discuss previous research on the association between the socio-economic origin of individuals and their educational outcomes in order to provide a general picture of the trend in and extent of educational inequality associated with socio-economic background. Traditionally, sociologists have considered a person's socio-economic origin as indicated by parental education and occupation, although they often differ in the way of measuring those variables. Some, for instance, prefer a categorical classification of parental occupation based on class perspective, while others use a continuous scale measuring occupational prestige or socio-economic status of occupation with emphasis on unidimensional hierarchy of occupational structure.[4] In this paper, I will discuss studies in both perspectives of measuring parental occupation so long as they empirically address the effects of parental occupation and/or other respects of socio-economic origin.

After examining educational inequality associated with gender and socio-economic origin, I will briefly review a number of studies addressing recent demographic changes in South Korea and their implications for children's education. South Korea has recently experienced unprecedented demographic changes of which major features are the rapid increase of divorce and the growing number of marriages between South Korean men and immigrant women, especially from other Asian countries. These demographic changes are likely to affect the traditional family structure and thus will have important consequences for children's overall well-being, including education, given the fundamental role of the family as a welfare agency in South Korean society.

In examining the effects of gender, socio-economic origin, and family structure, I primarily focus on two indicators of educational outcomes – educational attainment and achievement. Educational attainment, which indicates whether a person has completed a given level of education, has long been a major focus of sociologists whose main concerns are to examine family influences on individuals' life chances. On the other hand, educational achievement refers to students' 'ability to apply what they have learned [in school]'[5] and as such it is usually indicated by a student's performance on standardised academic tests. Educational achievement has been widely studied especially by educational researchers and policy analysts interested in schools and pedagogical practices affecting student learning as well as by sociologists whose interests mainly reside in the effects of family background on students' performance in school.[6]

Before turning to findings of educational inequality, in the next section I will briefly describe the degree of educational expansion South Korea has experienced during the past decades and the quality of education South Korean students demonstrate by referring to relevant statistics. I also provide a short introduction to the overall structure and some major features of the South Korean educational system. Theses descriptions will be useful for understanding overall educational contexts of South Korea.

## Contexts of South Korean Education

### Educational expansion

Recent educational statistics among OECD (Organisation for Economic Cooperation and Development) countries show the outstanding position of South Korea in terms of educational growth in comparative perspective.[7] The proportion of those aged between 25 and 34 who had attained at least upper secondary education was 95 per cent in South Korea in 2002, which was the highest level, along with Norway, among the 30 OECD countries. The differences between younger and older age groups are surprising. Only 31 per cent of 55 to 64 year-olds in South Korea had completed upper secondary education. In other words, the attainment of upper secondary education increased threefold within a single generation, which is the largest increase among OECD countries. The difference in South Korea between the two age groups is remarkable considering that the corresponding differences were 3 per cent in the United States, 14 per cent in the United Kingdom, and 14 per cent in Sweden.

Even more impressive is the fact that educational expansion in South Korea occurred not only at the primary or secondary levels but also at the tertiary level. In 2002, 41 per cent of 25 to 34 year-olds in South Korea had tertiary qualifications (including both tertiary-type B and tertiary-type A), which was the third highest level among the 30 OECD countries, followed by Canada and Japan.[8] The level for the age group of 25–34 is particularly astonishing compared to that for the older group of 55–64, among whom only 9 per cent had completed tertiary education. Again, cross-national comparisons highlight the expansion of tertiary education in South Korea: corresponding differences between the younger and older age groups were 7 per cent in the United States, 9 per cent in the United Kingdom, and 13 per cent in Sweden.

What does such a dramatic expansion of education in South Korea imply for changes over time in inequality of educational opportunity? How have different demographic groups fared in educational opportunities under the context of rapid educational expansion? Have certain groups of population enjoyed particularly greater benefits from educational expansion than have others? These are key issues I will attempt to address through a review of empirical findings.

*Quality of education*

Educational development in South Korea has achieved not only an extraordinary increase in quantity of education but also a high quality of education. International comparisons of student performance on academic tests have been considered useful for assessing a country's overall quality of education. The extraordinary performance of South Korean students, along with other East Asian students, has been documented in various comparative studies of student achievement. For instance, among fourth-grade students from more than 20 countries that participated in an international survey of student achievement, the Third International Mathematics and Science Study (TIMSS 95), South Korean students, along with students in Singapore and Japan, markedly outperformed their peers in other countries in both mathematics and science. South Korean eighth graders also achieved top performance among their counterparts from more than 40 countries in both subjects. In 1999, TIMSS was repeated for eighth graders in 38 countries and again South Korea and other East Asian countries achieved the highest scores.

In 2000–01, the OECD administered an international survey, the PISA (Programme for International Student Assessment), of literacy skills in reading, mathematics, and science among 15-year-olds students. The PISA is considered as one of the most comprehensive and carefully designed surveys of student achievement.[9] Among students from more than 40 countries in PISA, South Korean students, along with students in Japan and Hong Kong, showed the highest mean scores in mathematical and scientific literacy.

Some may criticise the remarkable performance of South Korean students on achievement tests as simply reflecting 'wrong' educational practices that make South Korean students accustomed to academic tests without encouraging flexibility and creativity. In 2003, the PISA assessed a student's capacity for solving 'problems that are not bound to specific areas of school knowledge'.[10] The problem sets administered to measure such ability were characterised to 'call on individuals to move among different, but sometimes related, representation and to exhibit a cretin degree of flexibility in the ways in which they access, manage, evaluate, and reflect on information'.[11] Interestingly, South Korean students showed the highest level of problem solving among the PISA countries. This story suggests that criticism of the remarkable performance of South Korean students on academic tests as only reflecting their educational practices of repetition and memorisation at the expense of flexibility and creativity is not proven.

*Educational expenditure from public and private Sources*

A widely used indicator of governmental involvement in education is the relative share of public and private spending on education. In particular, as tertiary education is costly, it is useful to focus on tertiary education in looking at the relative proportion of public and private funds. In 2000, South Korea (2.6 per cent) showed the highest level of overall (both public and private) expenditure on institutions for tertiary education as a percentage of GDP (growth domestic production) among OECD countries, along with the United States (2.7 per cent) and Canada (2.6 per cent). This level of educational expenditure is approximately three times the level in such countries as Czech Republic (0.9 per cent), Greece (0.9 per cent), Italy (0.9 per cent) and New Zealand (0.8 per cent).[12]

At the same time, South Korea showed the largest proportion of expenditures on tertiary education funded by the private sector – households and other private entities. The private sector funded 77 per cent of total expenditure on institutions for tertiary education in South Korea, which was the highest level among OECD countries followed by the United States (66 per cent) and Japan (55 per cent). Striking was the comparison with Nordic countries such as Denmark (2.4 per cent), Finland (2.8 per cent), and Norway (3.8 per cent), where most expenditures on tertiary education were funded by the public sector. Even in Greece (0.3 per cent) and Turkey (4.6 per cent), which had economic levels similar to or lower than that of South Korea, tertiary education was supported mostly by public funds.[13] Moreover, in South Korea most private expenditure comes from households, whereas in countries such as Germany a large portion of private expenditures on education are provided by private businesses.[14] The considerably higher responsibility of individual students and their families for tertiary education is reflected in the fact that more than 80 per cent of students attend private universities, which rely almost entirely on tuition fees from students for their budgets.[15] Moreover, the OECD figures on public and private expenditures on education include only payments to educational institutions. Thus, private payments to education outside institutions, such as payments for private tutoring, are not included in the figures.[16] Considering the high prevalence of private tutoring or lessons in private institutions outside school (*hakwon*) for admissions to university programmes among South Korean students, the actual proportion of private expenditures on tertiary education is likely to be even higher than the current figures revealed in the OECD study.

In short, these statistics indicate the far greater economic burden for individuals to cover the cost of tertiary education in South Korea in comparison with other countries. Given that cost is an essential element in educational decision-making, the high share of private funds may function as an important barrier to school continuation among students from disadvantaged families, preserving social inequality in educational attainment, particularly at the tertiary level. I will discuss the implications of such low levels of public support for educational inequality as I review studies that investigate the effects of socio-economic background.

*Structures and features of the south korean educational system*

In this section, I briefly describe selected features of the South Korean educational system. It should be clear that this description does not intend to summarise all the complicated aspects of the South Korean educational system and their evolution but aims only to highlight some features that may be relevant for understanding educational inequality.[17] The structure of the South Korean education system is relatively straightforward compared with those of other systems. It consists of six years of compulsory elementary school, three years of middle (lower secondary) school, and three years of high (upper secondary) school, and four years of university (or 2–3 years of junior college). There is no between-school tracking at the level of middle school. Upon graduation from middle school, however, students proceed to either academic high school or vocational high school, mostly depending on their grades and needs. Vocational high schools offer occupational training for students who enter job markets after graduation, whereas academic high schools are directed to prepare students for post-secondary education. Therefore, there are significant differences between the two types of schools in many respects, including curricula, academic pressures, and eventually access to opportunities for tertiary education. Vocational high schools are perceived as less prestigious than academic high schools. As of 2003, the proportion of students attending vocational high schools among total high school students was about 30 per cent.

Probably the most significant and controversial policy at the secondary level is the 'equalisation policy'. To reduce differences among high schools and relieve intense competition for admissions to the best high schools, the South Korean government abolished school-specific entrance examinations and replaced them with nationwide entrance examinations. Once they passed the examinations, students were assigned to (academic) high schools within their residential districts by a lottery.[18] In other words, students were randomly assigned to a school regardless of whether the school was private or public, single-sex or co-educational. Since it was first implemented in Seoul (the capital of South Korea) and major metropolitan areas in 1974, this policy has been extended to other areas. Furthermore, in 1998 entrance examinations for high schools were entirely abolished in four major cities including Seoul. In the cities students are selected only according to middle school activities records, while in other places the entrance examination score is still a major criterion for selection. Although there are controversies as to whether the South Korean government should continue this policy given increasing demand for diversity and choice of secondary education, the equalisation policy is considered to have contributed to demolishing the hierarchical structure of secondary education and alleviating extreme competition for high school admissions.

After graduating from high school, students may proceed to higher education. The two main types of post-secondary educational institutions are universities and junior colleges (and some teacher's colleges and industrial or technical colleges). A university programme typically takes four years and leads to a bachelor's degree, whilst most junior colleges offer two-year programmes aimed at practical and occupational skills. Students must take the national entrance examination to apply for admission to university or junior college programmes, and admissions are determined primarily by their scores in the examination. Although the relative importance of the examination score for determining admissions to university or junior college programmes has recently decreased in the face of severe criticisms of the entrance examination system, it still remains the most critical criterion for admissions, with a four-year university programme requiring usually much higher examination scores than does a junior college programme. Given the substantial impact of educational qualifications, particularly college degrees, on life chances in South Korea, competition and pressures on higher test scores among high school students are considerable.

At all levels of education, the South Korean education system shows a high degree of standardisation and centralisation with the same standards adopted nationwide. The government tightly regulates many aspects of education including teachers' training, school budgets, and curricula. It administers the national entrance examination and enforces government standards for teaching, learning, and evaluation. Although recent educational reform aims at allowing more autonomy to each school and teachers in school, the overall level of standardisation and centralisation of the South Korean educational system is still high in comparison with that of other countries. How has the high level of educational standardisation, of which the equalisation policy is a clear indication, affected educational inequality especially by family socio-economic background? I will discuss this issue below as we turn to socio-economic status.

**Gender and Educational Inequality**

During the past few decades, South Korean women's educational gains have been particularly significant, resulting in negligible gaps recently between males and females in educational attainment. For instance, in 2003 gender differences in educational attainment, represented as the number of years of formal education completed, were not present among the age group of 25 to 34 (13.6 years for males and 13.5 years for females), whereas differences in the average years of schooling favoured males (10.1 years) by 2 years among those aged between 55 and 64.[19] Gender disparities are not found among the younger generation in other major indicators such as graduation and advancement rates.[20]

Evidence of gender equality within the younger generation has stemmed from sociological research that tracks gender differences in the likelihood of attaining a given level of education across birth cohorts by applying sophisticated statistical methods to a national representative sample usually obtained from social surveys. Because data of reasonable quality on educational attainment at the national level had not been available until a couple of decade ago in South Korea, it is not practically feasible to track the changes in educational inequality over long-term periods. Alternatively, researchers can address temporal changes in educational inequality by comparing birth cohorts from the same years. By comparing old and new cohorts, a reasonable picture of the temporal changes in educational inequality can be drawn.

Several studies that compared the probabilities of graduating from high school and of attending (and completing) tertiary education across different birth cohorts consistently found across the cohorts a decline in gender gap in educational attainment, resulting in no significant differences between males and females among most recent cohorts.[21] Because studies were not consistent with cohorts examined and they used data collected in different years, it is not easy to ascertain exactly when gender differences started to decline in South Korea. But what is evident is the overall trend towards a decline in gender gap in educational attainment.

One could argue that the trend of increasing overall chances for tertiary education among women may obscure emerging gender disparities in the *type* of tertiary education women attain. For instance, Japanese women's gains in attaining tertiary education were more substantial at the level of junior college than at the university level, resulting in junior college education dominated by females.[22] As described above, junior college programmes usually with two years of education occupy the lower tier of tertiary education compared to four-year university programmes. This concern is consistent with the recent discussion in the sociology of education, which emphasises the implication of qualitative differentiation within a given level of education in inequality of opportunity.[23] As the overall attainment of a given level of education is rapidly growing, according to this perspective it is no longer whether a person attends a school at all but which type of school the person attends that becomes more important for an individual's life chances. Therefore, inequality of educational opportunity can be maintained, despite overall educational expansion, by the way in which advantaged families are more likely to succeed in sending their children to qualitatively different, better, placements at a given level of education.

Interestingly, there is no strong evidence for supporting this argument for South Korean women. Park's study, which compares separately the chances of attending university as opposed to no tertiary education upon high school completion; attending junior college to no tertiary education; and attending university to junior college, finds no significant gender differences among the most recent cohort (those born after 1971) in any of the three comparisons, while older women were disadvantaged in all of the comparisons, compared to their male counterparts.[24] In other words, South Korean women have achieved significant gains not only in the quantitative aspect (overall increase in educational attainment) but also in the qualitative aspect of educational development.

In contrast to gender equality among recent cohorts in educational attainment, interestingly gender differences are apparent in educational achievement. Differences between South Korean male and female students in academic performance particularly on mathematics and science are substantial. In most countries that participated in PISA 2000, 15-year-old males outperformed their female counterparts in mathematical literacy. However, countries showed wide variations in the degree of gender differences in this respect. The gap between average scores of male and female students was largest in South Korea (27 points) among more than 40 participating countries. The average gender difference in OECD countries as a whole was only 11 points and the gap was negligible in countries such as Iceland, New Zealand, and Finland. Higher performance of male than female students was also significant in science literacy among South Korean students. Again, South Korea showed the largest gender gap (19 points) favouring males. Meanwhile, the OECD average in gender difference in science was zero point. On the other hand, South Korea displayed the smallest (14 points) score gap between 15-year-old males and females in reading literacy favouring females. Also, in all the participating countries female students had much higher mean scores than did male students. 15-year-old females in Iceland, New Zealand, and Finland performed better than their male counterparts by 40 or more points.[25] South Korea's greater gender differences in mathematics and science in favour of males were not only found among 15 year-olds but also among those at younger ages. Among the participating countries in TIMSS, which assessed fourth and eighth graders during 1994–95, South Korea was one of the countries showing the largest gender gaps in mathematics and science for both grades.[26]

Although South Korean female students' lower achievement than male students in mathematics and science is apparent in comparison with the gender differences in other countries, little is known about the reasons for the lower achievement among female students in the two subjects. For instance, gender differences in attitudes towards mathematics or science, interest in the two subjects, and other learning habits have been pointed to as possible causes of the significant gender gaps in actual academic performance. However, evidence does not support that 15-year-old South Korean females have distinctive patterns in these aspects of learning compared to their male counterparts. Comparisons of relevant measures of learning attitudes and educational interests collected in PISA 2000 showed that gender differences in such measures as the index of interest in mathematics, the index of self-concept in mathematics, or the index of self-efficacy were not particularly distinctive in South Korea compared to those in other countries.[27]

One could expect that comparably lower achievement of 15-year-old female students compared to male students in mathematics and science would affect female students' selection of fields of study at the tertiary level, probably resulting in substantial gender gaps particularly in fields associated with mathematics and science. However, recent statistics showing percentages of female students who have received tertiary qualifications in mathematics- or science-related fields (such as computer science, engineering, manufacturing, and construction) indicate that South Korea actually has higher percentages of women in these fields than do many other industrial countries. Specifically, 43 per cent of degrees earned in mathematics and computer science in tertiary-type A (corresponding to university education) institutions and advanced research programmes in 2002 were awarded to women in South Korea, while the corresponding percentages were 28 per cent, 23 per cent, and 32 per cent in Australia, Germany, and the United States, respectively. Similarly, 25 per cent of tertiary-type A and advanced research students who received degrees in engineering, manufacturing, and construction were women in South Korea, which was similar to or even higher than the percentages in most other OECD countries.[28] The situation was similar in respect of tertiary-type B (corresponding to junior college) education.

In sum, women's educational gains in South Korea during the past few decades are remarkable. In major indicators of educational attainment, gender differences are no longer substantial. Gender differences in fields of study at tertiary level are actually smaller in cross-national comparative perspective. Although women occupy only less than one-quarter of advanced research graduates with degrees above bachelor level, the gap is also likely to decline as the current trends of educational attainment continue.

In contrast with such significant gains in educational attainment, the lower performance among South Korean female students than their male counterparts in mathematics and science is considerable in comparison with other industrial countries. Despite lower achievement among female students in the two subjects, however, South Korean female students are more likely than female students in many other countries to receive degrees in fields of study related to mathematics or science at the tertiary level. Although this finding may suggest that the lower performance among females in mathematics and science is not a critical issue, more studies are needed to investigate various sources at home or in school that may cause female students' lower achievement in the two subjects. In the era of information and technology, students' mathematical and scientific skills and knowledge will become more relevant for their labour market success. Even though the current selection of fields of study among female students does not seem to be restricted by their lower performance in mathematics and science, consequences of lower achievement in the two subjects may be of significance in other aspects of life chances such as types of work or wage. Therefore, it is important to address potential causes of lower achievement among female students and find effective policy intervention for boosting females' performance.

**Socio-economic Status and Education Inequality**

Because comparisons of South Korea with other countries in the magnitude of inequality of educational attainment are rare, I start this section with a discussion of inequality regarding educational achievement. Researchers of educational achievement have assessed cross-national differences in educational inequality by comparing the extent to which socio-economic status (SES) of the family is associated with the student's academic performance. For this exercise of cross-national comparison, it is essential to have comparable measures of family SES across countries in addition to comparable measures of achievement. PISA provides an excellent opportunity for looking into the relationship between family SES and student performance as it contains various measures of family SES including parental occupation and education. Careful collection and measurement of parental occupation is of particular importance for addressing educational inequality given that parental occupation has been a key element of family SES in literature of sociology of education and stratification. However, previous international surveys of student achievement such as TIMSS did not collect this information, which substantially constrained researchers in addressing the issue of educational inequality associated with family SES. In PISA, parental occupation was measured as an index that represents the status of each occupation (the International Socio-Economic Index of Occupational Status developed by Harry Ganzeboom and his colleagues).[29] Higher values of the index indicate higher levels of occupational status.

A straightforward comparison of the relationship between parental occupation and student performance across countries is to present for each country the difference between average scores of students in the top national quartile of the index of parental occupational status (representing students from wealthiest families) and their counterparts in the bottom quartile (representing students from poorest families). As expected, in all the participating countries wealthier students did better on average than poorer students. However, PISA also showed considerable variation across countries in the magnitude of the difference between scores of wealthier and poorer students. Students in South Korea who were wealthier outperformed poorer students by 33 points on average in reading literacy, which was the *smallest* gap among more than 40 countries that participated in PISA. The small score gap in South Korea is outstanding when compared to 115 points in Switzerland, 113 points in Germany, and 99 points in the United States.[30] Although to a lesser extent, the small gap between wealthier and poorer students in South Korea was apparent in mathematics and science literacy as well.

As discussed earlier, parental education is another major aspect of socio-economic background widely used in the literature. South Korea is, again, distinctive with its small gap between scores of students whose parents have the highest level of educational attainment and their counterparts whose parents have the lowest level of educational attainment. In PISA, South Korean 15 year-olds whose mother had completed tertiary education showed higher performance in reading literacy by 31 points on average than those whose mother had not completed upper secondary education. The gap in mean reading scores between the two groups of students was again *smallest* in South Korea than in other participating countries in PISA; they were 129 points in Germany, 119 points in the Czech Republic, and 88 points in the United States.

In short, results from PISA indicate a comparatively low degree of educational inequality in South Korea, represented by the weakest association between socio-economic background and student performance. The low level of educational inequality in South Korea is particularly impressive in that South Korean students show a high level of overall performance as well. As in other countries, South Korean students in the bottom quartile of the socio-economic index of parental occupation or those whose mother completed the lowest level of education had lower achievement than did their counterparts who had parents with the highest level of occupational status or education. However, the mean scores of those from low SES families in South Korea were actually higher than the OECD average scores (calculated by including students in all OECD countries) and still higher than the mean scores of students in the top quartile of the index of parental occupational status or whose mothers had completed tertiary education in some countries.

How has South Korean education achieved the considerably small difference among students from different socio-economic backgrounds maintaining comparably high educational performance? What characteristics of South Korean educational systems and policies account for the successful combination of a higher performance with a narrower gap? Previous literature on comparative education has paid attention mostly to pedagogical practices and cultural factors that may be able to explain the extraordinary performance of South Korean students. The considerably small gap in academic performance among South Korean students from different socio-economic backgrounds has not been highlighted. Because of the relative lack of interest in the issue especially in comparative perspective, current knowledge is quite limited for understanding factors that are related to the low degree of educational gap in South Korea.

Comparing the effect of family SES on student reading performance across 34 PISA countries including South Korea, a recent study by Park proposes that cross-national variations in the effects of family SES should be associated with differences across countries in institutional features of national educational systems.[31] One of the institutional characteristics examined in the study is the degree of curriculum standardisation. The empirical study shows that countries with highly standardised educational systems in terms of curricula tend to have less educational inequality (indicated by weaker impacts of family SES on student performance especially within schools). Along the same lines as a previous study that showed a significant reduction in socio-economic inequality especially associated with a change toward greater curriculum standardisation in Scottish secondary education,[32] Park highlights a role that curriculum standardisation plays in reducing the gap between students from higher and lower SES. Curriculum standardisation requires academic exposure to core subjects for all students and thus helps students possess at least a minimum level of academic knowledge. In contrast, in educational systems where the level of curriculum standardisation is low, the pattern of learning is more likely to differ between high performers, who are more likely to come from advantaged families, and low performers, who are more likely to come from disadvantaged families. Without standardised curricula for all students, low performers are less likely to take core and academically demanding subjects than high performers are. With less exposure to core subjects than low performers in standardised systems, a greater portion of low performers in non-standardised systems will fall below a minimum level of academic knowledge expected of students of a similar age.

In fact, this effect of educational standardisation is reflected in the finding discussed earlier that South Korean students with the lowest level of socio-economic background perform much better than their counterparts in other countries. In other words, South Korean students with lower socio-economic status are much more likely to master a relatively high level of literacy required by standardised curricula than their counterparts in other countries with non-standardised education, where they often fall below the average to such extent that they lack even a minimum level of literacy. In this regard, the equalisation policy might be an important factor for South Korean education in achieving the comparatively small difference in academic performance among students.

However, this conclusion on the association between curriculum standardisation and educational inequality should be treated with caution in view of the fairly small number of studies that explicitly examine the association in South Korea or in other industrial countries. As has been pointed out, more research needs to examine wide cross-national variations in academic gaps among students and to investigate various institutional features of educational systems that may help account for the differences between countries. Findings from those studies will be useful for educational policymakers in specific societies to assess the limitations and potential of their educational systems to reduce educational gaps between students from different socio-economic backgrounds.

Given its comparable data collection and internationally co-ordinated operation, educational achievement is a useful indicator of educational outcomes with which to compare cross-nationally the degree of educational inequality. However, major data collections on student achievement, in which South Korea has regularly participated, have been conducted only recently. Therefore, it is not feasible to track changes in educational inequality over time through educational *achievement*. Instead, studies have vigorously addressed the trends in educational attainment by comparing the effects of socio-economic background on attainment. As has been said regarding research on gender and educational attainment, the most common way of examining temporal trends in the effects of family SES has been to draw comparisons across birth cohorts constructed from social survey data. Therefore, I now move to discuss findings of trends in educational inequality from research on educational attainment.

In sociological literature, the main method of studying the effects of socio-economic background is to assess the extent to which measures of socio-economic background affect the probability of attending or completing a given level of education conditional upon completion of the previous level of education. In other words, the model is concerned with how people differ in the likelihood of continuing their educational careers to the next level, depending on their socio-economic background. The essential component of this method is to separate changes over time in the distribution of educational attainment from changes in the association between socio-economic background and educational attainment. The distribution of educational attainment is affected by educational *expansion* (i.e., the overall size of the pie), which is distinguished from educational *inequality* (i.e., the way in which the pie is divided among different groups of people).[33] Since the influential work by Robert Mare, this method as a dominant way of assessing trends in the effects of socio-economic background has been applied in the context of many countries.[34] Most studies conducted on educational inequality in South Korea have relied on this method.

Of course, these studies often differed in other aspects of their research design despite common usages of the educational transition model. Some studies measured parental occupation as the index of occupational status, while others preferred categorical representation (such as professional, managerial, clerical, service/sale, farming or skilled manual) of parental occupation. Similarly, parental education was measured either by a linear variable of the years of schooling completed or by categorical classification (such as primary/lower, secondary/upper or secondary/tertiary). Studies also varied on educational transitions examined. Some focused on the transitions at the lower stages of educational career such as from middle school to high school, while others looked at the transition from high school to tertiary education with a distinction between university and junior college. Some variations also existed as to whether researchers looked at the probabilities of *attending* a given level of education or *completing* it. Finally, there were differences among studies in the ways of constructing birth cohorts.[35]

Despite their differences in research design, what is remarkably consistent among these studies is the lack of evidence of a decline in the effects of parental education or occupation on educational attainment during the past few decades. The persistent effects of socio-economic background were found at both earlier and later transitions of educational career. Moreover, no decline in the influence of socio-economic background was detected in transitions to university or junior college upon high school completion. There is even some evidence that having a father with tertiary education has become *more* important over time in determining an individual's likelihood of attending university or junior college.[36] The robustness of the finding is impressive given the diversity of research designs utilised. In conclusion, evidence from studies on educational attainment strongly indicates stability of educational inequality in South Korea despite the dramatic expansion of educational attainment among the South Korean population during the past few decades.

## Recent Demographic Changes and Educational Inequality

In the United States and other Western countries that have substantial proportions of children living in single-parent families and stepfamilies, research has been concerned about the implications of family structure for children's well-being and education. Findings overall indicate that growing up with a single parent is negatively associated with children's educational attainment and achievement. The negative consequences of living with a single parent for a child's education are often explained by two factors: poorer socio-economic conditions of single-parent families compared to intact families and the lower degree of involvement in the child's education among single parents on account of their time constraints in combining work and parenting.[37] Research has documented trends of increasing prevalence of single parents associated with out-of-wedlock births and divorce, especially among mothers with the lowest level of education and poorest economic conditions, in many Western countries. The trends are likely to increase disparities in parental economic and time resources, which are key factors for boosting educational development, between children in single-parent and nuclear families.[38]

The relevance of family structure, particularly single parenthood, for children's education has not been a major concern in South Korean education, particularly as the prevalence of single parenthood was low in comparative perspective. In addition, the majority of single parenthood was caused by the death of a parent rather than by parents' divorce or non-marital childbearing. Evidence shows that compared to children with two parents, those with a widowed parent often do not show substantial differences in their educational outcomes, in sharp contrast to lower achievement and attainment among those living with a divorced parent.[39] Moreover, strong family ties in South Korean society have played an important role in providing economic and emotional support to single parents, buffering the negative consequences of single parenthood.

However, demographic changes that South Korean society has experienced during the past decade have rendered the question of family structure and its impact on children's education no longer a peripheral concern. One of the most apparent demographic changes in South Korea is the dramatic increase in divorce, especially since the late 1990s. Changes in crude divorce rate (CDR), which is a widely used indicator of divorce for cross-national and temporal trends indicating the number of divorces per 1,000 population, highlight a rapid increase during the past decade. Compared to 1.1 divorces in 1991, the rate doubled in 1998 (2.5) and then rose to 3.5 in 2003. It is also noted that the level of divorce in South Korea is now similar to or even higher than that in many Western countries except for the considerably higher rate in the United States.

The rapidly increasing rate of divorce has led to growing single parenthood. An important policy context regarding the growth in single parenthood is that South Korea has an overall conservative social welfare system with a very low level of spending by the government on social welfare. I have addressed above public expenditures on education. The low level of welfare provision is also evident in another indicator – public expenditures on family (including both cash and other kinds of benefits) expressed in terms of GDP. In 2000, public expenditure on families was only 0.1 per cent of GDP in South Korea, whereas the corresponding percentage in Nordic countries was about 3 per cent.[40]

As in other societies, single-parent families have poorer economic conditions than intact families in South Korea. Studies of economic comparisons between the two types of family in South Korea highlight particularly vulnerable single-mother families.[41] Less than half of South Korean women of working age participate in the labour force, which is significantly low in comparison with women in Western countries and even with other East Asian countries such as Japan and Taiwan. Moreover, labour market discrimination against women in terms of employment conditions and wages is considerable.[42] Such an economic environment for South Korean women places a child living with a single mother at particularly high risk of economic deprivation.

What does increasing single parenthood in South Korea imply for the future trend in educational inequality? In order to address the issue, it is essential to assess the extent to which children from single-parent families have lower attainment compared to those from intact families and to find factors related to the differences. Until recently, educational researchers in South Korea have paid little attention to family structure, as the traditional form of family structure has been prevalent in South Korean society. However, with the recent demographic changes, a small number of researchers have extended their focus to examine the impact of family structure.

Park's study aims to present an accurate description of educational differences between children from single-parent and intact families using data from a nationally representative sample.[43] An important advantage of this study is to distinguish single parenthood by the cause (divorced or widowed) and the gender of the single parent and thus provides a better understanding of differences among single-parent families. The study also tries to explain the effects of single parenthood by assessing the relative importance of household income and parenting practices. Comparing the probability of aspiring to a four-year university education among middle-school and high-school seniors, Park shows that students living with a divorced parent have significantly lower aspirations, while the difference between students with a widowed parent and those with two parents is relatively small. The negative effect of living with a widowed parent, moreover, disappears once household income is held constant, while the disadvantage of children with a divorced parent remains significant even after household income and parenting practices are taken into account.

Along with a few previous studies using rather limited data (e.g., students only in a specific area),[44] Park's study highlights significant disadvantages for children living with a single parent, especially one who was divorced. Given the increasing prevalence of divorce, this finding has important implications for educational inequality. As the South Korean government's low level of public support to the family and children's education remains unchanged, an increasing number of children from single-parent families, especially due to parental divorce, will be at high risk of poverty and other social and economic disadvantages, which may pose serious barriers to their educational progress and ultimately social achievement. Thus, as single parenthood grows in South Korea, family structure is emerging as an important mechanism through which inter-generational continuance of socio-economic status occurs.

Another recent demographic change relevant to children's education is a rapid increase in marriages between South Koreans and foreigners. The proportion of such marriages was only 1.2 per cent in 1990; it rose tenfold (11.4 per cent) in 2004. The majority (about 72 per cent) of marriages between South Koreans and foreigners have been between South Korean males and foreign females. Most females marrying South Korean males come from other Asian countries such as China, Vietnam, and the Philippines.[45]

As such marriages have become more prevalent since the late 1990s, the majority of children born in these families are now expected to reach the age of schooling. In fact, it has been widely reported that schools have difficulties in dealing with these students' educational needs because teachers have no experience of interacting with students born in such families, and educational and material resources for helping these students and families are scarce. For a long time, South Korean society has regarded itself homogeneous with a negligible number of immigrants. Emphasis on 'blood' and 'descent' has been considerable, resulting in very exclusive policies on immigration and cultural prejudices against foreigners. Thus, it is not difficult to expect strong social and cultural stigma on and discrimination against these students.

Currently, there is little research that systematically and extensively examines educational outcomes of children born to Korean/foreign parents. Only a small number of ethnographic studies, which interviewed a limited number of these children and their parents, are available, and no official statistics on demographic and other social characteristics of interracial children have so far been provided.[46] However, the increasing prevalence of marriages between South Koreans and foreigners and the growing number of children born in these families will pose a serious challenge to South Korean education and society. It is very likely that being born to a foreign parent will in the near future become a significant factor affecting an individual's educational opportunity and thus a new mechanism through which educational inequality is maintained.

**Conclusion**

South Korea's remarkable educational expansion during the past few decades should be acknowledged. South Korea has achieved the largest expansion of education in the world within a single generation. An important issue is the extent to which the South Korean government has contributed to expanding educational opportunities by providing financial or other support to families and by implementing educational policies that assist students from disadvantaged socio-economic background to continue their educational careers. Families and individuals in South Korea have taken a major responsibility for the high cost of tertiary education with comparatively little public support.

It is submitted that the South Korean government has made no significant efforts to reduce socio-economic disparities in educational opportunities. For instance, the South Korean government's policy for tertiary education has focused mostly on the number of students admitted in response to social demands for higher education rather than concrete actions such as lowering tuition fees or providing subsidies to poorer families.[47] Indeed, it is demand by individuals and willingness of parents to make sacrifices for their children's educational opportunities, rather than governmental efforts to reduce barriers to higher education, that has brought about the dramatic expansion of education in South Korea.

The negligible level of governmental support to families and children's education is related to the persistent effects of socio-economic background on educational transitions, especially the increasing importance of the father's education for educational advancement among the recent cohorts. Research has also attributed the persistent socio-economic differentials over time in educational opportunity to unchanging income inequality and stable differentials between social strata in other economic indicators.[48] Furthermore, evidence indicates that since the Asian financial crisis in the 1990s, income inequality in South Korea has worsened and poverty significantly increased.[49] Given these economic changes, socio-economic differentials in educational opportunity are likely to persist for the time being.

Although evidence of persistent inequality of opportunity over time for educational attainment is remarkably strong, it is difficult to assess the degree of educational inequality in South Korea in cross-national comparison because of the lack of comparative research on educational attainment. Although studies of educational achievement suggest that South Korea should display a relatively equal opportunity for education in comparative perspective, it is not reasonable to draw the conclusion for educational attainment from the finding for educational achievement, because key factors determining educational attainment and achievement may differ. For instance, the low level of financial support from government is more likely to affect a student's chance for continuing a given level of education and making a transition to the next level (i.e., educational attainment), while school-related factors such as the degree of standardisation or other pedagogical practices are more relevant to educational achievement. Of course, as educational achievement is a major determinant of educational attainment, factors affecting students' academic performance could potentially impact on those influencing their educational transitions. In short, it is possible that South Korea may show a relatively high degree of inequality with strong association between socio-economic background and educational attainment, despite the comparatively weak impact of socio-economic background on educational achievement. More research is needed to examine how the effects of socio-economic origin on attainment in South Korea compare with those in other countries and to address which factors may account for the difference, if any.

In contrast to the seemingly substantial inequality of educational *attainment*, especially associated with the low level of state financial support for tertiary education, the degree of equality in educational achievement in comparative perspective is impressive. Not only the higher overall performance among South Korean students but also the distinctively low performance gap among students from different socio-economic backgrounds in South Korea deserves more serious attention from educational researchers and policymakers.

However, researchers and policymakers have recently called for the abolition of the equalisation policy, claiming that it has failed to boost educational achievement especially among the best students as it does not allow separate curricula that match their high ability. Their main assumption is that the differentiation of students according to ability level would yield positive results for all students through more effective teaching with separate curricula appropriate to individual students' ability. Nonetheless, studies of ability grouping in the United States and other Western countries have found differential effects of ability grouping on students at high and low ability groups. Students in high ability groups or elite schools tend to score higher than would be expected, whereas those in low ability groups or below-average schools tend to achieve less than would be expected.[50] In other words, against the expectations of the positive views on curriculum differentiation, it does not help boost but actually hampers academic performance among lower achievers, who are more likely to come from disadvantaged backgrounds, resulting in larger differences between students. The argument against the educational equalisation policy and a high degree of educational standardisation can be understood due to the relatively lower performance of the best students in South Korea compared to those in other countries. For instance, in PISA South Korean students within the top 5 per cent scored lower (629 points) than those in Germany (650) and in the United States (669), while the mean score for South Korea was much higher than those for Germany and the United States.[51] However, to what extent can this concern over the relatively low achievement among the best students in South Korea justify the abolition of the equalisation policy in the face of previous findings that showed increasing inequality associated with ability grouping? How can the introduction of separate curricula and student ability grouping prevent low performers, who are also more likely to be poorer students, from falling further below average? Currently, South Korean education is at a critical point in its direction for reform. What is really needed is critical assessment of the features of the educational system that have contributed to South Korean education by combining equity and quality and how they can accommodate the growing concern for diversity and selection of students and families in the educational system.

Where is South Korean education going? How will inequality of educational opportunity change and will it remain in the years to come? The recent demographic changes, particularly the increasing prevalence of single parenthood caused by parental divorce and the growing number of children born to South Korean and foreign parents, will be serious challenges to the South Korean education system; the education system at present is not sufficiently competent to deal with such changes. Unless South Korean society as a whole questions its assumption of cultural homogeneity and is willing to embrace foreigners and immigrants, its education system will not be able to effectively address the educational disadvantages of children born in these families. Without significant social and cultural transformations, the emerging family types will become significant sources of variations in South Korean children's educational outcomes.

**Notes**

1. Richard Breen and John O. Jonsson, 'Inequality of Opportunity in Comparative Perspective: Recent Research on Educational Attainment and Social Mobility', *Annual Review of Sociology*, Vol.31 (2005), pp.223–43.
2. An indicator of significant gender inequality would be a markedly low rate of South Korean women's labour force participation. Only half of the South Korean women of working age were in the labour force in 2000, compared to 75 per cent of men. See Uhn Cho, 'Gender Inequality and Patriarchal Order Reexamined', *Korea Journal*, Vol.44, No.1 (2004), pp.22–41.
3. For example, see Catherine Freeman, *Trends in Educational Equity of Girls and Women: 2004* (NCES 2005-016) (Washington, DC: Government Printing Office, 2004), for recent findings of gender differences across several indicators of education in the United States.
4. Breen and Jonsson (note 1) p.224.
5. United Nations Children's Fund, *A League Table of Educational Disadvantages in Rich Nations* (Innocenti Report Card no. 4) (Florence: UNICEF Innocenti Research Centre, 2002), p.19.
6. Claudia Buchmann, 'Measuring Family Background in International Studies of Education: Conceptual issues and Methodological Challenges', in Andrew C. Porter and Adam Gamoran (eds), *Methodological Advances in Cross-National Surveys of Educational Achievement* (Washington, DC: National Academic Press 2002), pp.150–97. The author argues, at p.154, that compared to research on educational attainment where the effect

of socio-economic background has been a central concern, research on educational achievement especially led by educational researchers and policy analysts has been concerned more with identifying school factors that may contribute to student learning, sometimes not paying serious attention to the role of socio-economic background.

7. Organisation for Economic Cooperation and Development, *Education at a Glance 2004* (Paris: OECD, 2004).
8. OECD publications on education use the International Standard Classification of Education (ISCED 97) to distinguish levels of educational attainment. According to the classification, tertiary-type A refers to theory-based programmes that prepare students for professions with high skill requirements or for advanced research programmes such as graduate schools. Type B tertiary education is oriented towards practical and vocational education that usually prepares students for employment. See Glossary in OECD, *Education at a Glance 2004*, ibid.
9. For more information on PISA, see OECD, *Literacy Skills for the World of Tomorrow: Further Results from PISA 2000* (Paris: OECD 2003).
10. OECD, *Problem Solving for Tomorrow's World: First Measures of the Cross-Curricular Competencies from PISA 2003* (Paris: OECD 2004), p.16.
11. Ibid. p.27.
12. OECD, *Education at a Glance 2003* (Paris: OECD 2003), Table B2.1c. Among these countries, the Czech Republic (13,806 GDP per capita in 2000 in equivalent US dollars converted using Purchasing Power Parity calculations (PPPs)) and Greece (15,885) have the level of economic development similar to South Korea (15,186), while Italy (25,095) and New Zealand (20,372) have a higher level: ibid., Table X2.1.
13. Ibid., Table B3.2.
14. OECD, *Education at a Glance 1997* (Paris: OECD 1997).
15. In South Korean private universities, tuition fees amount over 95 per cent of budgets. OECD, *Education at a Glance 2003* (Paris: OECD 2003), p.215.
16. Ibid. pp.213–14.
17. More detailed discussions on various features of the South Korean educational system across different levels of education can be found in two previous studies: Hyunjoon Park, 'Educational Expansion and Inequality', *Research in Sociology of Education*, Vol.14 (2004), pp.33–58; Hyunjoon Park, 'Educational Expansion and Inequality of Opportunity for Higher Education in South Korea', in Y. Shavit, R. Arum, A. Gamoran and G. Menahem (eds), *Expansion, Differentiation and Stratification in Higher Education: A Comparative Study of 15 Countries* (in press).
18. Note that the equalisation policy has been applied to academic high schools only. Applicants for vocational schools have the opportunity to choose their schools.
19. OECD, *Education at a Glance 2005* (Paris: OECD 2005), Table A1.4.
20. For example, advancement rates from academic secondary education to tertiary education in 2004 were 89.8 per cent for both males and females. KEDI, *Educational Statistics System*, http://cesi.kedi.re.kr/jcgi-bin/index.jsp (accessed 1 December 2005).
21. Park, 'Educational Expansion and Inequality of Opportunity' (note 17); Sang-soo Chang, 'Patterns and Change of Educational Attainment in Korea', presented at the annual meeting of International Sociological Association, Research Committee 28, Tokyo, Japan, 1–3 March 2003; Hanam Phang and Kihun Kim, 'Educational Stratification of Korean Society', *Korean Journal of Sociology*, Vol.37, No.4 (2002), pp.31–65 (in Korean). Park compared four birth cohorts (those born before 1951, 1951–60, 1961–70, and 1971 or after) and Chang examined differences between four birth cohorts (1926–45, 1946–55, 1956–65 and 1966–75). Phang and Kim distinguished those aged 30 or below, 31–40, 41–50, and 51 or above, using data collected in 2001.
22. Mary C. Brinton and Sunhwa Lee, 'Women's Education and the Labour Market in Japan and South Korea', in Mary Brinton (ed.), *Women's Working Lives in East Asia* (Stanford, CA: Stanford University Press 2001), pp.204–32. According to Brinton and Lee, advancement rates among women from high school to junior college increased from 2.4 per cent in 1955 to over 20 per cent in 1995. During the same period, advancement rates among men remained stable at less than 5 per cent.
23. Richard Breen and John O. Jonsson, 'Analyzing Educational Career: A Multinomial Transition Model', *American Sociological Review*, Vol.65 (2000), pp.754–72; Samuel R. Lucas, 'Effectively Maintained Inequality: Educational Transitions, Track Mobility, and Social Background Effects', *American Journal of Sociology*, Vol.106 (2001), pp.1642–90.
24. Park, 'Educational Expansion and Inequality of Opportunity' (note 17). See also Kihun Kim and Hanam Phang, 'Social Class and Gender Differentials in Korean and Japanese Higher Education', *Korean*

*Journal of Sociology*, Vol.39, No.5 (2005), pp.119–51 (in Korean). Because of the small sample size for each cohort and the method of contrasting only with the oldest cohort of 1940–49, Kim and Phang's study is not quite sensitive enough for detecting changes over time. But the overall trends in gender differences observed in their study are generally consistent with what I have found.

25. OECD, *Literacy Skills for the World of Tomorrow* (note 9) Table 5.2a.
26. Ina V. S. Mullis *et al.*, *Gender Differences in Achievement: IEA's Third International Mathematics and Science (TIMSS)* (Chestnut Hill, MA: Boston College 2000). Also see OECD, *Literacy Skills for the World of Tomorrow* (note 9) p.142.
27. OECD, *Education at a Glance 2004* (note 7) Table A9.5.
28. Ibid. Table A4.2.
29. For more information on the index, see OECD, *Literacy Skills for the World of Tomorrow* (note 9) p.233. See also Harry B. G. Ganzeboom, Paul De Graff and Donald J. Treiman, 'A Standard International Socio-Economic Index of Occupational Status', *Social Science Research*, Vol.21, No.1 (1992), pp.1–56.
30. OECD, *Literacy Skills for the World of Tomorrow* (note 9) Table 6.1a.
31. Hyunjoon Park, 'Cross-National Variation in the Effects of Family Background on Educational Achievement: Relevance of Institutional and Policy Contexts' (PhD Dissertation, University of Wisconsin-Madison 2005).
32. Adam Gamoran, 'Curriculum Standardisation and Equality of Opportunity in Scottish Secondary Education: 1984–90', *Sociology of Education*, Vol.69, No.1 (1996), pp.1–21.
33. Breen and Jonsson (note 1) p.225; Robert Mare, 'Change and Stability in Educational Stratification', *American Sociological Review*, Vol.46, No.1 (1981), pp.72–87.
34. Mare (note 33). Yossi Shavit and Hans-Peter Blossfeld (eds), *Persistent Inequality: Expansion, Reform, and Opportunity in Thirteen Countries* (Boulder, CO: Westview Press 1993). The 13 studies included in the edited volume by Shavit and Blossfeld used basically the same model of educational transition.
35. See Park 'Educational Expansion and Inequality' (note 17) p.33; Park, 'Educational Expansion and Inequality of Opportunity' (note 17); Chang (note 21); Phang and Kim (note 21) p.31; Kim and Phang (note 24) p.119.
36. Park, 'Educational Expansion and Inequality of Opportunity' (note 17). Chang (note 21) has found that the increasing effects of the father's education are particularly apparent among women.
37. Sara McLanahan and Gary D. Sandefur, *Growing Up with a Single Parent* (Cambridge, MA: Harvard University Press 1994).
38. Sara McLanahan, 'Diverging Destinies: How Children are Faring under the Second Demographic Transitions', *Demography*, Vol.41, No.4 (2004), pp.607–27.
39. Timothy J. Biblarz and Greg Gottainer, 'Family Structure and Children's Success: A Comparison of Widowed and Divorced Single-Mother Families', *Journal of Marriage and the Family*, Vol.62, No.2 (2000), pp.533–48; Paul R. Amato and Bruce Keith, 'Separation from a Parent during Childhood and Adult Socioeconomic Attainment', *Social Forces*, Vol.70, No.1 (1991), pp.187–207.
40. OECD, *Social Expenditure Database 1980–2001* (2004), http://www.oecd.org/social/expenditure (accessed 1 December 2005).
41. Misook Kim *et al.*, *Life Conditions of Low Income Single-Mother Families and Policy* (Seoul: Korea Institute for Health and Social Affairs 2000) (in Korean).
42. Brinton (note 22).
43. Hyunjoon Park, 'Growing Up in a Single-Parent Family in Korea', Paper presented at the annual conference on Korean Education and Employment, Seoul, South Korea, 7 October 2005.
44. Kyehoon Oh and Kyunkyun Kim, 'Effects on Children's Academic Achievement of Family Structure', *Journal of Sociology of Education*, Vol.11 (2001), pp.101–23 (in Korean).
45. National Statistical Office (2005), http://www.kosis.nso.go.kr; Sung-bae Oh, 'A Case Study of Kosian Children's Development and Environment', *Journal of Korean Education* Vol.32, No.3 (2005), pp.61–82 at p.62.
46. Oh (note 45).
47. Park, 'Educational Expansion and Inequality' (note 17).
48. Chang (note 21).
49. Jiho Jang, 'Economic Crisis and its Consequences', in Doh C. Shin and Conrad P. Rutkowski (eds), *The Quality of Life in Korea: Comparative and Dynamic Perspectives* (Dordrecht, The Netherlands: Kluwer Academic Publishers 2003), pp.51–70.
50. Alan C. Kerckhoff, 'Effects of Ability Groups in British Secondary Schools', *American Sociological Review*, Vol.51 (1986), pp.842–58.
51. OECD, *Literacy Skills for the World of Tomorrow* (note 9) p.83.

# Official Languages and Bilingualism in the Courtroom: Hong Kong, Canada, the Republic of Ireland, and International Law

PHIL C. W. CHAN

Being the core means of human communication, language is at once universal and varied. As the Supreme Court of Canada in its *Reference re Language Rights in Manitoba*[1] maintained, '[t]he importance of language rights is grounded in the essential role that language plays in human existence, development and dignity. It is through language that we are able to form concepts; to structure and order the world around us. Language bridges the gap between isolation and community, allowing humans to delineate the rights and duties they hold in respect of one another, and thus to live in society.'[2]

Comparative law scholars should therefore find Hong Kong a stimulating exemplar. In addition to its legacy as a former Crown Colony of the United Kingdom now part of the People's Republic of China with its capitalist society[3] and common law legal system[4] constitutionally preserved, Hong Kong is amongst those few jurisdictions that embrace

English as an official language in addition to the language or languages spoken by the majority of their respective predominant or dominant populations. The predominant majority of the population in Hong Kong speaks Cantonese, a dialect of the Chinese language. As opposed to the simplified Chinese script in use in China, Hong Kong uses the traditional Chinese script developed since Chinese imperial times. Under Article 9 of the Basic Law of Hong Kong, which governs the constitutional framework of post-colonial Hong Kong: 'In addition to the Chinese language, English may also be used as an official language by the executive authorities, legislature and judiciary of the Hong Kong Special Administrative Region.'[5] The constitutional provision is reinforced by the Official Languages Ordinance, which states that '[t]he English and Chinese languages are declared to be the official languages of Hong Kong for the purposes of communication between the Government or any public officer and members of the public and for court proceedings'[6] and that '[t]he official languages possess equal status and, subject to the provisions of this Ordinance, enjoy equality of use.'[7] The status of English as official language and the significant role that an official language plays naturally permeate Hong Kong's legal profession, judiciary, and courtrooms, where being unequivocally understood is of paramount importance.

The issue of language use rights in the courtroom was given prominent scrutiny in *Re Cheng Kai Nam Gary*,[8] where a former legislator applied to the Hong Kong Court of First Instance for leave to apply for judicial review against the listing judge's refusal to cause his District Court criminal proceedings to be conducted in Cantonese and to direct a bilingual judge to be listed in the conduct of the matter on the basis of his right to fair trial as constitutionally and internationally enshrined.[9] The former legislator argued that the scheduled monolingual English-speaking judge's accurate examination of key witnesses including the defendant himself, who were to testify in Cantonese and whose testimony would thus have to be interpreted, would likely be frustrated. His application for leave was rejected.

As Hong Kong is a common law jurisdiction and various common law jurisdictions continue to adopt English as an official language notwithstanding the cessation of British rule, the experience which these jurisdictions have garnered with legal bilingualism, particularly in judicial proceedings, is of immense value to the development and protection of language use rights in Hong Kong. The strong French sentiments in the legal and political structures of Canada and their Irish counterparts in Ireland are particularly instructive and will be discussed in dissecting the anomaly in Hong Kong which *Re Cheng Kai Nam Gary* brought to light. *Re Cheng Kai Nam Gary* will also be used as a springboard for a wider discussion on whether international law may assist in furthering the development and protection of language rights in the courtroom.

### 1. The Right to Trial in One's Chosen Official Language

*Preliminary Issue: The Status of Cantonese in Hong Kong*

The Preamble to the Basic Law of Hong Kong states that

> Upholding national unity and territorial integrity, maintaining the prosperity and stability of Hong Kong, and taking account of its history and realities, the People's Republic of China has decided that upon China's resumption of the exercise of sovereignty over Hong Kong, a Hong Kong Special Administrative Region

will be established in accordance with the provisions of Article 31 of the Constitution of the People's Republic of China,[10] and that under the principle of 'one country, two systems', the socialist system and policies will not be practised in Hong Kong.[11]

In *Re Cheng Kai Nam Gary*, Justice Hartmann of the Hong Kong Court of First Instance maintained that the status of Chinese/Cantonese as one of Hong Kong's two official languages must therefore be qualified by Hong Kong's 'special history'.[12] Pointing out that Hong Kong's judiciary, including the Hong Kong Court of Final Appeal, is constitutionally empowered to continue after July 1997 to employ judges from other common law jurisdictions with no linguistic requirements,[13] Justice Hartmann inferred that the Basic Law Drafting Committee could not have intended that an individual in Hong Kong should have a constitutional right to be tried by a Cantonese-speaking judge.[14]

Ironically, in his syllogism Justice Hartmann overlooked the origins and consequences of Hong Kong's special history, namely, the transition of Hong Kong from being a Crown Colony of the United Kingdom to being now part of the People's Republic of China. In this respect, reference is had to Ireland and its predecessor the Irish Free State, whose 1922 Constitution[15] stated, in Article 4, that '[t]he National language of the Irish Free State (Saorstát Éireann) is the Irish language, but the English language shall be equally recognised as an official language.'[16] In *Ó Foghludha v. McClean*[17] in 1935, Supreme Court of Ireland Chief Justice Kennedy declared that

> One of the distinguishing marks of a nation, in the sense of a distinct people (though not a necessary or universal mark), is the possession of a common national language. This nation of ours possessed that distinguishing characteristic in the Irish language. It was the common speech of every Irishman down to comparatively recent times, when it yielded before immense pressure, compulsion in the schools, social, political and commercial forces. For some years before the Treaty of 1921,[18] there was an active but slow and difficult struggle to recover the lost ground. The language position at the date of the enactment to the Constitution is too fresh in our memories to need statement but the importance of it here is for the interpretation of Article 4. The declaration by the Constitution that the national language of the Saorstát is the Irish language does not mean that the Irish language is, or was at that historical moment, universally spoken by the people of the Saorstát, which would be untrue in fact, but it did mean that it is the historic distinctive speech of the Irish people, that it is to rank as such in the nation, and by implication, that the State is bound to do everything within its sphere of action (as for instance in State provided education) to establish and maintain it in its status as the national language and to recognise it for all official purposes as the national language. There is no doubt in my mind but that the term 'national' in the Article is wider than, but includes, 'official', in which respect only the English language is accorded constitutional equality. None of the organs of the State, legislative, executive or judicial, may derogate from the pre-eminent status of the Irish language as the National language of the State without offending against the constitutional provisions of Article 4.[19]

The Constitution of Ireland (Bunreacht na hÉireann) of 1937, replacing the 1922 Constitution of the Irish Free State,[20] is even more lucid, stating that '[t]he Irish language as the national language is the first official language'[21] whilst '[t]he English language is recognised as a second official language.'[22]

During British colonial rule over Hong Kong, Chinese was not recognised as an official language of Hong Kong notwithstanding the predominant use thereof within the population. Now, under the sovereignty of China, the Cantonese-speaking people of Hong Kong ought to be entitled to expect and demand the right to choose and to use Cantonese in judicial services and proceedings, particularly those that may undermine or threaten their freedom and liberty, for, in the words of Irish Supreme Court Justice Hardiman in *Ó Beoláin v. Fahy*,[23] 'the institution by a statutory official, and subsequently adjudication by a judge, of a criminal charge whether minor or otherwise is part of what I have called the public discourse of the nation and the official business of the State.'[24] Furthermore, it is doubtful that the Basic Law Drafting Committee, an organ of the People's Republic of China Government, intended to maintain the supremacy of English over Chinese in the official transactions in Hong Kong or to deprive its own nationals in Hong Kong of their right to use their own Chinese language in judicial services and proceedings. Above all, the concept of language is meaningless unless the language itself is capable of being used and directly understood; hence, 'a State duty grounded in the language itself rather than in the rights of its speakers would lend itself to weakened implementation obligations.'[25]

The spirit of the Basic Law of Hong Kong, and of the handover of sovereignty, is that Hong Kong and the people of Hong Kong are now 'an inalienable part of the People's Republic of China'.[26] In addition to indicating the rights and freedoms of persons residing in and to providing the groundwork for the infrastructure of post-colonial Hong Kong, the Basic Law of Hong Kong epitomises such a spirit in a written, referable form in a legally binding manner. The Supreme Court of Canada in its *Reference re Secession of Québec*[27] was adamant that '[a] political system must also possess legitimacy, and in our political culture, that requires an interaction between the rule of law and the democratic principle. The system must be capable of reflecting the aspirations of the people.'[28] Albie Sachs, now a Justice of the South African Constitutional Court, has observed that 'a constitution does much more than indicate the political and legal organization of the state. It serves as a symbol for the whole of society, as a point of reference for the nation. People like to feel that they have constitutional rights even if they do not exercise them. ... Above all, the constitution is a vehicle for expressing fundamental notions of freedom, at the conceptual, symbolic and practical levels.'[29]

The importance of equality in dignity and rights is explicitly recognised in Article 1 of the Universal Declaration of Human Rights,[30] which states that '[a]ll human beings are born free and equal in dignity and rights. They are endowed with reason and conscience and should act towards one another in a spirit of brotherhood.'[31] As the Explanatory Note to the Oslo Recommendations Regarding the Linguistic Rights of National Minorities,[32] reached and propounded by a group of experts in February 1998 under the auspices of the Organisation for Security and Co-operation in Europe, expounds, '[e]quality in dignity and rights presupposes respect for the individual's identity as a human being. Hence, respect for a person's dignity is intimately connected with respect for the person's identity and consequently for the person's language.'[33] The judiciary, especially one like Hong Kong's that is premised upon a political compromise, must, as Canadian Supreme Court Chief Justice Dickson in *R. v. Oakes*[34] categorically affirmed, be guided by the values and principles essential to a free and democratic society which I believe to embody, to name but a few, respect for the inherent dignity of the human person, commitment to social justice and equality, accommodation of a wide variety of beliefs, respect for cultural and group identity, and faith in social and political institutions which enhance the participation of individuals and groups in society.[35]

Indeed, as human beings are by their nature highly communicative, nothing can be more suppressive of and divisive to human society than linguistic barriers, particularly those that are imposed by a foreign or foreign-like oligarchy upon the majority masses. Speaking of Ireland, where the Irish language has systematically been dispensed with in the official business of the state, just as has Chinese in Hong Kong, Irish High Court Justice Costello in *Attorney General v. Paperlink Limited*[36] was adamant that '[a]s the act of communication is the exercise of such a basic human faculty ... a right to communication must inhere in the citizen by virtue of his human personality and must be guaranteed by the Constitution.'[37] In this light, Nic Shuibhne argues that 'recognition of a right to communicate must recognise implicitly the right to choice of language: otherwise its enunciation would be meaningless.'[38]

Language rights are all the more important where one's personal obligations *vis-à-vis* others or the state or where one's rights, freedom or personal liberty are at stake in a forum where being understood is of paramount importance. Yet it is not the only reason why legal bilingualism is essential for a society long suppressed such as Hong Kong or Ireland or, to a lesser degree, the Province of Québec within Canada, as Macdonald explains:

> The reason why it is important to be able to argue before a court in one's own language owes much to the rhetorical power of language. If the norm itself is available in one's language and if judicial judgment is simply the deductive application of the norm, pleading in one's language and receiving judgment in one's language is a superfluous luxury. But if a judgment is the rhetorical act of convincing, its presentational elements are equally important. The process of argumentation in law is more than a process of rational justification; it is also a process of presentational dialogue.[39]
>
> ... Law itself symbolizes a rationality that can never be fully achieved. We defer to the law as sound and principled, but we are not able to express in a definitive way the grounds for our deference. The presence of a second language at least serves to reassure us that this deference is not linguistically arbitrary. To claim that norms must be expressed and that their interpretation and application must be justified in more than one language is also to claim that whatever the semiotic importance of discursive, rationalistic modes for their apprehension, they must also be apprehended in presentational, deferential modes.[40]

Whilst it is true that Hong Kong's judiciary may continue to employ qualified judges from other common law jurisdictions without any linguistic requirements *expressly* stipulated, what was sought in *Re Cheng Kai Nam Gary* was the right to request that one's trial be presided over by a judge who understands one's own chosen official language. As Pupavac points out,

Linguistic identity is regarded by linguistic human rights proponents as crucial to a stable personality or community. Linguistic human rights are now being argued for in terms of securing the psychosocial development of individuals as well as their economic, political and social well-being. The linguistic repertoire to be protected is not just language acquisition but specific linguistic identification. Identification with a mother tongue is regarded as a universal fundamental need by advocates, although the notion that self-identity necessarily involves identification with the mother tongue has been contested by cross-cultural research. Nevertheless, advocates believe that identification with the mother tongue is crucial to self-identity and should be promoted. Consequently linguistic human rights are proposed to support individuals to 'identify positively with their mother tongue, and to have that identification respected by others'.[41]

In his previous study of the issue,[42] the present author, relying on the Supreme Court of Canada decision in *Société des Acadiens du Nouveau-Brunswick v. Association of Parents for Fairness in Education*[43] and the Court's subsequent *Reference re Bill 30, An Act to Amend the Education Act (Ontario)*,[44] asserted that Justice Hartmann erred in not upholding the spirit of the Sino-British Joint Declaration and consequently the Basic Law of Hong Kong by refusing to effectuate the attendant political compromise that inheres.[45]

However, upon a closer perusal of authorities, particularly the subsequent Supreme Court of Canada decision in *R. v. Beaulac*,[46] the present author wishes to take one step further from his previous position on the importance of effectuating such political compromise as inheres in the two documents and argue that language rights are *not* to be compromised and that politics should be disregarded in the calculus, in line with *Beaulac* which explicitly rejected as confined the political compromise doctrine propounded in *Société des Acadiens du Nouveau-Brunswick*;[47] with what language rights in Hong Kong should be perceived to constitute and originate from, namely, to address past suppression and injustice; and thus squarely with Hong Kong's special history as reflected in the Preamble to the Basic Law of Hong Kong. It is submitted, thus, that a judge in Hong Kong or elsewhere does not have the jurisdiction to deny an individual's right to use his or her chosen official language throughout his or her proceedings, civil or criminal, and that the presiding trial judge in a particular case ought to be required to be proficient in that chosen language. As the Supreme Court of Canada affirmed in *Veuillette*,[48] a 1919 decision concerning the composition of a jury in the Province of Québec where the French population did and continues to outnumber its English counterpart, 'the right of an English- or French-speaker to be tried in the province [of Québec] by at least six of his fellow citizens who speak his mother tongue is an absolute one. The judge does not even have the discretion to decide whether to grant the accused's request for a mixed jury. It is an absolute and indefensible right; and once he has expressed the wish, the judge must note it and ensure that the jury is mixed.'[49] In *Groener v. Minister for Education and the City of Dublin Vocational Educational Committee*[50] concerning the legality of imposition of linguistic requirements for a lectureship position in Ireland, the Court of Justice of the European Communities reaffirmed that

> a permanent full-time post of lecturer in public vocational education institutions is *a post of such a nature as to justify the requirement of linguistic knowledge*, within the meaning of the last subparagraph of Article 3(1) of Regulation No. 1612/68 of the

Council (which concerns the illegality of members states' restrictions, through otherwise ostensibly neutral measures, upon the free movement of workers and their access to employment within the European Economic Community), provided that the linguistic requirement in question is imposed as part of a policy for the promotion of the national language which is, at the same time, the first official language and provided that that requirement is applied in a proportionate and non-discriminatory manner.[51]

The Oslo Recommendations Regarding the Linguistic Rights of National Minorities state that '[i]n those regions and localities in which persons belonging to a national minority live in significant numbers and where the desire for it has been expressed, States should give due consideration to the feasibility of conducting all judicial proceedings affecting such persons in the language of the minority.'[52] The Explanatory Note to Oslo Recommendation 19 elucidates:

> Insofar as access to justice is vital to the enjoyment of human rights, the degree to which one may participate directly and easily in available procedures is an important measure of such access. The availability of judicial procedures functioning in the language(s) of persons belonging to national minorities, therefore, renders access to justice more direct and easy for such persons.
>
> On this basis, Article 9 of the *European Charter for Regional or Minority Languages* provides that, to the extent feasible and pursuant to the request of one of the affected parties, all judicial proceedings should be conducted in the regional or minority language. The Parliamentary Assembly of the Council of Europe has come to the same conclusion in *Recommendation 1201* which provides that 'In regions in which *substantial numbers* of a national minority are settled, the persons belonging to a national minority shall have the right to use their mother tongue in their contacts with the administrative authorities and in proceedings before the courts and legal authorities'. Accordingly, States should adopt appropriate recruitment and training policies for the judiciary.[53]

As Packer and Siemienski point out, the Oslo Recommendations

> are not – and never were intended to be – new standards. Rather, they should be viewed as an attempt to provide further specificity with regard to the application of existing international standards. To this end, the experts endeavoured to interpret and add further detail to the existing standards through a consistent and coherent understanding of international human rights law, including the rights of persons belonging to national minorities. The ultimate objective was to render useful guidance for domestic authorities in policy- and law-making in relation to the practical and full implementation of minority language rights.[54]

Similarly, Article 27 of the International Covenant on Civil and Political Rights requires that '[i]n those States in which ethnic, religious or linguistic minorities exist, persons belonging to such minorities shall not be denied the right, in community with the other members of their group, to enjoy their own culture, to profess and practise their own religion, or to use their own language.'[55] This provision is to be read in conjunction with

Article 2(1) of the Covenant, which states that '[e]ach State Party to the present Covenant undertakes to respect and to ensure to all individuals within its territory and subject to its jurisdiction the rights recognised in the present Covenant, without distinction of any kind, such as race, colour, sex, language, religion, political or other opinion, national or social origin, property, birth or other status.'[56] As Buergenthal explains, '[t]he obligation "to ensure" these rights encompasses the duty "to respect" them, but it is substantially broader. ... the provision implies an affirmative obligation by the state to take whatever measures are necessary to enable individuals to enjoy or exercise the rights guaranteed in the Covenant, including the removal of governmental and possibly also some private obstacles to the enjoyment of these rights.'[57]

One may argue that the Oslo Recommendations and Article 27 of the International Covenant on Civil and Political Rights are applicable to minorities only and thus do not apply to the Cantonese-speaking population in Hong Kong as it does not constitute a minority within the definition proffered by Special Rapporteur Francesco Capotorti of the United Nations Sub-Commission on the Prevention of Discrimination and Protection of Minorities, that is, 'a group numerically inferior to the rest of the population of a State, *in a non-dominant position*, whose members – being nationals of the State – possess ethnic, religious or linguistic characteristics differing from those of the rest of the population and show, if only implicitly, a sense of solidarity, directed towards preserving their culture, traditions, religion or language.'[58] However, one must not overlook the disquiet amongst international law scholars as to the constitution of a minority. Packer points out that

> It has been correctly observed that international law supposes the existence of minorities both in general and of specific types. However, while the existence of human beings and states are 'axiomatic' in international law, the existence of human groups is problematic. Conceptually, international law struggles with definitions of actors beyond the 'State'; indeed, the problem of defining actors has always troubled political theory in general and international relations in particular. ... while the catalogue and content of individual human rights has become relatively clear, the specificity of protections for groups, particularly minorities, has remained largely uncertain. Paramount among this uncertainty has been the very definition of 'the' or 'a minority' to whom any rights may accrue.[59]

Before the United Nations Human Rights Committee in *Ballantyne, Davidson, McIntyre v. Canada*,[60] the applicants alleged that their language rights, freedom of expression, and right of equality before the law had all been violated by the Province of Québec (and thus Canada), as the province through legislation forbade the use of English in public bill-posting and commercial advertising outdoors within its jurisdiction.[61] The Committee refused to lend credence to the enlargement of the concept, and protection, of minority rights to include individuals who otherwise constitute the majority of the State Party to the International Covenant on Civil and Political Rights. However, the Committee held that the equality and non-discrimination guarantee in Article 26 of the Covenant was inapplicable as the Québec legislative provisions in question

> operate to prohibit the use of commercial advertising outdoors in other than the French language. This prohibition applies to French speakers as well as English

speakers, so that a French speaking person wishing to advertise in English, in order to reach those of his or her clientele who are English speaking, may not do so. Accordingly, the Committee finds that the authors have not been discriminated against on the ground of their language, and concludes that there has been no violation of article 26 of the Covenant.[62]

Rodley discerns that the Committee might merely be seeking to ensure the interests of the Canadian francophone minority (despite their majority status and presence in the Province of Québec).[63] The author reiterates that 'Article 26 implicates indirect as well as direct discrimination and is not only concerned with minorities. It is arguable that the Committee's exclusion of legal equality/nondiscrimination considerations should be restricted to commercial expression.'[64] In her individual opinion joined by Nisuke Ando, Marco Tulio Bruni Celli, and Vojin Dimitrijevic, Elizabeth Evatt related her difficulty with the majority Views, that

> it interprets the term 'minorities' in article 27 solely on the basis of the number of members of the group in question in the State party. The reasoning is that because English-speaking Canadians are not a numerical minority in Canada they cannot be a minority for the purposes of article 27.
>
> I do not agree, however, that persons are necessarily excluded from the protection of article 27 where their group is an ethnic, linguistic or cultural minority in an autonomous province of a State, but is not clearly a numerical minority in the State itself, taken as a whole entity. The criteria for determining what is a minority in a State (in the sense of article 27) had not yet been considered by the Committee, and did not need to be foreclosed by a decision in the present matter, which can in any event be determined on other grounds. The history of the protection of minorities in international law shows that the question of definition has been difficult and controversial and that many different criteria have been proposed. For example, it has been argued that factors other than strictly numerical ones need to be taken into account.[65]

Indeed, in human society, what is capable of suppression is not necessarily the numerical supremacy of a given community but *always* its possession of power. As Ramaga maintains:

> Without the need for protection, the numerical criterion in defining 'minority' lacks relevance. The concurrent application of this criterion, the subjective test of group will to preserve identity, and the dominance criterion create a concept in which the apparently cardinal element of numerical inferiority is, actually, an expression of dominance. Only because of the natures of different international measures against dominance by minorities does minority status appear to be based on numerical inferiority rather than dominance. Otherwise, dominance alone could explain the whole concept of minority identification and status.[66]

The mechanism of power perforce inheres in the legal and judicial system, through the powerful tool of the law, and, as Thornton asserts, '[n]o forum, public or private, can overcome the advantage of power.'[67] Indeed, the law serves as justification for a particular *manner* of exercise of power. That the Chinese-speaking residents in Hong Kong do not constitute a minority in the territory is admittedly true, but it is precisely this truth that is tainted with and demonstrates *real* oppression. Within Hong Kong's judicial system, the fact that English continues to be the *lingua franca* attests that majority power is vested in the English-speaking judges in Hong Kong whilst minority oppression is manifest in scenarios such as in *Re Cheng Kai Nam Gary*. The situation as it persists in Hong Kong, to borrow the words of Irish Supreme Court Justice Hardiman in *Ó Beoláin v. Fahy*, is thus 'a constant, officially tolerated, discouragement or actual preclusion from the conduct of legal business in the [Chinese] language. In these circumstances it is no wonder that the [Chinese] language and [Chinese] speakers have made little progress in the routine use of the [Chinese] language in the courts.'[68] Speaking in the Irish context, Castellino laments that '[i]t is clear that the manner of the decimation of the Irish language during the colonial era is responsible for the lack of Irish spoken in modern-day Ireland',[69] which the author denounces as 'cultural genocide'.[70] Bertil Wennergren in his individual opinion in *Ballantyne, Davidson, McIntyre v. Canada* maintained that 'the issue of what constitutes a minority in a State must be decided on a case by case basis, due regard being given to the particular circumstances of each case.'[71]

Meanwhile, Veitch discerns in respect of Canada that

> The fact that francophones must use a second language in the marketplace or at work [or, in the case of Hong Kong, at university or in the courtroom] does not appear, in the eyes of the majority, to be any diminution of the status of the minority as Canadians. The position of the majority is to be explained by their belief that their language and culture are divisible, which represents the sharpest difference of attitude between the two groups. The francophone minority urge that language and culture are indivisible and that government intervention is needed in all sectors of society to ensure the equality of the francophones.[72]

The truth of the matter, however, is that a language with which an individual person identifies most intimately

> has intrinsic value as a cultural inheritance and part of an ongoing way of life. Participation in communal forms of human creativity such as language is an intrinsic part of the value of human life. The particular linguistic or cultural form it takes for a particular group of people has intrinsic value *for them* because it is *their* creation. This value of language, as a manifestation of human creativity with which its speakers identify, is the key to understanding the claim to its protection.[73]

Ó Riagáin dissects this value most astutely:

> The vocabulary, morphology, even accentuation, of a people's speech all bear evidence of their development as a distinct group, their lifestyle, contacts with other peoples and their shared historical experience.
>
> To suppress or deliberately restrict the use of a people's language is to attack their dignity in a most profound manner and to infringe their human rights. To attack a people's language or culture can often be more brutal, more damaging, than to displace them from their ancestral homelands or to marginalise them economically.

It will inevitably lead to resentment, to alienation, to a lowering of their self-esteem and ultimately to a breakdown of their social strictures.[74]

Fawcett is adamant that 'membership of a majority is based on the freedom to deny that one belongs to a minority, a *freedom* in the definition of oneself which the member of a minority cannot have!'[75] Thus, it cannot be denied that the Chinese-speaking residents in Hong Kong, from the perspective of language use, constitute a minority within Hong Kong's English-speaking dominant judicial system not yet rectified despite China's resumption of sovereignty over Hong Kong since 1 July 1997. It must be remembered that the importance of language rights, including the right to use a particular official language, lies in the fact that citizens 'are concerned as well with ensuring that the courts and their decisions in some sense belong to minority language communities.'[76] As McHugh maintains, '[a]ll law functions within the foundational values and parameters that the constitutional structure establishes and enforces. The creation of professional distance between the public and its law undermines the sovereignty of a democratic polity.'[77]

*A positive duty for the courts?*

It is important to emphasise that the right which the applicant in *Re Cheng Kai Nam Gary* was asserting was an individual's right to be tried by a judge capable of understanding directly the testimony given by any particular witness in the particular official language in the relevant proceedings. The right asserted is thus confined to trial proceedings and does not affect the participation of a monolingual judge in appellate proceedings, where evidence testimony is mostly not present.

However, Justice Hartmann refused to concede to the applicant's limited request, concluding that

> the constitutional right of a person to use the Chinese language in a court of law in Hong Kong means no more than the right of that person to employ that language, that is, to utilize it, for the purpose of forwarding or protecting his interests. That right to employ or utilize the language does not imply a reciprocal obligation on the part of the court to speak and read that language. It is sufficient if processes, such as the employment of interpreters or translators, exist to facilitate the court comprehending what is said or written.[78]

It is submitted that this position was from both constitutional and democratic perspectives a misguided one. The importance of institutional bilingualism in Hong Kong is recognised and inheres in both the Basic Law of Hong Kong and the Official Languages Ordinance. In this respect, reference is had to Canada's longstanding experience with official bilingualism *vis-à-vis* English and French as entrenched in its constitutional structures within the Canadian Charter of Rights and Freedoms.[79] The Canadian Minister of Justice, in 1978, stated in the House of Commons in Ottawa that

> It seems to me that all persons living in a [jurisdiction] which recognizes two official languages must have the right to use and be understood in either of those languages when on trial before courts of criminal jurisdiction. I repeat that a trial before a judge and jury who understand the accused's language should be a fundamental right and

not a privilege. The right to be heard in a criminal proceeding by a judge or a judge and jury who speak the accused's own official language, even if it is the minority language..., surely is a right that is a bare minimum in terms of serving the interests of both justice and [national] unity. It is essentially a question of fairness which is involved.[80]

As Jones points out, a right is 'conceptually tied'[81] to a commensurate duty. In Hong Kong, the right to choose to use one of the two official languages, as enshrined in the Basic Law of Hong Kong and reinforced by the Official Languages Ordinance, is intertwined with the commensurate constitutional duty, in the words of Canadian Supreme Court Justice Bastarache in his decision in *Beaulac*, upon which Justice Hartmann relied exclusively yet erroneously (as will be seen later in this paper), to

[maintain] a proper institutional infrastructure and [provide] services in both official languages on an equal basis. As mentioned earlier, in the context of institutional bilingualism, an application for service [or proceeding] in the language of the official minority language group must not be treated as though there was one primary official language and a duty to accommodate with regard to the use of the other official language. The governing principle is that of the equality of both official languages[82] [as stipulated in section 3(2) of the Official Languages Ordinance].

It is worth noting that Justice Bastarache is in his own right a leading Canadian authority on language rights.[83] In respect of Ireland, Nic Shuibhne argues that '[a] mere declaration that the Irish language is the national and first official language is utterly meaningless without a determination on the part of the State to create a climate favourable to its implementation in reality.'[84]

One would hope that international law would be able to assist in the development and protection of language use rights. Unfortunately, the United Nations Human Rights Committee has proven to be disappointing. In *Diergaardt et al. v. Namibia*,[85] the applicants complained that their minority language rights under Article 27 and their right to fair trial under Article 14 of the International Covenant on Civil and Political Rights were violated by virtue of the fact that the relevant civil proceedings affecting them were conducted in English and not in their native Afrikaans language, only with the Committee dismissing their allegations premised on both provisions.[86] Nisuke Ando and P. N. Bhagwati together with Lord Colville and Maxwell Yalden in their individual opinions maintained that 'each sovereign State may choose its own official language and that the official language may be treated differently from non-official languages, I conclude that this differentiation constitutes objective and reasonable distinction which is permitted under article 26';[87] and that

So far as the administration is concerned, English being the official language of the State party, it is obvious that no other language could be allowed to be used in the administration or in the Courts or in public life. The authors could not legitimately contend that they should be allowed to use their mother tongue in administration or in the Courts or in public life, and the insistence of the State party that only the official language shall be used cannot be regarded as violation of their right under article 19, paragraph 2 [which guarantees one's freedom of expression].[88]

Such reasoning, however, deviates from the advisory opinion of the Permanent Court of International Justice in *Minority Schools in Albania*[89] in 1935, where the court concluded that 'the plea of the Albanian Government that, as the abolition of private schools in Albania constitutes a general measure applicable to the majority as well as to the minority, it is in conformity with the letter and spirit of the stipulations laid down in article 5, first paragraph, of the Declaration of October 2nd, 1921,[90] is not well founded.'[91] Indeed, Pejic argues that the very existence of Article 27 connotes the duty of States Parties to the Covenant to ensure compliance with the provision through positive measures where necessary.[92] It must also be borne in mind that *Diergaardt et al. v. Namibia* is not applicable to the Chinese language in Hong Kong, Irish in Ireland, or French in Canada, as these languages are official and not non-official languages of the respective jurisdictions.

Meanwhile, as Castellino points out, '[i]n the classical challenge of linguistic protection the nationality or ethnicity of the person is synonymous with their language, and the protection of the language is a symptom of seeking to guarantee the protection of the civil, political, economic, social and cultural rights of group in question.'[93] Whilst the concept of ethnicity is different from that of race, their close correlation engages the International Convention on the Elimination of All Forms of Racial Discrimination[94] as applicable to Hong Kong:

> States Parties shall, when the circumstances so warrant, take, in the social, economic, cultural and other fields, special and concrete measures to ensure the adequate development and protection of certain racial groups or individuals belonging to them, for the purpose of guaranteeing them the full and equal enjoyment of human rights and fundamental freedoms. These measures shall in no case entail as a consequence the maintenance of unequal or separate rights for different racial groups after the objectives for which they were taken have been achieved.[95]

The purpose of such positive measures is not to unduly offer advantage to a particular group as opposed to the whole of society but to address, for the sake of the integrity of society, a past wrong. It is submitted that in his judgment in *Re Cheng Kai Nam Gary* Justice Hartmann overlooked the need to 'reflect the new reality by redressing past injustice while respecting pluralism and the rights of minorities.'[96] Counsel for the applicant in the case asked how an Italian speaker would feel if he or she were to be tried in Rome in a language other than Italian, only with Justice Hartmann stating that Hong Kong was not Rome.[97] In Justice Hartmann's view, '[a]s a consequence, language rights in our courts of law are different too',[98] and His Honour acknowledged that '[i]n passing, I stop only to observe that Hong Kong is not the only common law jurisdiction which preserves English as an official language of the courts even though the majority of the people are not native English speakers.'[99]

Of course Hong Kong was not Rome. However, it was because Rome (and Italy) has never been colonised by a foreign power since the Italian unification in 1870 that its majority Italian speakers are able to use their native language in their own courts. Hong Kong, on the other hand, endured colonialism for 155 years; Ireland for centuries. As Castellino points out:

> Law is a tool that has been in the hands of the privileged, and to this extent, has reflected the belief systems of the privileged. Human rights law as a specific

sub-branch of law, is seeking to enter a new dynamic: rather than having at its centre the notion of order and justice, it seeks to give high priority to the creation of a system of entitlements that is accessible to all, based on the notion of humanity rather than entitlement.[100]

The equality of status between Chinese and English in Hong Kong as indicated in section 3(2) of the Official Languages Ordinance; between Irish and English in Ireland in section 8 of the Official Languages Act 2003;[101] and between English and French in Canada in section 16(1) of the Canadian Charter of Rights and Freedoms and section 2 of the Official Languages Act 1988,[102] thus cannot disguise the need for positive measures where necessary. Rodley warns that

> a neutral norm applied to parties in an unequal condition can have an unequal effect. That unequal effect may be intentional or accidental. But it is real, and, once it is consciously perceived, is apt to generate a profoundly alienating sense of injustice. High sounding principles can have the ring of hypocrisy in their application. It may be hazarded that no single factor was more potent in the Marxist debunking of concepts such as the rule of law and human rights as mere 'bourgeois legality' than this disparity between normative rhetoric and practical reality.[103]

*The question of fluency in the dominant official language*

As a result of colonialism and its lingering effects, Chinese speakers in Hong Kong, and Irish speakers in Ireland, need to be immersed in the English language in order to succeed in the professions – certainly in the legal profession and on the Bench. Individuals in these jurisdictions therefore naturally consider fluency in English as an important goal for which to strive. As Ramaga discerns, '[m]inorities usually recognize their status of domination. Such recognition often enhances their efforts to maintain solidarity. But situations have existed where an oppressed group appears to accept the status quo. Such situations may not imply the group's acquiescence to domination if it has not had any voice to challenge that domination.'[104] The late psychoanalyst Erikson attests that '[t]herapeutic as well as reformist efforts verify the sad truth that in any system based on suppression, exclusion, and exploitation, the suppressed, excluded, and exploited unconsciously accept the evil image they are made to represent by those who are dominant.'[105]

Nonetheless, such linguistic fluency has not been credited but merely taken for granted by the authorities. Whilst Justice Hartmann's judgment referred to the applicant's fluency in English in passing,[106] Justice Geoghegan in his Supreme Court of Ireland dissenting opinion in *Ó Beoláin v. Fahy* discussed at length the appellant's residence in Dublin as perforce indicating his fluency in English and thus the lack of disadvantages from proceedings against him being conducted in that language. Justice Geoghegan stated that '*I am assuming, as I think that I am entitled to assume*, that the applicant being a defendant in a Dublin prosecution is able to speak and understand English and that, therefore, in so far as he is insisting on rules and forms to be in Irish he is not making any natural justice point.'[107] His Honour further stated that '[t]he due administration of justice is itself a constitutional requirement and must, I think, take precedence over an alleged constitutional right to procure an Irish translation of a statutory instrument in circumstances where the person seeking it can be *presumed* to be proficient in English. ... any judge trying a case in Dublin, in my view, is *entitled to assume* unless informed otherwise that a litigant is able to speak English.'[108]

As our discussion below on the issue of the right to fair trial will show, such deduction of linguistic fluency in *Ó Beoláin v. Fahy*, upon which defence arguments as to the right to fair trial were summarily dismissed, was flawed, particularly as we must not forget that 'in times of crisis or when we have something important to express, we revert to the language we know best, our mother tongue.'[109] Moreover, Justice Geoghegan's presumption of Dubliners' fluency in English merely on the basis of their residence in Dublin reflected precisely and furthermore perpetrated the dominance of the English language in Ireland. (Significantly, Justice Geoghegan's presumption must be rejected in the context of Hong Kong, where only the educated *may* be proficient in English. In fact, even legal practitioners in Hong Kong, who have perforce received the best of education in the territory – many overseas – are generally criticised for their poor grasp of the English language.) In addition, His Honour's indication that it was the accused's obligation to inform the particular trial judge concerned that he or she was not proficient in English, failing which his or her proficiency would be presumed, shifted the state's obligations to ensure compliance with constitutional language rights and the principles of fundamental/natural justice through, in particular, the right to fair trial into a heavy and unfair burden upon individual citizens or residents many of whom may be unaware of their constitutional language rights. It must be remembered that language rights are rights that inhere in the individual citizen or resident and that it is the state in which corresponding duties are vested.

Discouragingly, international law, through the voice of the United Nations Human Rights Committee, has failed to rectify such deprivation of language use rights. In *Guesdon v. France*,[110] the applicant alleged that his language rights under Article 27 and his right to fair trial under Article 14 of the International Covenant on Civil and Political Rights, amongst others, were violated by France. The complainant alleged that all of the witnesses, including himself, had indicated their wishes in respect of the relevant proceedings to testify in their native Breton language which was then to be interpreted into French, which use of Breton was refused by all trial and appellate judges as the applicant and witnesses were deemed to be capable of expressing themselves in and understanding the French language.[111] Language rights, more specifically minority language rights, were clearly at issue. However, the Committee concluded without elaboration that the facts of the communication raised no issue under Article 27 and that accordingly it need not examine the scope of France's reservation.[112] In respect of the applicant's allegations of a violation of his right to fair trial as enshrined in Article 14, the Committee dismissed his complaint on the grounds that the provision was concerned only with procedural equality[113] and that

> The provision for the use of one official court language by States parties to the Covenant does not, in the Committee's opinion, violate article 14. Nor does the requirement of a fair hearing mandate States parties to make available to a citizen whose mother tongue differs from the official court language, the services of an interpreter, if this citizen is capable of expressing himself adequately in the official language. Only if the accused or the defence witnesses have difficulties in understanding, or in expressing themselves in the *court* language, must the services of an interpreter be made available.[114]

Subsequently, in *Ballantyne, Davidson, McIntyre v. Canada*, where the complainants alleged that their language rights, freedom of expression, and right of equality before the law had been violated by the Province of Québec (and thus Canada), as the province through legislation forbade the use of English in public bill-posting and commercial advertising outdoors within its jurisdiction,[115] the Committee dismissed the complainants' allegations over violations of language rights on a different basis. In its majority views, the Committee maintained:

> As to article 27, the Committee observes that this provision refers to minorities in States; this refers, as do all references to the 'State' or to 'States' in the provisions of the Covenant, to ratifying States .... Accordingly, the minorities referred to in article 27 are minorities within such a State, and not minorities within any province. A group may constitute a majority in a province but still be a minority in a State and thus be entitled to the benefits of article 27. English-speaking citizens of Canada cannot be considered a linguistic minority. The authors therefore have no claim under article 27 of the Covenant.[116]

Such reasoning, if applied in Hong Kong and within the analogous confines of the courtroom, would mean that speakers of English would be able to claim minority language rights outside the courtroom, even though within the confines of the courtroom, if not elsewhere, they have clearly a double and significant advantage over their majority counterparts whose native language is Chinese. A number of Committee members were not hesitant to express their individual opinions on the issue. Birame Ndiaye, in particular, maintained that '[t]he *rationale* of article 27 is the preservation of the [ethnic, religious, and linguistic] minorities, and not the protection of the rights enunciated therein, merely for the sake of protection.'[117]

*The insufficiency of available interpretation*

The question of whether the availability of interpretation may be sufficient, whereby an individual's choice to use a particular official language in the judicial proceedings affecting that individual may be dismissed, must presently be resolved. In *Re Cheng Kai Nam Gary*, Justice Hartmann answered in the affirmative. However, as the present author in his previous study on the issue pointed out, the availability of interpreters or translators does not resolve and is not capable of resolving the denial of one's language use rights. In *Paquette v. R. in Right of Canada*,[118] a Court of Queen's Bench of Alberta decision, Justice Sinclair maintained that '[i]t seems to me that if one person speaks a language to another man who is unable to *directly* understand what is being said, the language is not being used for its fundamental purpose of effective communication.'[119]

Furthermore, the nature of interpretation necessarily entails that the quality of testimony interpreted by another person is perforce not on par with that of testimony given by that very person in his or her chosen official language to be then directly understood by the adjudicator. Macdonald observes that the delicacy of human language is such that

> Each human language, and each dialect within each human language, is a distinctive symbol system – as divergent and as productive of insight as music and painting. Each human language and each dialect within each human language permits each

speaker or listener, writer or reader, to fashion a different communicative *timbre*. Grammatical differences between active and passive voices or among indicative, subjunctive and imperative moods within a language, permit us, and at the same time oblige us, to fashion what we wish to say in particular ways. This is even more so the case with grammatical and syntactical differences as among human languages.[120]

... It is not just vocabulary that has the capacity to imprison; so too do grammar and syntax. The structure of everyday language typically is linear and episodic, channelling *our apprehension of the world and our expression of ideas*. For this reason, language frequently seems incapable of reflecting the complexities of spatial and temporal relations. Linguistic presuppositions and stereotypes become so ingrained that they create habits of thought – intellectual 'boilerplate' – which are almost impossible to penetrate without a conscious departure from conventional syntax and grammar. More significantly, syntactical structures carry with them assumptions about individuation, causation and human agency.[121]

The author then proceeds to point out the unsatisfactory outcome of courtroom interpretation as a result of such delicacy of human language:

From a practical point of view, the problem of legal dualism is that it enhances justificatory confusion by a continual process of self-referential citation. This self-reference necessarily truncates the search for meaning. Many of the possible interpretations of legal rules are lost, or at least are not consciously present, in the mind of the interpreter who looks to the rules in only one language. Rather than seizing upon a second language in order to enrich legal understanding and to gain more sophistication in legal interpretation, the jurist [or interpreter] who looks to only one text accepts incomplete normative descriptions and relies on jejune interpretive methods.[122]

Where personal liberty is at stake, such qualitative disparity constitutes a heavy burden upon the accused, as in *Re Cheng Kai Nam Gary*, whose trial may include witnesses who are to testify in an official language not directly understood. This burden is, however, not so imposed upon one who desires English to be used in his or her proceedings, where all judges in Hong Kong and those in Ireland must be capable of understanding English directly, or one who desires to use French in proceedings conducted in the Province of Québec. One wonders why the English-speaking residents in Hong Kong, and those in Ireland and their French counterparts in the Province of Québec, need not endure courtroom interpretation and the attendant qualitative disparity as aforementioned. In *Delap v. An tAire Dlí agus Cirt*[123] approved by the Supreme Court of Ireland in *Ó Beoláin v. Fahy*, Irish High Court Justice O'Hanlon was adamant that '[u]nder the Constitution he is entitled to conduct his side of the proceedings entirely through Irish, if he wishes to choose the first official language. I am of the opinion that he faces a great obstacle if he wishes to use Irish and it happens, at the same time, that ... he is not being treated in an equal manner to those members of the population who are fully content to use the English version at all times.'[124]

Thus, a manifestation of unlawful discrimination, or discriminatory practice, is apparent in Hong Kong's courtrooms, which has been rectified in Ireland and Canada (including

Québec). It is helpful to dissect the constitution of discrimination and its nemesis equality, and the relevant guidance of Canadian Supreme Court Justice McIntyre in *Andrews v. Law Society of British Columbia*[125] was apposite. In His Honour's opinion, discrimination

> may be described as a distinction, whether intentional or not but based on grounds relating to personal characteristics of the individual or group, which has the effect of imposing burdens, obligations, or disadvantages on such individual or group not imposed upon others, or which withholds or limits access to opportunities, benefits, and advantages available to other members of society. Distinctions based on personal characteristics attributed to an individual solely on the basis of association with a group will rarely escape the charge of discrimination, while those based on an individual's merits and capacities will rarely be so classed.[126]

In order to tackle discrimination and effectuate the guarantee of equality in the Canadian Charter of Rights and Freedoms[127] – in the case of Hong Kong, in the Basic Law of Hong Kong[128] and the Hong Kong Bill of Rights Ordinance[129] – His Honour maintained:

> To approach the ideal of full equality before and under the law – and in human affairs an approach is all that can be expected – the main consideration must be the impact of the law on the individual or the group concerned. Recognizing that there will always be an infinite variety of personal characteristics, capacities, entitlements and merits among those subject to a law, there must be accorded, as nearly as may be possible, an equality of benefit and protection and no more of the restrictions, penalties or burdens imposed upon one than another. In other words, the admittedly unattainable ideal should be that a law expressed to bind all should not because of irrelevant personal differences have a more burdensome or less beneficial impact on one than another.[130]

Here, to resolve such actual and manifested discrimination in the courtroom, it is essential that the state facilitate 'a climate favourable to its implementation in reality'[131] such as by causing, in the case of Hong Kong, a bilingual judge to preside over a trial which the accused has indicated his or her desire to be conducted in Chinese. As Réaume argues, 'it is the use of a *particular* language – the official language preferred by a given claimant – that official language use rights protect.'[132] Fernand de Varennes asserts that '[w]henever the number of individuals speaking a [non-preferred] language in a state is substantial, especially if they are mainly citizens [or residents as understood *vis-à-vis* Hong Kong], public authorities ... should be able to respond to their requests as well as offer public services in their primary language. Failure to do so could constitute a violation of the right to non-discrimination.'[133] Significantly, the United Nations Human Rights Committee in its General Comment No. 18 on non-discrimination[134] affirmed that

> the principle of equality sometimes requires States parties to take affirmative action in order to diminish or eliminate conditions which cause or help to perpetuate discrimination prohibited by the Covenant. For example, in a State where *the general conditions of a certain part of the population prevent or impair their enjoyment of human rights*, the State should take specific action to correct those conditions. Such

action may involve granting for a time to the part of the population concerned certain preferential treatment in specific matters as compared with the rest of the population.[135]

It is worth noting that in Canada an individual's right to demand that his or her trial judge understand directly the working language of the trial within the jurisdiction of Canadian federal courts (save the Supreme Court of Canada) is explicitly recognised in section 16(1) of the Official Languages Act 1988.[136] The same issue in respect of Canadian provincial courts was definitively resolved by the Supreme Court in *Beaulac* in favour of language use rights.

*Concluding remarks*

Unfortunately, Justice Hartmann did not enjoy legal arguments relating to non-discrimination or language rights as they were not raised by defence counsel who had the conduct of the matter. Instead, defence counsel focused their arguments exclusively on the applicant's right to fair trial – a tactic from which Réaume dissuades as '[t]he reduction of official language rights to the natural justice rationale falls into the trap of treating language as nothing more than an instrument of communication. Consequently, this approach construes the purpose of language rights in wholly instrumental terms'[137] – only with Justice Hartmann summarily dismissing the argument on the grounds, in erroneous reliance upon the Supreme Court of Canada authority of *Beaulac*, that language rights are not synonymous with the principles of fundamental/natural justice, each with their own origin and purpose.[138] His Honour deduced conclusively without elaboration that '[i]f language rights are distinct from the principles of fundamental justice, it is not therefore a denial of the applicant's fundamental right to a fair trial to be denied a judge who speaks the official language that the applicant chooses to employ.'[139] As will be seen immediately, His Honour mistook and consequentially misapplied the *ratio decidendi* of *Beaulac*.

## 2. The Implications of the Right to Fair Trial

It is noted that the applicant in *Re Cheng Kai Nam Gary* was to be tried in the Hong Kong District Court (there is only one, in the Wanchai District), where jury trial is not available in criminal proceedings.[140] It was therefore paramount that the presiding trial judge concerned was able to fully comprehend all evidence and testimony as well as the manner in which the same was to be rendered. Thus, the applicant argued that his impending trial by a monolingual judge notwithstanding the defence's preference for a bilingual judge would *ipso facto* render the trial unfair and thus unconstitutional.

Justice Hartmann, relying on *Beaulac*, dismissed the defence's argument. However, in doing so, His Honour appropriated from the entire Canadian judgment a single sentence only, without appreciating the real significance of the decision (or, indeed, of that sentence). In *Beaulac*, Supreme Court of Canada Justice Bastarache, in drawing a differentiation between language rights and the right to fair trial, in fact maintained that the two branches of rights are not mutually exclusive and that the '[f]airness of the trial is not to be considered at this stage and is certainly not a threshold that, if satisfied, can be used to deny the accused his language rights under s.530 [of the Canadian Criminal Code].'[141] Justice Bastarache then proceeded to indicate:

> Language rights are not subsumed by the right to a fair trial. If the right of the accused to use his or her official language in court proceedings was limited because of language proficiency in the other official language, there would in effect be no distinct language right. ... But language rights are not meant to enforce minimum conditions under which a trial will be considered fair, or even to ensure the greatest efficiency of the defence. Language rights may no doubt enhance the quality of the legal proceedings, but their source lies elsewhere.[142]

Furthermore, the asymmetry between language rights and the principles of fundamental/natural justice is not *in se* a sufficient answer to a charge of an, or a potential, unfair trial. As Supreme Court of Canada Justice Beetz in *Société des Acadiens du Nouveau-Brunswick* stated:

> The common law right of the parties to be heard and understood by a court and the right to understand what is going on in court is not a language right but *an aspect of the right to a fair hearing. It is a broader and more universal right than language rights*. It extends to everyone including those who speak or understand neither official language. It belongs to the category of rights which in the *Charter* are designated as legal rights and indeed it is protected at least in part by provisions such as those of ss. 7 [due process] and 14 [right to an interpreter] of the *Charter*.[143]

The majority of the Supreme Court of Canada in *R. v. Mercure*,[144] a decision in 1988, was adamant that 'the right to be understood is not a language right but one arising out of the requirements of due process.'[145] We also refer to the Irish Court of Criminal Appeal decision in *Attorney-General v. Joyce and Walsh*[146] in 1929:

> The Irish language is not merely the vernacular language of most, if not all, of the witnesses in question in the present case, but it holds a special position by virtue of the Constitution of the Saorstát, in which its status is recognised and established as the national language of the Saorstát, from which it follows that, *whether it be the vernacular language of a particular citizen or not*, if he is competent to use the language he is entitled to do so. Therefore, it may be said that all those who gave their evidence in the Irish language in the present case had, as it were, a double right to do so: first on general principles of natural justice as their vernacular language; and secondly, as a matter of Constitutional right.[147]

Fernand de Varennes argues:

> Whilst a state is free to designate whatever language it prefers as official, and thus recognise its legal obligation to respond in the official language (or languages) – subject to appropriate limitations – such a designation can never entitle public authorities to violate the fundamental human rights of individuals. Judicial interpretation, legal provisions or administrative practices which view official language

status as a green light for any type of conduct favouring the official language(s) are [unacceptable], if the result is an infringement of human rights.[148]

Given that constitutional language rights and the principles of fundamental/natural justice, upon which modern democratic society is built, carry heavy and important implications, a violation of any of them accordingly 'is by its very constitutional nature a serious error of law'[149] and 'constitutes a *substantial wrong* and not a procedural irregularity'.[150] A violation of these fundamental rights or principles is further exacerbated by any potential abridgment of liberty, as in *Re Cheng Kai Nam Gary* where the applicant was to face a criminal trial that may and did lead to his imprisonment. Justice Hartmann's hasty refusal to grant leave to the accused to apply for judicial review was thus most unfortunate.

### 3. The Common Law Tradition in Jeopardy

Worse still, Justice Hartmann in turn complained about the 'reasonably lengthy and complex arguments needed to be analysed to understand what lay at their core. Were they, despite the clothing of constitutional importance and the excitement of public interest, applications that were doomed to failure?'[151]

The application should not have failed but for Justice Hartmann's neglect of the real implications of the handover of sovereignty over Hong Kong, the importance of constitutional language rights, and the correlations between constitutional language rights and the principles of fundamental/natural justice. As Supreme Court of Canada Justice Bastarache in *Beaulac* reminded us, 'the exercise of language rights must not be considered exceptional, or as something in the nature of a request for an accommodation.'[152]

Last but not least, immediately upon referring to that same Canadian decision – *Beaulac* – exclusively without elaboration in his disposal of the accused's application for leave to apply for judicial review, Justice Hartmann decried that 'little is to be gained in looking at the manner in which language rights are protected in other constitutions. We must look to the Basic Law and why it is that English is preserved as an official language for our courts.'[153] The quintessence of the common law tradition, the prime reason why qualified judges from other common law jurisdictions who may not be able to speak Chinese continue to be employed within Hong Kong's judiciary, is precisely that we are thus enabled to inquire as to how our common law brethren apply and adapt the common law to their own local circumstances – and constitutions – which perforce vary amongst jurisdictions, so that we may appreciate better the common law and our own constitution and apply the same accordingly. This is also the reason why English continues to be used in Hong Kong's courtrooms. It was thus Justice Hartmann himself who neglected Hong Kong's special history, only that in addition His Honour rendered a severe disservice to the common law tradition by denigrating its importance and centrality to the legal and judicial system of Hong Kong.

### 4. Conclusion

The fundamental principle that a government, which includes its judicial branch, is not merely to rule but essentially to serve its people and that its continued existence derives from and is inextricably bound to its legitimacy underlies the decline and eventual cessation of colonialism and the advent of the right of self-determination upon the end of the Second World War. In Hong Kong and Ireland where local populations were for long periods of time systematically subjugated by their British colonial masters, or in Canada where on account of the unrelenting solitudes between them the English and French communities view each other with great animosity, such political legitimacy is ever more imperative.

The legacy of British colonial rule, nevertheless, continues to prevail in the three jurisdictions, particularly within their legal professions and judiciaries through the close correlation between the common law and the English language. As Macdonald discerns, 'a direct connection between a language and a legal tradition is implied: the common law and the English language are inexorably connected such that the possibility of "common law French" is fatally compromised',[154] a state of affairs which the author finds 'deeply troubling'.[155] To insist, directly or indirectly, upon a party to a set of judicial proceedings using English, albeit an official language of the three jurisdictions yet which may not be the language with which that party self-identifies most intimately, in such proceedings is to perpetuate and not redress a past wrong, with its effects only worsened and exacerbated by the essential nature of language in relation to a person's identity and individuality.

Finnis asserts that '[i]ndividuals can only be *selves* – i.e., have the "dignity" of being "responsible agents" – if they are not made to live their lives for the convenience of others but are allowed and assisted to create a subsisting identity across a "lifetime".'[156] The right of a person to use a particular official language in judicial proceedings affecting him or her civilly or criminally is thus of paramount value and importance *in se*, which in turn enhances the legitimacy of the government, 'by making the state and its institutions full participants in the life of the community',[157] and ultimately 'a community's self-respect'.[158] As Macdonald enunciates, '[w]ords limit; words liberate; words confound; and words enfranchise.'[159]

## Acknowledgements

This study was prompted by the Author's preparations for a survey on certain Hong Kong court decisions: Phil C. W. Chan, 'Important Decisions of Hong Kong Courts in 2002 (Part I): Language Rights, Foreign Offenders' Sentencing, and Immigration and Refugee Laws', *Chinese Journal of International Law*, Vol.4 (2005), p.219. The Author wishes to express his gratitude to his good friend and colleague Aisling O'Sullivan, Doctoral Fellow at the Irish Centre for Human Rights at the National University of Ireland, Galway, for assembling the materials on Ireland and reviewing an earlier draft of this paper. The Author also thanks Jill Cottrell, Richard Gardiner, Professor Paul Rishworth, and Paul Serfaty for their helpful comments on subsequent versions of this paper, which was presented at the Centre for International and Public Law at the Australian National University (22 November 2006). Responsibility for any error or omission remains with the Author alone.

## Notes

1. [1985] 1 SCR 721.
2. Ibid. *per* The Court, p.744.

3. The Basic Law of the Hong Kong Special Administrative Region of the People's Republic of China as adopted by the Seventh National People's Congress at its Third Session on 4 April 1990, 29 ILM 1519 (1990), Art.5, in pursuance of the 1984 Joint Declaration of the Government of the United Kingdom of Great Britain and Northern Ireland and the Government of the People's Republic of China on the Question of Hong Kong, 23 ILM 1366 (1984).
4. Ibid. Art.8; see also Arts.18, 84, and 87.
5. Ibid. Art.9.
6. Official Languages Ordinance (Cap.5), s.3(1).
7. Ibid. s.3(2).
8. [2002] 1 HKC 41.
9. Basic Law of Hong Kong, Arts.82 and 92; International Covenant on Civil and Political Rights, Art.14.
10. Article 31 of the Constitution of the People's Republic of China states that '[t]he state may establish special administrative regions when necessary. The systems to be instituted in special administrative regions shall be prescribed by law enacted by the National People's Congress in the light of the specific conditions.'
11. Basic Law of Hong Kong, Preamble.
12. *Re Cheng Kai Nam Gary* (note 8) *per* Hartmann J., pp.47–8.
13. Basic Law of Hong Kong, Arts.82 and 92; see also Art.93.
14. *Re Cheng Kai Nam Gary* (note 8) *per* Hartmann J., pp.47–8.
15. Irish Free State Constitution Act 1922, 13 Geo. 5 (Session 2), c.1, s.1 and Sch.1.
16. Ibid. Sch.1, Art.4.
17. [1934] IR 469.
18. That is, the Anglo-Irish Treaty of 6 December 1921 as scheduled to the Irish Free State (Agreement) Act 1922, 12 Geo. 5, c.4, whereby the Irish Free State as a co-equal Dominion of the British Empire, modelled upon the Dominion of Canada founded under the British North America Act 1867, 30 Vic., c.3, was founded.
19. *Ó Foghludha v. McClean* (note 17) *per* Kennedy C.J., p.482.
20. Constitution of Ireland of 1937, Art.48.
21. Ibid. Art.8(1).
22. Ibid. Art.8(2).
23. [2001] 2 IR 279.
24. Ibid. *per* Hardiman J., p.340.
25. Niamh Nic Shuibhne, 'State Duty and the Irish Language', *Dublin University Law Journal*, Vol.19 (1997), p.33 at p.48.
26. Basic Law of Hong Kong, Art.1.
27. [1998] 2 SCR 217.
28. Ibid. *per* The Court, p.256.
29. Albie Sachs, *Protecting Human Rights in a New South Africa* (Cape Town: Oxford University Press 1990), p.189.
30. Adopted and proclaimed by United Nations General Assembly Resolution 217A(III) of 10 December 1948.
31. Ibid. Art.1.
32. See http://www.osce.org/documents/hcnm/1998/02/2699_en.pdf, reproduced in *International Journal on Minority and Group Rights*, Vol.6 (1999) Special Issue: *Linguistic Rights of National Minorities*, p.359.
33. Ibid. Explanatory Note to the Oslo Recommendations Regarding the Linguistic Rights of National Minorities, General Introduction.
34. (1986) 26 DLR (4th) 200.
35. Ibid. *per* Dickson C.J., p.225.
36. [1984] ILRM 373.
37. Ibid. *per* Costello J., p.381.
38. Nic Shuibhne (note 25) p.38.
39. Roderick A. Macdonald, 'Legal Bilingualism', *McGill Law Journal*, Vol.42 (1997), p.119 at p.139.
40. Ibid.
41. Vanessa Pupavac, 'Language Rights in Conflict and the Denial of Language as Communication', *International Journal of Human Rights*, Vol.10 (2006), p.61 at pp.65–6, quoting Robert Phillipson, Tove Skutnabb-Kangas and Mart Rannut, 'Introduction', in Tove Skutnabb-Kangas and Robert Phillipson (eds), *Linguistic Human Rights: Overcoming Linguistic Discrimination* (Berlin and New York: Mouton de Gruyter 1994), p.2.

42. Phil C. W. Chan, 'Important Decisions of Hong Kong Courts in 2002 (Part I): Language Rights, Foreign Offenders' Sentencing, and Immigration and Refugee Laws', *Chinese Journal of International Law*, Vol.4 (2005), p.219.
43. [1986] 1 SCR 549.
44. [1987] 1 SCR 1148.
45. Chan (note 42) p.222.
46. (1999) 173 DLR (4th) 193.
47. Ibid. *per* Bastarache J., p.215: 'Language Rights must in all cases be interpreted purposively, in a manner consistent with the preservation and development of official language communities in Canada. To the extent that *Société des Acadiens du Nouveau-Brunswick* stands for a restrictive interpretation of language rights, it is to be rejected.'
48. (1919) 58 SCR 414.
49. Ibid. *per* Brodeur J., p.423.
50. Case No.379/87, 28 November 1989.
51. Ibid. para.24 (emphasis added).
52. Oslo Recommendations (note 32) Recommendation 19.
53. Ibid. Explanatory Note to the Oslo Recommendations Regarding the Linguistic Rights of National Minorities.
54. John Packer and Guillaume Siemienski, 'The Language of Equity: The Origin and Development of the Oslo Recommendations Regarding the Linguistic Rights of National Minorities', *International Journal on Minority and Group Rights*, Vol.6 (1999) Special Issue: *Linguistic Rights of National Minorities*, p.329.
55. International Covenant on Civil and Political Rights, Art.27.
56. Ibid. Art.2(1).
57. Thomas Buergenthal, 'To Respect and to Ensure: State Obligations and Permissible Derogations', in Louis Henkin (ed.), *The International Bill of Rights: The Covenant on Civil and Political Rights* (New York: Columbia University Press 1981), pp.77–8.
58. Francesco Capotorti (as Special Rapporteur of the United Nations Sub-Commission on the Prevention of Discrimination and Protection of Minorities), *Study on the Rights of Persons Belonging to Ethnic, Religious and Linguistic Minorities*, Report to the United Nations Sub-Commission on the Prevention of Discrimination and Protection of Minorities, UN Doc. E/CN.4/Sub.2/384/Rev.1 (1979); also as Francesco Capotorti, *Study on the Rights of Persons Belonging to Ethnic, Religious and Linguistic Minorities* (New York: United Nations 1991), para.568 (emphasis added).
59. John Packer, 'On the Definition of Minorities', in John Packer and Kristian Myntti (eds), *The Protection of Ethnic and Linguistic Minorities in Europe* (Turku/Åbo, Finland: Institute for Human Rights, Åbo Akademi University 1993), p.23.
60. United Nations Human Rights Committee, Views on Communications Nos.359/1989 and 385/1989, UN Doc. CCPR/C/47/D/359/1989 and 385/1989/Rev.1 (47th Session, 5 May 1993).
61. Ibid. paras.3.1–3.3, 4.1–4.7, 6.1–6.10, 9.1–9.10, and 11.1.
62. Ibid. para.11.5.
63. Nigel S. Rodley, 'Conceptual Problems in the Protection of Minorities: International Legal Developments', *Human Rights Quarterly*, Vol.17 (1995), p.48 at p.55.
64. Ibid.
65. *Ballantyne, Davidson, McIntyre v. Canada* (note 60) E. Individual Opinion of Elizabeth Evatt, co-signed by Nisuke Ando, Marco Tulio Bruni Celli, and Vojin Dimitrijevic (concurring and elaborating).
66. Philip Vuciri Ramaga, 'Relativity of the Minority Concept', *Human Rights Quarterly*, Vol.14 (1992), p.104 at p.119.
67. Margaret Thornton, 'The Public/Private Dichotomy: Gendered and Discriminatory', *Journal of Law and Society*, Vol.18 (1991), p.448 at p.457.
68. *Ó Beoláin v. Fahy* (note 23) *per* Hardiman J., p.350 (modified).
69. Joshua Castellino, 'Affirmative Action for the Protection of Linguistic Rights: An Analysis of International Human Rights: Legal Standards in the Context of the Protection of the Irish Language', *Dublin University Law Journal*, Vol.25 (2003), pp.1 at p.24.
70. Ibid.
71. *Ballantyne, Davidson, McIntyre v. Canada* (note 60) D. Individual Opinion of Bertil Wennergren (concurring).

72. Edward Veitch, 'Language, Culture and Freedom of Expression in Canada', *International and Comparative Law Quarterly*, Vol.39 (1990), p.101 at p.110.
73. Denise G. Réaume, 'The Demise of the Political Compromise Doctrine: Have Official Language Use Rights Been Revived?', *McGill Law Journal*, Vol.47 (2002), p.593 at pp.617–8.
74. Dónall Ó Riagáin, 'The Importance of Linguistic Rights for Speakers of Lesser Used Languages', *International Journal on Minority and Group Rights*, Vol.6 (1999) Special Issue: *Linguistic Rights of National Minorities*, p.289.
75. James Fawcett, *Minority Rights Group Report No. 41: The International Protection of Minorities* (London: Minority Rights Group 1979), p.4.
76. Macdonald (note 39) p.138.
77. James T. McHugh, 'Making Public Law, "Public": An Analysis of the *Québec Reference Case* and its Significance for Comparative Constitutional Analysis', *International and Comparative Law Quarterly*, Vol.49 (2000), p.445 at p.445.
78. *Re Cheng Kai Nam Gary* (note 8) *per* Hartmann J., p.48.
79. Canadian Charter of Rights and Freedoms (Part I, Constitution Act 1982, Statutes of Canada 1982, c.79; Canada Act 1982 (United Kingdom), c.11), ss.16–22. See also Official Languages Act 1988, RSC 1988, c.38.
80. *House of Commons Debates*, Vol.5, 3rd Session, 30th Parliament, 5087; affirmed in *Beaulac* (note 46) *per* Bastarache J., p.214.
81. Peter Jones, 'Human Rights, Group Rights, and Peoples' Rights', *Human Rights Quarterly*, Vol.21 (1999), p.80 at p.83.
82. *Beaulac* (note 46) *per* Bastarache J., p.221.
83. See, e.g., Michel Bastarache (ed.), *Les droits linguistiques au Canada* (Montreal: Editions Yvon Blais 1986); Michel Bastarache (ed.), *Language Rights in Canada* (Montreal: Editions Yvon Blais 1987).
84. Nic Shuibhne (note 25) p.46.
85. United Nations Human Rights Committee, Views on Communication No.760/1997, UN Doc. CCPR/C/69/D/760/1997 (69th Session, 6 September 2000).
86. Ibid. paras.10.6 and 10.9.
87. Ibid. Individual Opinion of Nisuke Ando (dissenting).
88. Ibid. Individual Opinion of P. N. Bhagwati, Lord Colville and Maxwell Yalden (dissenting), para.2.
89. PCIJ Series A/B Judgments, No.64 (1935), *World Court Reports*, Vol.III (1932–35), p.484.
90. Article 5, first paragraph, of the Albanian Declaration, as quoted in *Minority Schools in Albania*, ibid. p.485, provided that 'Albanian nationals who belong to racial, religious or linguistic minorities will enjoy the same treatment and security in law and in fact as other Albanian nationals. In particular, they shall have an equal right to maintain, manage and control at their own expense or to establish in the future, charitable, religious and social institutions, schools and other educational establishments, with the right to use their own language and to exercise their religion freely therein.'
91. *Minority Schools in Albania*, ibid. p.502.
92. Jelena Pejic, 'Minority Rights in International Law', *Human Rights Quarterly*, Vol.19 (1997), p.666 at pp.676–7.
93. Castellino (note 69) p.32.
94. Adopted and opened for signature and ratification by UN GA Res. 2106 (XX) of 21 December 1965 and entered into force on 4 January 1969.
95. Ibid. Art.2(2).
96. Guillaume Siemienski, 'Vienna Seminar on the Linguistic Rights of National Minorities 27–28 February 1998: Seminar Report', *International Journal on Minority and Group Rights*, Vol.6 (1999) Special Issue: *Linguistic Rights of National Minorities*, p.351.
97. *Re Cheng Kai Nam Gary* (note 8) *per* Hartmann J., p.48.
98. Ibid.
99. Ibid.
100. Castellino (note 69) pp.39–40.
101. Section 8 of the Official Languages Act 2003 (No.32) elucidates an individual's language use rights in the administration of justice. In particular, sub-section (1) provides that '[a] person may use either of the official languages in, or in any pleading in or document issuing from, any court.' Sub-section (2) then demands that '[e]very court has, in any proceedings before it, the duty to ensure that any person appearing in or giving evidence before it may be heard in the official language of his or her choice, and that in being so heard

the person will not be placed at a disadvantage by not being heard in the other official language.' An individual's language use rights are then accorded superiority over the State's choice of a particular official language in civil proceedings, by sub-section (4) which states that '[w]here the State or a public body is a party to civil proceedings before a court – (a) the State or the public body shall use in the proceedings, the official language chosen by the other party, and (b) if two or more persons (other than the State or a public body) are party to the proceedings and they fail to choose or agree on the official language to be used in the proceedings, the State or, as appropriate, the public body shall use in the proceedings such official language as appears to it to be reasonable, having regard to the circumstances.' Lastly, one must not overlook that it is the State which carries the burden of ensuring compliance with an individual's language use rights, as sub-section (6) mandates: 'In choosing to use a particular official language in any proceedings before a court, a person shall not be put by the court or a public body to any inconvenience or expense over and above that which would have been incurred had he or she chosen to use the other official language.'

102. Section 2 of the Official Languages Act 1988, RSC 1988, c.38, states that '[t]he purpose of this Act is to (a) ensure respect for English and French as the official languages of Canada and ensure equality of status and equal rights and privileges as to their use in all federal institutions, in particular with respect to their use in parliamentary proceedings, in legislative and other instruments, in the administration of justice, in communicating with or providing services to the public and in carrying out the work of federal institutions; (b) support the development of English and French linguistic minority communities and generally advance the equality of status and use of the English and French languages within Canadian society; and (c) set out the powers, duties and functions of federal institutions with respect to the official languages of Canada.'
103. Rodley (note 63) p.50.
104. Ramaga (note 66) p.115.
105. Erik H. Erikson, *Identity: Youth and Crisis* (New York and London: W.W. Norton 1968), p.59.
106. *Re Cheng Kai Nam Gary* (note 8) *per* Hartmann J., p.44.
107. *Ó Beoláin v. Fahy* (note 23) *per* Geoghegan J., p.359 (emphasis added).
108. Ibid. p.361 (emphasis added).
109. Richard Silver, 'The Right to English Health and Social Services in Québec: A Legal and Political Analysis', *McGill Law Journal*, Vol.45 (2000), p.681 at p.686.
110. United Nations Human Rights Committee, Views on Communication No.219/1986, UN Doc. CCPR/C/39/D/219/1986 (39th Session, 23 August 1990).
111. Ibid. paras.2.2–2.3. The Human Rights Committee noted, ibid. para.5.6, that France had entered into a reservation to Article 27 as the French Republic and its Constitution does not recognise the existence of minorities in its territory.
112. Ibid. para.7.3.
113. Ibid. para.10.2.
114. Ibid.
115. *Ballantyne, Davidson, McIntyre v. Canada* (note 60) paras.3.1–3.3, 4.1–4.7, 6.1–6.10, 9.1–9.10, and 11.1.
116. Ibid. para.11.2.
117. Ibid. B. Individual Opinion of Birame Ndiaye (dissenting).
118. [1985] 6 WWR 594.
119. Ibid. *per* Sinclair J., p.629.
120. Macdonald (note 38) p.123.
121. Ibid. pp.133–4 (emphasis added).
122. Ibid. p.156.
123. (1990) TÉ 46.
124. Ibid. *per* O'Hanlon J.; as quoted in *Ó Beoláin v. Fahy* (note 23) *per* Hardiman J., p.342 (trans. O'Malley).
125. [1989] 1 SCR 143.
126. Ibid. *per* McIntyre J., pp.174–5.
127. Section 15(1) of the Canadian Charter of Rights and Freedoms states that '[e]very individual is equal before and under the law and has the right to the equal protection and equal benefit of the law without discrimination and, in particular, without discrimination based on race, national or ethnic origin, colour, religion, sex, age or mental or physical disability.' When promulgating the Charter, Parliament considered language rights to be of such importance that specific provisions are stipulated therefor, in sections 16 to 23, inclusive.
128. Basic Law of Hong Kong, Art.25.

129. Article 22 of the Hong Kong Bill of Rights Ordinance, modelled upon and giving effect to Article 26 of the International Covenant on Civil and Political Rights, states that '[a]ll persons are equal before the law and are entitled without any discrimination to the equal protection of the law. In this respect, the law shall prohibit any discrimination and guarantee to all persons equal and effective protection against discrimination on any ground such as race, colour, sex, religion, political or other opinion, national or social origin, property, birth or *other* status' (emphasis added).
130. *Andrews v. Law Society of British Columbia* (note 125) *per* McIntyre J., p.165.
131. Nic Shuibhne (note 25) p.46.
132. Réaume (note 73) p.613.
133. Fernand de Varennes, *Language, Minorities and Human Rights* (The Hague: Martinus Nijhoff Publishers 1996), p.176.
134. United Nations Human Rights Committee, *International Covenant on Civil and Political Rights General Comment No.18: Non-discrimination* (37th Session, 10 November 1989).
135. Ibid. para.10 (emphasis added).
136. Section 16(1) of the Official Languages Act 1988 states that '[e]very federal court, other than the Supreme Court of Canada, has the duty to ensure that (a) if English is the language chosen by the parties for proceedings conducted before it in any particular case, every judge or other officer who hears those proceedings is able to understand English without the assistance of an interpreter; (b) if French is the language chosen by the parties for proceedings conducted before it in any particular case, every judge or other officer who hears those proceedings is able to understand French without the assistance of an interpreter; and (c) if both English and French are the languages chosen by the parties for proceedings conducted before it in any particular case, every judge or other officer who hears those proceedings is able to understand both languages without the assistance of an interpreter.'
137. Réaume (note 73) p.597.
138. *Beaulac* (note 46) *per* Bastarache J., p.215.
139. *Re Cheng Kai Nam Gary* (note 8) *per* Hartmann J., p.48.
140. District Court Ordinance (Cap.336), s.79(5)(b).
141. *Beaulac* (note 46) *per* Bastarache J., p.222.
142. Ibid. p.224.
143. *Société des Acadiens du Nouveau-Brunswick* (note 43) *per* Beetz J., p.577 (emphasis added).
144. [1988] SCR 234.
145. Ibid. *per* Dickson C.J., joined by Beetz, Lamer, Wilson, Le Dain, and La Forest JJ., p.238.
146. [1929] IR 526.
147. Ibid. *per* Kennedy C.J., p.531 (emphasis added).
148. de Varennes (note 133) pp.175–6.
149. *R. v. Tran* [1994] 2 SCR 951, *per* Lamer C.J., p.1009.
150. *Beaulac* (note 46) *per* Bastarache J., p.226.
151. *Re Cheng Kai Nam Gary* (note 8) *per* Hartmann J., p.52.
152. *Beaulac* (note 46) *per* Bastarache J., p.215.
153. *Re Cheng Kai Nam Gary* (note 8) *per* Hartmann J., p.48.
154. Macdonald (note 39) p.151.
155. Ibid.
156. John Finnis, *Natural Law and Natural Rights* (Oxford: Clarendon Press 1980), p.272.
157. Réaume (note 73) p.618.
158. Ibid.
159. Macdonald (note 39) p.133.

# Constitutionalising Affirmative Action in the Fiji Islands

JILL COTTRELL AND YASH GHAI

**Introduction**

> Equality includes the full and equal enjoyment of all rights and freedoms. To promote the achievement of equality, legislative and other measures designed to protect or advance persons, or categories of persons, disadvantaged by unfair discrimination may be taken.

This provision comes from the South African Constitution (section 9(2)) and neatly encapsulates the connection between equality and affirmative action. It is not unusual today to have constitutions permit affirmative action (and thus remove doubts whether this is legal in the face of an equality provision, as in the South African example). It is also recognised that anti-discrimination laws are often not sufficient by themselves to bring about equality. However, it is rare for constitutions to require affirmative action – Malaysia[1] and to a limited extent India[2] are examples. This paper analyses the attempt to achieve equality through constitutional provisions for mandating affirmative action in the Fiji Islands, with particular reference to the ethnic context.

Affirmative action can be and often is undertaken without a constitutional provision. This is how the extensive affirmative action, for example in the United States and Australia is undertaken.[3] When affirmative action is statutory or administrative (without objectives stated in the Constitution), there is considerable discretion in structuring these schemes, and different rationales and approaches can be adopted. This gives flexibility, but can also cause controversy. Whether or not constitutionally mandated or protected, affirmative action programmes almost always generate litigation, as the experiences of the United States, Canada, India, and South Africa have shown.[4]

*Justifying affirmative action*

The 'politics' of affirmative action can have quite different manifestations and consequences, depending on the size of ethnic groups and the structure of ethnic relations. Redress for a small, marginalised community (e.g., aboriginals in Australia) may raise no acute political problems, other than expressions of prejudice. When applied to larger communities, the issue becomes more politicised, for reasons either of economic benefits or access to state power. In the former case, policies may have a class bias, although the beneficiaries may themselves be identified only through ethnic affiliation (the United States is an obvious illustration). In the latter case, the principal focus is on ethnic affiliation, where ethnicity is already politicised or becomes so through the politics of affirmative action (of which two leading illustrations are Malaysia and Fiji). When the beneficiaries are small, deprived communities, the thrust of affirmative action is social justice; when it becomes intertwined in ethnic politics, it is often about domination.

A principal purpose of affirmative action is to assist members of a disadvantaged community to gain opportunities for social and economic advancement, and the justification is the effective, rather than a formal, equality of all citizens. Those communities will often comprise groups who have historically been disadvantaged (slaves, indentured labourers, low caste and social classes, women, the disabled, victims of systematic discrimination, or minorities who have, for example, suffered appropriations of their traditional land by outsiders). In these cases affirmative action is also based on compensation for past wrongs and social justice. Another objective of affirmative action is social harmony through the economic and political integration of different communities; the latter objective is often secured through reforms to the electoral system enabling greater representation of social or ethnic minorities.

In India's case, for example, all these objectives were important as its leaders worked on the Constitution after independence. The critical issue was the social discrimination and general subordination of social groups known as casteism. Casteism was seen by many nationalists as the enemy of Indian unity and civic spirit, as a blot on India, which could only be redressed by its total abolition. Therefore the abolition of caste distinctions and discrimination was important not only to help lower castes, but also to provide a new moral basis for the Indian state.[5]

Affirmative action of this kind inevitably tends to have integrative and even assimilative tendencies. Until recently the model of 'upward mobility' implicit in this tendency was little questioned. But now there is considerable emphasis on identities and the protection of cultural differences that mark off one community from another.[6] Affirmative action is advocated to maintain the cultural values and institutions of community, rather than to facilitate their phasing out by reference to some 'universal' principles. Affirmative action takes the form of special representation in state institutions, protection for cultural practices even if they may be inconsistent with general national norms, control over land, and forms of self-government. This presumably does not rule out economic advancement (although economic development has an important impact on values and organisation). The focus in this approach to affirmative action shifts from the individual to the community, places a heavy emphasis on the political, and implicates group rights.

There is controversy as to whether affirmative action for recognition and for economic and social justice are in conflict or mutually supportive. Nancy Fraser supports the former position.[7] She says that the two paradigms call for remedies that point in different directions. Distributive remedies emphasise the equal worth of each individual and accordingly aim 'to put the group out of business as a group' because group identities form the axis of economic injustice. By contrast, recognition promotes group differentiation, because it positively affirms the value of group identity. But Iris Young argues that justice must necessarily combine distribution and recognition, using the latter as the means to the former; 'the cultural denigration of groups produces or reinforces structural economic oppression'.[8] A particular justification for recognition as affirmative action is that it preserves the integrity of the group and the value orientation of individuals so that they are better able to cope with the broader national economy and politics – the example of aboriginals in Australia, many of whom have had difficulties in dealing with the arrival of a foreign culture and political domination, being often regarded as a compelling argument. Kymlicka argues for affirmative action on the basis of the cultural vulnerability of indigenous people.[9] It is thus clear that we are talking of a very different policy and approach when we consider affirmative action in this form from that of racial minorities such as in the United States or of the lower castes in India.

A more fundamental controversy arises as to whether affirmative action should be undertaken at all, legally or morally. The opposition is based both on unfairness to persons who suffer discrimination in what is often called 'reverse discrimination', based on quotas, in favour of members of the beneficiary community, even if they are seen as more meritorious, and the consequences of such discrimination in terms of efficiency. Moreover, even if some measure of affirmative action is accepted, there can be controversy as to what measures may validly be taken. The major difference centres on whether the measures should increase the capacity and opportunities of the beneficiary community to compete on equal terms with others[10] or whether, at least on a temporary basis, to reserve a certain number of jobs and other opportunities for them.[11]

Courts have to deal with affirmative action at a rather different level: less concerned with whether it is justified at a moral or policy level than with how it achieves its ends and whether particular programmes fit constitutional mandates or permissions or even whether applications to particular individuals fit with the constitutional or statutory scheme.

*The context of Fiji*

Fiji provides an interesting example of the dilemmas that surround affirmative action. It is an unusual study of the interaction of the two paradigms mentioned above. This conjuncture has ancient roots, from the very beginnings of colonialism over a century ago. In these circumstances affirmative action becomes deeply implicated in inter-community politics as well as in the structure of the state. For this to be clear it is necessary to sketch the origins of the ethnic dilemmas that face the country.

Fiji became a British colony in 1874 when its principal chiefs signed a Deed of Cession of their islands to the British Crown in the hope of securing, in their own words, 'civilisation and Christianity'. Unlike other colonies with outside settlement, British policy in Fiji was to maintain the culture, traditions and institutions of indigenous Fijians, and thus to insulate them as far as possible from the modern, semi-market economic system established by colonial rule and protect them from the kind of exploitation that other indigenous peoples in the region – and further afield – had faced. At the same time, Britain was anxious to develop the resources of the colony so that it could become self-sufficient and meet the costs of administration. For this purpose it invited external investment, principally by a sugar company from Australia, and secured cheap labour through recruitment from India (then also under British control), sowing the seeds of a market, albeit administered, economy. By the time of independence in 1970, Indo-Fijians outnumbered indigenous Fijians, though that position is now reversed.

The policies of protection of indigenous Fijians through the preservation of their traditional system and economic development by importing capital, management and labour cast Fiji in a deep contradiction. The traditional system was incompatible with a market economy and yet could not be entirely isolated from it. To develop sugar plantations, land was required. However, land was owned collectively by indigenous clans and held under rules which did not permit easy alienation.[12] Alienation would in any case have deeply disrupted traditional political and social orders, since land, as in feudalism, was central to them. Colonial policies went further: Fijians' movements were restricted, and a special system of administration for Fijians was established, while participation of Fijians in colonial administration was limited. The system propped up, and to some extent even created, the Fijian chiefly system. The impacts on ordinary Fijians are an important aspect of the background to current affirmative action debates – though they are not phrased in these terms.

To this conflict between tradition and modernity was added another – the conflict of interests between the three major racial communities. Land was provided on terms that were congenial neither for sound economic development nor good for relations between the racial communities. The segregation of these communities and the isolation of the indigenous people from the market meant that the relations among them were largely determined by administrative policies. Colonial history is interpreted largely in terms of administrative regulation of racial claims and relations.[13] Many of the current political and economic difficulties facing Fiji stem from these policies,[14] which could not be sustained in the latter part of the twentieth century as the market became the dominant mode of economy and access to economic opportunities, while the state penetrated most aspects of the lives of all communities – this fact was then compounded by the inclination of Britain to give up sovereignty over Fiji.

The transition to independence for indigenous Fijians was less traumatic than they had feared. Although, then, less numerous than Indo-Fijians, they inherited the colonial state and dominated both the government and the armed forces. Upon independence in 1970, Fiji acquired a constitution which largely adopted the colonial framework, adjusting it, but only slightly, to the reality of British departure. The absence of Britain in the dual role of participant-umpire left no option but for local communities to negotiate agreements on contentious issues. For better or for worse, the Fiji Constitution served that purpose for 17 years during which Fiji enjoyed considerable stability and prosperity, even if in that period indigenous Fijian hegemony was firmly established. Overall the Fiji Constitution was on a fairly orthodox Westminster model including a standard Bill of Rights. However, the ethnic factor affected a number of aspects. Most seats in Parliament were elected on ethnic lines.[15] The voting set-up was particularly unusual, although something similar to it was not unknown in colonies with settler populations, or otherwise ethnically diverse.

The Constitution also entrenched a number of pieces of legislation protecting the interests of indigenous Fijians, especially in relation to land, most of which was reserved for them; in their large representation in the Senate, which gave the community a veto on amendment of legislation which secured special rights of indigenous Fijians; and in the constitutionalisation of the Great Council of Chiefs and the Fijian administration which gave considerable autonomy to Fijian provincial councils.[16]

The maintenance of the traditional system was one of the key assumptions underlying the 1970 constitutional settlement. The steady undermining of these assumptions greatly reduced the Constitution's ability to handle Fiji's problems and intricate racial relations. Nor did the military coup in 1987 (following the defeat of the traditional Fijian political party by a coalition committed to non-racial politics) produce more workable instruments of governance. The Constitution of 1990 which the military imposed further elevated the status of indigenous Fijians and gave the government a *carte blanche* to establish affirmative action policies for them. This Constitution, and the government that acquired power under it, lacked legitimacy, and was inapt as well as corrupt. It became increasingly evident that a new dispensation broadly fair and acceptable to all the communities was necessary to restore stability, revive the economy, and produce a modicum of national consensus, and that it had to cut loose from the racial moorings of Fiji towards another mode of accommodation. Under considerable external and internal pressures, the government agreed to review, and if necessary, amend it.

## 'Disadvantage'

The provisions of the 1997 Constitution were based on the recommendations of a Constitution Review Commission (known as the Reeves' Commission after the chair, a former Governor-General of New Zealand), which identified the main areas for affirmative action as education and training, land and housing, participation in commerce, and public employment.[17]

Yet it is also necessary to look at a factor that was very important in the reasoning of the Reeves Commission, that is, overall poverty. Living standards in Fiji are by no means as grindingly poor as in some developing countries. The starting point for most discussions on poverty in Fiji is still a 1997 study, itself using figures mainly from 1990–91. It estimated that overall the proportion of poor households was around 25 per cent.[18] What this shows is that most of the really poor were found among Indo-Fijians, but other figures showed that there was a very wide range within groups. In fact, if the class of 'others' was disaggregated to separate Europeans, Chinese, mixed race people and other Pacific Islanders, it would probably be shown that the poorest were among the last group.[19] Far fewer Fijians were in the money economy, and more were reliant upon land than other communities, which tends to make measurement of poverty more difficult. Movement of more Fijians to urban areas, and increase in landlessness among

Fijians has also increased Fijian poverty since 1997. The key significance of land suggests that it ought to be looked at first.

*Land*

Land has an almost mystic importance in modern political discourse in Fiji; land is said to represent 'life, sustenance, identity and culture'.[20] Large numbers of Indians have been small-scale farmers, mainly cane farmers leasing their farms for 30 years at a time from Fijians. Most land (over 80 per cent) is owned on a customary, communal basis and not by individuals. It is linked to lineage or *mataqali*. Revenues from land are allocated on a hierarchical basis; the Native Land Trust Board receives 25 per cent, three levels of chiefs (sometimes the same person) receive a share and members of the clan are left with 52.5 per cent; the benefits received by most members of the community from the land are therefore very small.[21] Thus it is not just the Fijian–Indian relationship which is rooted in land, but also relationships within the indigenous community. About 8 per cent is freehold land held mostly by Europeans and part-Europeans, with the rest government-owned.

Yet it is arguable that much of this place of land in Fijian society has an element of myth, and is to some extent a creation of the colonial policies referred to earlier; As Ratuva writes: 'the notion of land inalienability was part of Governor Sir Arthur Gordon's colonial Native Policy to keep Fijians in a state of communal cohesion in the context of slow evolutionary changes amidst dramatic changes'.[22] As late as the 1940s and 1950s the colonial regime imposed restrictions on the possibility of Fijians becoming truly independent farmers – they were to remain within the Fijian Administration system, performing all their customary obligations.[23]

The truth is that the land available simply does not produce enough to support the burdens and expectations placed upon it – at least not through cane farming. The cane farmers are not made wealthy through their often small farms, and the rent they pay is essentially used to finance the maintenance of the Fijian social, especially chiefly, structure.

Interestingly, the inclusion of land as one of the targets of affirmative action was seen by the Reeves Commission as catering for one of the demands of the Indo-Fijian community.[24] But there are also now landless Fijians. It has been estimated that overall about 50 per cent of the population is landless.[25]

Arguments to the effect that 'Fijians own 87 per cent of the land'[26] while true do not greatly advance the discussion. Much land occupied by Fijians is not productive, being hilly, while the most productive land has traditionally been leased for cane, or is freehold. The whole land issue is tremendously complex and emotionally charged. Both main groups profess attachment to land. Many tenant farmers, but equally many Fijian owners, do not understand the implications of a lease.[27] In recent years many Fijian land owners, with politically motivated encouragement, have declined to renew cane leases[28] – an example, in many instances, of cutting off one's nose to spite one's face in the case of owners who are then unable to use the land productively. There is some evidence to show that much of the land not re-leased is lying idle.

*Commerce*

Differences between Fijians and Indo-Fijians seem, superficially, both obvious and pronounced and cause greatest resentment in the area of commercial activity. Until recently, few Fijians have gone into business. And there are some very wealthy Indian businessmen, while even the small shopkeepers in town will seem wealthy to the poor Fijian who comes to town, to try his luck because he is landless, perhaps. Far higher proportions of Indians than Fijians tend to be in business. In 1993 F$10.7 million (F$2 = US$1) tax revenue derived from Indian individuals in business, but only F$1.2 million from Fijian individuals in business. And there were 36,502 Indian taxpayers as opposed to 33,987 Fijian, although by that time the overall ethnic balance in the country was in favour of the latter. In 1996 the census showed that 45.6 per cent of the employed population were Fijian, and 48.5 per cent Indo-Fijians.[29] Of corporate managers, 15.2 per cent were Fijian and 64 per cent Indo-Fijian,[30] though it is undoubtedly true that 'the largest and key industries in Fiji are either owned by foreigners or controlled by large domestic interests supported by the successive Fijian governments. For example, shipping, oil and petroleum, the automobile industry, banking, mining and accounting services are largely controlled by foreign interests',[31] this is presumably not appreciated by the average Fijian, nor does it alleviate the sense of grievance stemming from the sight of rows of Indian-owned shops in towns.

The reasons for these discrepancies are much debated. Undoubtedly colonial policies that kept Fijians in rural areas and a traditional economy and culture were important. On the other hand, there is the familiar phenomenon of the immigrant community, and the impetus that is given to entrepreneurship by the sense of insecurity that immigrants often feel. Landlessness (in the sense of limited opportunities to obtain rural land other than on lease for sugar cane purposes) among Indo-Fijians has restricted their options. Being forced to live in town, and in a country with little industry, trading has been one of their outlets. One of the richest Indo-Fijian businessmen, Hari Punja, loves to describe how his father walked the hills from village to village with his peddler's tray.[32]

Some have suggested that cultural factors have also inhibited Fijian success in business. H. C. Sharma, a Member of Parliament said: 'Why do businesses run successfully by other races come to a grinding halt when run by our Fijian brothers?'[33] This should not be dismissed as simply a racial stereotype. Fijians have a self-image of not being interested in business. If prices go up, it is said, a Fijian may work less because it will take less time to earn what he needs. Fijian businessmen often find that they are under pressure to give goods to their relatives and clansmen, rather than sell them. Precedence is often given to obligations to church and community over investment and commercial success. Some Fijians distrust even members of their own community who have been successful in business. Wanting to do business is perceived as an Indian attribute.[34] Obviously attitudes are complex: Fijians feel simultaneously inferior in terms of capacity and superior in terms of absence of entrepreneurial acquisitiveness – and unjustly deprived in terms of the result! All these are perfectly human feelings.

Fijian land holding can also be an obstacle to success in business or even in commercial farming. Like communities in Africa, or elsewhere in the Pacific, including Maoris in New Zealand, they may find it difficult to raise money on the security of land, because the land is not theirs to alienate.[35]

Reality is of course much more complex than ethnic stereotypes, whether they are of one's own community or of others. There are many Fijians who sell their own produce in the markets. Yet until recently there have been few successful businesses of any size owned by Fijians, and many examples of failures.[36] But things are changing, and more Fijians are showing interest in business.

## Housing

The 1997 poverty study gave the following information about poor housing conditions, indicating that there is no clear relationship between ethnicity and housing inadequacy, as shown in Table 1. Squatter housing is another serious problem, and one that has been getting worse. A survey carried out in 1995 found that in one town squatter settlements had multiplied tenfold since 1986. Squatting is not the preserve of any community: in 1994 there were said to be 5,000 Fijian squatters in Suva, the capital of Fiji, and 5,200 Indo-Fijian squatters. Overall figures have recently suggested about 82,350 squatters.[37] Squatting is obviously increasing, many being Indo-Fijians who have been evicted at the expiry of cane leases; in fact Indo-Fijians outnumber Fijians except in the capital, Suva. However, it has been stated that Fijians move to town because the traditional system denies them a chance of land, and to avoid their customary obligations, and Fijian women for the freer lifestyle.[38]

## Education

The earliest schools for Fijians were for children of chiefs only. Before independence education in Fiji was largely segregated, and more was spent per capita on the education of European children than Indo-Fijian children, and more on the latter than on Fijians.[39] In 1970, 44.4 per cent of Fijian candidates passed the secondary school entrance examinations, as against 69.7 per cent of Indo-Fijians; 22.3 per cent of Fijian candidates for New Zealand university entrance passed as opposed to 33.3 per cent of Indo-Fijians. Gaps may have narrowed over the years but remain significant. It seems that Fijian children drop out of school more often than Indo-Fijian.[40] Also, even if passing rates for public examinations have narrowed, there may still be a grade gap. Thus for the Fiji Junior Certificate (Secondary) examinations in 1987, 16 per cent of Indo-Fijian candidates obtained an A grade, but only 4 per cent of Fijian children.[41] Some explain the differences in terms of motivation, including the parental push factor. It is often said that cultural factors, including the tendency of Fijian teachers to be frequently absent in order to meet their communal obligations, contribute to the poor performance of Fijian children. Fijian children also do better in Indian than in Fijian schools.[42] However, other research has also suggested that quality of schooling – especially the quality of leadership in schools – rather than ethnicity is important.[43] Affirmative action in the sense of giving responsibility to Fijian teachers despite relative inexperience may be a factor, although providing Fijian children with no Fijian teachers is also detrimental. High dropout rates have been reported from schools as a result of inability to pay fees or levies, with the rates being higher for

**Table 1.** Ethnicity and Housing

|  | No safe water source | No electricity | Pit toilet |
|---|---|---|---|
| National | 16.9 | 33.4 | 43.7 |
| Fijian | 11.5 | 62.1 | 34.9 |
| Indo-Fijian | 21.6 | 29.2 | 54.5 |
| Other | 6.4 | 34.1 | 12.7 |

*Source*: The 1997 Fiji Poverty Study, Table 17.

Fijian children. About 35,000 children failed to complete primary school over the five years prior to 2005.[44] A recent report indicates that 17,000 children drop out annually.[45]

The government attributes these differences to poor schools in rural areas, especially small schools, which are more often than not attended by Fijian children. The size of schools, and the proliferation of very small schools, is a product of the policy under which most schools are set up by religious or other groups and provided with grants in aid. However, the policy has also led to an increase in the number of schools, and there seems little power to require schools to close or even to amalgamate.[46] Expenditure on rural schools remains below that on those in towns.[47] The recent Fiji Teacher Association study attributed dropout rates largely to rural Fijian parents' inability to meet costs, often because they give priority to church and communal obligations.

At university level there is also a higher dropout rate among Fijian students, and generally lower achievement; the Great Council of Chiefs recently asked the Fijian Affairs Board (which administers scholarships for Fijians) to take action on Fijian students' failures in external and tertiary exams.[48]

*Public employment*

At the time of the first coup, while the proportions of general and administrative grades were not grossly disproportionate to population (41 per cent Fijian:55 per cent Indo-Fijian) and the same is true of teaching (44:54), the differences were far greater in the more highly qualified grades, such as in respect of medical officers (29:57).[49]

One of the most dramatic changes in the country in the years following the initial coups has been the shift in this balance. Some of the changes have been due to Indo-Fijian emigration. This has itself been attributable to the reduction in public employment opportunities, but also to a general belief that there was not much of a future for Indo-Fijians in the country, and also to physical insecurity, particularly following the 2000 coup.

By the end of the 1990s, most civil servants were Fijians. There were some significant variations, some of which (in terms of numbers between Fijians and Indo-Fijians) show the impact both of strenuous affirmative action for Fijians and of the discrepancy in certain professional areas:[50]

> Office of the President 16:0
> Foreign Affairs 57:8
> Ministry of Justice 23:13
> Judiciary 95:91
> Auditor-General 22:23.
> Education 4,003:3,297

The Fiji Human Rights Commission has supplied figures for January 2006 as given in Table 2. These also show that in the four highest civil service grades grouped together the ethnic ratio is 125:17:3:1. Distribution in the police force is 1,353 Fijian and Rotuman officers (62.3 per cent), 765 Indian officers (35.2 per cent), and 54 others.[51]

*The nature of disadvantage: comment*

Fijian culture was not denigrated under the colonial regime, and perhaps it is not appropriate to describe the treatment of Fijians under this system as 'discrimination'.

Table 2. Ethnicity of civil servants as at 31 January 2006

| Ethnicity | Fijian male (female) | Indo-Fijian male (female) | Others male (female) | Expatriate male (female) | Total by gender: male (female) |
|---|---|---|---|---|---|
| Number | 5,706 (5,911) | 3,631 (2,675) | 200 (206) | 101 (44) | 9,638 (8,836) |
| Total (%) by ethnicity | 11,617 (62.9) | 6,306 (34.1) | 406 (2.2) | 145 (0.78) | 18,474 |

Source: FHRC, *Report on Government's Affirmative Action Programmes, 2020 Plan for Indigenous Fijians and Rotumans and the Blueprint* (Suva: FHRC 2006), http://www.humanrights.org.fj/pdf/AA_report.pdf (accessed 5 October 2006), percentages added.

It was of course patronising, and was destructive of self-confidence in the Fijian community. At least since independence, any lack of access to opportunities for Fijians now (except no doubt in some individual instances) is not based on discrimination *per se*. Rather it is based on historical policies, which appear with the benefit of hindsight to have been unwise, community choices and pressures, and lack of experience. Attitudes and aptitudes, as we know from other societies, replicate themselves from generation to generation.

In Fiji there was a community to blame, that is, the Indo-Fijians. Even if it was appropriate to describe the treatment of Fijians as 'discriminatory', it was not Indo-Fijians who formulated those policies; they were as much victims of colonial policies as were the Fijians. Yet ethnic stereotypes are as prevalent in Fiji as elsewhere: Indo-Fijians think of Fijians as lazy; Fijians think of Indo-Fijians as greedy, scheming (and rich). Even more sophisticated, not to mention governmental, analysis tends to be simplistic. Distinctions within communities are ignored or downplayed, including distinctions, ethnic and other, within the Indo-Fijian community. The true 'villains of the piece' – the colonial regime, the Fijian elite, and globalisation – are ignored.[52]

**Affirmative Action in the Past**

Some sort of affirmative action has been a feature of Fiji since independence. It did not have constitutional protection until 1990 when, in the aftermath of the 1987 coups, and in the heyday of Fijian chauvinism, the Constitution not only entrenched Fijian institutions, and Fijian dominance over the political system but provided (in language taken from Article 15(2) of the Canadian Charter of Rights and Freedoms):

> 18. Nothing contained in section 16 of this Constitution shall preclude the enactment of any law or any programme or activity that has as its object and purpose the amelioration of conditions of disadvantaged individuals or groups including those that are disadvantaged because of race, sex, place of origin, political opinions, colour, religion or creed.

It went further, to provide that notwithstanding the Bill of Rights Parliament must enact laws with the object of promoting and safeguarding the economic, social, educational, cultural, traditional and other interests of the Fijian and Rotuman people, and direct the government to adopt any programme or activity for the attainment of those interests. The government could give directions for the reservation of certain proportions of scholarships, training privileges or other special facilities and also for the reservation of permits and licences for businesses.[53]

## The Reeves Commission's Vision

The Reeves Commission was aware of the tension discussed earlier between identity rooted in tradition and removal of disadvantage which might require departure from tradition. Yet the Commission considered that it was important for national stability that disparities in economic status should be addressed, pointing out that such disparities were not as straightforward as ethnicity. The Commission appreciated the force of arguments made, especially in the joint submission of the National Federation Party and the Fiji Labour Party to the Commission on problems with affirmative action programmes.[54] Although the submission recognised 'the need for inter-community equity' the two parties would have preferred affirmative action not to be based on racial criteria. The Reeves Commission also emphasised the inequality suffered by women, disabled persons, and the elderly. However, the Commission rejected the suggestion that need should be the sole criterion – this, it maintained, 'would overlook the reasons why it is necessary to achieve ethnic justice'.[55] The proposals of the Commission took the form of a draft, which was ultimately adopted (as section 44 of the Constitution) albeit with some significant changes, and which we will shortly analyse in some detail.

Fijians embraced with some enthusiasm the concept of 'indigenousness', believing that this gave them sufficient justification in international law for special measures in their favour. The Commission took a different view, and indigenousness did not play a prominent part in its approach to the issues.[56]

## Affirmative Action Elsewhere in the 1997 Constitution

The Constitution seeks to balance the claims and interests of communities and of individuals. The 'Compact'[57] commits the state in a comprehensive yet tendentious manner to 'affirmative action and social justice programmes to secure effective equality of access to opportunities, amenities or services for the Fijian and Rotuman people, as well as for the other communities, for women as well as men, and for all disadvantaged citizens or groups, are based on an allocation of resources broadly acceptable to all communities' (section 6(k)). The community angle also appears in section 6(l), which suggests a trade-off, such that the gains of one community will need to be balanced with those of another: 'the equitable sharing of political power among all communities is matched by an equitable sharing of economic and commercial power to ensure that all communities fully benefit from the nation's economic progress' (the underlying implication of which is that indigenous Fijians will be prepared to share political power with Indo-Fijians in return for a greater share in the economy, allegedly dominated by Indo-Fijians).

Section 6(b) protects indigenous Fijians' land rights (which means basically that the prospects for members of other communities of acquiring access to land depend substantially on the decisions of indigenous Fijians).[58] Section 6(d) protects the rights of indigenous Fijians and Rotumans to 'governance through their separate administrative systems' (and thus not only privileges these communities over others, but also minimises possibilities of inter-racial co-operation). The Compact also recognises the paramountcy of Fijian interests 'as a protective principle ... to ensure that the interests of the Fijian community are not subordinated to the interests of other communities'.[59] Other provisions which discriminate against other communities include the vesting of important functions in the purely indigenous institution, the Great Council of Chiefs ('Bose Levu Vakaturaga') (section 116), as a general advisory body to the government. More specifically, 14 members of the Senate (out of a total of 32 and with effectively the power of veto over legislation which they regard as contrary to indigenous interests) are appointed upon the nomination of the Great Council (section 64), as are the country's President and Vice-President (after consultation with the Prime Minister (section 90)). Chapter 13 is devoted to 'Group Rights'; its principal purpose is to entrench the protection of entitlements of indigenous communities to land, fishing, and minerals, as well as to provide for the application of their customary laws and rights and the resolution of disputes in accordance with 'traditional Fijian processes' (section 186).

These politics and provisions complicate the design and implementation of affirmative action under section 44. Many of these provisions are designed to preserve the nature of Fijian society – affirmative action for identity. Yet some aspects of Chapter 13 especially are distinctly economic as well as 'way of life' oriented. Indo-Fijians remained barred from land, fishing, and some aspects of administration but there are no protected traditional areas of occupation and living for Indians.

A brief focus on the military may be illuminating. The government is very coy about the ethnic distribution in the military, and affirmative action programmes do not mention this disparity when aiming at 50 per cent Fijian employment in the public service. Some have described the military as 99.9 per cent Fijian; the Fiji Human Rights Commission has stated that of those who have applied for recruitment since 1987, 2.6 per cent were Indo-Fijians and 5 per cent 'others'.[60]

The issue of the military is not merely a matter of public employment, nor is it just a question of loyalty: whether Indo-Fijian members of the forces could be trusted to defend the country. The work of Halapua shows the nexus between the military, Fijian traditional leadership and Fijian 'modern' class structures, religion, and access to state power.[61] Viewed in this context, section 44 with its ostensibly race-blind affirmative action provisions may seem rather different.

*The scheme of section 44*

Section 44 belongs to the more traditional type of affirmative action, focused on members of disadvantaged communities. It cannot be looked at in isolation. The Constitution provides a good general Bill of Rights, which precludes discrimination on grounds of 'actual or supposed personal characteristics or circumstances, including race, ethnic origin, colour, place of origin, gender, sexual orientation,[62] birth, primary language, economic status, age or disability'.[63] Like other provisions, this is applicable to public bodies, including courts, and also to individuals performing the functions of a public office; it is not, therefore, unlike the Bill of Rights in the South African Constitution, applicable 'horizontally'. There is no general provision for limitation on this article, although law dealing with governance of the Fijian community, chiefly status, traditional fishing rights or restrictions on land alienation under customary law is protected, as is personal law on some subject matters – the latter provided that the law is reasonable and satisfies the 'democratic society' principle. Overlooked in much of the discussion is the 'economic status' prohibited ground of discrimination, which on the face of it would mean not only that poor people may not be discriminated against, but rich people also.[64] However, it is important to note also that only 'unfair' discrimination is outlawed:[65] to discriminate in favour of a person with disadvantaged economic status, at least in relation to economic benefits, is not unfair.

The Bill of Rights is mainly concerned with civil and political rights, but there is a right to education – 'to basic education and to equal access to educational institutions'. However, there is no right to food, health or housing.

Section 140 states that recruitment, and promotion and management of persons within a state service must be based on principles including merit, adequate and equal opportunities for training and advancement for men and women equally and for members of all ethnic groups; and that 'the composition of the state service at all levels should reflect as closely as possible the ethnic composition of the population, taking account, when appropriate, of occupational preferences'. State services are defined to include the military, but no serious substantive effort seems to have been made to bring about any such reflection. Possibly the government may argue that since only 2.6 per cent of applications have been from Indo-Fijians they have an occupational preference against military service. Such an argument might be convenient, but possibly as unconvincing as one which alleges that women had an occupational preference not to be engineers (see also comments relating to section 44 (1)(c) below).

Section 44 provides a broad mandate of access to equal opportunity. But in spite, or more accurately because, of the broad mandate, there are not enough resources to satisfy all persons in need. Thus, some criteria have to be established, even if it is the concept of the 'least well off'. Affirmative action raises questions of institutional responsibilities, criteria, and procedures, matters for ordinary legislation but nonetheless prescribed here in the Constitution. The reason for this prescription was to move to a new form of affirmative action, away from communities to individuals as beneficiaries, and in part to deal with problems that have bedevilled affirmative action in other countries. Section 44 perhaps does not provide clearly whether the emphasis is to be on the individual or the community (authorising both types of benefits).

The principal features of section 44 are that there is a mandatory requirement of programmes, approved by Parliament, for the benefit of all disadvantaged groups. There is no indication of the nature of beneficiary groups – no mention of ethnicity, gender or disability. There is a clear intention that programmes are not to be permanent, but to last only until their objectives are achieved. Therefore, target groups, criteria for selection within these groups, and performance indicators are all to be specified by Parliament. Programmes are to be monitored and annual reports made to Parliament.

Before looking more closely at these provisions and the programmes ostensibly introduced under them, we look briefly at developments since they came into force.

**After the Constitution**

Two years after the adoption of the Constitution the Labour Party, headed by an Indo-Fijian, took office after elections.[66] The new government moved rapidly to implement the provisions of the Constitution, as it was obliged to do, since existing programmes were protected for only two years. It commissioned a draft poverty strategy in 1999,[67] a document concerned with the fulfilment of the party's electoral platform, which did not mention affirmative action or indeed ethnicity. In 2000 it drafted a Social

Justice Bill to implement Chapter 5 of the Constitution, seeking the advice of the Fiji Human Rights Commission about the drafting of the bill and commissioning a report on affirmative action through the International Labour Organisation.[68]

On the day the Social Justice Bill was introduced into Parliament, George Speight, ostensibly motivated by concerns for the well-being of *taukei*,[69] invaded Parliament, seized most of the government and other MPs and kept them incarcerated for up to 55 days.[70] A state of emergency was declared and the army took over, which ultimately installed a civilian government, the leader of which was returned as Prime Minister in the 2001 elections. Some have implicated the affirmative action programme as among the causes of the coup. Others have attributed this to simple ethnic antagonism, specific fears about land, intra-Fijian tensions, ethnic Indo-Fijian Prime Minister Mahendra Chaudhry's arrogance, or the Constitution.[71]

After the coup the new government introduced first of all a Blueprint for the Enhancement of Indigenous Fijian and Rotuman Participation in Commerce and Business,[72] which was followed up in 2002 with a 20 year development plan with similar aims, sometimes referred to as '50:50 by 2020'.[73]

The development plan insists that it is in accordance with the 'spirit' of the 1997 Constitution, which it finds mainly in the Compact provisions, quoted earlier, on the paramountcy of Fijian interests and affirmative action. It barely mentions section 44, and when discussing poverty it slides over evidence of the extent of poverty in the Indo-Fijian community. Its 200-plus pages are replete with proposals for development, in education, commerce, health, tourism, public enterprise reform, culture and others, all directed towards the achievement of a vision of a society 'where the special place of indigenous Fijians and Rotumans as the host communities are recognized and accepted, and where their rights are fully safeguarded'.[74]

In 2001 a Social Justice Act was enacted. The text of the Act was very similar to that proposed by the previous government in 2000. But the devil, as always, was in the detail; in this case in the Schedule. The 2000 Bill had scheduled 14 schemes: two limited to Fijians and one to non-Fijians. The 2001 Act schedules 29 schemes, ten limited to Fijians, and one with more favourable conditions for Fijians than for others. Two are limited to non-Fijians. The 2000 Bill and the 2001 Act both assert that 'programs of affirmative action listed in the Schedule ... comply with section 44 of the Constitution' – something which, the Fiji Human Rights Commission has pointed out, cannot be achieved by simple legislative assertion.[75]

The government's report to the United Nations Committee on the Elimination of Racial Discrimination was similarly disingenuous: 'The poorest and most disadvantaged people in Fiji are Fijians. Fijian households generally have the lowest incomes.'[76]

The policies have been criticised by the Committee on the Elimination of Racial Discrimination,[77] by the Committee on the Elimination of Discrimination Against Women for not including a gender perspective,[78] by the Commonwealth Human Rights Initiative,[79] by many Fiji non-governmental organisations,[80] and most recently by its own Human Rights Commission,[81] which concluded that the Social Justice Act was inconsistent with the Constitution (both section 38 and section 44), and that the Act and government policies were inconsistent with the Convention on the Elimination of All Forms of Racial Discrimination. The Commission analysed all 29 'programmes' appended to the Social Justice Act and concluded that eight were acceptable as not discriminatory on racial grounds; three were acceptable on racial ground but suffered from gender imbalance; nine were discriminatory in racial terms (one because the scheme was not means-tested for Fijian applicants but for others, and one because the administration of the scheme added racial quotas); one was indirectly discriminatory (that is discriminatory in effect though not in conception); three were inadequately resourced and did not meet the Act criteria; two did not address disadvantage; one did not have performance requirements; and on two there was insufficient information.[82]

### Section 44 Analysed and Evaluated

*Mandatory programmes – for what and for whom?*

The first striking requirement is that there be programmes for all disadvantaged groups. This is impossible for a poor country, and very difficult even for wealthier ones. It is also impossible also for certain reasons internal to section 44, as we will see. Meanwhile, there are few programmes for women, for persons with disability, and for other Pacific Islanders who are among the poorest groups within the main statutory vehicle for affirmative action, the Social Justice Act (and absolutely none for gay men and lesbians).

The objective must be to secure 'equality of access' to the benefits of certain specific areas of life: education, land and housing, commerce, and the service of the state.[83] The Constitution does not include an omnibus category 'other opportunities, amenities or services essential to an adequate standard of living' as proposed by the Reeves Commission. The Commission did not give examples, suggesting that it should be a matter for political judgment.[84] Health would be an obvious example, and it is regrettable that this sort of benefits were excluded, although of course such exclusion does not mean that government may not strive for equality of access to health care; indeed discriminatory government health care policies would violate section 38.[85]

Affirmative action must take the form of 'programmes'. The Reeves Commission stated that this 'means a particular scheme of assistance',[86] which suggests something that occurs over a period and is not an event. The Commission wanted any programmes to be both 'reasonable' and 'necessary', and explained that the function of 'necessary' was to require a connection between the programme and the purpose.[87] Arguably, 'necessary' is implied; if a group does not really need a programme in order to achieve a result, then that group is not disadvantaged. Also, it may be argued that 'necessary' was too narrow; there may be a number of ways in which to achieve a certain result; no one particular route is necessary, even if something is necessary.

The absence of 'reasonable' may be more serious. The reasonableness standard does not mean that the court will substitute its judgment for that of the legislature. As the South African Constitutional Court maintained,

> A court considering reasonableness will not enquire whether other more desirable or favourable measures could have been adopted, or whether public money could have been better spent. The question would be whether the measures that have been adopted are reasonable. It is necessary to recognise that a wide range of possible measures could be adopted by the state to meet its obligations. Many of these would meet the requirement of reasonableness. Once it is shown that the measures do so, this requirement is met.[88]

The Commission explained that the reasonableness standard was to allow the courts to be able to decide on the validity of a programme while deferring to the government's setting of the programme's priorities. In the absence of the word, there is no way of exercising discipline: will the government, for example, choose expensive or ineffective, inadequately thought through or unfair techniques without any judicial scrutiny? Many of the programmes involve quotas: certain percentages of licences, scholarships, and grants are reserved (usually) for Fijians. The absence of the reasonableness standard makes it much more difficult for the courts to scrutinise such quotas, scrutiny which might have been able to be drawn on the experience in other jurisdictions. It is true that a court may read some sort of reasonableness requirement into the provision – at least to the extent that something that is unreasonable in the sense of not responding adequately to the needs of the intended beneficiaries may not be an affirmative action programme at all. Yet, attacking a programme on the basis of its being, although potentially effective, excessively expensive or unbalanced in the sense that it ignores the needs of other groups, may be difficult for any but the most creative court.[89]

A programme must be for the benefit of a 'group' or a 'category' (or for more than one group or category); there is no definition in the Constitution of either 'group' or 'category'. The Reeves Commission proposed specific mention of Fijians and Rotumans, and then of other groups.[90] But this language was used in the Compact and not in section 44 itself.

Arguably, 'group' is used where the purpose of the programme is to achieve the upliftment of a group as a whole, rather than of individuals. This is relevant where groups, defined in terms of ethnicity, gender, geographical origin, or disability, are concerned. The particular group generally must be disadvantaged in some respect, although some members of the group may not be. This interpretation is supported by the fact that section 44(2)(d) states that if the programme is for the benefit of a group, criteria for participation within the group must be specified. There is no requirement of criteria within a category. A 'category', it is suggested, is a class where the criteria of identification are the very criteria that define eligibility.

No criteria having been provided to identify groups, any plausibly disadvantaged group will be permissible. Thus if the government ascertains that Fijians are disadvantaged in some respect, a programme that benefits Fijians is a section 44 programme (as in programmes 1, 2, 7, 9, 12).[91] It is suggested that some of the Fiji Human Rights Commission criticisms are misconceived when they seem to be suggesting that a programme for the benefit of a racial group is not within the section.

Nonetheless, many of the beneficiary groups under the Social Justice Act do not seem to meet the constitutional requirement. A target group of 'Women, youths, disabled (mental and physical), unemployed and low-income earners'; (Programme 6) is not really a 'group' at all; it lacks any coherence. 'Other communities' (as in programme 13) by definition cannot be disadvantaged.

*Disadvantage*

The Reeves Commission did not discuss 'disadvantage' as a legal term, and the Constitution does not define it. There is a definition in the Social Justice Act: '"disadvantaged", in relation to a group or category of persons, means that the group or category does not have equality of access by virtue of the actual or supposed personal characteristics of the members of the group or category or by virtue of the location or educational level of the category or group.'[92] This is both a curious and, it is suggested, arguably unnecessary provision;[93] 'equality of access' is defined to mean access to the list of benefits identified in Section 44 of the Constitution. Was this necessary disadvantaged as the statute defines it? Various disadvantaged groups may be excluded. For example, are 'poor farmers' a group or a category disadvantaged as the statute defines it? It is suggested that there should be no objection to defining a group as 'poor' and then devising a scheme to benefit that group without having to agonise over whether that poverty resulted from inadequate access to something specific. Access is constitutionally the remedy and not the cause. A further oddity is the introduction of the concept 'actual or supposed personal characteristics', which comes close to suggesting that the introduction must be discrimination – something which the Commission and the Constitution carefully avoided; it was, perhaps, felt necessary because of its link with section 38 – discrimination on grounds of personal characteristics is not permitted – unless it also falls under section 44.

The scope of section 44 is whittled down – including by the omission of 'or circumstances' included in section 38. 'Location or educational level' is a circumstance, but by no means the only possible circumstance. Prisoners (programme 11), for example, may be disadvantaged by virtue of their personal circumstances (though not 'location or educational level'), but not their characteristics as prisoners. The value of this addition is presumably to make it clear that it would be legitimate to have a scheme for rural schools, or for people with less than a certain educational level, and almost certainly with Fijians in mind in both instances.

If a programme is challenged in court, how would disadvantage be established? How far would or should the courts defer to the administration in defining disadvantage? The Indian courts have wrestled with such definitional issues, and have concluded that there must be evidence of a sociological kind that identifies groups as backward. Yet, beyond insisting that there is a plausible case for identifying a group as disadvantaged, there is a limit to what one can reasonably expect the courts to do. Interestingly, the South Africans have set up an equality court in which the judiciary, the presiding judges or magistrates must have undergone 'social context training'.[94]

*The criteria*

Once a 'group' is identified, there is an obligation for the group to meet certain criteria of eligibility. The Reeves Commission deliberately decided not to propose that criteria be specified – and none are thus provided in the Constitution. If the purpose is to uplift the group it may be positively counter-productive to concentrate efforts on the weakest members of the group, as the Commission pointed out.[95] A scholarship scheme may have financial criteria. It will also have criteria related to ability to benefit. These may well not overlap entirely. A student from a better-off household may be better equipped to benefit from university. The Commission pointed out that in the case of encouraging business enterprise it may not be the most deprived member of a group who is the most able to benefit.

On the other hand, public funds should not be used to subsidise people who refuse to educate their own children. Suppose that parents have unconstitutional notions about education of women, but would be persuaded to have their daughters educated if scholarships were available. The objective of affirmative action programmes is not merely to benefit individuals but to make the entire disadvantaged group feel that it is receiving its fair share of opportunities. It may be to offer role models, so that other members of the community are encouraged to follow on. This may justify, at least at the early stages of an affirmative action programme, benefits of this type of incentive.

There is the problem of what in India has been termed the 'creamy layer', that is, those who have already floated to the top of the class.[96] One possible function of criteria within the target group is to ensure that creamy layer members of an otherwise disadvantaged group are excluded. However, it must be recognised that the fact that one generation has risen above the general level does not necessarily mean that disadvantage has ended. Cultural inhibitions, and discrimination, may survive the uplifting of one generation, or may recur in the next. A person whose father has done well financially may still be disadvantaged for other reasons – by attending a rural school, or not having parental support needed to do well in school. Again the criteria must be related to the intended benefit. It may continue to be justified to have a favourable admissions or recruitment policy, but not to have a system of special loans or grants, for those whose financial resources put them in the creamy layer.

Someone has to decide what the criteria should be when devising a scheme. There being no constitutional touchstone, can the courts be called upon to decide whether the criteria are valid, provided they are spelled out in the legislation? On the face of the language of section 44, they cannot. This is unsatisfactory as it opens the possibility of purely token criteria; if there must be criteria presumably they must be meaningful. Again, this would be difficult for courts to decide. Nonetheless the requirement, 'Must comply with other requirements and conditions specified by the government or relevant agencies' (one of the programme 6 criteria), clearly fails the constitutional test of specificity. The following criteria for benefiting within the class of Fijians whose ancestral land has been alienated are not the sort of identification criteria the Constitution envisages: 'owner of freehold land must be a willing seller; purchase price of the freehold land must be based on the market value; landowning unit must have the capacity to pay back loan grant' (programme 10).

The Constitution does not contain a particular provision recommended by the Commission. Yet this could be implied. If fishermen as a whole are disadvantaged, a group defined as 'fishermen' would be acceptable. Although perhaps there are few Indo-Fijian fishermen in Fiji and so the provision of support for fishermen could be thought of as indirectly discriminatory in favour of Fijian fishermen, it would not be unfairly discriminatory. Within the group there must be selection criteria; perhaps age and income. It would not be permissible to add, as a matter of administrative practice, an exclusion of Indo-Fijian fishermen as it would breach section 38. The Human Rights Commission has indicated that precisely such discrimination has arisen in some instances. Under programme 6, Small and Micro Enterprise Development, which targets women, youths, disabled (mental and physical), unemployed and low-income earners, 95–97 per cent of the beneficiaries have been Fijians; since Fijians do not comprise such an overwhelming dominance of these groups, some discrimination – and more likely direct rather than indirect discrimination – must have been at work.

*The benefit*

Section 44 programmes are to 'achieve effective equality of access to' the benefits. This stipulation can also be found in the South African Constitution.[97] A narrow view could be that access to education simply refers to admissions to educational programmes and access to participation in commerce means the chance to get started. Access to 'all levels' of public service clearly means promotion as well as employment opportunities, but does it mean more? The Commission made it clear that more was required by the word 'effective': equality of result, not equality of opportunity, is needed.[98] The Constitutional Court of South Africa explained 'access' in the context of housing:

> For a person to have access to adequate housing all of these conditions need to be met: there must be land, there must be services, there must be a dwelling. Access to land for the purpose of housing is therefore included in the right of access to adequate housing in section 26. A right of access to adequate housing also suggests that it is not only the state who is responsible for the provision of houses, but that other agents within our society, including individuals themselves, must be enabled by legislative and other measures to provide housing.[99]

This suggests that programmes need not be for the government itself to provide access; this is also suggested by the use of the word 'achieve' rather than 'provide'. The South African example does point to another aspect of the Fiji provision: the absence of the word 'adequate', which is most relevant to housing. If people have any sort of housing, however inadequate, does this mean that there can be no section 44 programme to benefit them? One may read an element of security into the concept of housing, so that squatters who may have a roof over their heads can still benefit. But quality of construction, access to water, and so forth is central to adequacy. A programme to benefit those who have no piped water would be perfectly legitimate under section 38 of course, provided that it did not discriminate on other irrelevant grounds such as ethnicity.

*Legislative fulfilment*

The Constitution requires that a programme be set up by legislation. The Reeves Commission wanted Parliament to approve the details, which means that the legislation would be – or ought to be – far more detailed than one would normally expect to find in principal legislation (as opposed to regulations). In fact the Act violates this principle by permitting the Minister responsible to amend the Schedule, which entails approval of the cabinet but not of Parliament.[100] Also in violation of the Constitution, the Social Justice Regulations add certain other programmes; they provide the legal framework for the reservation of Government contracts, licenses and permits to Fijians and Rotumans and, since 2004, for 50 per cent of licenses and permits issued under the Land Transport Authority Act to be reserved for them.[101]

The fact that rather complex legislation is called for under section 44 would suggest that section 44 programmes should generally be substantial. Section 44 should be reserved for those programmes which the government wishes to highlight as fulfilling the social justice mandate of the Constitution, and also for programmes which constitutionally require to be under section 44 because they contain elements which genuinely infringe the guarantee of equality in section 38 (equality). This could be a weakness of the Constitution. To this extent the permissive approach of the South African Constitution is perhaps to be preferred. Alternatively, it would have been possible to require that criteria and standards be laid down and made public without actually requiring them to be expressly specified in the Act.

The government has in fact had some problems in complying with these requirements, and many programmes that it puts forward as being affirmative action do not meet constitutional requirements and many are not actually set up by legislation at all but by administrative action alone.

Lastly, there is a 'sunset clause' in the Constitution: an Act establishing programmes automatically expires after ten years, although programmes may be continued by new legislation if their objective has not been achieved, that is, 'unless the benefited persons or groups have demonstrably ceased to be in need of it',[102] which suggests the onus of proof to be upon one who argues that the programme should not be continued. What if the programmes have been merely ineffective? Arguably, this is left to political judgment.

## The link with equality

Many programmes can be undertaken without infringing section 38, and therefore without the necessity to invoke the complications of section 44. These possibilities are opened up by the concept of 'unfair' discrimination. Meeting needs is not by itself unfair. Extra resources for rural schools, scholarships for poor children, or resources for people wishing to set up businesses would not be a problem *per se*, even if tageted largely on one ethnic group. Indeed, programmes for the explicit benefit of a certain ethnic group need not be prohibited.

However, if a programme would otherwise violate section 38, it will only be valid if it also falls under section 44. According to section 38(3) special measures may be taken with the purpose of achieving substantial equality between different groups or different categories of persons, and the taking of such measures does not amount to section 38 discrimination (sub-s.(4)).[103] These provisions serve as a shield against actions based on section 38; they would not give a right to one who has been denied favourable action. It is suggested that section 44 does not give one the right to sue either.[104]

The phrase 'special measures' was not recommended by the Reeves Commission, though it did refer to its use in the South African Constitution. It is a phrase from international law, including the Convention on the Elimination of all Forms of Racial Discrimination (CERD) and the Convention on the Elimination of all Forms of Discrimination Against Women (CEDAW), and the International Labour Organisation (ILO) Convention 169 on Indigenous Peoples, and its use here was presumably intended, or at least should have the effect, of bringing international jurisprudence into Fiji domestic law.[105]

## Goals, standards and monitoring

Legislation setting up an affirmative action programme must set out the goals of the programme and the performance indicators for measuring its success in attaining those goals (s.44(2)(d)), and the administering agency must monitor the efficacy of a programme established under the section by reference to the specified performance indicators (s.44(6)).

Some have suggested that performance indicators should not be only numerical, but should be directed towards measuring social impact and effectiveness. A South African White Paper on Public Service Education and Training in 1997[106] stated that evaluation should be concerned with effectiveness, efficiency, adequacy, equity, responsiveness and appropriateness. Many of these indicators are not capable of being measured in statistical terms. However, if annual reports are to be useful as indicators of progress they must include indicators that are quantifiable.

Goals, in addition to being measurable, must also be achievable, and a global objective is difficult to fit into the constitutional scheme: 'the ending of Fijian disadvantage' is enormously broad, subjective and immeasurable. The goal of achieving equality of access for persons with disability will never materialise, if only because there will always be more persons with disabilities 'coming on stream'. Programmes for students with disability cannot meet section 44 unless they are designed to change behaviour of the rest of the community; provision of special equipment and overseas training of teachers cannot have this effect (programme 5). At one level this is not a problem, because an affirmative action programme for persons with disability would not be a violation of section 38. Yet persons with disability might reasonably expect to be viewed as a disadvantaged category or group; and would find it unfair and indeed unconstitutional if there were not any section 44 affirmative action programmes for them.

The great majority of the statutory programmes listed in the Schedule to the Social Justice Act do not satisfy the constitutional requirements in relation to goals and performance indicators. In the Schedule, goals and the performance criteria by which progress towards goals is to be measured include such immeasurables as 'to enable the target group to pursue excellence at all levels' and 'uplift standards of living of target group' for the small/micro enterprise development programme. In other words, the government and its lawyers have great difficulty in fitting what they want to do into the constitutional framework. At one level the framework is clear, but when applied in detail it creates real problems; there seems to have been little appreciation of the complexities of section 44.

**Non-statutory Programmes**

A variety of affirmative action programmes, especially those outlined in the '50:50 by 2020' document, have no statutory backing. Many of these programmes do not require such sanction because they are not discriminatory, or at least are not unfairly so. Some, however, are. A notable example concerns the Fiji Holdings Limited, as described below.

An interesting example is the provision of rural health services. The government stated that Fijians are prepared to work in rural areas, while Indo-Fijians and expatriates are less inclined. But doctors who work in rural areas have less access to good equipment, and thus their professional experience and prospects tend to be reduced. The government has suggested that the disparity be dealt with on a non-affirmative action basis, including incentives and requirements about spending time in rural areas,[107] which would thus not infringe section 38. Already there is a predominance of ethnic Fijians in the health services. The government plans to increase the proportion because it anticipates that emigration will continue (an example of self-fulfilling prophecy). This would not be permissible as an affirmative action programme in the public employment context, because there is no under-representation of Fijians; indeed there ought to be affirmative action for Indo-Fijians).

## The Record of Affirmative Action

For decades successive governments have sought to close what they have perceived to be the gap between the two main groups. These efforts have been on the whole unsuccessful. It was possible to change the ethnic balance of the public service, quite dramatically as we have seen, partly as a result of emigration and partly as the result of recruiting policies. But success in education and business is less easily achievable. A scheme in the 1970s designed to increase sugar cane cultivation which favoured Fijians (448 farmers) over Indo-Fijians (339) was regarded as a success. Yet only 30 per cent of Fijian farmers met their repayment obligations, as opposed to 97.6 per cent of Indo-Fijian farmers.[108] It was possible to make the entire Fijian community in a sense capitalists by the creation of the Fijian Holdings Limited:

> Its shareholders include Provincial Councils, the Native Land Trust Board, the Fijian Affairs Board, Tikina and village groups, Fijian co-operatives, individual Fijians and family companies. Its investments give Fijians significant shareholding in major companies thus helping to achieve the national objective of bringing indigenous Fijians fully into the mainstream of the country's economic life.[109]

This may create capitalists, although through the quasi-feudal mechanisms of Fijian institutions, and through money raised by traditional means, but it does not create entrepreneurs; nor do schemes that set Fijians up in business and then abandoned them without proper training or support, in a setting where competition was fierce.[110] A recent Asian Development Bank report has suggested that even systems of concessionary loans and reserving of licences for tuna fishing to Fijians have a low success rate and that the problem is not so much lack of capital but the necessary 'blend of fishing skills and high level business skills'[111] – a suggestive comment since 'must have the necessary skills and experience in the relevant fishing industry activity' is a criterion for this scheme under the Social Justice Act.[112] It also suggests that some schemes are having a deleterious impact on the overall performance of the sector.

The constitutional requirements of clear criteria and standards ought to improve standards of administration. But corruption and ineptitude have characterised many of the affirmative action programmes that have operated in Fiji. Some of the worst examples involved grant and loan schemes that have perhaps offered temptations that other types of administrative actions do not. Favourable loans, especially to prominent Fijians, coupled with precipitate Fijianisation of the management, were a major cause of the near collapse of the National Bank of Fiji.[113] The Auditor General of Fiji commented in reports on various affirmative action programmes: 'Generally, the investigation revealed that there was no system of authorisation, lack of forecasting and planning, poor channel of communication and co-ordination and no means of performance monitoring and control.'[114] Also, the Auditor General observed: 'It did not really benefit the eligible farmers but favours prominent indigenous Fijians in the community.'[115]

Somewhat similarly, university failure and dropout rates remain higher among Fijians than other groups, which suggests that scholarship schemes for Fijian students have not guaranteed the level of motivation, parental support and study skills necessary to succeed at university. The government has commented that the monitoring of programmes by agencies has not been satisfactory, with the result that it is difficult to judge how successful programmes have been. Speaking of the '50:50 by 2020' plan, the government has commented that '[t]here is an urgent need for an effective monitoring mechanism to be established so that beneficiaries of the Plan are well targeted and its goals achieved.'[116] However, as we have suggested, often targets and measures are so vague that drawing conclusions that they have been achieved would be difficult in any case.

## Concluding Thoughts

We do not oppose the use of affirmative action in appropriate circumstances, including programmes for the benefit of specific ethnic communities in Fiji. Nonetheless, the conceptualisation and implementation of affirmative action programmes in Fiji have largely been faulty and ineffective.

The core of the problem lies in the whole dilemma of the purpose of affirmative action. This dilemma is at the heart of Fijian society: can Fijian values, society and tradition (or perhaps a parody of tradition) be preserved, and how far is this compatible with the market, globalisation and individualism? The dilemma would be there even if there were no *vulagi*[117] communities. The Fijian chiefly, military, political, and now economic elites have tried to maintain their privileges and the subjection of the masses in Fijian society. Some of the policies of affirmative action serve to bolster that increasingly irrelevant societal structure, yet at the same time that structure itself adds to the problems of poverty within the Fijian community – which gives rise to more calls for affirmative action. Affirmative action for identity and affirmative action for equality in Fiji are tugging largely in opposite directions.

The existence of the Indo-Fijian community provides a scapegoat and an excuse, for individuals and for the government. The realities of the community are misconceived – indeed misrepresented – to justify extensive affirmative action programmes. Problems are not properly confronted because of the myths surrounding the positions of both communities. Issues that ought to be confronted as ones of personal responsibility, of economic development and general policy become transformed into issues of ethnicity, and government largesse.

The Reeves Commission wanted to downplay ethnicity in the Constitution; politicians kept more of this than the Commission would have wanted (especially in the political structure). As long as ethnicity is the dominant discourse, fundamental problems will be skirted, while resentment on both sides is stoked. Indo-Fijians will continue to emigrate and aspects of the economy and services will continue to decline (and now Fijians are migrating in increasing numbers, too).

The drafting of the affirmative action provisions has not helped. Some of this can be laid at the door of the Commission; but some at that of the politicians (removing the 'reasonable and necessary' requirement). A Fijian-dominated government has been able to pass through a Fijian-dominated Parliament legislation that cannot be scrutinised by the courts in the manner of the courts in the United States and South Africa, so there is no gradual accumulation of principles or check on whether the programmes are grounded in sound evidence and have any real chance of success.[118]

The efforts of the government in terms of legislation are unimpressive. One has only to look at the South African Employment Equity Act, for example, to see how complex an affirmative action programme, balancing all the issues of justice and effectiveness, may be. To some extent this is the result of the rush imposed by the Constitution: the original Social Justice Act was hastily drafted to deal with the expiry of existing programmes and its successor is essentially the same. In other words, the government has simply not taken the constitutional requirements seriously enough.

The Commission wanted change. Nonetheless, it has not indicated how, but only that some sort of ethnic preference would be permissible, or even necessary, and yet gave little indication as to what would be acceptable. The end result was that it was all too easy for government to continue its old, tired – and mostly failed – policies without any fundamental change. The circumstances of the Fijian community were described recently by Mahendra Chaudhry, ethnic Indo-Fijian Prime Minister of Fiji removed from power in the 2000 coup:[119]

It is well known, Sir, that:

(a) 13,000 Fijian families line up each month for the State's family assistance allowance;
(b) Fijians make up the majority of the 90,000 people, who exist in overcrowded squatter settlements along the Suva/Nausori corridor;
(c) there is an alarming increase in the death rate of Fijian babies when the infant mortality rate for other races show a marked decline;
(d) Fijian youths constitute the majority of the prison population; and
(e) the educational achievements of Fijian students are way below that of other races.

This requirement of affirmative action gives legitimacy to the government's tendency to turn policymaking on its head. An affirmative action programme should be one driven by the realisation that in order to achieve certain social goals some temporary distortion of equality principles is necessary – and this is what the Commission sought to achieve. Instead of focusing on what is needed to achieve a result, the focus has so far tended to be 'what can we do to show we are providing affirmative action?' – especially for Fijians. Programmes that are not in fact discriminatory are labelled 'affirmative action' for political reasons. There is, for example, no need to trumpet giving more resources to under-resourced rural schools as affirmative action (and thus somehow detrimental to Indo-Fijians) – it is simple fairness. The obsession with affirmative action has the tendency to distort many aspects of government policy and national debate. Who has the land has more attention than what the land is used for.

Possibly a better approach would have been to introduce a fuller range of economic, social and cultural rights (rather than education alone). As in the South African Constitution, this could have built in the notion of providing access progressively, to the maximum of available resources (there being no such moderating provisions in the Fijian Constitution). The neediest can be – should be – given priority (not affirmative action),[120] which could *then* be aided with affirmative action as provided for in the 1990 Constitution, with the possibility of judicial scrutiny.

While this paper was being written Fiji had another general election. The same party returned to power, but, unlike the two previous general elections held under the Constitution, this time the government complied, albeit half-heartedly, with the constitutional requirement that it offer cabinet positions proportional to seats in the House of Representatives and to other major parties. A slightly more conciliatory tone is detectable, perhaps in consequence of these changes, and the President's Speech at the opening of Parliament included the following passage:

Affirmative Action is integral to the Government's drive to achieve social justice and greater equality of economic and social development opportunities. Assistance under this programme will continue to apply to the needy and disadvantaged of all communities.

Government will conduct a comprehensive review of the Social Justice Act and the affirmative action policies and programmes which have been implemented under it. This is to ensure that they conform with the requirements of the Constitution.[121]

The government has also indicated that there may be some review of the constitutional provisions.[122]

## Addendum

The reader will naturally wonder whether the coup of December 2006 affects the issues discussed in this paper. The full implications are as yet unclear. The military have appointed a government which includes members of both communities, including former Prime Minister Mahendra Chaudhry, and it insists that it is committed to protection of human rights and eradication of corruption. The ostensible motivation for the coup did include at least one affirmative action element, namely the indigenous fisheries rights Bill 'Qoliqoli Bill', criticised as being racist. And recently the new government has suspended the affirmative action programme in education for Fijian students because it is 'racially discriminatory, in breach of the constitution and unfair to other indigenous Fijian students who attend schools managed by other communities but who do not have access to these benefits'.[123]

## Acknowledgements

The Authors were active in the process that led to Fiji's 1997 Constitution. They also advised the government of Fiji in 2000 on the implementation of affirmative action policies. Yash Ghai's research has been supported by the Distinguished Researcher Award of the University of Hong Kong.

## Notes

1. Article 153(2) of the Constitution of Malaysia provides that 'the [government] shall exercise [its] functions under this Constitution and federal law in such manner as may be necessary to safeguard the special provision of the Malays and natives of any of the States of Sabah and Sarawak and to ensure the reservation for Malays and natives of any of the States of Sabah and Sarawak of such proportion as he may deem reasonable of positions in the public service . . . and of scholarships, exhibitions and other similar educational or training privileges or special facilities given or accorded by the Federal Government and, when any permit or licence for the operation of any trade or business is required by federal law, then, subject to the provisions of that law and this Article, of such permits and licences'.
2. Article 15(2) and 16(4) permit respectively 'special provision for women and children' and 'reservation of appointments or posts in favour of any backward class of citizens which, in the opinion of the State, is not adequately represented in the services under the State'. More positive obligations are imposed on the state by article 46 which requires it to 'promote with special care the educational and economic interests of the weaker sections of the people, and, in particular, of the Scheduled Castes and Scheduled Tribes' and to 'protect them from social injustice and all forms of exploitation'. A fixed proportion of seats are, in general, reserved for these two groups in the national (Art. 330) and state legislatures (Art. 332) in proportion to their presence of the population (articles 325, 330–34).

3. In the United States affirmative action was introduced by an Executive Order of the President, although today its primary basis is statutory; for example, the Small Business Act requires that contracting with small companies be given publicity – this is to encourage others to emulate the government.
4. Well-known American examples include the *Bakke* case (*Regents of the University of California v. Bakke* 438 US 265 (1978), and the more recent cases of *Gratz v. Bollinger* 539 US 244 (2003) and *Grutter v. Bollinger* 539 US 306 (2003). See Marc Galanter's aptly entitled study of Indian provisions and experience of affirmative action, *Competing Equalities: Law and the Backward Classes in India* (Berkeley, CA: University of California Press 1984).
5. As Galanter (ibid. p.28) writes: 'Untouchability (and the excesses of caste hierarchy) presented a problem whose solution was required to unlock India's national destiny.'
6. There is now an enormous literature on this, sparked off in part by the writings of Charles Taylor, including 'The Politics of Recognition', in Amy Gutmann (ed.), *Multiculturalism and the Politics of Recognition* (Princeton, NJ: Princeton University Press 1991), and Will Kymlicka, including *Liberalism, Community and Culture* (Oxford: Clarendon Press 1989), and by the political campaigns and struggles of indigenous peoples and ethnic communities.
7. Nancy Fraser, 'Rethinking Recognition: Overcoming Displacement and Reification in Cultural Politics', *New Left Review*, Vol.3 (2000), p.107.
8. Iris Young, 'Unruly Categories: A Critique of Nancy Fraser's Dual Systems Theory', *New Left Review*, Vol.222 (1997), pp.147, 159.
9. See Kymlicka (note 6).
10. Canada (other than for aboriginal and francophone communities) and Australia follow this approach. In Australia the Public Service Act 1999 (Commonwealth) provides that a public agency head must establish a workplace diversity programme to assist in giving effect to the Australian Public Service (APS) Values, which include employment decisions based on merit; freedom from discrimination; and recognising and utilising the diversity of the Australian community which it serves; promoting equity in employment; and providing a reasonable opportunity to all eligible members of the community to apply for APS employment. In Canada, the Employment Equity Act provides for the benefit of members of the First Nations (aboriginal peoples); women; visible minorities; and persons with disabilities. Governmental departments and agencies must determine the representation of the four designated groups in their organisation and compare the results with the availability of these groups in the Canadian workforce. Where under-representation is found, a review of employment systems, policies and practices must be conducted to identify potential barriers. A plan, developed in consultation with unions and employees, then representatives, must be prepared that will ensure reasonable progress in attaining a fair degree of representation of the designated groups in each occupational category.
11. In India, the Persons with Disabilities (Equal Opportunities, Protection of Rights and Full Participation) Act 1996 requires government at all levels to institute schemes for allocation of land at preferential rates for housing for people with disabilities. It also provides for them free education up to the age of 18; special schools; part-time classes if necessary; special transport; restructuring of curricula; scholarships; and removal of architectural barriers. India also provides quotas for the 'scheduled tribes', 'scheduled castes', and 'other backward classes', under which members of these classes can enter institutions of higher education with lower examination grades. Malaysia has a quota system under which admissions to places for Indian and Chinese Malaysians in national educational institutions are restricted in order to benefit Malays.
12. At least this was the colonial orthodox view. For our present purposes, it is sufficient to note that this view prevailed, with far-reaching consequences both internally within the indigenous communities and their relations with others. See Peter France, 'The Founding of an Orthodoxy: Sir Arthur Gordon and the Doctrine of the Fijian Way of Life', *Journal of the Polynesian Society*, Vol.77, No.1 (1968), pp.6–32; Peter France, *The Charter of the Land: Custom and Colonisation in Fiji* (Melbourne: Oxford University Press 1969).
13. See Brij Lal, *Broken Waves: A History of the Fiji Islands in the Twentieth Century* Honolulu: University of Hawaii 1992), for an outstanding study of Fiji's history.
14. The negative impacts of this sort of policy are stressed by Carmen M. White, 'Affirmative Action and Education in Fiji: Legitimation, Contestation and Colonial Discourse', *Harvard Educational Review*, Vol.71, No.2 (2001), p.240, citing A. F. Mamak, 'Pluralism and Social Change in Suva City, Fiji' (unpublished PhD dissertation, University of Hawaii 1974).
15. For further details see Jill Cottrell and Yash Ghai, 'Constitution Making in Fiji: Context and Process' (Stockholm, International Institute of Democracy and Electoral Assistance 2004), http://www.idea.int/conflict/cbp/upload/CBP-Fiji.pdf (accessed 5 October 2006).

16. The Great Council of Chiefs (GCC – often now known by its Fijian name of Bose Levu Vakataraga or BLV) was something of a colonial creation.
17. Reeves *et al.* (hereafter 'Reeves'), 'Towards a United Future: Report of the Fiji Constitution Review Commission', Parliamentary Paper No.34 of 1996 (Suva: Parliament of Fiji 1996).
18. From the United Nations Development Programme (UNDP), *Fiji Poverty Study*, http://www.undp.org.fj/HTMLper cent20docs/Povertyper cent20Reduction.htm (accessed 5 October 2006).
19. See for example Vincent D. Nomae *et al.*, *Poverty Amongst Minority Melanesians In Fiji: A Case Study of Six Settlements in Suva*, http://www.usp.ac.fj/fileadmin/files/schools/ssed/economics/working_papers/2004/wp2004_15.pdf (accessed 5 October 2006).
20. Kalivati Bakani, General Manager of the Native Land Trust Board, in *What are Good Land Policies for Fiji in the 21st Century? National Land Workshop Report* (Suva: Citizens' Constitutional Forum 2002), p.10.
21. Steven Ratuva, 'Anatomizing the Vanua Complex: Intra-Communal Land Disputes and Implications on the Fijian Community', paper presented at conference on South Pacific Land Tenure Conflict Symposium, University of the South Pacific, Suva, Fiji, 2 April 2002, http://www.usp.ac.fj/fileadmin/files/Institutes/piasdg/governance_papers/ratuva_vanua.pdf (accessed 5 October 2006). Ratuva cites for the figures J. Kamikamican and T. Davey, 'Trust on Trial: The Development of the Customary Land Trust Concept in Fiji', in Y. Ghai (ed.), *Law, Government and Politics in the Pacific Island States* (Suva, Fiji: Institute of Pacific Studies 1988), p.289, though there the figures are slightly different.
22. Ratuva (note 21).
23. Ministry of Finance and National Planning, *20-year Development Plan (2001–2020) for the Enhancement of Participation of the Indigenous Fijians and Rotumans in the Socio-Economic Development of Fiji*, Parliamentary Paper No.73 of 2002, para.2.3.6.
24. Ibid. para.8.69.
25. Bakani (note 20) p.90.
26. Government policies to return government-held land to Fijian communities has raised this figure from about 83 per cent in recent years.
27. These points came out in the *Land Workshop Report*, (note 21).
28. Between 1997 and 2001 only 27.6 per cent of the expired leases were renewed. Of these 20.1 per cent were sugarcane leases, 4.3 per cent were other leases including other agricultural crops and commercial leases, and 3.2 per cent were residential leases. About 45 per cent of the land of which leases had expired has been given to new tenants and about 30 per cent has not been allocated.
29. Ministry of Finance and National Planning (note 23) section 2.8 Table 2.5.
30. Ibid. Table 2.6.
31. Mahendra Reddy and Biman C. Prasad, 'Affirmative Action Policies and Poverty Alleviation in Fiji: An Examination of Post-Coup Policies and Programmes', *Development Bulletin No. 60* (2002), http://devnet.anu.edu.au/db60pdfs.php (accessed 5 October 2006).
32. Personal information.
33. 30 June 1997, p.567 (in the debate on the Constitution, Parliament of Fiji, Parliamentary Debates, House of Representatives).
34. See Solrun Williksen-Bakker, 'Fijian Business – A Bone of Contention: Was it One of the Factors Leading to the Political Crisis of 2000?', *Australian Journal of Anthropology*, Vol.13 (2002), p.72.
35. This point is made by the government itself: Ministry of Finance and National Planning (note 23) para.2.3.9.
36. Ibid.
37. See Abdul Hassan, 'A Preliminary Study on the Supply of Low Cost Housing in Fiji', Pacific Rim Real Estate Conference, University of Melbourne, January 2005, http://www.prres.net/index.htm?http://www.prres.net/Proceedings/2005proceedings.asp (accessed 5 October 2006).
38. Ibid.
39. S. Ratuva, 'Ethnic Politics, Communalism and Affirmative Action in Fiji: A Critical and Comparative Study' (PhD Dissertation, University of Sussex 1999) ch. 6.
40. Helen Tavola, *Secondary Education in Fiji: A Key to the Future* (Suva, Fiji: Institute of Pacific Studies 1991), p.113.
41. Ibid. p.116.
42. Professor Tupeni Baba, a professor of education at the University of the South Pacific (and later Minister of Education in the short-lived government elected in 2000), made observations on these lines at a meeting of the Citizens' Constitutional Forum on Multiculturalism: *Educating for Multiculturalism* (Suva: CCF 1998), p.71.

43. Tavola (note 40) p.118.
44. Pratap Chand, Member of Parliament, stated that the per capita grant in aid to secondary schools has dropped by 50 per cent, and that secondary children have to pay an average of F$200 a year in levies, *Fiji Times* 17 November 2005.
45. From a study by the Fiji Teachers Association, reported by news agencies on 12 July 2006: e.g. *People's Daily*, http://english.people.com.cn/200607/12/eng20060712_282340.html (accessed 5 October 2006).
46. Tavola (note 40) p.158.
47. According to the governing party's (SDL) manifesto for the 2006 General Election.
48. Reported in *Fiji Times*, 1 December 2005.
49. The public service figures are taken from Asesela Ravuvu, *The Facade of Democracy: Fijian Struggle for Political Control* (Suva: Reader Publishing House 1991), p.77, attributed to the *Fiji Public Service Commission Report 1987*.
50. Taken from tables compiled in connection with the plans of the People's Coalition Government in 2000.
51. Fiji Human Rights Commission (FHRC), *Report on Government's Affirmative Action Programmes, 2020 Plan for Indigenous Fijians and Rotumans and the Blueprint* (Suva: FHRC 2006), http://www.humanrights.org.fj/pdf/AA_report.pdf (accessed 5 October 2006), p.64.
52. See R. Robertson and William Sutherland, *Government by the Gun: The Unfinished Business of Fiji's 2000 Coup* (Annandale, NSW and London: Pluto Press and Zed Press 2001).
53. Constitution 1990, Chapter III.
54. The submission stated that '[e]xperience elsewhere suggests that affirmative action can cause great resentment among those who are not its beneficiaries unless it is very clearly directed at the really disadvantaged groups. It also produces resentment if it is applied to cover most employment opportunities and other resources. Politically it is hard to resist the continual prolongation of affirmative action. In most instances the beneficiaries of affirmative action are the better off in the target communities, and its benefit eludes those most in need. Affirmative action often lends itself to corrupt practices, and there is inadequate accountability of implementation. It can lead to the lowering of efficiency in the delivery of services and the lowering of morale. Most international conventions which authorise or require affirmative action stipulate that it be used only for the disadvantaged groups and for only so long as is strictly necessary', National Federation Party and the Fiji Labour Party, *Towards Racial Harmony and National Unity* (August 1995), pp.52–3.
55. Ibid., note 17, Para.8.38.
56. Space constraints preclude more detailed discussion; see Jill Cottrell and Yash Ghai, 'Constitutional Engineering and Impact: The Case of Fiji', in Said Arjomand (ed.), *Constitutionalism and Political Reconstruction* (Brill, 2007 in press).
57. The Compact, beginning with: 'The people of the Fiji Islands recognise that, within the framework of this Constitution and the other laws of the State, the conduct of government is based on the following principles', is in section 6. Section 7 states that the Compact is non-justiciable but should be used in the interpretation of the Constitution or laws made under it.
58. The provision on the right of equality (section 38) exempts Fijian land law and customs from its application.
59. This formulation of paramountcy as a 'protective principle' is different from its interpretation as advanced by the then leading party of indigenous Fijians in its submission to the Reeves Commission as the basis of political domination (submission of SVT, *Respect and Understanding: Fijian Sovereignty, the Recipe for Peace, Stability and Progress* – excerpts are in Brij V. Lal, *Another Way: The Politics of Constitutional Reform in Post-Coup Fiji* (Canberra: National Centre for Development Studies/Asia Pacific Press 1998), pp.143–54.
60. FHRC, *Report* (note 51) p.62.
61. Winston Halapua, *Tradition, Lotu, and Militarism in Fiji* (Lautoka: Fiji Institute of Applied Studies 2003), p.154: 'poverty [among indigenous Fijians] was a direct consequence of the exploitation of the ordinary ethnic Fijians by the new ruling class which ethnic Fijians themselves brought to life. A new system of exploitation entrenched itself in Fiji after 1987. This system, which we call *turagaism* [traditional chiefly system] saw the emergence of a new ruling class which not only placed its own pecuniary and political interests ahead of the *vanua* [the community] or the ordinary people, but whose survival depended fundamentally on the exploitation of their own people.' Indeed the system was in place well before 1987 but the victory of the opposition groups in that year led to the 1990 constitution after the coup which formally entrenched the principal features of the system.
62. This little bombshell was introduced by the legal draftsmen; it does not appear in the Reeves Commission report. It caused something of a frenzy (people seemed to imagine Fiji becoming a haven

for gay matrimonials!) and a draft bill was prepared to remove this from the Constitution. This was forestalled, incidentally, by the 2000 coup, and has not yet been reintroduced. The criminal law on the books still discriminates in nineteenth century British fashion as two men found to their cost in 2005. They were convicted by a magistrate who had obviously never heard of gay rights, but appealed successfully, *Nadan v. The State* [2005] FJHC 1, http://www.paclii.org (accessed 5 October 2006), on the ground of the right to privacy.
63. Constitution 1997, s.38.
64. The use of this stipulation was recommended by the Reeves Commission (para.7.283).
65. This was not part of the Reeves recommendations, but is no doubt derived from the South African Constitution, as is the prohibition on indirect as well as direct discrimination.
66. See Cottrell and Ghai (note 56) for an account of the electoral system and the events in 1999.
67. Vijay Naidu, Kevin Barr, Robert Lee and Kesaia Seniloli, 'Fiji's Poverty Alleviation and Eradication Strategy Framework: Opening Doors to an Inclusive Society', Draft prepared for the United Nations Development Programme and Fiji's Ministry for National Planning, July 1999.
68. Yash Ghai, assisted by Jill Cottrell, was commissioned to prepare this report.
69. Fijians, often contrasted with *vulagi* or guests – meaning particularly in this context the Indo-Fijians.
70. For an account see Michael Field, Tupeni Baba and Unaisi Nabobo-Baba, *Speight of Violence: Inside Fiji's 2000 Coup* (Auckland: Reed 2005).
71. Notably Field *et al.*, ibid., do not mention affirmative action. At p.63 they note the achievements of the first six months of the Labour (or People's Coalition) government and that after that period Chaudhry's approval rating was 60 per cent.
72. A summary is available at 'Scoop' Independent News, 17 July 2000, http://www.scoop.co.nz/stories/WO0007/S00055.htm (accessed 5 October 2006).
73. Ibid., note 24.
74. From the Plan's 'vision and mission'.
75. A group of non-governmental organisations rightly commented that '[t]he State has attempted to prevent any challenge to nullify the social justice legislation by stating that the legislation effectively overrides the 1997 Constitution (section 8), a clear violation of Constitutional principles and the rule of law': *NGO Report on the Status of Women in the Republic of the Fiji Islands*, by the Fiji Women's Rights Movement, the Fiji Women's Crisis Centre, and the Ecumenical Centre for Research Education and Advocacy (2002), section B.1, available on the Ecumenical Centre for Research Education and Advocacy website, http://www.ecrea.org.fj/webpages/publications_files/Submissions/cerd.doc (accessed 5 October 2006).
76. State Party report CERD/C/429/Add.1, 15 November 2002, para.41.
77. *Concluding Observations of the Committee on the Elimination of Racial Discrimination: Fiji*. 02/06/2003. CERD/C/62/CO/3. See also Margot Salomon, 'Masking Inequality in the Name of Rights: The Examination of Fiji's State Report under the International Convention on the Elimination of Racial Discrimination', *Asia-Pacific Journal on Human Rights and the Law*, Vol.1 (2003), p.52.
78. *Committee on the Elimination of Discrimination against Women: Fiji. 07/05/2002. A/57/38 (Part I)*, paras.24–70, at para.48.
79. *Recommendations to the Commonwealth Ministerial Action Group on the Political and Human Rights Situation in the Fiji Islands*, compiled by Mitchell O'Brien (New Delhi: CHRI 2002).
80. See the collection of documents, including State Party report (note 76) in Ganesh Chand (ed.), *Papers on Racial Discrimination (Volume 1) The CERD Papers* (Lautoka: Fiji Institute of Applied Studies 2005), available on the institute's website at http://www.fijianstudies.org/fias_pord_vol1.htm (accessed 5 October 2006).
81. FHRC, *Report* (note 51).
82. Ibid. pp.69–90.
83. The definition is that proposed by the CRC; it seems to include the military.
84. Para.8.67. Of the omission, Counsel to the Commission, Alison Quentin-Baxter, commented that '[w]hile there is probably a certain logic in not laying an open-ended duty upon Parliament to make provision for social justice and affirmative action programmes, the provision does not have the effect intended by the Reeves Commission of requiring all affirmative action and social justice programmes to be specifically authorised by an Act conforming with the constitutional requirements', see 'Ethnic Accommodation in the Republic of the Fiji Islands' (prepared for the School of Law, University of Waikato 1999), http://www.undp.org.fj/elections/reports/index.htm (accessed 5 October 2006).

85. Perhaps it does make it easier for the government to take little note of the fact, as its own '50:50 by 2020' document states, that while maternal mortality rates declined among the Fijian community between 1997 and 1999, the rates increased within the Indo-Fijian community – see para.9.2.6.
86. Para.8.87.
87. Para.8.58.
88. *Republic of South Africa v. Grootboom* 2001 (1) SA 46, 68–9.
89. It must be recognised that the Fiji courts are not entirely lacking in creativity and even boldness. They, for example, held that the 2000 coup was illegal (*Republic of Fiji v. Chandrika Prasad*, Civil Appeal No. ABU0078/2000S, [2001] FJCA 2).
90. Para.8.55. It is not clear where the Reeves Commission's language went to: the Report of the Joint Parliamentary Select Committee (Parliamentary paper No.17 of 1997), on which the draft was based, stated (para.E2) that the 1990 Constitution provisions should be replaced as recommended by the Commission. The Commission language was defective as it seemed to assume that everyone was disadvantaged: 'Fijian and Rotuman people and other ethnic communities, and for women as well as men, and for all other disadvantaged citizens or groups of citizens.'
91. The references are to the Schedule of the Social Justice Act.
92. Social Justice Act 2001, Section 3.
93. Incidentally, this defines a word that does not otherwise appear in the Act at all. It can perhaps be laid at the door of the Fiji Human Rights Commission which had asked that these terms be defined by the Act when it commented on the draft Bill. However, an Act of Parliament may elaborate but cannot define words for the purposes of a Constitution.
94. Promotion of Equality and Prevention of Unfair Discrimination Act 4 of 2000 as amended in 2003, s.31(4), 'The Chief Justice must, in consultation with the Judicial Service Commission and the Magistrates Commission, develop the content of training courses with a view to building a dedicated and experienced pool of trained and specialised presiding officers, for purposes of presiding in court proceedings as contemplated in this Act, by providing (a) social context training for presiding officers.'
95. Ibid., note 17, para.8.77.
96. *Indra Sawhney v. Union of India* AIR, 1993 SC 447.
97. Here 'equitable access to' is used in relation to natural resources, 'access to' adequate housing, health care, food, water, social security, and 'effective access' to the right to education.
98. Ibid., note 17, paras.8.63–6.
99. *Grootboom* (note 90) p.67.
100. Section 7. Perhaps it would have been compliant with the Constitution to make it possible for a resolution of Parliament to amend the schedule. Apparently at present subsidiary legislation is not even tabled in Parliament: Reddy *et al.*, *Public Finance Management in Fiji: The Institutional Environment and the New Financial Management Bill* (Lautoka and Suva: Fiji Institute of Applied Studies 2004).
101. Based on government press release (15 December 2004), http://www.fiji.gov.fj/publish/page_3796.shtml (accessed 5 October 2006). We have not been able to read the text of the regulations.
102. Section 44(7).
103. 'A person' would include a private individual: so it would be permissible for government to require governments contractors to employ a certain percentage of Fijians and the contractors would not be guilty of discriminating – though in fact they would not be liable for this under the Constitution anyway.
104. Cf. the South African Employment Equity Act: 'However, having regard to the fact that the Act requires an employer to take measures to eliminate discrimination in the workplace it also serves as a sword.' *Harmse v. City of Cape Town* (2003) 24 I.L.J. 1130, 1141–42, Labour Court per Waglay J. See Saras Jagwanth, 'Affirmative Action in a Transformative Context: The South African Experience', *Connecticut Law Review*, Vol.36 (2004), p.725.
105. The more so as section 3 provides that 'developments in the understanding of ... human rights' are to be taken into account in interpreting the Constitution.
106. See http://www.polity.org.za/govdocs/white_papers/pst&e.html (accessed 5 October 2006).
107. Ibid., note 17, para.9.5.3.
108. This extrapolates from the Government's own figures, and assumes that all the 802 farmers in the scheme were included in the information given – see '50:50 by 2020', paras.2.5.1–2.
109. See http://www.fijianholdings.com.fj (accessed 5 October 2006).
110. As with the Equity Investment Management Company in the 1990s, see Ratuva, thesis (note 38) ch.7.

111. ADB report by Tony Hand et al., Technical Assistance Consultant's Report, *Republic of the Fiji Islands: Fisheries Sector Review* (June 2005), para.104.
112. Schedule to Act, Programme 17.
113. Ratuva (note 21) ch.7.
114. *Special Report of The Auditor General of The Republic of The Fiji Islands – February 2002*, 0020 Ministry of Agriculture: Affirmative Action Plan Parliamentary Paper No 11 of 2002, available on the website of the Office of the Auditor General www.oag.gov.fj (accessed 5 October 2006), p.2. See also Report for 2004, *Volume 5 Infrastructure* (Parliamentary Paper No. 113 of 2005): 'The Social Justice Regulations [have] been misinterpreted by some Ministries and are not following the specific requirements of the social justice regulation and procedures on procurements' (Part 3, p.3)
115. 2002 Report, *Volume 4 Audit Report on the Economic Services Sector* (Parliamentary Paper No.91 of 2003), para.37.2.
116. *Draft Strategic Plan for 2007–11* (released in September 2006), http://www.fiji.gov.fj/uploads/Draft_SDP_2007_11.pdf (accessed 5 October 2006), p.9.
117. See above note 69.
118. There is of course a huge literature on this. Pretorius, 'Constitutional Standards for Affirmative Action in South Africa: A Comparative Overview', *Zeitschrift für ausländisches öffentliches Recht und Völkerrecht*, Vol.61 (2001), pp.403–57, discusses cases from the US and Canada as well as South Africa.
119. Responding to the President's Speech on the opening of Parliament, 8 June 2006 (Hansard), http://www.parliament.gov.fj/hansard/index.aspx (accessed 6 October 2006). A Minister quoted this with approval.
120. As is clear from the *Grootboom* case above.
121. 6 June 2006; most readily available as 'HE's Address 2006.doc', http://www.fiji.gov.fj/uploads/ (accessed 5 October 2006). Incidentally, the undertaking is repeated in the *Draft Strategic Plan for 2007-11* (note 118). The Plan (p.9) stated that '[s]ome of the issues raised in the [Fiji Human Rights Commission] report would be addressed in a comprehensive review to be undertaken by Government on all its affirmative action policies and programmes. A Cabinet Sub-Committee on Equal Opportunities and Human Rights has been established to oversee the review process that will involve wide consultations throughout the country.' This despite the fact that the Prime Minister's response to the Commission report was virulent: 'the Commission has handled this entire question very badly and brought its credibility into doubt'. Media Briefing 30 June 2006, http://www.fiji.gov.fj/publish/page_6976.shtml (accessed 5 October 2006).
122. *Draft Strategic Plan* (note 116), p.70.
123. Citizens Constitutional Forum, Coup Update 16, received 9 February 2007.

# Notes on Contributors

**Wei Bu** is Professor of Communication and Media Studies at the Institute of Journalism and Communication at the Chinese Academy of Social Sciences in Beijing. She has conducted research on Internet usage and the digital divide in China, the media rights of children, gender and the media, and empowerment through communication and has published widely in Chinese. In English she has recently published 'Women and the Internet in China', in *Promises of Empowerment: Women in Asia and Latin America* edited by P. H. Smith, S. L. Troutner and C. Hünefeldt (Rowman & Littlefield, 2004), and 'Looking for "the Insider's Perspective": Human Trafficking in Sichuan', in *Doing Fieldwork in China* edited by M. Heimer and S. Thøgersen (NIAS Press, 2006).

**Phil C. W. Chan** is currently Visiting Scholar/Visiting Professor at the Faculty of Law, Common Law Section, University of Ottawa, and Visiting Scholar at the Asian Institute, Munk Centre for International Studies, University of Toronto. Since graduating from the University of Hong Kong with his LL.B. and Rowdget W. Young Medal in Law in 2002 at the age of 19 and from the University of Durham with his LL.M. in 2004, he has been pursuing independent academic research and has authored over 20 articles on human rights, international law and affairs, constitutional law, and copyright published or forthcoming in various refereed international journals. In addition to this Special Double Issue, he is Guest Editor of the *Journal*'s forthcoming Special Double Issue on *Protection of Sexual Minorities since Stonewall: Progress and Stalemate in Developed and Developing Countries* (Vol.12 Nos.3/4 hardback by Routledge with Foreword by Archbishop Desmond Tutu). He is a Member of the Editorial Boards of this *Journal* and the *Journal of Homosexuality*, and *Sexuality & Culture*. Previously he has served as Researcher at energy law practice Baker Botts and has held visiting positions at the British Institute of International and Comparative Law, Keele University School of Law (Gender, Sexuality and Law Research Group), the Lauterpacht Research Centre for International Law at the University of Cambridge, the Asia-Pacific College of Diplomacy at the Australian National University, and the Institute of Chinese Studies at the University of Heidelberg. He is currently working on the psychosocial and legal implications of school bullying. His book fee for the book version of this Special Double Issue has been donated to the UNICEF Tsunami Fund.

**Jill Cottrell** was Senior Lecturer in Law at the University of Hong Kong until 2003 where she continued to teach on a part-time basis until 2006. Previously she had taught in Nigeria and England. Now she is mainly involved in writing and consultancy work on constitutional issues. With Yash Ghai she has written on constitutional issues in Fiji, including a paper on the constitution-making process (in press by the United States Institute of Peace), one for the International Institute for Democracy and Electoral Assistance in

Stockholm, and 'Constitutional Engineering and Impact: The Case of Fiji', in *Constitutionalism and Political Reconstruction* edited by S. Arjomand (in press by Brill).

**Yash Ghai** held until recently the Sir Y. K. Pao Chair of Public Law at the University of Hong Kong, where he is currently Honorary Professor of Law, and is now engaged in consultancy work on constitutional issues in various countries as well as in research on constitutions and ethnicity. He advised the opposition parties in Fiji during the country's constitution-making process. He was also Chairman of the Constitution of Kenya Review Commission between 2000 and 2004 and is currently the United Nations Secretary-General's Special Representative for human rights in Cambodia. His publications cover constitutions, ethnic relations, human rights, and sociology of law. His books include *Public Law and Political Change in Kenya* (with J.P.W.B. McAuslan) (Oxford University Press, 1970; reprinted with introduction by Y. Ghai in 2001); *Hong Kong's New Constitutional Order: The Resumption of Chinese Sovereignty and Basic Law* (Hong Kong University Press, 1997; 2nd ed. 1998; 3rd ed. in preparation), and *Autonomy and Ethnicity: Negotiating Competing Claims in Multi-Ethnic States* (as editor and contributor) (Cambridge University Press, 2000). He is a Fellow of the British Academy.

**Clare Hemmings** is Senior Lecturer in Gender Studies at the London School of Economics and Political Science, where she teaches interdisciplinary feminist and sexuality studies. She has published *Bisexual Spaces: A Geography of Sexuality and Gender* (Routledge, 2002) and is currently working on the importance of feminist historiography for intervening in global gendered discourse. She is a member of the *Feminist Review* collective.

**Cecilia Milwertz** is Senior Researcher at the Nordic Institute of Asian Studies in Copenhagen. She is engaged in research on non-governmental organising to address gender equality issues in China. She has authored *Beijing Women Organizing for Change – A New Wave of the Chinese Women's Movement* (NIAS Press, 2002) and co-edited *Chinese Women Organizing – Cadres, Feminists, Muslims, Queers* (Berg, 2001) and *Gender Politics in Asia – Processes of Change and Empowerment* (NIAS Press, 2005).

**Michael Palmer** is Professor of Law, Chair of the Centre of East Asian Law and Associate Dean for Research at the Faculty of Law and Social Sciences at the School of Oriental and African Studies, University of London, and is a barrister of Lincoln's Inn. He is Member of the Editorial Board of the *Journal* and Associate Member of the International Academy of Comparative Law. He is co-author (with S. Roberts) of the leading text in Europe on alternative dispute resolution: *Dispute Processes: ADR and the Primary Forms of Decision Making* (Cambridge University Press, 2nd ed. 2005; 3rd ed. in preparation). He has published widely in the area of Chinese law and his recent and forthcoming publications include 'Patriarchy, Privacy and Protection: Slowly Conceptualising Domestic Violence in Chinese Law', in N. Iu. Erpyleva, M. E. Gashi-Butler, and J. E. Henderson (eds), *Forging a Common Legal Destiny: Liber Amicorum in Honour of William E. Butler* (Wildy, Simmonds & Hill, 2005); 'The Emergence of Consumer Rights: Consumer Protection Law in the People's Republic of China', in S. Thompson, K. Latham, and J. Klein (eds), *Consuming China* (Routledge-Curzon, 2006); 'Towards a Greener China? Accessing Environmental Justice in the People's Republic of China', in A. J. Harding (ed.), *Access to Environmental Justice* (Leiden University Press, 2007); and 'Mediation in China's Practice of Administrative Litigation', in *Transnational Law & Contemporary Problems* Special Issue on *China: Law, Finance and Security* (2007, ed. L. Backer).

**Hyunjoon Park** is Korea Foundation Assistant Professor of Sociology at the University of Pennsylvania. His research interests include social stratification, education, health, and transition to adulthood in Korea and other Asian countries. His recent publications include 'Educational Expansion and Inequality in Korea' (*Research in Sociology of Education*, 2004); 'Age and Self-Rated Health in Korea' (*Social Forces*, 2005); and 'Transition to Adulthood in Japan and Korea: An Overview' (*Sociological Studies of Children and Youth*, 2005). Currently he is investigating the consequences of recent demographic changes on children's well-being in Korea and other Asian countries.

**Paul Rishworth** is Dean and Professor of Law at the University of Auckland. His research interests are in constitutional law, particularly in the fields of judicial review and human rights. He is co-author of *The New Zealand Bill of Rights* (Oxford University Press, 2002).

**Kristen Walker** is Associate Professor of Law at the University of Melbourne. She teaches and researches Australian constitutional law, international law, and law and sexuality. She is also a practising barrister at the Victorian Bar, specialising in public law.

# Index

Numbers in *italics* represent tables.

abortion issues in China 163–164
Adams, Vincanne 13
affirmative action 5, 218–242
Afrikaans language 202–203
Aggleton, Peter 20–21
AIDS 17, 20, 33, 44, 51, 87, 94
Albania 203
Altman, Denis 13, 21
America *see* United States
Anglican Church (NZ) 85
Asian Development Bank 239
Assiter, Alison 136–137
Australia 3: affirmative action 219; Australian Marriage Equality 105; churches 111; civil unions 114, 120; constitutional aspects of marriage 107–116; decriminalisation of homosexuality 84; educational statistics 180; High Court 108; Marriage Act (1961) 104, 105, 106, 113–114, 116; Marriage Amendment Act (2004) 107; legal benefits of marriage 105–106; negative aspects of same-sex marriage 117–119; originalism in constitutional interpretation 108–111; political debate over same-sex marriage 116–117; recognition of foreign marriages 106–107; registration of same-sex relationships 115–116; same-sex marriage 33, 63, 104–120; state legislation 113–116
Australian Capital Territory (ACT) 105: Civil Unions Act (2006) 120; Civil Partnerships Bill (2006) 120

Bainham, Andrew 56
Bala, Nicholas 64
Balfour, David 81–83, 98
Ball, Carlos A. 51
Barlow, Tani 127

Barnard, Ian 16, 17
Belgium 30, 38–39, 107
Bhutan 6
biblical views on homosexuality 2, 55, 58–59, 60
bilingualism in the courtroom 5, 191–212
blackmail 31, 37
Binnie, Jon 17
bisexuality 1–2, 16–22: as a neutral practice 20–22; attitudes towards 9–11; erasure of 17–20
Boyce, Paul 14, 15, 19
Brazil 21
Breton language 205
Britain *see* United Kingdom
Bromwich, Rebecca Jaremko 64
Buddhists 6
Buergenthal, Thomas 64
Bush, George W. 30, 55, 61, 62
Bush, Jeb 61
Butler, Judith 10, 15, 16

Canada 2, 5: affirmative action 219; Charter of Rights and Freedoms 34, 88, 89, 201–202, 208, 227; educational statistics 174, 176; language issues 192ff.; same-sex marriage 30, 31, 46, 48, 53, 54, 56, 58, 92, 105, 107; Supreme Court 34, 38, 39, 46, 48, 50, 53, 56ff., 194ff.
Cantonese: status in Hong Kong 5, 192–209
Cantú, Lionel, Jr 14
Capotorti, Francesco 198
Castellino, Joshua 200, 203
censorship issues (New Zealand) 94–96
Chan-Tiberghien, Jennifer 128
Chao, Y. Antonia 17
Chau, L. C. 40
Chaudhry, Mahenda 231, 241, 242
Chiang, Mark 13–14

254  Index

China 4, 6, 14, 20, 35, 126–166, 186: abortion issues 163–164; All-China Women's Federation 126, 129, 130ff, 146, 150, 155, 163, 165; Beijing–Tianjin Facilitators Team on Gender and Development 138; Boxer Rebellion (1899–1901) 44, 148; *China Women's News* 129, 131, 134; Civil Code (1931) 148; Civil Law (1985) 155; Communist Party 126, 148, 164; Constitution (1982) 147, 159; Criminal Law (1979/1997) 147, 155, 156; Cultural Revolution (1966–1976) 164; domestic violence 128–135, 160–161; Domestic Violence Network 128–129, 138, 139; education for women 151–152; employment rights for women 153; family laws 157–164; family planning 161–164; financial position of women 159; gender equality 126–141, 151; General Principles of Civil Law (1986) 159; Inheritance Law (1985) 152; Labour Law (1994) 146; Law for the Protection of the Health of Women and Children (1994) 161, 162; Law for the Protection of Women's Rights and Interests (1992) 149ff, 160, 162; Legal Advice Centre 129, 133; Maple Women's Psychological Counselling Centre 129, 138, 139; Marriage Law (1950/1980) 146, 159; Marriage Law (2001) 130, 138, 139, 147, 155ff.; National People's Congress 137, 138, 163, 164; People's Political Consultative Conference (1993) 138; personal rights of women 154–156, 160; political representation of women 164–165; Population and Birth Planning Law (2001) 161–164; property rights of women 152–153, 159–160; re-education towards gender equality 135–141; *Rural Women* magazine 129, 131, 133; Sex/Gender Education Forum 130; sex-selective abortion 163–164; status of Hong Kong 191–192, 194; Supreme People's Court 156; Tiananmen Massacre 35; Villagers' Committees 164; Women's Centre for Law Studies and Legal Services 129, 133; Women's Hotline 131, 132, 134; Women's Media Watch Network 129, 133; Women's Protection Law (2005) 4, 145–166; Women's Research Institute 129, 131; women's rights 145–166; World Women's Conference (1995) 126, 127, 130ff, 140, 164; *see also* Hong Kong
Chinese cultural attitudes 42–43
Chinese language: status in Hong Kong 5, 192–209
Christianity 2, 43–44, 56–57, 58–59, 60, 95, 221
civil unions/partnerships 3, 53, 90, 120: registration of same-sex relationships 115–116; *see also* same-sex marriage
Clarke, Desmond M. 57
colonialism: and attitudes to sexuality 2, 5, 11, 41, 43–44; and the English language 212
common law tradition 211
Commonwealth Human Rights Commission 231
Confucianism 2, 42, 43, 45, 134, 146
Costa Rica 21
Czech Republic 176, 181

DeLay, Tom 61
demographic change and education (South Korea) 184–186
Denmark 176
Desai, Manisha 127
divorce rates 184–185
domestic violence in China 4, 128–135: raising awareness 137–139
Dunne, Gillian 19
Dworkin, Ronald 46, 50

educational inequality: China 151–152; South Korea 4–5, 172–188
English language: and common law 211; in Canada 196, 207; in Hong Kong 5, 191–192, 204, 211; in Ireland 193, 194, 204, 205, 207; in Namibia 202–203
Erikson, Erik H. 204
European Charter for Regional or Minority Languages 197
European Convention on Human Rights 2, 32, 33, 53, 61
European Court of Human Rights 2, 33, 53, 57, 61
European Union Charter of Fundamental Rights and Freedoms 34
Evatt, Elizabeth 199
Eyerman, R. 129

families: changing structure 184–186; in Chinese culture 42–43; legal changes in China 157–164
Fawcett, Jamie 201
feminist studies 11, 22, 127, 136; *see also* gender equality, women's rights
Fields, A. Belden 31
Fiji: affirmative action 5–6, 218–242; benefits of affirmative action 235–236; Bill of Rights 222, 227, 229–230; Chinese minority 222; colonial regime 221, 222; commerce 223–224; Constitution (1970/1990) 221–222, 241; Constitution (1997) 222, 228–238, 241; criteria for affirmative action 234–235; Deed of Cession 221; disadvantage, nature of 226–227, 233–234; education 225–226; Europeans 222, 223; failure of affirmative action measures 239–240; Fiji Holdings Limited 238, 239; Great Council of Chiefs 229; history 220–222, 227–228, 230–232; housing 225, *225*; Human Rights Commission 226, 229ff.; indigenous Fijians 221ff., *225*, *226*; Indo-Fijians 5, 6, 221ff., *225*, *226*; Labour Party 228, 230; land ownership 223, 235; Land Transport Authority Act 236; legislation for affirmative action 236–237; military coups (1987, 2000, 2006) 222, 227, 231, 242; monitoring affirmative action 237–238; National Bank of Fiji 239; National Federation Party 228; Native Policy 223; poverty 222–223, 225; programmes of affirmative action 232–233, 238; public employment 226, *226*; Reeves Commission 222, 228, 232ff.; Rotuman people 226, 227, 228, 233; Section 44 229–230, 232–238; Social Justice Act (2001) 231–232, 236ff.; Social Justice Bill (2000) 230–231
Fijians 221ff., *225*, *226*
Finland 176, 179
Finnis, John 55–56, 59
Fletcher, Ruth 44
foreign marriages 106–107
France 205
Fraser, Mariam 14
Fraser, Nancy 220
French language: in Canada 196ff.; in France 205
Freud, Sigmund 10

Gaita, Raymond 118
Galloway, J. Donald C. 49–50
Ganzeboom, Harry 181
gay identities 13, 14, 15, 16, 18
gender equality: China 126–141; South Korea 173, 178; *see also* inequality in education, women's rights
Gender Institute (London School of Economics) 11
Germany: educational statistics 176, 180, 181, 188; legalisation of homosexuality 32
Gert, Bernard 49
Gilmartin, Christina 129
Goldsworthy, Geoffrey 109, 110
Gordon, Arthur 223
Great Britain *see* United Kingdom
Greece 176
Green, James 21
Gu Cheng 136

Hague Convention on Celebration and Recognition of the Validity of Marriages 107
Hahm, Chaihark 44–45
Halapua, Winston 229
Han Feizi 45
Hawaii State Supreme Court 61
Heinze, Eric 66
Heitlinger, Alena 127
Helminiak, Daniel A. 59
Hepworth, Mike 37
Herman, Didi 52
Hindus 6
HIV/AIDS 17, 20, 33, 44, 51, 87, 94
Ho, Cyd 37
Ho, David F. 42
homosexuality 2, 31–33: Chinese attitudes 42–43; decriminalisation 32–34, 83–85; legal developments in Hong Kong 33–41; post-colonial attitudes 44; religious attitudes 56–60, 97–98; *see also* gay identities, lesbian identities
Hong Kong 2–3, 5, 29–66: attitudes towards homosexuality 31–33; Basic Law 30, 35, 37, 45, 46, 192–193, 194, 196, 201, 202, 208, 211; bilingualism in the courtroom 191–212; Bill of Rights Ordinance (1991) 30, 35, 37, 38, 39, 45, 46, 49; Court of Appeal 36, 37–38, 39, 51, 193; Court of First Instance 51, 192, 193; Crimes (Amendment) Bill (1991) 35–36; Crimes Ordinance 36; decriminalisation

of homosexuality 34–41; Disability Discrimination Bill 40; educational statistics 175; Equal Opportunities Bill 40; Equal Opportunities Commission 40, 41; importance of all-inclusive equality 46–55; international obligations 63; Law Reform Commission 35; Legislative Council Home Affairs Panel 36–37, 40; Matrimonial Ordinances 59; Offences Against the Person Ordinance (1865) 34; Official Languages Ordinance 201, 202; Operation Rockcorry 35; Public Security Bureau 156; Race Discrimination Ordinance 46; right to same-sex marriage 41–46, 55–65; Sex Discrimination Bill 40; Sexual Orientation Discrimination Ordinance 41; Society for Truth and Light 43, 49, 51; *see also* China

Iceland 179
India 14, 16, 19, 235: caste system 219, 220
Indo-Fijians 5, 6, 221ff., *225*, *226*
inequality in education: China 151–152; South Korea 4–5, 172–188
International Covenant on Civil and Political Rights (ICCPR) 2, 30, 33, 35, 37, 63, 86, 93, 111–112, 115, 197–198, 202
International Covenant on Economic, Social and Cultural Rights 64
International Labour Organisation (ILO) 237
International Socio-Economic Index of Occupational Status 181
Ireland: attitudes to abortion 44; constitution 56, 57; Court of Criminal Appeal 209; High Court 58, 195; Homosexual Law Reform Committee 59; language issues 5, 192ff.; Supreme Court 56–57, 194, 195, 200, 204–205
Irish Free State 193–194
Irish language, status of 193–194, 200ff.
Italy 176, 203

Jackson, Peter 14, 17
Jamison, A. 129
Japan 6, 18, 128, 185: educational statistics 174, 175, 176, 178
Jolly, Susan 12, 15
Judaism 58

Katyal, Sonia K. 45
Kelly, Paul J. 49

Khan, Shivananda 20
Kimlicka, Will 45
Kinsey, Alfred 32, 83
Kirk, Jeremy 110–111
Klerk, Yvonne 64–65
Koppelman, Andrew 51
Korea *see* South Korea
Krafft-Ebing, Wilhelm von 10

Lacey, Nicola 39–40
Lambevski, Sasho 15
language issues 191–212
Lather, Patti 136
Latin America 14
Lave, Jean 4, 135
Lee Cheuk-yan 40
Lee Kuan Yew 42
lesbian identities 13, 15, 16, 18, 19
Leung Wai-tung 45
Liguori, Ana Luisa 21
Lin, Timothy E. 51–52
Locke, Kenneth A. 58–59
London School of Economics Gender Institute 11
Lubhéid, Eithne 14, 15

McCarthy, Joseph 32
McClelland, Mark 18–19
MacDonald, Roderick A. 206–207, 212
Macedonia 15
McMorland, Don 85
Malaysia 219
male domination 130–135; *see also* domestic violence
Manalansan, Martin F. 14
Mao Zedong 145, 146, 148, 166
Mare, Robert 183
marriage 3–4: constititutional aspects 107–116; domestic violence 4, 128–135; hetero-normativity 31, 109, 111; legal benefits (Australia) 105–106; legal changes in China 157–161; linkage to the state 3, 4; nature of marriage 119; foreign marriages 106–107; mixed marriages 186; women with gay men 18; *see also* civil unions/partnerships, same-sex marriage
Massachusetts (USA): same-sex marriage 30, 54, 57, 62, 65, 92, 107; Supreme Judicial Court 30, 46, 54, 63, 65
Meagher, Dan 111
Mexico 14

Millibank, Jenni 104
Morgan, Wayne 52, 104
Morocco 13, 21
Muslims 6

Nagar, Richard 12, 13, 17
Namibia 202–203
Narr, Wolf-Dieter 31
Narrain, Arvind 16
Nepal 6
Netherlands: same-sex marriage 30, 105, 107
New Zealand 3, 81–99: anti-discrimination principle 86–89; Bill of Rights Act (1990) 83, 89–91, 92, 98; Broadcasting Act (1989) 96; censorship issues 94–96; Christian Coalition of Concerned Citizens 85; churches 85, 97–98; Civil Union Act (2004) 93, 99; civil unions 90, 93–94, 114; Consistency 2000 project 88–89, 90; Court of Appeal 82, 92, 94, 95; Crimes Act (1961) 85; decriminalisation of homosexuality 83–85; Department of Education 82; educational statistics 176, 179; Film and Literature Board of Review 95; Films, Videos and Publications Classification Act (1993) 94; Government Administration Committee 95, 96; Homosexual Law Reform Act (1986) 85; Homosexual Law Reform Bill 82–83, 85, 86; Homosexual Reform Society (NZHRS) 84; Human Rights Act (1993) 83, 87, 88, 90, 91, 94, 96, 97, 98; Human Rights Action Group 94, 95; Human Rights Commission 88, 89, 97, 98; Human Rights Commission Act (1977) 86; Human Rights Review Tribunal 90; Maoris 224; Marriage Act (1955) 91–92, 93–94; Mazengarb Report 83; National Gay Rights Coalition 84; Office of Film and Literature Classification 94, 95; Race Relations Act (1971) 86; Relationships (Statutory References) Act (2005) 90–91; same-sex marriages 63–64, 91–93, 112; Supreme Court 94
Newsome, Gavin 62
Ng, Vivien 14, 17
Nie, Jing-bao 127
Nissinen, Martti 52
non-originalism in constitutional interpretation 111–113
Norway 174, 176

Ó Riagáin, Dónall 200–201
official languages, status of 191–212
Organisation for Economic Cooperation and Development (OECD) 174, 175, 176, 181: Programme for International Student Assessment (PISA 2000) 175, 179, 181, 182, 188
Organisation for Security and Cooperation in Europe 194
originalism in constitutional interpretation 108–111
Oslo Recommendations Regarding the Linguistic Rights of National Minorities 194, 197, 198
O'Sullivan, Aisling 56

Packer, John 197
Pan, Suiming 20–21
Parker, Richard 20
Pelec, Jelena 203
Petersen, Carole J.
Philippines 6, 14, 186
Phillips, Oliver 44
Pi Xiaoming 132, 133–134, 139
Pigg, Stacey Leigh 13
PISA 2000 (OECD) 175, 179, 181, 182, 188
post-colonial attitudes to sexuality 2, 5, 11, 41, 43–44
Presbyterian Church (NZ) 85, 97–98
Prondzynski, F. F. V. R. 57
Puar, Jasbir 16, 17
Punja, Hari 224
Pupavac, Vanessa 195–196
Puri, Jyoti 15

Québec Province 194, 195, 198–199, 206, 207
queer theory 9, 10, 15–16, 22

Ramaga, Philip Vuciri 199, 204
Ratuva, Stephen 223
Rawls, John 57
Raz, Joseph 51
Réaume, Denise G. 208
Reinig, Timothy W. 58
registration of same-sex relationships 115–116
religious attitudes to homosexuality 97–98
reverse discrimination *see* affirmative action
Rodley, Nigel S. 199
Roman Catholicism 44, 49, 56, 85

Sachs, Albie 194
same-sex marriage 2, 3, 53, 54: Australia 104–120; Hong Kong 41–46, 63–65; negative aspects 117–119; originalism 108–111; registration of same-sex relationships 115–116; right to same-sex marriage 55–60; *see also* civil unions/partnerships
Schiavo, Terry
Schwartz, Shalom 41–42
Sedgwick, Eve Kosofsky 9, 15, 16, 19, 22
sexual health 17, 20
sexual translations 12–15
Sharma, H. C. 224
Shuibhne, Nic 195, 202
Siemienski, Guillaume 197
Singapore 42
single parenthood 184, 185
socio-economic status and education (South Korea) 173, 180–184
South Africa 2, 34, 234: Constitution 218, 229, 236–237, 241; Constitutional Court 46, 47, 48, 56, 232; Employment Equity Act 240; same-sex marriage 30, 31, 46, 47–48, 56, 59, 107; Supreme Court of Appeal 47, 59; White Paper on Public Service Education and Training (1997) 237–238
South Australia 105
South Korea: demographic change 184–186; divorce rates 184–185; educational inequality 4–5, 172–188; educational system 174–178; equalisation policy in education 177, 187; expansion in education 174–175, 183, 186; expenditure on education 175–176; family structure and education 173, 184–186; gender inequality in education 173, 178–180; higher education 177; place of Confucianism 44–45; socio-economic status and education 173, 180–184; structure of education 176–178
Spain 30, 107
Spakowski, Nicola 127
Stern, Minna 14
Storr, Merl 10
Summerhawk, Barbara 18
Swarr, Amanda Lock 12, 13, 17
Sweden 174
Switzerland 181

Taiwan 185
Tasmania 106: civil unions 114; Same-Sex Marriage Bill (2004) 113
Thailand 14, 17
Thatcher, Margaret 33
Third International Mathematics and Science Study (TIMSS 95) 175, 179
Thomas Aquinas 55, 56
Thornton, Margaret 199
tolerance as a concept 52
transgender studies 9
transnational sexuality studies 9–16, 22
Trinidad 17
Turkey 176

United Kingdom 2, 3, 14, 19, 61: attitudes to homosexuality, 32, 33, 34; Buggery Act (1533) 3, 31; Civil Partnership Act (2004) 33, 53; educational statistics 174; former colonies *see* Fiji, Hong Kong; High Court of Justice (Family Division) 53–54; Human Rights Act (1998) 90; Offences Against the Person Act (1861) 31; Section 28 33; Sexual Offences Act (1967) 32; Sexual Offences Act (2003) 34; Wolfenden Report 32, 83, 84
United Nations: Commission on Social, Economic and Cultural Rights 64; Convention on the Elimination of All Forms of Racial Discrimination (CERD) 86, 231, 237; Convention on the Elimination of All Forms of Discrimination Against Women (CEDAW) 149, 157, 163, 166, 231, 237; Convention on the Rights of the Child 45, 48; Human Rights Committee 33, 63, 93, 112, 115, 198, 205, 208–209; Non-Governmental Organisation (NGO) Forum 126, 127, 132; World Conference on Human Rights (Vienna, 1993) 126; World Women's Conference (Beijing, 1995) 126, 127, 130ff, 140, 164
United States 2, 14, 15, 16, 53: affirmative action 219, 240; Bill of Rights 89; Court of Appeals for the Seventh Circuit 48; Defense of Marriage Act (1996) 62; divorce rates 184; educational statistics 174, 176, 180, 181, 187, 188; Kinsey Report 32, 83; Marriage Protection Amendment 62; originalism in constitutional interpretation 108; racial

minorities 220; same-sex marriage 31, 54, 55, 61–62, 92; Stonewall Riots 32; Supreme Court 33, 49, 51–52, 55, 61–62, 94
Universal Declaration of Human Rights (1948) 1, 6, 194

Vance, Carole 13
Varennes, Fernand de 208, 209–210
Veitch, Edward 200
Victoria (Australia) 104
Vietnam 186

Wenger, Etienne 4, 135
Wennergren, Bertil 200

Western values, imposition of 11–12, 41–42, 127
Wild, Fran 84
Wilson, Ara 17
Wintemute, Robert 58
women's rights 59: China 4, 126, 145–166; *see also* gender equality
Wu, Anna 40
Wu Changzhen 156

Yang Dawen 156
Young, Iris 220
Yau, Eliza 36, 37

Zhang Naihua 128
Zimbabwe 44